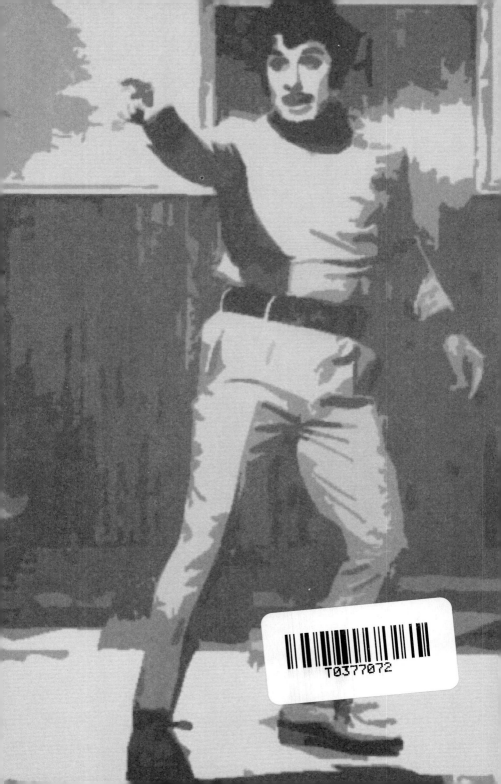

Popular Cinema and Politics in South India

The research methodologies of Dr Rajanayagam are exemplary for those who want to do in-depth research in the issues concerning the influences of cinema and its impacts on political, social, economic and cultural planes.

— **S. Raguram**
Eastern University, Sri Lanka

This book uses a media-inclusive approach to provide a comprehensive and brilliant semiotic, psychoanalytical, and feminist analysis of image-politicking of two dramatis personae of Thamizh film: MGR and Rajinikanth. Apart from deconstructing the most significant films of these two heroes, the book also uses several secondary sources such as fanzines, news articles, gossip magazines, published research on films, interviews with fans, and case studies of fan clubs to provide a multidisciplinary, multi-site, multi-layer analysis.

— **Srividya Ramasubramanian**
Texas A&M University, USA

The book delves into the cultural-literary roots of significant patterns observed in films; particularly, the psycho-cultural mapping of body and cultural tetrad are new to Thamizh/Indian film studies. I recommend this book especially to the media scholars and critics to derive inspiration and interest in the area of media and politics.

— **Bernd Trocholepczy**,
Johann Wolfgang Goethe-Universitaet,
Frankfurt am Main, Germany

Popular Cinema and Politics in South India

Reimagining MGR and Rajinikanth

S. Rajanayagam

First published 2015 in India
by Routledge
912 Tolstoy House, 15–17 Tolstoy Marg, Connaught Place, New Delhi 110 001

Simultaneously published in the UK
by Routledge
2 Park Square, Milton Park, Abingdon, Oxon OX14 4RN

Routledge is an imprint of the Taylor & Francis Group, an informa business

© 2015 S. Rajanayagam

Typeset by
Glyph Graphics Private Limited
23 Khosla Complex
Vasundhara Enclave
Delhi 110 096

Printed and bound in India by
Avantika Printers Private Limited
194/2 Ramesh Market, Garhi, East of Kailash
New Delhi 110 065

All rights reserved. No part of this book may be reproduced or utilised in any form or by any electronic, mechanical or other means, now known or hereafter invented, including photocopying and recording, or in any information storage and retrieval system without permission in writing from the publishers.

British Library Cataloguing-in-Publication Data
A catalogue record of this book is available from the British Library

ISBN 978-1-138-82203-0

to

my parents
Salethammal
Salethu Pillai

CONTENTS

Figures and Tables	ix
Abbreviations	xi
Acknowledgements	xiii
Note on Transliteration	xiv
Introduction: Popular as Political	xv

Part I: Politics of Narrative

1. Assemblage Structure	3
2. Image-Building Devices	12

Part II: Politics of Body

3. Imaging Male Body	33
4. On Being a *Man*'s Woman	43
5. Psycho-Cultural Mapping of Body	51
6. Double-Bodied Migrantcy	62
7. Wealth of Poverty	73
8. Dispensation of Justice	80

Part III: Politics of Imaging Politics

9. Image and Imagining	105
10. Politically Loaded Octa-Motifs	125
11. Imaging by Tactexting	143
12. MGR: Politics as Co-text	152
13. RK: Politics as Context	168

viii   CONTENTS

14. Cinelating Politiking   184
15. Politics Beyond Politics: Trans–Image Voting   200

Filmography   268
Select Bibliography   278
About the Author   289
Index   290

FIGURES AND TABLES

Figures

1.1	Hero-Centric Model of Dramatis Personae	8
2.1	Hierarchy of Villains	13
2.2	Hero–Villain Continuum	14
2.3	Double-Roles — An Analytical Model	17
2.4	On-Going Circulation of Cine Song Massaging	19
2.5	Tea-Stall Politiking	21
5.1	Women — A Cultural Tetrad	52
5.2	Male-Female Inter-Relationship	53
5.3	Mother Fixation — MGR	57
5.4	Mother Fixation — RK	58
6.1	Universification of Multiverse	63
6.2	Double-Bodied Migrantcy	65
7.1	Attitude Towards Wealth — General Pattern	76
7.2	Attitude Towards Wealth — Hero vis-à-vis Heroine	78
8.1	Justice — MGR's Version	85
8.2	Justice — RK's Version	86
8.3	Terrain Switching	98
9.1	Cinema Theatre as a Liminal Zone	106
9.2	Circles of *Thiruvizhaa*	108
9.3	Psycho-Political Mapping of Cinemenon	111
9.4	Cine-Viewing as a 'Rite of Passage'	112
9.5	Psycho-Political Dynamics of Hero Worship	114
9.6	Learning from Cinema	119

x ◼ FIGURES AND TABLES

10.1 Comparative Fantasy Space   127
10.2 The Orphan Syndrome   133
10.3 Politically Loaded Octa-Motif Interlace   139

11.1 Metaleptical Tactexting   145
11.2 Synonymisation and Self-Reflexivity   146

Tables

1.0 CBFC Data on Annual Output of Feature Films   xviii

4.1 Haughty Woman   44
4.2 Comparative Approaches to the Shrew   45

6.1 Aspects of Embodying and Disembodying   69

15.1 Era of Radicalism-turned-Rhetoric
      Electoral Performance: 1957–71   202
15.2 Era of Promise-turned-Pathos
      Electoral Performance: 1977–84   208
15.3 Era of Gender Politiking
      Electoral Performance: 1989–96   216
15.4 Era of Minor Parties
      Electoral Performance: 1998–2004   222
15.5 Era of Alternative-turned-Ally
      Electoral Performance: 2006–14   235

ABBREVIATIONS

AIADMK/ADMK	All India Anna Dravida Munnetra Kazhakam
Anna	C. N. Annadurai
BJP	Bharathiya Janata Party
CM	Chief Minister
CPI	Communist Party of India
CPI(M)/CPM	Communist Party of India (Marxist)
DMDK	Daesiya Murpoakku Dravida Kazhakam
DMK	Dravida Munnetra Kazhakam
EVR/Periyar	E V Ramasamy Naickar
INC/CONG.	Indian National Congress
LTTE	Liberation Tigers of Thamizh Eezham
MDMK	Marumalarchi Dravida Munnetra Kazhakam
MGR	M G Ramachandran
MLA	Member of Legislative Assembly
MP	Member of Parliament
PM	Prime Minister
PMK	Paattaali Makkal Katchi
PS	People Studies
RK	Rajinikanth/Rajini
VCK	Viduthalai Chiruthaikal Katchi

Acknowledgements

I would like to thank my mother and father who till their death showed incomparable love and concern for me; my sister Kulanthai Therese who has made sure that I don't miss my mother; other sisters, brothers, nephews, nieces, and their partners, grand-children, and all in the families for their understanding and support; Chitraa for her gentle and caring accompaniment, Venky for his encouragement; Josephine Joseph for her guidance and concern; A. Victor, Selvanayagam, and Rajarathinam for their emotional support.

My thanks are due to the members of People Studies' survey teams, especially Adaikalaraj and family, Henry Jerome, Karthik and John Victor Xavier; my 'students' during the last quarter century from whom I have learnt profound insights into media and life; the fans of MGR, Rajinikanth and other stars whom I have interviewed.

I am grateful to scholars David Raj, V. S. Albert, Pragasan, Raju, Donald D'Silva, Uma Vangal, Deepa Viswam, Stephen Joe, P. Subramaniam, S. Innacimuthu, Stephen Martin for their feedback on the manuscript; Miranda Alophonso, Leo Paul, and Rex Angelo for corrections.

I am greatly indebted to academicians of international repute Richard Reuben, Bernd Trocholepczy, Selvaraj Velayutham, Srividya Ramasubramanian and Raguram Sivasubramaniam for their valuable endorsements.

My special thanks to the editorial team at Routledge, New Delhi, for their stimulating queries and admirable guidance.

Note on Transliteration

In the transliteration of 'Tamil' words I have opted for their spoken form and avoided the use of diacritical marks. Even the otherwise anglicised words like 'Tamil' are also not exempted; thus, for example, it is 'Thamizh', not 'Tamil', unless it occurs in a quoted text or refers to the official/statutory usage (as in 'the Government of Tamil Nadu'). The short/long, soft/hard sounds are differentiated by doubling the corresponding letter (as in anpu/**aa**ru, satam/sa**tt**am).

Introduction

POPULAR AS POLITICAL

The 'popular' cinema[1] in India, labelled variously as 'commercial', '*masala*',[2] 'entertainment', 'conventional', 'dominant' or 'mainstream' cinema, has been severely criticised by the 'new wave', 'alternative', 'off-beat', 'parallel', or 'art' film-makers, some of whom are considered great auteurs, for its staple ingredients.[3] Not only these 'elite', 'highbrow' filmmakers but also film critics and media scholars have been treating popular cinema with condescension and contempt.[4]

While granting that the popular cinema in India as elsewhere lacks realism, creativity, and indepth analysis of social issues, and gives rise to the *phenomenon of star*,[5] it indeed has its own distinct identity and a 'power' of its own. What is peculiar to Indian popular cinema is the 'politicisability'[6] of the screen-constructed popular image of the star. While many studies are available on the subject of popular cinema, approaching it from varied inter-related perspectives including the semiotic,[7] the psychoanalytic[8] and the feminist[9] perspectives, studies from a political perspective are comparatively fewer and highly cine-deterministic by exaggerating the 'power' of cinema and assigning a passive role to the viewers, particularly the fans, who are, according to these studies, mesmerised by the screen-constructed star-images and are vulnerable to be exploited by the stars.

Cinemas and Politics: The Pan-Indian Scenario

The connection between popular cinema and direct politics caught the imagination of film critics and media scholars, and became an esoteric, 'notorious' subject of study, when the mass(ive) hero M. G. Ramachandran (MGR) of Thamizh Nadu demonstrated the power of popular cinema by an inventive 'synonymisation' of cinema and politics through the agency of fan clubs. He floated his own political party the All India Anna Dravida Munnetra Kazhakam (AIADMK/ADMK) in 1972 and eventually captured power in the State in 1977. The 'MGR phenomenon' soon had its Telugu incarnation in the neighbouring State of Andhra Pradesh in the person of N. T. Rama Rao (NTR). The political success of NTR is even more astounding than MGR's. His Telugu Desam Party (TDP) came to power in 1983 within nine months after its formation; what is surprising is that even before the party could get any formal recognition from the Election Commission, the TDP candidates contested as independents. The MGR phenomenon has become an established tradition, albeit with a reduced and scattered impact, thanks to the involvement of prominent stars in Thamizh Nadu such as 'nadikar thilakam' Sivaji, 'super star' Rajinikanth (Rajini/Rajni/RK), and now 'puratchi kalaignar' Vijayakanth whose party Daesiya Murpoakku Dravida Kazhakam (DMDK) presently enjoys 29 MLAs (securing 7.9 per cent votes in 2011 elections[10]); and in Andhra Pradesh 'mega star' Chiranjeevi's Praja Rajyam Party[11] has won 18 assembly seats (with 18 per cent vote share in 2009 elections).

While MGR and NTR succeeded, at least initially, in synonymising cinema and politics, the neighbouring south Indian states of Karnataka and Kerala witnessed an entirely different dynamics of politicising popular screen image. In Karnataka, Rajkumar emerged as a key political figure in the 1980s by spearheading a movement to make Kannada the medium of primary education in the state, which immediately dissipated into an uncontrollable anti–Thamizh riot. In Kerala, one of the most literate States of India, Prem Nazir, a Guinness record-holder for acting in the largest number of films (over 700!), enjoying a massive fan following, tried his hands in politics but was unsuccessful. However, both Rajkumar and Prem Nazir remained till their death as supremos in cinema *and* as potential threats to other political parties in their respective States.

Politicising popular screen image is not exclusive to the south Indian States. The political stage in the Hindi belt, for example, witnessed the 'pan-Indian' hero Amitabh Bachchan in the electoral fray in 1984 as an Indian National Congress (INC) candidate thanks to his friend Rajiv Gandhi. When the Bofors scandal stormed the nation, Bachchan quit

INTRODUCTION ◾ xvii

politics temporarily and when he came out of the limbo after a decade he had changed his allegiance to Samajwadi Party of which his wife Jaya Bachchan is a sitting Rajya Sabha MP. Not only the Bachchans, dozens of Hindi stars have been active in politics as MPs, nominated or elected. Some notable examples are: Sunil Dutt (INC MP elected for five terms from Mumbai North-West; also minister in the Union cabinet in 2004) and his wife Nargis (nominated to Rajya Sabha by Indira Gandhi), Shatrughan Sinha (BJP MP in both houses of parliament; also Union minister in BJP government during 2003–04), Raj Babbar (initially Samajwadi Party MP; then INC MP from Firozabad after defeating the daugher-in-law of his former party's chief Mulayam Singh Yadav!), Vinod Khanna (BJP MP from Gurdaspur), Vyjayanthimala Bali (initially INC MP; after finishing the term, joined the BJP because the INC refused her MP ticket), and Dharmendra (BJP MP from Bikaner in Rajasthan) and his wife Hema Malini (BJP Rajya Sabha MP).

In a striking contrast to the south Indian counterparts, the north Indian Hindi star-politicians have not been able to achieve anything substantial in Indian (Hindi) politics primarily because the Hindi films do not have the geo-cultural specificities which the south Indian films possess, uphold and nurture. While the governments in the centre (irrespective of the party ruling) have been persistent in promoting and 'imposing' Hindi as *the* national language, and to a great extent they have even succeeded in it, there are not many specific traits definable as 'Hindi culture' in India, except may be in the States of Uttar Pradesh and Madhya Pradesh; and in all other states, remarkably even in the States where Hindi is very prevalent — it has been and is still a Bhojpuri, Maithili, Haryanvi, Gujarathi, Sindhi, Rajasthani, Marathi, Bengali, Odisha, or a tribal, and not Hindi, culture. As we go from the Hindi heartland towards the south, the individual cultural identities become more and more pronounced. Hindi is a meta-language superimposed on other originary cultures with unique and individualised ethnic, linguistic, national identities, and with clear geo-political markers.[12] As a consequence, the Hindi films and politics create a 'fictitious' and 'base-less' meta-culture subsuming and transcending specific cultures, and politically synonymising Hindi with 'India that is Bharat'. Such a notional unitary meta-culture (a political-legal construction) in an otherwise loosely knit federation of diverse national cultures (a cultural–psychological existentiality) has been immensely helpful to Hindi films to have a market (wherever Hindi is spoken or understood) many times huger than that available to any south Indian language films.[13]

A comparative look into the annual output of feature films would further augment this point. Of the overall total output, according to the Central Board of Film Certification (CBFC),[14] the Hindi films constitute hardly one-fifth, closely followed by Telugu and Thamizh; and, if we add Kannada and Malayalam, the four south Indian languages alone would constitute more than 50 per cent of the national total. Marathi[15] and Bengali come next in order with an average of around 100 films a year. The pattern is consistent as Table 1.0 demonstrates. The Hindi film industry, evidently, has not been representative of India neither in terms of film output nor in terms of cumulative film-business turnover, though it might have an edge over others because of, as noted earlier, some sort of pan-Indian market it enjoys. Any attempt towards 'Bollywoodisation' of Indian cinemas is therefore unjustifiable and deliberately political.[16]

Table 1.0
CBFC Data on Annual Output of Feature Films

	2009	2010	2011
Total	**1288**	**1274**	**1255**
Hindi	235	215	206
Telugu	218	181	192
Tamil	190	202	185
Kannada	177	143	138
Malayalam	94	105	95
Bengali	84	110	122
Marathi	99	116	107

Source: All tables provided by the author.

This politics apart, when it comes to stars entering politics, the very business advantage the Hindi films have become a severe handicap because the Hindi film stars do not culturally belong anywhere. To succeed in politics the 'leader' should be perceived to *represent* a people and they in turn should be able to *identify* themselves with and *own* the 'leader' as 'our man' (or 'didi' or 'ammaa' for that matter!), which is possible for the south Indian stars, thanks to the distinct Thamizh, Malayalam, Kannada or Telugu identity in films.[17] Because of this, the Hindi stars with political ambitions, though with a widespread fan following, have not been able to successfully float their own party; instead they have been forced to join some existing 'national' party or other at the most as a value addition to that party. In effect, it is only the star's popularity — the *familiarity* of his/her face to the public — that is used by the party and *not* the screen-constructed image of the star. That explains why even an 'all-time favourite' hero[18] like Bachchan could not shine in politics: he could not outshine Rajiv Gandhi in charisma; nor was his fan-base extensive enough to outdo the INC cadre-base.[19] Moreover, once elected an MP, his 'subservient' position[20] in the party and governance did not correspond on the one hand to the stature of the all-powerful, invincible super-hero, and on the other hand to the image of the angry young action-hero who constantly confronted, challenged and often deposed the establishment. Such a hero certainly cannot, and should not, be a part of the establishment, that too accused of scams. Probably Bachchan himself felt the discomfort, and announced he was quitting politics.

There are a few interesting studies in star politiking, particularly comparing Hindi film icon Bachchan and the star-CMs MGR and NTR. But they have been very cine-centric, as for example, Vachani who notes, 'Bachchan's lack of credibility as state functionary was a failure of the Outsider archetype to make the transition from cinema to politics (that is, from 'outside' to 'inside' society)'.[21] But the 'failure', it may be underscored, is not in the 'transition'; it concerns what he promises in *real* politiking and the credibility and believability of such promises. If only Bachchan was in a position, let us say, to offer a new or alternative government under his leadership, then probably the 'outsider archetype' would not have been the root cause for his 'lack of credibility as state functionary'. If that were to have happened, he should have been in the place of Rajiv Gandhi in the INC or he should not have contested in one constituency as a candidate of 'somebody else's party', even if it is his friend's. Das Gupta is more cine-deterministic than Vachani when he concludes: 'The fundamental difference between the two star-Chief Ministers and other star-politicians of India lies in the fact that in the case of the former, the films themselves created the politics and the politicians; the latter are merely film stars who decided to move into politics or were persuaded to do so as vote catchers'.[22] He categorically asserts: 'The Indian actor-Chief Ministers became political leaders *because* they were the superstars of their cinema'.[23] Though not so emphatic, similar cine-centric bias is found in other studies[24] on popular culture and politics. It may be noted that media 'scholars' and 'critics' have been too quick to construe a 'cause-and-effect link' between film and politics in Thamizh Nadu because of two reasons. First, they have been carried away by the superficial data on the prevalence of cinema in Thamizh Nadu. Though the number of theatres has been on the decline over the years (for example, from 1633 in 2006–07 to 1033 in 2014–15), Thamizh Nadu still enjoys a high number and, interestingly, the film output has not significantly changed. According to the Government of Thamizh Nadu data,[25] in 2014–15, the number of permanent cinema theatres is 996 (in 2006–07, 1293), semi-permanent 20 (in 2006–07, 109), touring 14 (in 2006–07, 221), and open-air 3 (in 2006–07, 10). While granting that the number of theatres is certainly an index of the popularity — even inevitability — of cinema as a mass entertainment in Thamizh Nadu, these data alone do not suffice to construe a 'symbiotic' relationship between cinema and politics. Second, it is significant that invariably all these studies, barring an exception or two, have been done *after* the action hero MGR had become the chief minister or at least after the 'Puratchi Nadikar' (Revolutionary Actor) had turned into the 'Puratchi Thalaivar' (Revolutionary Leader)[26] and had come to occupy the centre stage in Thamizh Nadu politics; as a result, these studies are so excessively obsessed with the *actor face* of MGR that they fail to recognise his other concomitant faces and to identify factors other than cinema operative in electoral politics.

The present study, while acknowledging the powerful role of cinema in influencing and moulding popular culture, makes a definitive departure from the aforementioned studies by problematising the very 'cause-and-effect', 'symbiotic' 'nexus' between film and politics, which other studies tend to assume, either explicitly or implicitly. Focusing on Thamizh Nadu, and subjecting the films of MGR and RK to a multi-disciplinary analysis, this study unveils the cultural and political ramifications of popular screen-constructed images, and the intricate cumulative effect of 'on-screen' and 'trans-screen' factors on the *seemingly pro-image* voting behaviour vis-à-vis the election results. In the process, this study on the one hand succeeds in deconstructing several scholarly myths and establishing that cinema has had and can have only a *limited* role at the most as a *surrogate propaganda* tool; on the other, it revisits the entire political history of post-Independent Thamizh Nadu through cinema (as) lens, and presents a refreshing psycho-political map of contemporary Thamizh Nadu.

***

Cinema and Politics: The Thamizh Scenario

When cinema started talking Thamizh during the mid-1930s, it was largely confined to a few urban centres, and it was speaking the lingo of puranic-nationalistic ideology. The INC in general indulged in an 'image-aversive' politics. As cinema started spreading its fantasy wings over hitherto unknown rural areas, thanks primarily to rural electrification project initiated by the passionate leaders of the burgeoning democracy, it was speaking yet another lingo – the *lingo of the Dravida Kazhakam* (DK) spearheaded by E. V. Ramasamy Naickar (EVR or Periyar), with his secular-rationalist ideology. The DMK, the political offshoot of the DK headed by C. N. Annadurai (Anna) with a committed band of youngsters including M. Karunanidhi, quickly grasped the political potential of the popular cinema. Propagating through an agitational strategy an opportunistic mix of the rationalism of EVR, linguistic chauvinism and the secessionist demand for a separate statehood, the DMK was soon promoting its own party film star in the person of MGR, and ushered in the saga of screen image-dependent politics. With his assiduously built Good Samaritan image and subaltern lingo MGR continued to march through the royal road laid for him by the DMK, and inaugurated the magnificent saga of apparently image-reigning politics with a nebulous populist ideology which he christened as 'Anna-ism'.

Almost coinciding with MGR's retirement from cinema RK 'invaded' the filmdom like a thunderbolt. With his initial deviant image and anger-filled sub-cultural lingo — the exact opposite of MGR on many counts — RK soon emerged as the 'super star'. Having played a prophetic role for a while through an image-intervening politics with an ambiguous spiritualistic ideology, he is now at the pinnacle of his acting career as a 'global hero'[27] who is paid — as the grapevine goes — the highest in India.

While so many stars have dabbled in image-politiking in Thamizh Nadu, I have been particularly attracted by MGR and RK because, though their screen-constructed images are poles apart (starting from their skin complexion to type of on-screen roles assumed), they have been able to wield immense political power through a devout fan following. This is the question that daunted me and eventually led to this study: How come they both clicked with the popular psyche? What are

xxii ■ POPULAR CINEMA AND POLITICS IN SOUTH INDIA

the dimensions of the cultural mutations that have paved the way for this paradigm shift in the Thamizh psyche that seems to have undergone a metamorphosis from approving and accepting as saviour MGR's 'Mr Perfect' image to approving RK's 'Anti-Hero' image?

The journey into the dynamics of image-politiking triggers off a series of interlocked questions which need to be addressed. First of all, one of the most intriguing facts is that both MGR and RK are 'outsiders'. There are equally creative and talented artistes of Thamizh origin. Sivaji, for example, is more versatile an actor than MGR, and Kamal Haasan than RK. Ironically, only MGR and to a certain extent RK have been successful in politics, while a seasoned Thamizh artiste like Sivaji, in spite of being widely recognised, has met with political debacle. Why? Does the 'outsider' image help them transcend the insurmountably rampant caste barriers?

Second, the exit of MGR from filmdom, interestingly, coincides more or less with the entry of RK. If it is assumed that the latter starts from where MGR left, how is it that the MGR fan clubs continue to be active, even while RK fan clubs seem to have sweeping influence over Thamizh politics? Does this imply that RK has not replaced MGR, but fills a cultural vacuum created by some other factors?

Third, it is perplexing that, contrary to their 'all-powerful' political image, both MGR and RK have met with disappointing election results. MGR who won in 1977 assembly elections, for example, drew a blank in 1980 parliamentary elections, but returned to power with a thumping majority in the assembly elections in the same year. Similarly, RK who seemed to work miracles in 1996 parliamentary elections through a brief television interview had to cut a sorry figure in 2004 elections. Does this mean that, when it comes to voting, there are other more decisive factors than the size of the fan following?

Fourth, hero-worship is not specific to cine stars. When Karunanidhi was arrested first by MGR government and later by the Jayalalithaa government, so many party-men self-immolated in favour of Karunanidhi. When Vaiko (formerly, Vai Gopalasamy) was dismissed from the DMK, some of his followers self-immolated. When M. K. Azhagiri (son of Karunanidhi) was once dismissed from the DMK because of feud in the first families, there were followers ready to burn themselves! How do we understand this phenomenon? Is it a part of the Thamizh 'cultural script' itself? Does this have its roots in the masochistic religious rituals? Is 'hero-worshipping' cine stars any different from performing the same to political 'stars'?

Fifth, there was a mushrooming of unauthorised RK fan clubs foreshadowing the 1996 elections. Clashes between rival RK fan clubs were not uncommon. Some of his fans even dared to defy the order of their 'deity' by contesting in elections. Similarly, foreshadowing the 2009 elections, RK fans displayed an attitude of defiance by announcing they would float a party in RK's name. While forming clubs, therefore, the fans may have their own agenda that is different from that of their star. What exactly is their ulterior motive? How far are these clubs genuinely committed to their star? What is their strategic location in the process of politicising the screen image? What are the salient psycho-social characteristics of the fan phenomenon, particularly the way the fans negotiate meaning against the backdrop of image politiking?

Unraveling these critical queries is like opening up a Pandora's box, and the study, therefore, is exploratory. Differing from other scholarly studies on contemporary 'historizing' which are either media-deterministic or media-negligent in the context of Thamizh Nadu, I have adopted a more authentic media-inclusive perspective. Being multi-disciplinary, the study draws theoretical insights from a wide range of disciplines: from subaltern history to counter-cultural movements, from semiotics to stylistics, from post-modernism to neo-Marxism, from deconstruction to popular religion, from gyno-criticism to socio-linguistics, from psychoanalysis to aesthetics. Consequently, the topic of image-politiking is approached from different — even diametrically opposed — angles, with different analytical tools. In actual application, these tools are innovatively 'composited' and employed simultaneously so that the interpretation of the data is coherent and the result, valid and reliable.

Since it is of paramount importance, in the process of deconstructing the screen image, to trace back syntagmatically to identify the constituent elements of such image, the selection of films becomes very crucial. From his first appearance on the screen in 1936 MGR has to his credit an amazing repertoire of 133 Thamizh films (136 including films in other languages). More impressive is the repertoire of RK. From 1975 till date RK has acted in around 165 films (including *Koachadaiyaan*) of which over 100 are in Thamizh (excluding 'guest' appearances). Though it would be ideal to access all the films for the study, I have made, for obvious practical reasons, a chronological selection spanning the entire film career at the rate of at least one film a year, and when MGR or RK happens to be at crossroads (political or personal), I have considered more than one in order to understand the fuller ramifications of such a situation. Also, I have made it a point to view all their 'silver jubilee' films (i.e., films that ran continuously for 25 weeks at least in one theatre — 11 for MGR during the period covered, and 15 for RK), and in the case of RK, I have further made sure all the 15 films of his choice (screened as a part of *Rajini-25* celebrations) were viewed. Besides these films, some 'also-runs' (neither spectacular hits nor miserable flops) are also included so that our probe into the dynamics of *image sustenance* could be more complete. In so far as they are relevant to the study of MGR and RK, some select films of other actors including Sivaji and Kamal are also referred to in the study.

Besides the aforementioned films which serve as the primary sources for this study, the secondary sources include the official and unofficial *fanzines, e-zines and popular biographies* of MGR, RK and other artistes referred to in this study; *news items and gossips* related to these artistes published in the mainstream popular magazines and newspapers; journals, books and other publications devoted to film and media studies. Given the extensive and multi-directional nature of the study, as the supplementary sources I have resorted to case studies of select fan clubs and depth interviews with office-bearers of select fan clubs, hardcore fans and professionals from the Thamizh cinema industry who have been closely associated with the artistes under study. With these, I have made a generous use of the findings of the series of field studies I have undertaken for People Studies, a multi-disciplinary research institute.[28]

***

An Overview

The book is divided into three major parts. It starts with one of the oft-overlooked areas, viz., the narrative structure, and proceeds through the dominant themes to the politicising dynamics.

Structurally, an MGR or RK starrer, like any typical Indian masala film, is a spectacular *assemblage* of 'nava rasas' and a synthesis of dominant and subaltern cultures. Moreover, interval, an apparently commercial

INTRODUCTION xxv

or convenience device, radically transforms the narrative into a 'double climax' structure, having a very limited number of narrative scenarios, though. MGR and RK creatively combine all these ingredients into a unique 'masala mix', a *pre-set formula*, with a hero-centric arrangement of the *dramatis personae*. The image formation is an evolutionary process, involving snowball dynamics, making their films stereotypical, redundant and serial-episodic.

Stunts, double roles, comedy, song-and-dance, punch dialogues, mini-narratives, dramatic entry, and end clips are some of the narrative devices which MGR and RK employ to the extent that they suit their political agendas.

The second part revolves around 'body' as the critical *locus standi* and pivotal focal point. The ideological core of the politiking of MGR and RK rests on the most obvious, concretely visible feature of their respective physical (male) bodies — the fair or dark complexion. Their universe is *phallo-centric*, and there is a remarkable agreement between them in the portrayal of the female body. However, there are significant differences as well: When a woman dares to be unconforming to the patriarchal norms, MGR shifts the locus from gender to social, as a question of rich-versus-poor, whereas RK resorts to 'precipitation' technique and is bent on defeating the woman. Likewise, in the cultural mapping of body, MGR pays almost exclusive attention to the *valorous* man, whereas RK often goes beyond the valorous to emphasise the *virile* man. In the context of mother fixation, MGR and RK tend to exhibit, in conformity with their respective 'affable darling' and 'enfant terrible' images, 'castration anxiety' and 'exposure anxiety' respectively.

Construction of the 'social body' consists of the phenomenon of 'double bodied migrantcy', i.e., the simultaneous process of subalternising and elitising through 'spasmodic liminal spurts' in a universified multi-verse. Concerning wealth, MGR and RK as a rule become rich or retain their wealth, and they never challenge the overall socio-economic structure. If they remain poor, *they choose* to be so, for greater moral or political gains.

Certain epistemological privilege marks their attitude towards justice, which varies according to their role as 'victims' or 'custodians' or both. While MGR emerges as the embodiment and the custodian of the moral values of the middle class, RK by and large embodies the subaltern morality. The essentially political struggle between the powerless and the powerful is switched to the moral terrain and presented as 'MGR/RK versus the villain' through the process of 'metaphorical symbolisation' and 'metonymical iconisation'.

The third part on the *politicising dynamics* starts with delineating the psycho-social nuances of theatrical viewing, which is a modernised recreation of the *thiruvizhaa* drama, fun and free-play. Hero-worship, the distinguishing mark of fan-centred politiking has its historical antecedent in the cultural practice of *nadukal* worship.

In the fantasy–politics *interface* there operate at least eight politically loaded motifs (*octa-motifs*) — the *thaaikulam*, the *fan-bond*, the *subaltern*, the *Thamizhness*, the *orphan*, the *renouncer*, the *donor*, and the *god* — which contribute to constituting the politiking formula.

The degree of success of the image politiking of MGR and RK largely depends on how they image politics through *tactexting* (tactical texting). The metaleptical *blurring-and-blending* of the public, private and screen realms transforms the image politics into real politics of real MGR/RK. Every film, in turn, becomes a political statement. While MGR treats films and corresponding contemporary political events as co-texts, RK treats politics mainly as *a context* to his films, and turns his political limelight into a profitable business.

A crucial difference between MGR and RK which many studies have ignored concerns the 'twin centre' politiking. MGR maintains a *revolving* twin centre (in the centre of the DMK and of the *mandram*); in the case of RK's fans, it is a *satellite* twin centre (as fans, RK; as party members, somebody else). In terms of *cinelation* (cinema + simulation) MGR's 'politician-cum-actor' model of politiking exemplifies *isomorphic* cinelation, whereas RK's 'star-intervening-politics' model is an example of *isolated* cinelation.

An analysis of the 'trans-image' voting behaviour of the people manifests that the voters in the context of Thamizh Nadu have been consistently 'image discriminative' and the success of MGR lies precisely in his intuitive awareness that the voters, when it comes to exercising their franchise, are image discriminative, and consistently choose the better, given the limited political options available within the ambit of the first-past-the-post electoral system.

Of the five successive chief ministers who have had the so-called 'cine-background' (Anna, Karunanidhi, MGR, Janaki, and Jayalalithaa), for example, Anna the very founder-leader of DMK was personally defeated in 1962. Karunanidhi's DMK had been voted out of power half a dozen times (1977, 1980, 1984, 1991, 2001, and 2011). MGR's ADMK had been routed in a parliamentary election (1980). Even in the assembly elections (1980 and 1984), it was, enigmatically, the victim, not the saviour, MGR who was voted to power. In the case of Janaki, her political presence was too brief to notice, and she vanished immediately after the rout in 1989. Jayalalithaa had been personally defeated and the ADMK under her leadership has suffered heavy electoral losses many times both for parliament and assembly. Regarding actors who floated their own parties, actors like Sivaji and T. Rajendar had been personally defeated; Vijayakanth could not take his party beyond a single assembly seat until he aligned with the ADMK. Similar is the story of Sarath Kumar. Concerning other actors, only when s/he was fielded as an official candidate of parties like the ADMK or the DMK, had s/he any chance of winning.

Notes

1. A terminological clarification regarding the terms 'film', 'cinema' and 'movie' is called for at the outset. While the word 'film' in general encompasses the social dimension, the word 'cinema' is confined to the aesthetic dimension. The word 'movie' refers to the economic aspects. The differentiation could be elucidated albeit naively thus: '"movies", like popcorn, are to be consumed; "cinema"(at least in American parlance) is high art, redolent of aesthetics; "film" is the most general term with the fewest connotations' (see Monaco 1981: 195). It is obvious that these three terms are inter-related and often there is a considerable overlapping. Sometimes, a fourth word 'talkie' is also used, but its use is mainly in the context of distinguishing it from the 'silent' films. In popular parlance, at least in Thamizh Nadu (Tamil Nadu/TN), the word 'picture' also is used as a synonym of 'film'. The term 'cinema theatre' or simply 'theatre' stands for the place where a film is exhibited. In the present study, 'film' is also employed to denote the individual work. When the context of discussion does not require this subtle differentiation, both 'film' and 'cinema' are interchangeably used.
2. '*Masala*' is a well-ground mix of various condiments like chilly, pepper, turmeric, coriander, cardamom, and other spices. It means, figuratively, the admixture of a variety of elements which 'spice up' the narrative. Its

Western equivalent is 'kitsch'. From the point of view of film business (distribution and exhibition) in TN, the audiences are differentiated taste-wise and geographical location-wise into (*a*) rural, lowbrow C-centres, (*b*) urban, highbrow A-centres and (*c*) the mid-way B-centres; and the *masala* films are associated with the C-centres. It must be quickly added, however, that the audience tastes and preferences have gone beyond these conventional differentiations, and have become very unpredictable, making the film-making business a high-risk gamble.

3. See, for example, Ray (1976: 90–91).

4. These distinctions, however, are becoming obsolete today even in academic circles. Though some filmmakers and critics continue to deride the 'popular' films with a certain royal distain, and often tinged with overt contempt, the 'popular' films have emerged as truly 'political' films. Moreover, invariably all the box-office hits are the 'popular' ones. No wonder, most of the former 'new wave' filmmakers have eventually settled for a low to medium budget 'middle' or 'realist' cinema — the commercial(ly viable) cinema masquerading as 'new wave'. Conversely, we could identify most, if not all, of the 'commercial' elements in the few 'middle cinema' films which were successful at the box-office.

5. While the star-phenomenon implies fan-following and box-office returns, it inevitably makes the stars become 'super auteurs' exerting an overwhelming influence over every aspect of filmmaking, including, not infrequently, 'directing' the directors. MGR and RK are such super auteurs; hence the films they act are referred to in this work as *their* films.

6. The century-old Indian cinema ('cinemas', to be meaningful to the cultural diversities) has produced some significant, explicitly political films both before and after Independence. However, in a state — democratic or otherwise — where films are censored and certified by the government through authorised bodies such as the Central Board of Film Certification (CBFC) in India to ensure that the contents are culturally appropriate and politically correct, any film *merely allowed* to be screened has to be necessarily political. Being 'politically correct' implies being an ideological state apparatus, and therefore it cannot be apolitical. While in a broad sense this being so, we use the term 'politicisability' to mean the link with direct political involvement.

7. For example, Metz (1974) and Barthes (1981). For an approach to popular culture from a postmodern perspective, see Collins (1989).

8. Metz (1982) and Denzin (1995).

9. Mulvey (1989), Mayne (1990) and Josephine (1991).

10. Interestingly, the DMDK's performance was apparently better when it had gone on its own. The vote share in 2006 was 8.38 per cent, at par with the INC's, and it went up to 10.3 per cent in the 2009 parliamentary elections.

But it fell down to 7.88 per cent when it contested in 2011 elections in alliance with the ADMK. The low per cent may also be because of the limited number of seats (41) allotted to the DMDK, the number which the ADMK deemed appropriate to the DMDK's strength. More on the intricacies of vote sharing, later.

11. When the Telugu mega star Chiranjeevi launched his Praja Rajyam party in a mammoth gathering in Thiruppathi in August 2008, he proclaimed that his party would be an alternative to the INC and the TDP, and the media on their part projected him as another NTR. In the 2009 elections, while his nascent party emerged as the third strongest in the State, he himself met with a baffling response — of the two constituencies he contested, the 'mega star' could win only one (he won Thiruppathi but lost Palakollu). After running the party for about 30 months, he did a volte-face in February 2011 and merged it with the INC for good.

12. Besides Hindi, there is Urdu, a close associate of and a competitor to Hindi. Urdu is the predominant language of the Muslim community in India, even in the south.

13. The 'pan-Indian' market the Hindi films enjoy is something similar to Hollywood films being released all over the world, wherever English is spoken or understood.

14. The CBFC data are available online at its official website: http://cbfcindia. gov.in/html/uniquepage.aspx?unique_page_id=30 (accessed 12 September 2014). See the annual reports for 2010 and 2011.

15. Paradoxically, Mumbai, the capital of Hindi cinema (named Bollywood after Bombay) is also the home for the aggressive, 'ethno-centric' ('maraathi manoos') politics of the Senas of Thackeray cousins against people from the Hindi-belt settled in Maharashtra (particularly targeting the migrants from UP and Bihar); and Marathi films nationally ranking fifth or sixth in terms of total annual film output have to compete with the Hindi films in their own home State.

16. As a recent media example for how subtly Bollywoodisation is perpetrated we could cite the presentation of the top five responses to the question, 'In the history of Indian cinema, who is the greatest actor of all time?' according to an opinion poll commissioned by NDTV. As the segment began after the commercial break, the anchor (Prannoy Roy) quizzed the panelists, 'to try and tell me who... what turned out to be the top five greatest actors of all time — we asked this across the country — we didn't prompt anybody...' To this, the spontaneous answer of a panelist was, 'Rajinikanth, MGR...' The anchor interrupted at this point and prompted, 'All India', as if to say that Rajinikanth and MGR were not to be in the 'all India' list. Interestingly, even after this 'correction' by the anchor one more panelist still included Rajinikanth in the list. However, according

xxx POPULAR CINEMA AND POLITICS IN SOUTH INDIA

to the survey, all the five actors were from the Hindi cinema, to which all the panelists expressed surprise, 'So all from Hindi cinema...?!' Making his comment on the list, the anchor concluded, 'If you take the southern States it woudn't be these, of course — but if you take the whole country, the dominance of Bollywood...' What is significant is the contrast made here: *the southern States versus the whole country.* If the response in 'the southern States' would be different, what is presented as the finding in fact represents the opinions of 'the northern States' only. Therefore, presenting this as the preference of 'the whole country' indeed amounts to uncritically (or deliberately) endorsing Bollywoodisation. (The opinion poll telecast on 27 August 2012 was part of the mid-term poll commissioned by NDTV with a sample size, the channel claimed, of almost 30,000 respondents, covering 125 out of the 543 Lok Sabha seats in the 18 big states. The findings were telecast on NDTV 24×7 from 27 to 31 August 2012 in a special show anchored by Prannoy Roy. Visit also: http//:www.ndtv. com/ [accessed 2 November 2014]).
In the academic circles there have been serious attempts in the recent years to correct the distorted historiography of the cinemas of India. See Velayutham (2008).

17. As this identification/representation process goes down to the grassroots, there come into play other more sensitive factors than race and ethnicity at the level of concrete electoral praxis; the foremost among such divisive-unifying factors is one's caste identity.

18. According to the opinion poll by NDTV mentioned above, the 'top 5 great actors of all time' are: Amitabh Bachchan, Aamir Khan, Salman Khan, Shah Rukh Khan, and Dilip Kumar (in the descending order of popularity).

19. Bachchan was elected in 1984 in the tremendous sympathy wave and it is very difficult to assess the extent of impact of Bachchan's popularity on the elections; the situation then was calamitously tragic after the murder of Indira Gandhi leading to an outrageous butchering of the Sikhs in thousands.

20. The political clout and the consequent extra dose of media attention Bachchan had were because of his close association with Rajiv Gandhi.

21. Vachani (1999: 221).

22. Das Gupta (1991: 234) betrays an attitude of carelessness and a tendency to blow up the figures. For example, he says on page 201 that MGR had acted in 292 films; it is 'more than 250' on page 200; the sentence structure on page 199 implies 262 — whereas MGR had acted only in 136 films, including his non-Thamizh films. The same mistake one finds also in Thoraval (2000: 322), who probably borrowed the figures from Das Gupta.

INTRODUCTION ■ xxxi

23. Das Gupta (1991: 199, emphasis added).
24. See, for example: Hardgrave and Neidhart (1975), Ramasamy (1979), Sivathamby (1981), Samuel (1983), David (1983), Pandian (1992), Dicky (1993a and b), Baskaran (1996), Azhagesan (1999), Rajadurai and Geetha (2000), and Velayutham (2008).
25. For details, see the *Policy Notes 2006–07* and *2014–15* of Information and Publicity, Government of Tamil Nadu, available at the official website: http://www.tn.gov.in/ (accessed 12 September 2014).
26. The title 'Puratchi Nadikar' was given to MGR by his erstwhile friend-turned-arch-enemy Karunanidhi when *Naadoadi Mannan* became a super-hit. The title 'Puratchi Thalaivar' was conferred on him by his lieutenant and the ADMK's first organising secretary K. A. Krishnaswamy on 17 October 1972 when MGR launched his new party. The changeover from 'nadikar' to 'thalaivar' marks the finality of MGR's political transfiguration, while retaining 'puratchi' symbolises the continuity of the Dravidian rhetorics. The legacy of MGR's 'puratchi' survives to this day in 'Puratchi Thalaivi', one of the prefixes to Jayalalithaa. In fact, the word is appropriated by any actor with political inclinations, such as 'puratchi kalaignar' Vijayakanth and 'puratchi thalapathi' Vishal, a young actor.
27. It is really surprising that *Outlook*, in its 4 June 2012 issue, with the special coverage, 'Cinema Century — 100 years of the world's most mesmerising moviedom', featured in its cover of all the people Rajinikanth, seated in a rotating chair, with the caption: 'Global hero Rajnikanth'. It is unusual for an English magazine to have a non-Bollywood star, particularly in a 'cinema century' special. Probably, this is another indication that a growing number of people tend to perceive the Indian cinema as no more a monopoly of the Hindi cinema. It may also be mentioned that RK's 'global popularity' thanks to unprecedented publicity to his *Enthiran* so overwhelmed the Bollywood super star Shah Rukh Khan that he was keen on roping in RK for his blockbuster *Ra.One*. He also later dedicated a song publicised as '*lungi* dance' in his *Chennai Express* to 'thalaivaa' RK, exhorting his fans 'not to miss' the film.
28. The references to the field studies in this book (denoted by the term *PS Study*) concern the series of macro-level studies planned and executed by me under the banner of People Studies, Chennai, supported initially by Culture and Communication, Chennai. A unique feature of these studies is the innovative social-psychological approach blending qualitative with quantitative aspects. The findings, released to the press after each study, are now available in a single volume. See Rajanayagam (2013).

Part I: Politics of Narrative

1

ASSEMBLAGE STRUCTURE

The Indian commercial film — any *Indian* feature film for that matter — has as its core the structure of the 'universal' classical drama, while sporting at the same time a unique, culture-specific structure of its own, a fact that makes it difficult for a Westerner, not familiar with the national cultures in the Indian subcontinent, to comprehend and appreciate this peculiar narrative layout.

Classical Core

To begin with, a typical classical drama starts with *protasis* (exposition), followed by *epitasis* (complication) and *catastasis* (new and further element of complication), reaching *catastrophe* (resolution), and is wound up with *epilogue*. The *catastrophe* consists of *peripeteia* (reversal of fortune or *conversio*) and *anagnorisis* (transition from ignorance to knowledge or *cognitio*). *Epitasis* and *catastasis* are achieved by creatively combining elements of *suspense* and *surprise* with narrative *knots* and *twists*.

This traditional *linear* structure of *conflict–development–climax–denouement* model[1] is 'inculturated' into the *Indian screen* by incorporating elements of the grand *kaavya* literature and folk cultural *kooththu* performance. While the main story moves forward *vertically* in different storylines, it is interspersed with *horizontally* laid out branch stories, and 'non-story' components such as song-and-dance inserts, parallel comedy tracks and stunt sequences. When these 'stories', 'storylines', and the 'non-story' components of a film are woven together, the resultant narrative has the structure of a more or less coherently laid out 'assemblage', and the whole film in effect becomes a spectacular feast of *nava rasas*.[2] Thus, in contrast to the single-genred Western film,

4 ■ POPULAR CINEMA AND POLITICS IN SOUTH INDIA

each Indian film (including many of the so-called 'new wave' ones) is an innovative admixture of a wide *range of genres*.

Popular stars like MGR and Sivaji of the past, and RK, Kamal, Vijayakanth, Vijay, and Vishal of the present, adroitly exploit these 'assembled' elements to establish their respective screen images.

Forms from Culture

Kaavya, meaning epic, has a well-knit grand narrative structure, subsuming innumerable little narratives as 'branches', which are employed either as illustrative examples or as biographies of related characters. *Kaavya* is essentially hero-centric, and the characters are assigned values vis-à-vis their bond(age) to the hero. The inherent ideology is statusquoist, and the overall tone is characterised by grandeur, beauty and ethics. All these aspects of *kaavya* are applicable to film as well. In fact, these aspects form the very backbone of the deep narrative structure of the films starring popular heroes.

Kooththu, meaning 'play' in rural parlance, has, as opposed to *kaavya*, a loosely-knit narrative structure, replete with folk songs, dances, stunts and double entrendres. *Kooththu* is performed as an inseparable part of the annual village festival (*oor thiruvizhaa*) in honour of the village deity, for the twin-purpose of entertaining and giving a socio-religious message. Such a festive context also provides *kooththu* performance with certain 'liminal freedom', which manifests itself as social criticism, mainly through the character of the 'buffoon', who plays a variety of roles including that of a jester and a commentator.

Kooththu, which is characterised, therefore, by religiosity, entertainment and social criticism, often has as its contents the quasi-historical and semi-mythological folk heroes and heroines. Sometimes, the folk derivatives of the branch stories from *kaavya* also constitute the contents of *kooththu*.[3] Film as a mass medium appropriates these features of *kooththu*, empties them of their radical and subversive potential, if any, and incorporates them with its *kaavya* core. Thus, film in effect is *a kaavya performed as a kooththu*.

It may be pertinent here to note that during the early years of cinema the elite sections of society viewed the film artistes with condescension, if not always with contempt. Even at a time when cinema held a complete sway over the masses, the elite and the Congressmen perceived cinema as a mere picturised version of *koooththu*. Noted Congress leader Kamaraj, one of the former chief ministers of Thamizh Nadu, referred to the then DMK front-rung leaders including Anna, M. Karunanidhi and MGR as *kooththaadikal* (literally, performers of *kooththu*) because of their links with the cinema industry.[4]

Contents from Culture

If the structure of the commercial film is an assemblage of *kaavya* and *kooththu*, when it comes to the *contents*, it is not rare to find specific motifs, themes, and even plots[5] drawn from three divergent cultural sources: the pan-Indian *kaavyas* and *puranas,* the region-specific *kooththu* folktales and myths of oral traditions, and the corpus of Thamizh classical literature starting from the *Sangam* age. The use, however, is very subtle and the motifs are *re-enunciated* metaphorically or metonymically within the universe of contemporary discourse.

The frequently recurring archetypal characters in Thamizh films include: *Rama–Sita* (ideal husband-wife relationship), *Kovalan–Mathavi* (extramarital sex), *Kannahi* ('queen of chastity'), *Surpanaka* (falling in love with another's husband), Draupadi (polyandry), Pandavas versus Kauravas (feud between in-laws), *Rama–Ravana* (good versus evil), *Krishna–Gopis* ('lila,' the play; by extension, eve-teasing), *Lakshman* (ideal brother), *Karnan* (ideal friend), *Saguni* (the schemer), *Kunthi* (virgin mother; by extension, one who gives birth through premarital sex), *Murugan–Valli–Theivanai* ('legal' bigamy), *Nallathangaal* (folk version of *pieta*, the suffering mother), *Mathurai Veeran* (folk hero from an untouchable community), *King Manu* (symbol of justice), *Thiruvalluvar* (the Great Intellectual), *Avvaiyaar* (the Wise Old Lady), and munificent nobles and chieftains like *Paari*.

The popular or commercial films, therefore, serve as a *synthesis* of dominant and subaltern cultures both in form *and* in content.

Double Climax

Since a film is screened in the movie houses in India as two halves to make provision for *interval* — a short break for about 15 minutes so that the viewers could refresh themselves — it has become *normative* that the narrative also is divided into two more or less equal halves. This has given rise to the practice of 'double climax' structuring of the narrative.[6] The narrative climaxes with an unexpected 'turning point' just preceding the interval, and this apparent 'narrative discrepancy' is sorted out in the post-interval half.

The following narrative schema highlights the general double climax structure centred on interval:

Phase 01 (The Beginning): It consists of establishing the narrative context, introducing the main characters, and initiating the central conflict.

Phase 02 (The Pre-Interval Development): The conflict initiated in the first phase undergoes a series of mutations with many twists and turns, acquires newer dimensions and gets more complex and intensified as the story moves ahead. Tension builds up, and as the interval approaches, it reaches its peak with a turning point.

Phase 03 (The First Climax): This 'climax' is a riveting turning point. It may involve an unexpected setback to the hero or villain, or a new mission entrusted to the hero, or the surfacing of a totally new problem. This keeps the viewers guessing during the interval as to what is in store for them during the next phase.

INTERVAL

Phase 04 (The Post-Interval Development): This phase starts with a twist, suspense or surprise, and with further turns and twists, the story moves forward towards the final showdown. The viewers are provided, through timely doses of back-story information, with additional and newer insights into the characters. Tension mounts as the climax approaches, the viewers' involvement and expectations soar high, and the conflict swells up in magnitude and intensity.

Phase 05 (The Final Climax): It marks the direct confrontation of the hero and the villain. The climactic fight is the fiercest and the longest. The villain is defeated, the hero emerges victorious, the victims of villainy are rescued, and the core conflict is resolved with reversal of fortunes.

Phase 06 (The Denouement): The viewers are greatly relieved of their tension as the hero triumphs. In the denouement that follows, loose strings are tied up and the story is rounded off with a few finishing touches.

ASSEMBLAGE STRUCTURE   7

The intervention of interval then further 'Indianises' the narrative structure by radically transforming it to *two* 'narratives' *disjointed and conjointed* by the interval. In this sense, interval is a *narrative*, in as much as a commercial or convenience, device. In the films of MGR and RK special attention is being paid to the point at which the narrative is to be divided, because a bad break may fail to pull the viewers back into the movie house after the interval. Moreover, the double climax structure makes the 'point of attack' (the point at which the narrative opens) a lot more challenging, compared to the conventional single climax structure. In fact, the risk involved in deciding the three major points — the point of attack, the interval break point, and the final climax — is so great that even seasoned filmmakers find it unnerving to guess which combination would click with the audience.

Hero-Centricity

A functional analysis of the dramatis personae in a typical masala film reveals that there is only one *prime* character (the protagonist or hero), one *significant active* character (the antagonist or villain), one *significant passive* character (the heroine), one *subordinate passive* character (the victim), two sets of *subordinate active* characters (hero's allies and villain's aides), and other characters used as mere *human props*. This could be represented diagrammatically as shown in Figure 1.1.

Obviously, all the films of the popular stars are as a rule hero-centric. Characters other than the hero — significant or subordinate, active or passive — are clipped[7] to heighten hero-centricity. These characters are linked up with the hero in a strict hierarchy, actualised through one or more of the following narrative cum technical devices:

- *social*[8] positioning of the characters in terms of their relationship with the hero as per the narrative
- *spatial* positioning of these characters vis-à-vis the hero in the overall mise-en-scène
- *visual perceptual* positioning in terms of composition of shots and camera angles regarding the characters vis-à-vis the hero
- *auro-lingual* positioning of sound and language aspects concerning the characters vis-à-vis the hero
- *temporal* positioning in terms of duration of their screen presence vis-à-vis the hero

Figure 1.1
Hero-Centric Model of Dramatis Personae

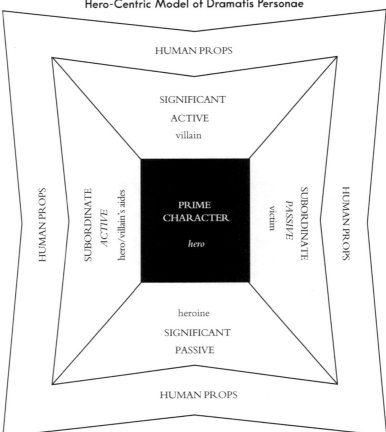

Source: All figures provided by the author.

The aforesaid and other such devices utilised are mixed with other masala elements within the selectively replicated socio–cultural universe. As the combined effect of this, the hero's image emerges profoundly and prominently.

Snowball Dynamics

The image formation concerning commercially successful, politically motivated stars like MGR and RK is an evolutionary process, involving *snowball dynamics.* The core image created in one film is carried over to the next, reinforcing the previously constructed image and adding an embellishing and enhancing layer to it. The choice of the themes, the treatment and the characterisation are most often stereotypical, redundant and serial-episodic. By contrast, the films of Sivaji and Kamal, the foremost rivals of MGR and RK respectively, have an 'insulatory additive' dynamics. That is, the image created in a film is self-contained and self-insulated (single-episodic), and is not, in general, carried over to the next film. Their films are, therefore, vibrantly entropic, and the *divergent* roles they play 'add' up to their image as 'great actors'.

Sivaji, for example, dabbles in a variety of genres and subjects — historical, mythological and social-familial — but always rendering the character come alive with his excellent, often exaggerated, performance. His roles range from hero to anti-hero, from handsome young man to respectable elder, from upright and law-abiding man to a man of loose morals, from 'the man who lives happily ever after' to the one who dies. Even the films in which Sivaji plays double or more roles are primarily designed to exhibit his acting skill.[9] The roles are so divergent that the image painted in a film is immediately erased or undone by the next film and a new image is painted, which in turn is erased.

Same thing could be said of Kamal, known for his dedication to on-going experimentation and innovation. His roles range from heavy to shallow, complex to naive, patriot to betrayer: compulsive obsessive neurotic (*Guna*), foreign-returned feudal lord (*Thaevar Magan*), bigamist (*Sathi Leelavathi*), divorcee masquerading as a woman (*Avvai Shanmugi*), hindu 'fundamentalist' (*Hei! Ram*), Marxist trade unionist (*Anbae Sivam*), small-time rowdy trying to study medicine (*Vasool Raja MBBS*), high-tech 'common man' (*Unnaipoal Oruvan*), patriotic Indian residing in the US, who helps the US destroy the Talibans in Afghanistan (*Vishwaroopam*)!

Sivaji and Kamal compete with their own performance by trying to outdo one performance by the next. They achieve this primarily through expert 'acting', which establishes the *difference* between characters. This could be seen vividly in the films where they play double or more roles — they pay meticulous attention to differentiate roles, rendering through acting each role with a unique personality. That explains why their films are invariably entropic, and they are appreciated as '*character* artistes'. On the contrary, MGR and RK, revered as '*charismatic* artistes', rely on 'action', and compete with their own performance, paradoxically, by *concurrence* of one performance with the previous one. While their films are not as entropic as that of Sivaji and Kamal, they take extreme care to *inventively* chisel their roles — a semblance of being entropic is offered by introducing a new style in fight or mannerism, new and more glamorous heroines, exotic outdoor locations for song–dance sequences, and political overtones — to *converge* on their image as 'super-powers'.

Notes

1. The genre-based narrative is essentially linear and logical, and is distinctly divided into 'acts'. Already the Greek philosopher Aristotle talks of *three* acts (protasis, epitasis and catastrophe). German playwright Gustav Freytag advocated *five* acts (exposition, rising action, climax, falling action, and denouement). Contemporary American screen writing author Syd Field has popularised the three-act structure. For more details on the structure of classical drama and its varied modern forms, see Neale and Krutnik (1990).
2. According to the Indian *classical* aesthetics, *bhava* refers to facial expression. There are nine *bhava*s, each expressing a lasting emotion such as love (*rathi*), laughter (*hasa*), sorrow (*soka*), anger (*krodha*), high-spiritedness (*uthsaha*), fear (*bhaya*), disgust (*jugupsa*), astonishment (*vismaya*), and peace (*shantha*). The experience of the expression of these emotions is called *rasa*. There are nine corresponding *rasas* (*navarasas*] of *sringara* or erotic, *hasya* or comedy, *karuna* or pathos, *raudra* or fury, *vira* or heroic, *bhayanka* or terror, *bibhastha* or indignation, *adbhutha* or wonder, and the ninth rasa is of peace and serenity. See Anand (1957).
3. Paradoxical it might seem, that *kooththu* sometimes draws its contents from *kaavya*. The paradox will be resolved, if we become aware of the fact that the grand epic by its very nature unceasingly absorbs or co-opts the popular little narratives. It may be reiterated that all the 'branch stories' of the great epics had once been the folktales of the subalterns. *Kooththu*, therefore, only 'retrieves' from the 'usurper' what had once rightfully belonged to it. It may be noticed that the *actual kooththu* performance of the 'retrieved' stories varies considerably from the epic source. The *kooththu* version might at times even be diametrically opposed to that of the epic.
4. Vestiges of this attitude continue even today among certain sections of the elite and the Congressmen. Ironically, however, having wonder-struck

by the enormous crowd-pulling power of these *koooththaadikal* particularly during election campaigns, the Congress also started, albeit reluctantly, to prune and promote its own version of *koooththaadikal*, epitomised in Sivaji.

5. Some of MGR's films, for example, are 're-makes' of *koooththu* performances themselves: 'Mathurai Veeran' and 'Raajaa Daesingu' draw heavily from *koooththu*. 'Gule Bakaavali' is an Arabic folklore, and it had also been filmed earlier. 'Jenoavaa' is a typical Western folklore.

6. Here is an instance of the *context deciding the content*. Much like the TV soaps closing each episode with a 'hook' to pull back the viewers for the next episode, the commercial cinema has devised the double climax tactic — a device too contrived to be spontaneous. But the interval break also means a big business, especially in multiplexes, where the viewers are not allowed to carry edibles from outside.

7. Characters other than the hero are clipped and mutilated to such an extent that, by and large, they lack any personality of their own. They are often stereotypical, flat and two-dimensional.

8. 'Social positioning' refers to the character's caste-cum-class status vis-à-vis the hero's. Indian society, it may be remembered, is marked by rigid caste hierarchy and cinema replicates the hierarchy either explicitly or implicitly. Even films that purport to decry caste division, ironically, tend to betray caste superiority.

9. Karunanidhi, who scripted *Raajaa Raani*, says years later that he included the rehearsals of four plays 'to show the acting skill of Sivaji to the people'. In the film Sivaji comes as the 'elderly' Socrates, the 'valorous' Chera king Senguttuvan, the 'serene' sage, and the 'comical' Abinaya Sundara Mudaliyar (Narayanan (1994: 223). Incidentally, when Sivaji died, the *Los Angeles Times* (23 July 2001), in its 'Passings' section described Sivaji as 'an intense actor considered the Marlon Brando of south India's film industry'. No wonder why Sivaji is called *Nadikar Thilakam*, whereas MGR is *Makkal Thilakam* and belongs to Fairbanks–Flynn school.

2

IMAGE-BUILDING DEVICES

Given the fact that MGR and RK are more image-conscious than their respective contemporaries, they are seen to appropriate all available narrative devices, not merely for the purpose of expert story-telling, but primarily as vehicles of effective image-building. For this reason, the way they employ these devices is more *functional* than aesthetic. The most commonly deployed ones are, surprisingly, the very 'easily disposable' 'non-story' components having little direct bearing on the film's story but exerting an enormous influence over the exercise of image-construction.[1] Of these, stunts, double-roles, comedy, songs, punch dialogues, mini-narratives, dramatic entry and end clips are discussed below.

Stunts and Villainy

MGR and RK portray their villains as though they are 'evil incarnate', reducing them to single-agenda existence — they exist only to oppose and eliminate the hero, who, however, is invincible and undefeatable. Such a reduction of personality is obviously based on the logic of 'the worst villain makes the best hero'. The evil-doings of the villain are exaggerated only to accentuate the unconquerable power of the hero. Besides the narrative details, technical aspects such as the camera angles and movements, and sound effects are so manipulated as to heavily distort the image of the villain, who comes across as an evil personified.

It is to be remembered, however, that a film would normally have more than one person set against the hero. There is, in fact, a 'hierarchy' of villains, as Figure 2.1 illustrates.

IMAGE-BUILDING DEVICES 13

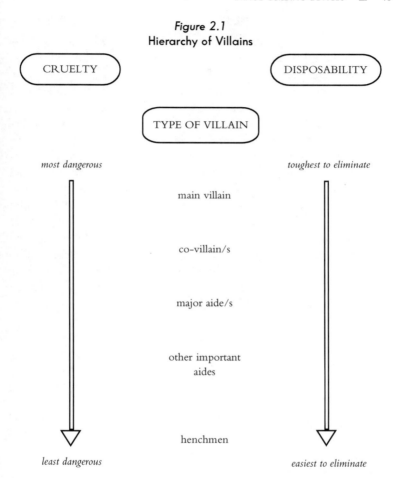

Figure 2.1
Hierarchy of Villains

It is the 'villainy' actualised in different degrees at different points in the narrative by the hierarchised gang[2] of villains that makes the mission of the hero look insurmountable. The importance is in the descending order, as one goes down from the 'main villain' to the 'henchman'. Accordingly, the effort put in by the hero is the least while tackling the henchmen, and it increases as he moves up the ladder. Figure 2.1 shows the relative effort required of the hero, corresponding to the type of villain he confronts. In minor fights, the hero's body is not touched. In major fights he may receive a blow or two, that too initially, in order to provoke him. In very major fights, there is reciprocal physical assault, but it is more on the villain. In the climactic fight, violence is let loose on both sides (usually there will be other people with the hero) with physical assaults.

While granting that the war between the villain and the hero is reminiscent of the mythological war between the good and the evil, the *deva*s and the *asura*s, a critical look at the films of MGR and RK would tell us that the villains are not without any good, and, conversely, the heroes are not without any blemish. In many films the villains do have a 'positive side' — however thin it may be — and the heroes, their 'darker side'. MGR's image, as we have noted earlier, is one of 'do-gooder' with an 'anti-social' streak popping up now and then. RK's image accommodates much more 'deviance' as an integral part of his personality structure. Leaving this aspect aside, the ruthless and inhuman way in which the hero eliminates the villain's men and often the villain himself would be sufficient enough to militate against the 'good' hero! This means that the villain and the hero have something in common, as Figure 2.2 highlights.

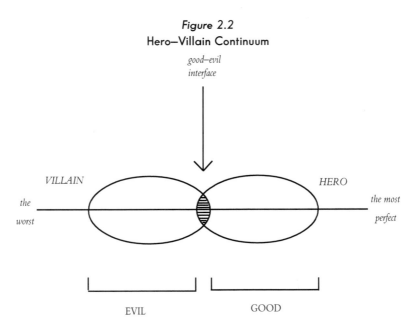

Figure 2.2
Hero–Villain Continuum

What attracts our attention is the dynamics of 'good–evil interface' in the 'hero–villain continuum'. The 'evil' in the hero is justified because of the noble 'end' — 'the end justifies the means' — an unacceptable or at least debatable ethical principle. The 'good' in the villain is actualised in his act of surrendering to the hero and repenting for his evil-doings.[3]

Double-Roles

'Double-roles', or 'double-acts' as it is popularly called, is a technologically constructed narrative device, which enables a person (the hero as a norm; occasionally also the heroine) to play simultaneously two distinctly different characters.

When the 'double-roles' technique was introduced in the 1950s, it was surely a *novelty*, and was received by the audience with excitement. That this technique is still a popular narrative device — at a time when we have super computers generating amazing virtual realities — indicates that its prevalence is for reasons *other than* being novel.

This device is more often seen in the films of *mega stars* (for example MGR, Sivaji, RK, and Kamal) or mega directors (for example, Shankar's *Jeans*). An obvious reason for this phenomenon is the space it gives the hero to *monopolise* the film. The hero, playing two roles simultaneously, inevitably occupies more time. Thus, the centrality of the hero, which might otherwise be criticised as 'undue', is justified thanks to this device.[4] Added to this is the opportunity the hero gets to act with *two heroines* at a time. This can be a real feast to the fans, because they, with their hero, have the *voyeuristic pleasure* of gazing at two beautiful damsels.[5]

That this device gives a golden opportunity for the hero to *exhibit his histrionic skills* can be another valid reason. Versatile actors like Sivaji and Kamal, who have played double-roles in more films than their respective rivals (MGR and RK), are known for using this device to show their audience how multifaceted they are. In the case of MGR and RK, often it is not the case. In fact, their double-acting in general is poor, and they differentiate the two roles primarily through heavy make-up and contrasting costume, and not through acting. MGR, who invariably struggles in double roles, for example, tries to manage by means of exaggerated mannerisms. *Naadoadi Mannan* is a case in point: his mannerism in his role as the king-in-waiting is overdone to the point of annoyance.

16 POPULAR CINEMA AND POLITICS IN SOUTH INDIA

A majority of films, however, attempt to provide an interesting plot through double-acting. Disappointingly, even here, barring a very few exceptions, most of the double roles could be dispensed with, without affecting the main story because of 'narrative superfluity'. What is interesting, however, is the clever use of double acting as a cinematic variant of the psychological game of Jekyll-and-Hide. Sometimes one role may act as the 'conscience' personified. In any case, this device helps the hero keep his moral image intact while indulging in amoral, anti-social activities.

Based on the above observations, the double-acting of MGR and RK could be compared. In both MGR and RK films, one role is inevitably the hero, and the other is either a villain or a victim or a helper. In some films where one role is on par with the other, in terms of character strength and centrality, the hero may also be a helper, in which case the other role will assume 'heroship'. In some other cases, the victim becomes a helper, but after being 'redeemed' by the hero.

There are three possible relationships between the two roles as shown in Figure 2.3. In the *hero–villain* relationship, the hero confronts the villain, who is either 'condemned' to death at the end (*Raajaa Daesingu*; in *Billaa* the villain is condemned but not by the hero) or 'condoned' after he repents (*Netrikkann*). In *hero–victim* relationship, the hero takes on himself the task of rescuing the victim from the clutches of the villain (not of the double roles). Sometimes, the victim is rescued early, in which case he becomes hero's collaborator (*Siriththu Vaazha Vaendum*). In *hero–helper* relationship, both of them collaborate in tackling the common villain.

In MGR and RK films, the roles chosen to be paired reflect an *asymmetrical*[6] social system. MGR, in his twin roles, *confronts* the divided society and, through *legal* justice, *neutralises* the disparities. RK, on the contrary, while *acknowledging* the disparities, *naturalises* them through *spiritualising* them. Both, however, *evade* the core issues, which continue to remain unresolved — a point to be discussed in later chapters.

Comedy and Inversion

In a film that effectively tells the story, the comedy normally plays a crucial role, especially when the story involves a heavy theme. Any effective narrative would also take the viewer along as it progresses towards peak moments, building up tension both within the story and

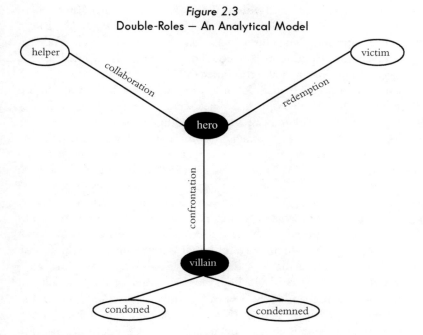

Figure 2.3
Double-Roles — An Analytical Model

outside of it, that is, in the viewer. Comedy comes as a welcome relief during such moments. Sadly though, such a creative interpolation of comedy with the story is a rarity in Thamizh films.

Often enough, comedy is treated as a convenient time-filler — in order to stretch the film for about two-and-a-half hours, an average length of a typical Thamizh film. The comedy moves parallel to the main story as a separate 'track', and the hero is not physically present in most of such sequences. The only 'connection' is that the comedian will be given the identity as hero's friend. Surprisingly, even RK films are no exceptions, particularly the ones in which RK combines with another professional comedian. The 'narrative autonomy' of the comedy track has become almost a tradition in Thamizh filmdom. As an unavoidable corollary, the comedy actors also function 'autonomously', evolving the content themselves *independently* of the director!

The 'positive' side of the 'narrative autonomy' enjoyed by comedy (and the comedians) is its use in commenting on socio-political issues of the day, by satirising, parodying, belittling or passing derogatory remarks. The pioneer in metamorphosing comedy into an effective

18 POPULAR CINEMA AND POLITICS IN SOUTH INDIA

weapon of socio-political critique is N. S. Krishnan (NSK),[7] later known as 'Kalaivaanar'. His 'kinthanaar kathaa kaalakshepam' in *Nalla Thampi*, and 'Aimpathum Arupathum' in *Manamagal* are classic examples of what a socially conscientious person could do with comedy. Comedians like Nagesh and Chandra Babu continued the NSK tradition, but very much toned down — so toned down at times as to reach the point of no significance. Of late, comedian Vivek seems to imitate NSK in criticising what he considers as superstitious cultural and religious practices.

An interesting use of comedy is 'comical inversion', i.e., making the comedy an 'inverse' of the main story; the comedian in turn becomes an 'inverse hero'. In *Raaman Thaediya Seethai*, for example, the hero MGR in his search for an ideal woman administers tests on several of them before ticking off one. His comedian friend inverts this story by falling in love blindly, and getting married in a haphazard manner. His weak body (exposed in a boxing contest) is an inversion of the hero's handsome body. The message of comical inversion is clear: a foolish and weak man like the comedian deserves only such a wedding; conversely, 'selecting' an ideal wife is the prerogative of a rich, intelligent and handsome man like MGR. Similar inversions could be found in a number of MGR starrers (*Naadoadi Mannan, Urimai Kural*, etc.). Comical inversion is not very uncommon in RK films. In *Padaiyappaa*, for example, the comedian Senthil, who is of same dark complexion as RK, is presented as an inverse hero. In the pretty long sequence of introducing the hero to the heroine, constant comparison is made between the comedian and RK. In another sequence when the friends go for the engagement of the comedian, he is lent the hero's attire, only to be stripped shortly!

A clever use of the comedy is to make the comedian the mouthpiece of the hero. In *Ithaya Kani*, for example, the comedian refers to seeing the 'vaaththiyaar' film *Thaikkuppin Thaaram* seven times and is in all praise for the bull-fight. In *Enga Veettu Pillai*, the comedian declares that the whole country has adopted MGR as their 'household son'. In RK's *Annaamalai*, the comedian constantly describes the attractiveness of RK, and speaks on his behalf (and on behalf of the 'poor').

Song Massage

The most regular and popular imaging device concerns the cine songs. Since cine songs have a peculiar existence and circulation of their own (see Figure 2.4), they serve both as an ongoing massage for the receivers, and as an unceasing flying-carrier of political messages of the stars concerned.

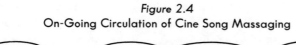

Figure 2.4
On-Going Circulation of Cine Song Massaging

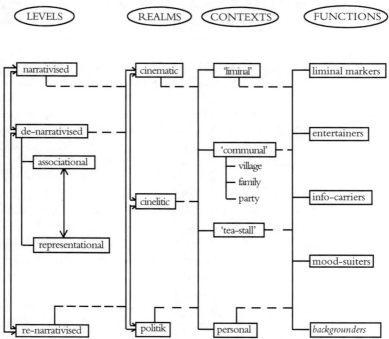

The cine song operates at three *levels*. Whether a song-dance (S-D) sequence is intrinsically bound up with the story or added only as an appendage (which often is the case), it is assigned a place in the original narrative as filmed. This is the first level (the 'narrativised' level). The second level concerns the repackaging of these S-D sequences in other (non-movie) media by lifting them out of their original narrative contexts. The non-movie media, which constantly churn out a variety of 'cine-based' programmes, encompass the industries of television, radio and audio-players. Though at this level the S-D sequences are 'de-narrativised', they are still connected to the star. This 'connection'

20 POPULAR CINEMA AND POLITICS IN SOUTH INDIA

in the case of TV is 'associational' (the image of the star in the audio-visual clippings obviously link the song to the star), whereas it is 'representational' in the case of audio-only programmes (though the song is delinked from the star because it is the voice of the singer, it is all the same linked to him because it is identified as occurring in that star's film). The third ('re-narrativised') level, seen primarily from the point of view of the viewers/listeners, is the imaginative repackaging of S-Ds (video or audio), induced by different realms and contexts, wherein the viewers/listeners are able to freely weave their own fantasies as narratives.

The cine songs (and S-Ds) offer their users the feel of getting massaged by performing one or more of the following *functions*:

- They serve as *liminal markers* when they are blasted through cones and loud speakers during *family* celebrations like weddings, deaths and births, *socio-religious* festivals involving the whole village, and *political* revelries over anniversaries and election victories.
- They are one of the cheapest and easily available 'entertainers' and time-fillers. They can be heard at leisure and according to one's convenience for a longer or shorter duration. They could be endlessly repeated to one's heart's content.
- Listening to cine songs for the sake of their content makes them powerful *info-carriers*. It should be emphasised here that though each song has a central theme based on which it could be categorised as the romantic, the social (particularly in praise of the subaltern identity), the motivational, the moral, the political, the sentimental (concerning fraternal, maternal and other familial relationships), the spiritual, the philosophical and so on, each is *polyphonic* and often characterised by multiple tonalities.
- The cine songs become very soothing and comforting 'mood-suiters' by catering to the personal moods and preferences of the users. More than the content, it is music that does this function (light, sad, fast, melodious, heavy, joyous, slow, etc.).
- Another taken-for-granted but widely prevalent function of the cine songs is serving as *backgrounders*, providing 'unlistened sound effect'.

The cine songs are spread across three *realms* marked by four inter-related contexts. The 'cinematic' realm is the one in which a film is seen and experienced in the theatrical 'liminal' context. The 'cinelitic' refers to the realm of the fan club activities, which is the interface of cinema and politics. The 'politik' is the directly political realm, which is party-based. In terms of magnitude, the S-Ds or just the songs are consumed more outside the theatrical contexts than inside. The most 'silent' of such non-theatrical use is private listening, the 'noisiest' is the 'communal' celebration, be it at the level of village, family or political party, and the most complex is its use at the 'tea-stall' (see Figure 2.5).

In the rural socio-political system, the tea-stall is an important 'centre', a 'melting pot', a meeting point, where collective opinions are

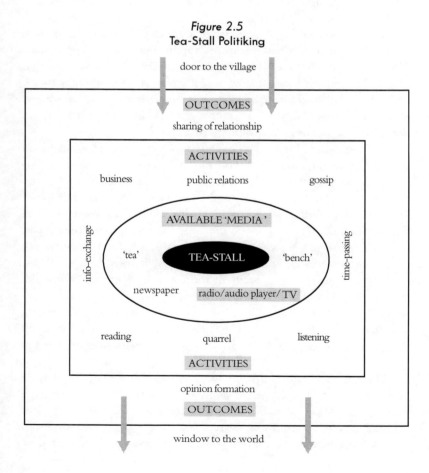

Figure 2.5
Tea-Stall Politiking

22 ▄ POPULAR CINEMA AND POLITICS IN SOUTH INDIA

formed and relationships shared.[8] The tea-stall is not merely a point of buying and selling, but a 'door to the village' and a 'window to the world'. It is surrounded with metaleptically overlapping hostile and friendly activities of sharing and disputing, gossiping and problem solving, reading and listening, voyeuring and just time-passing, and so on. The available 'media', which constitute the substance of and the milieu for the plethora of activities, are 'tea' (or anything that is consumed), 'bench' (normally the wooden bench to sit; who sits when will depend on the relative ranking in the caste hierarchy), 'newspaper' (or any paper or magazine meant for reading; one's ability to read is a mark of one's social status), and radio or audio player (and sometimes TV also).

From the point of view of the formation of political opinions, the radio/audio player plays a crucial role. Though these technological devices may appear to be the non-interrupting but noisy backgrounders, they often take on provoking, inspiring, and even instigating roles. They also frequently become *reference points* to clarify and judge issues, to gather additional information, to solve problems, etc. Interestingly, the content that is disseminated through radio/audio player is by and large cine-based, *cine songs* to be specific.

Strikingly, the bulk of the conversation is cine-related interspersed with other matters ranging from the most trivial to the gravest. The conversation in general does not follow any logic and order, any passer-by could become an active partner in the chat and anyone could drop out any time. This indeed is very peculiar — while the chat partners are in a constant flux, the chat goes on non-stop (till the shop is closed). This aspect of tea-stall politiking resembles surprisingly the *chat on the net*, with one vital difference of the net chat being marked by anonymity.

The *informality* that prevails in the tea-stall, as distinct from the formality and rigidity of the village *panchayat*, contributes to the effectiveness of the tea-stall politiking. Most of the decisions concerning the affairs of the village, it could be said, are *announced* in the *panchayat*, while the necessary *ground* for arriving at such decisions is prepared at the tea-stall.

Though each stall will have an assortment of CDs (representing various stars) to be played on request (if need be), it is a common phenomenon that the stalls blare out songs from RK starrers, and not infrequently also from MGR starrers. It is noteworthy that songs from MGR films, particularly the *kolhai paadalkal* (ideological songs), have a lasting value cutting across generations because of their ethical content and celebration of subalternity.

Punch Dialogues

A punch dialogue is an utterance accompanied by dramatised action usually delivered by the hero. It is an art involving the syntactics of verbal composition and the stylistics of acting that out. The 'punch' comes because of the conglomeration of poetic exaggeration, wit, philosophical overtone, political sarcasm, etc., often tinged with oxymoron, metaphor and other figures of speech. The emotional intensity of the narrative setting (confrontational, as a norm), the camera angles and the special sound effects make the punch effective; the catchiness and the simplicity of the rhymes make it memorable; the inventiveness of the style makes it worth practiceable.

Just as in the field of advertising the USP (Unique Selling Proposition) is critical to the effective positioning of a brand, in the field of cinema, 'punch dialogue' has been successfully applied by RK as a USP to 'position' his image. The beginnings of this could already be seen in MGR starrers, though he did not extensively use this devise. For example, MGR's statement in *Marma Yoagi*: 'If I aim, it will not miss (to hit the target); if it is going to miss, I will not aim', was such a hit that it almost became a proverb. In *Naadoadi Mannan* he says, 'There are many who have ruined themselves without trusting me; there is none who has trusted me got ruined'.

By combining such 'propositions' with his 'style' and making them sound political (particularly in the films released during the 1990s) RK has managed to strike the right formula to evolve a saleable USP for each film: 'Don't provoke me; if you do, I'll do what I say and what I have not said' (*Annaamalai*); 'I am the union, I am the leader – always' (*Mannan*); 'If I say once, it is like saying a hundred times', 'God tests the good, but does not forsake; He gives plenty to the bad, but forsakes them' (*Baatshaa*); 'No one knows when I'll come, how I'll come; but I'll come right at the right moment' (*Muththu*); 'God says thus, and Arunaachalam accomplishes it' (*Arunaachalam*), 'My way is a unique way, don't interfere' (*Padaiyappaa*); 'Only pigs come as a herd; a lion comes single' (*Sivaji*). The USPs are too numerous to be listed here (more could be found in the later chapter on tactexting in RK films).

24 ■ POPULAR CINEMA AND POLITICS IN SOUTH INDIA

Even a cursory reading of these pronouncements of RK would indicate how these are politically motivated. But what interests us here is the way these USPs are advertised to promote his films. These statements were given the status of the Vedas and included in all the publicity materials of the films — posters, hoardings, newspaper ads and stills, and trailers. RK politicised the narrative; narrativised the politics; and commercialised both to make profits in crores — an aspect to be looked into later. No other Thamizh actor to this day has made such a successful use of this narrative device to promote his/her business.[9]

Mini-Narratives

A mini-narrative is any minuscule narrative form such as a 'short' story or a snippet that is not directly connected (or only remotely connected) to the main story of the film. As a narrative device, it encompasses:

- Unrelated plays or side-stories deliberately inserted
- Court scenes, often too contrived to flow with the main story
- Documentary footages, both audio and visual
- Snippets or 'pass-by' mini-narratives
- Icons in the mise-en-scene
- Cues prefacing the film

The early DMK activists, especially from 1949 to the late 1950s, extensively used this mini-narrative device to deliver alliterative *rhetorical* monologues as a response to the current socio-political happenings. Their film rhetoric in conjunction with the overall media rhetoric helped the DMK in a number of ways: in the political front, to propagandise its 'anti-North, anti-Brahmin, and anti-theist' ideology; in the socio-cultural front, to advocate social reforms and to campaign against the prevailing social evils; and in the linguistic front, to champion the revival of the Thamizh language and cultural heritage.

To this end, the DMK activists frequently resorted to highly dramatic 'confrontational scenes', which would lend themselves for the hero to deliver his rhetorical pronouncements in the form of presenting his arguments. Thus, through the court scenes in *Vaelaikkaari* (1949) the DMK founder Anna comes up with his scathing attack on the deceit of religious heads. In *Paraasakthi* (1952), Anna's disciple M. Karunanidhi (MK) goes a step further in his vitriolic attack on religion. Similar criticisms are found, though in a much diluted and mutilated form, in later films such as MK's *Manohara* and Anna's *Sorka Vaasal* (both 1954).

Rhetorical *plays*, ranging from plays proper to play rehearsals and musical story-telling form of *kathaa kaalakshepam*, have been employed with varying degrees of success. The trend starts with Anna's *Nalla Thampi* in which is featured 'kinthanaar kathaa kaalakshepam'. Commenting on the film, Anna himself jovially remarked, 'Between *kinthanaar kathaa kaalakshepam* and campaign on prohibition my story has also been skilfully packaged!' (Narayanan 1994: 96). The story of 'Anarkali' in Kannadasan's *Illara Jothi*, the rehearsal of the play on 'Cheran Senguttuvan' in M. Karunanidhi's *Raja Rani*, and the play of 'Samrat Ashokan' in Murasoli Maran's *Annayin Aanai* are replete with 'anti-Delhi, anti-North, and anti-Congress' sentiments. Sometimes, even *documentary* footage is also used, as in N. S. Krishnan's *Panam* where a documentary footage featuring the proceedings of the DMK's First State Level Conference held in December 1951 finds a strategic place.

MGR, as a DMK artiste, identifies himself with the DMK mainstream by *selectively* adopting the mini-narrative forms. He does not, for example, entertain play-inserts.[10] He does adopt court scenes, but prefers *dialogical* settings to elongated monologues, as exemplified in the court-inserts in the early films scripted especially by the DMK activists like MK and Kannadasan. There are court scenes in MK's *Raaja Kumaari* and *Manthiri Kumaari*, A. S. A. Swamy's *Marma Yoagi*, Thanjai Ramaiyadoss' *Gule Bakaavali*, and Kannadasan's *Mathurai Veeran*. On rare occasions MGR has used documentary footage also, as *Ulagam Sutrum Vaalipan*, which uses clippings of leaders like Gandhi, Nehru and Anna speaking on harnessing scientific inventions for social development.

Without intruding into his action hero image, MGR subtly manipulates other forms of mini-narratives to maintain his identity as a DMK artiste, and at the same time to propagate his own vision of society. He frequently places the party symbols, photographs of party leaders, and names of party leaders, Thamizh kings and Thamizh scholars, both contemporary and legendary, as *icons* in the mise-en-scene, the 'setting' of a scene. In *Ithaya Kani*, for example, he introduces the AIADMK's symbol of twin-leaves; in *Rikshaakaaran*, pictures of Gandhi, Anna, Bharati and Crucifix are among the props in MGR's hut; in *Neethikku Thalai Vanangu*, a street is named after Thalamuthu, a DMK martyr; similarly, in *Thirudaathae*, an orphanage is named after the Thamizh scholar Thiru Vi Ka.

26 ⬛ POPULAR CINEMA AND POLITICS IN SOUTH INDIA

What is amazing is MGR's resourcefulness in inventing new forms or putting the existing forms to *new use*. The foremost invention is the 'pass-by' mini-narrative, an 'event' that gets his attention only momentarily as he 'passes by'. In *Oli Vilakku*, for example, as MGR walks along the street, he would pause for a while to enquire into the health of an old lady. In *Meenava Nanpan*, he would, in a 'split-second' encounter, 'adopt' parents for him. These are all trivial things but have terrific impact on the formation of his image.

Prefacing refers to placing 'cues' before or as the film commences informing the viewer from what perspective the film needs to be interpreted. Thus, in *Ithaya Kani* he prefaces the film with a voice over quote of Anna acknowledging him as his 'ithaya kani' (dynamic equivalent of 'the apple of the eye'). In *Naadoadi Mannan* he does the prefacing through the title song exalting the Thamizh language and the Dravida Nation. In *Nam Naadu*, a directorial voice over sets the tone of the film.

Besides these, even songs, especially moral and political ones, are occasionally *narrativised*.[11] For instance, a narrative context is created for the take-off of the song advising the kids not to steal (*Thirudaathae*), and to obey parents (*Nam Naadu*).

In the case of RK, there are numerous instances of his employing the mini-narrative device, but the practice is not *consciously and consistently* political till the early nineties, and in a curious turn is *deliberately a-political* after *Baba*, as will be seen later in the tactextual analysis of his films.

Dramatic Entry

To emphasise the importance and centrality of the hero, he is often introduced dramatically. The hero's entry happens as a sudden 'intrusion' in the story. In sharp contrast to the conventional entry, where the hero's entry realistically flows with the narrative, in the dramatic entry, it is as though he appears from nowhere, and this 'suddenness' may not be justified at all. This type of entry is very common in the films of MGR (like *Periya Idaththu Penn*, *Kumari Koattam*, *Meenava Nanpan*, and *Mathuraiyai Meetta Sunthara Paandiyan*) and in the films of RK (for example, *Padaiyappaa*). The context in which such a dramatic entry occurs always corresponds to their image as the representatives

IMAGE-BUILDING DEVICES 27

of the poor and the marginalised, or as the saviours and protectors of women in danger. Interestingly, all such entries happen in a confrontational situation.

Foreshadowing the entry is yet another popular way of introducing the hero, especially in the case of RK. Other characters in the film are shown, in a chain of events, to compliment, adore and revere the hero, who is yet to be introduced. This makes the viewer wait with expectation for his arrival, and finally the hero appears, much in the fashion of a divine apparition, amidst singing and dancing. This 'delay-expectation-arrival' technique in films like *Baatshaa*, *Arunaachalam*, and *Baba* symbolises his 'supermanship' or 'divinity'. This may be extended even to the initial titles, for example, an eerie BGM accompanies the computer-generated title of RK.

End-Clips

The story comes to a close, in a typical film, when the climax is completed with a denouement. But in quite a few films, it could be noticed, a set of visual clippings come after the formal closure and just preceding or accompanying the credits (the 'end-clips'). These clips apparently have no bearings whatsoever on the story proper, but they do have an important role to play in giving a 'finishing touch' to the image. While the denouement winds up the story, it is the end-clip that marks the closure of the tone and mood of the film. Interestingly, from the image-building point of view, the tone and mood commence already in the title and close with the credit. Thus, the image construction is a 'title-to-credit' process. If the presentation of the titles (with subsequent but more impactful dramatic entry of the hero) is designed to attract the viewer based on the law of *primacy*, the end-clips work on the law of *recency* by subtly persuading the viewer as to the kind of image they are to remember and the message to be taken home.

The typically conventional ending would stop with the freeze frame of the 'union of lovers' (hero and heroine). The most popular ending involves the repeat of the first/title ('inaugural') song of the hero either in full or a segment. Such songs in MGR films often justify the titles, as in *Thani Piravi* ('Only once I've spoken with you, you are unique by birth…'). In many of his films, however, a brief, often two-stroke, dialogue justifying the title precedes, as in *Siriththu Vaazha Vaendum*, the song repeat 'I am an actor in the stage of world' is preceded by a two-stroke conversation justifying the title:

'If only a good man cries, others will laugh.'
'Yes, all must live laughing...'

While in MGR films the end-line justifies the title, in RK films it is the ridicule of the conventional denouement, as in *Nallavanukku Nallavan* and *Mister Bhaarath*, where a character mocks at the stereotypical ending of the police coming to arrest the culprits.

Other Devices

The most contemporary and the most fascinating narrative device concerns the use of technology, including computer graphics, special effects and innovations in sound — besides manoeuvring camera, lighting, and editing. These are increasingly employed with other narrative devices to boost, as evident in the recent RK starrers from *Baatshaa* onwards, the invincible image of the hero.

Notes

1. The importance of these devices in image-construction for the stars particularly with a political agenda could be understood from the way the viewers respond to their use by 'non-star' actors — comedians and heroes as well. In the hands of 'non-stars' they degenerate into a spoof, which the viewers brush aside as a nonsense or enjoy as a comedy. The punch dialogue is a case in point: its use by anyone except RK amounts to a comedy, and in fact it is used frequently by comedians to provoke laughter. In another extreme, *Thamizhpadam*, a spoof that deconstructs heroism in Thamizh films, epitomises the 'comedy of heroism'.
2. Most films depict the villains to form a well-knit, cohesive but hierarchised group — something like a 'community of gangsters' — with their own norms and ethics. Discipline and obedience to the leader are the watchwords.
3. It must be reiterated that the present post-/modern trend is towards *obliterating* the good–evil continuum, making the hero *converge* on the

villain. For a fuller treatment of this trend, see later our discussion on RK's *Enthiran*.

4. However, we should remember that for the mega stars their 'centrality' is their life-blood, their survival, and it would be achieved even without having recourse to double acting.

5. To be seen with young and beautiful girls may also be a desperate need for the aging hero, as noted earlier in the case of MGR.

6. For a descriptive account of the asymmetry, see our later discussion on universe and multiverse.

7. 'Any average Tamil film would have its 'serious' side in which the trials and tribulations of the hero and the heroine are portrayed, and this would provide all the rasas except *Hasya* and that was provided by the comedian (the film version of the traditional Vidusaka/buffoon) whose antics, either as a fool or a man with foolish habits, provide the laughter to the audience. N. S. Krishnan used this pattern to provide a parallel theme within the main film dealing with the incongruent social features. This parallel theme would be an autonomous one — it forms a sub-plot within the major plot of the film — and the relevance it would have to the main theme would only be minimal and nominal. Very often the comedian is a friend of the hero and would perhaps help the hero at some crucial moments'. See Sivathamby (1981: 27–28).

8. It may be noted that in many villages the 'barber-shop' also does most of the functions of the 'tea-stall'.

9. It is interesting that RK is interpreted as a 'management guru' and his punch dialogues as 'value statements on business and life management'. See Balasubramanian and Krishnamoorthy (2010).

10. MGR does not entertain play-inserts, because that would make high demands on his acting skill. He knows that he is not a 'character' artiste like Sivaji, so he prefers the action-oriented stuff. He is not a 'talker' but a 'doer'.

11. Since songs enjoy greater reach than the films themselves, MGR has been paying utmost attention to their composition and positioning in the overall narrative.

Part II: Politics of Body

3

IMAGING MALE BODY

The most obvious and perceptible of the differences between MGR and RK lies in the presentation of their (male) bodies, especially the 'look' and the body structure. The 'body presentation' remains as the remarkably visible 'differentiation marker' because it is MGR and RK, as 'em-bodied' heroes, who dominate vast chunk of scenes in each film. Their persistent 'bodily' presence, in effect, is the medium through which the narrative unfolds.

The skin complexion and the body-build are often hereditary, and are in ordinary circumstances unchangeable. That these seemingly superficial, surface characteristics can have far-reaching consequences is evident from the manner in which both MGR and RK have ingeniously handled their bodies on-screen to construct each one's unique and lasting image.

Male Body Exhibition

MGR is fair-skinned and enjoys a well-built muscular body. He is ever-young and handsome[1] like the mythological *Markandaeya*, and defies death even in the most deadly encounters. He possesses enormous strength and can tackle a battalion of foes with relative ease. According to classical and dominant aesthetics, such a body type is considered attractive and desirable.[2]

RK, on the contrary, is of dark complexion, and the structure of his body consists of too slender a leg to match the rather broad bust. 'In every company I approach, they say', RK broods with self-pity in *Raajaa Chinna Roajaa*, 'have you seen your face in the mirror? How can you, with your black skin, unkempt hair, and small eyes, become a hero? Do you think the people are fools? Only if an extraordinary

34 POPULAR CINEMA AND POLITICS IN SOUTH INDIA

miracle happens in this world, can you become a hero!' Such a body type with aesthetically undesirable features would only be considered a handicap for an average male. With respect to valour and bravado, however, RK is on a par with MGR, and in 'style', he outsmarts him.

While MGR and RK differ in many respects, both take pleasure in exhibiting the male body. They do this through the following four ways:

Clothing

MGR revels in selectively exhibiting his body through clothing. Whether a cowherd or a rickshaw-puller, he is seen in half-sleeved shirts, revealing the well-formed muscles of the upper arms. His favourite tight-fitting shirts and pants display the contours of his body structure. Occasionally he is also seen bare-bodied (*Nallavan Vaazhvaan, Urimai Kural*), and with just a loin-cloth around his waist (*Mahaadaevi*). Even after growing relatively old, MGR would still remain romantically more daring, as in *Ulagam Sutrum Vaalipan*, indulging in under-water romance in a swim-suit.

Barring a difference or two (for example, RK is more frequently seen in long sleeves), RK resembles MGR in selective exhibition of his body features. Often that is in the direction of proving his machismo. Much like MGR, RK is seen to be more body-conscious as he grows older. For example, in *Padaiyappaa*, a young man stands wonder-struck by his well-built bare body. In later films such as *Enthiran* he would go for the romantic feel rather than exposing his body.

Character Choice

The way MGR and RK like their bodies to be perceived by the audience is linked up with the kind of roles they play. MGR, who has been derisively labeled 'aged actor' (*kizhattunadigan*) from mid-1950s onwards, has paid meticulous attention to the choice of characters. Thus, he would not grow old; he would not be an elder brother (with very few exceptions like *En Thangai* and *Panakkaara Kudumbam*); he would not have grown-up daughters. With only a handful of exceptions, his films would end with marriage of lovers. He is always young and smart. His last film *Mathuraiyai Meetta Sunthara Paandiyan* witnesses a 61-year old man acting as a youth in his early twenties. He is handsome and without any blemish or handicap;[3] and as a general rule, MGR does not die.[4]

IMAGING MALE BODY ◼ 35

While RK is particular with his 'formula', he is not so obsessed like MGR with looking young. His predominant concern is that he must emerge as the 'super star' at the end, whether he is young or old. Often he combines in the same film being young and old, either by structuring the story to extend over two or three generations (as in *Nallavanukku Nallavan* and *Padaiyappaa*), or by taking recourse to the narrative device of double act (as in *Netri Kann* and *Muththu*).

Stunt

Stunt sequences are one sure way of proving to the fans that MGR and RK are young. Each film has at least two major stunt sequences, with the climactic one being longer and fiercer, involving violent physical assaults. The duration of each sequence depends on the person with whom the hero fights and the narrative point at which the fight occurs.

MGR and RK are versatile 'fighters,' but each has his own unique style of fighting. MGR is seen to be more proficient with 'traditional' weapons[5] like sword and *silambam*,[6] inserted more as a *display of his expertise* in wielding these weapons rather than for decimating the villains.[7] RK, on the contrary, is more *physical* in his stunts. He cleverly combines, to the merriment of his fans, mischievous comedy and violence with 'style'.

Adulation

Singing the praise of the hero, usually by the heroine, is yet another way of manifesting male exhibitionism. It is mandatory that in all the films of MGR and RK there will be at least one song depicting their ineffable physical beauty and charm. Besides songs, there is a generous sprinkling of dialogues and passing references by other characters glorifying every aspect of physicality, including face, complexion, eyes, smile, speech, chest, mannerism, walking, mischief and recklessness, valour, and youthfulness.

In the case of MGR, for example, the lover (in *Meenava Nanpan*) wonders if he is the god of lust (*kaaman*):

> Face made of gold
> Body made of sandalwood
> Is it you who have come like *Kaaman*!
> Is it you the king of the divine world!

36 ■ POPULAR CINEMA AND POLITICS IN SOUTH INDIA

The exhibition of MGR's body through adulation could be summed up in the fantasy of his heroines in three different films: MGR is a 'beautiful man! beautiful man! extraordinarily beautiful man!' (*Thozhilaali*). 'Is she a woman who has not seen' this 'well-built beautiful darling?' (*Kudumpa Thalaivan*). 'Only once', she has talked with him, and discovered that he is 'unique by birth'. This makes her 'faint', and she screams, 'Enough! Enough! Why do I need another birth?' (*Thani Piravi*).

Similar adjectives that qualify the 'fair-skinned' MGR are employed for the 'dark-skinned' RK as well to describe the 'body beauty'. In *Billaa*, the woman in love with RK says that 'beauty and personality' are the things that attract her to him. In *Raajaathi Raajaa*, when someone wonders how he managed to get a job so quickly, RK declares, 'It is because of my lucky face (*muharaasi*)!' In *Paandiyan*, his lover extravagantly praises him comparing him to *Krishna*, *Kaaman*, thief (*kalvan*), *Indira*, 'the golden moon which intoxicates women's mind', 'the *Pandiya* (king) of the rhyme-filled Thamizh of *Sangam*', and showers adjectives such as 'well-structured beauty', 'immense beauty', and 'male beauty'.

One significant feature associated with RK's body — not so much present in MGR — that is praised as a norm is the 'style' which could be best summed up in the song of the heroine in *Baatshaa*:

When you walk, your walking is beautiful!
When you laugh, your laughter is beautiful!
The Thamizh you speak is beautiful!
Only you are beautiful!
The long hair that falls on the forehead is beautiful!
The five fingers that run through that hair are beautiful!

Gaze at Male Body

The male body (of the hero), exhibited through clothing, character choice, stunt, and adulation, is meant to be voyeuristically consumed by other characters within the narrative and the viewers, both men and women. At least six such voyeuristic looks could be identified in the films of MGR and RK.

Protective Look of the Mother

The male body is presented to the mother as something beautiful, longing to be fondled, and waiting to be shown affection. She can touch, feed, and kiss her 'baby' irrespective of his age. Such a presentation gets more dramatic and sentimental, when the hero plays the role of an 'orphan'. In fact, the films in which the hero (MGR or RK) does not have a mother far outnumber those in which he has a mother. Interestingly, it is MGR, more than RK, who readily places his body in the protective hands of the extended 'community of mothers' (*thaai kulam*). In return, he assures the security-seeking mother of a brave manly body.

Infatuated Look of the Fiancée

The male body for the fiancée (usually the heroine) is a romantic object to be admired and fantasised. Erotic touch, embrace and kiss are permitted. MGR, however, distances himself generally from this objectified romantic body by subordinating romance to 'duty'. This 'distance' gives him the freedom to be a duty-conscious man, while enabling him at the same time to lend his body to be reduced by the infatuated lover to a fetish.

The 'duality' of MGR is by and large absent in the case of RK, who willingly exposes his body to his fiancée. A striking example is *Paandiyan*, in which RK's stark naked body is exposed to his lover. The girl after seeing the naked body utters the phrase 'O God!' repeatedly, a response modelled on RK's in *Annaamalai*.[8] Though set in a comical context, the scintillating way she recites the phrase with eyes closed indicates that she is trying to freeze and reify the naked body as it has been encountered. RK's friends praise him for this achievement, observing that others usually 'show women jewels, money and sari to attract them', but he has made her 'come round without latching', meaning that he has won over her without 'showing' her any of the things listed (but 'showing' her his body).

Incestuous Look of the Sister

The sister looks at the male body with sisterly affection and concern. Physical touch, including occasional embrace and kiss is permitted. But this sisterly love often acquires contours of incest. This is more evident in MGR than RK, in spite of the fact that, compared to MGR, RK has played the role of a brother in more films. It becomes possible for MGR because of the recurrent practice of extending his fraternal

38 POPULAR CINEMA AND POLITICS IN SOUTH INDIA

body to all young women other than his fiancée. What is extraordinary is that these 'proxy' sisters, before being declared as such by MGR, entertain erotic dreams of romancing with him.[9] That such a sequence is a regular pattern in MGR films makes us believe that he encourages 'proxy' incest. The underlying logic seems to be: 'MGR is so beautiful that it is okay for his "sister" to sleep with him!'

Reverential Look of the Wife

In quite a few films of MGR and RK, the story would end with the union of lovers. Comparatively, RK has more films in which the wife plays a major or significant role. An analysis of such films reveals that there is, both for MGR and RK, a conspicuous difference between the look of the lover and that of the wife. This is more evident when the lover turns into a wife. The passionate look of the lover is transformed into the reverential and gratuitous look of the wife. Thus, the lover who is shortly going to marry MGR tells him in *Kanni Thaai* with gratitude, 'There would have been many women who thought of possessing you, but only I am fortunate to have you'. Similar is the attitude of RK's newly-wed wife in *Padaiyappaa*. Touch of male (husband's) body gets ritualised and remains very formal in the presence of others.

Lustful Look of the Seducer

The male body is presented to the 'seducer' as an object of lust or as something to be conquered. Depending upon who the 'seducer' is — whether she is a villain's aide or his daughter or villain herself, or any girl other than the heroine — the way the male body is gazed at, considerably varies. When the seducer from the villain's camp attempts to conquer the body, MGR would either ignore her or win her over to his side as in *Ulagam Sutrum Vaalipan*. RK, on the other hand, would either defeat her by taking possession of her as his wife (as in *Thampikku Entha Ooru* and *Mannan*) or eliminate her (as in *Moondru Mukam* and *Padaiyappaa*).

Envious/Queer Look of Other Men

A peculiar feature in exhibiting the male body to be voyeured is to present it as the envy of other men. There are occasional references to this

IMAGING MALE BODY   39

in the films of both MGR and RK, comparatively more so in MGR's. In *Siriththu Vaazha Vaendum*, for example, the excited girl hypothesises, 'If only you were a woman, all the adolescent boys would be mad after you'. A friend of MGR in *Raaman Thaedia Seethai* would kiss him, much like a lover does. He kisses thus because the body of MGR, who is going to get married soon, would not be available for him. In RK's *Annaamalai*, the comedian friend, who remains single throughout the film, frequently indulges in praising RK, employing adjectives, which are, strangely enough, similar to those used by RK's lover.

Cultural-Literary Roots

While accepting that in Thamizh culture and literature, 'physical beauty' is predominantly associated with female body, one must hasten to add that this association has not been exclusive. Describing the male body by or for women is not an unknown practice. Already in *Tholkappaiyam*, the oldest book of grammar, talks of 'paadaan thinai', i.e., a literary genre meant to praise men of valour and status. Epics like *Perungathai, Seevaka Chinthamani* and Kambar's *Ramayanam* devote a section to the 'royal procession' during which women, irrespective of their age, fall in love with the hero. This 'royal procession' later evolves into a distinct literary genre called 'Ulaa'. This is defined as a genre that praises the knowledge, wealth, valour, love, charity, and beauty of the hero, when he comes in royal procession after coronation or wedding. It also explains his caste, family, and genealogy. If he is a king, his mountain, river, country, town, elephant, horse, garland, drum, flag, and sceptre (together called '*thasaangam*') are also sometimes included. Most importantly, it portrays how women of all seven age groups (starting from five and ending at 40) fall in love with him. Other genres like 'Pillai Thamizh' (Child's Thamizh, meaning, poem in praise of the child), and 'Parani' (poem in praise of valour exhibited in the battlefield) come close to *Ulaa* in describing the male body.

When it comes to the little tradition, not much importance is attached to male bodily features. This aspect of the little tradition could be considered as the survival of the remnants of the bygone *Sangam* era. The practice of describing the male body is not prevalent in the earliest *Sangam* literature, which, however, is replete with praises of valour and munificence. It is only after the Thamizh culture's absorption of

40 ■ POPULAR CINEMA AND POLITICS IN SOUTH INDIA

Sanskritic aesthetics, that the depiction of the male physicality gained prominence in literature. The little tradition even now does not consider 'looks' to be very important for a man.

Obviously, therefore, the approaches of MGR and RK to male body have their roots in Thamizh culture and literature. The major difference between MGR and RK is that MGR draws more heavily upon the Sanskriticised great tradition, while RK is closer to the little traditions.

'Looks' and 'Style'

The foremost reason for the success of MGR and RK as 'charismatic' actors lies in their respective body and how each has in his unique way presented it. This will become more evident if we compare them with their contemporaries.

When compared to Sivaji Ganesan, MGR is not a versatile actor, a fact that led MGR to specialise in 'action' roles modelled on Errol Flynn. When Sivaji made his debut as hero in *Paraasakthi*, he was just 24, but MGR was then at least 35. By the time MGR established himself in the cine-industry as a force to reckon with, he was already in his late forties. Faced with the stamp of 'aged hero', and the consequent anxiety to prove young, MGR resorted to stories which would depict him young. For the same reason, he handpicked his female counterparts — younger, newer, and multiple heroines — as he grew older (atypical example is *Ulagam Sutrum Vaalipan*, in which he romances in double roles with four teenage girls). It is in this context that he manipulated his fair skin and 'beautiful look' to have an edge over his 'young' rival Sivaji Ganesan, who lacked these qualities. MGR even over-played with his 'look', especially in films having double roles, as in *Enga Veettu Pillai* and *Maattukkaara Vaelan*. In these films, the girls in love with different MGRs are shown to be struggling to decide which MGR they are in love with — is it the MGR of their heart or the MGR who is physically present? They finally settle, according to the stories, for the physically present MGR. Such is the power of his 'beautiful face!' Thus, by emphasising his 'beauty', a concept traditionally associated with the female, and combining it with the traditional manly qualities of valour and action, MGR struck a unique style of presenting the male body.

While MGR emphasised the combination of *action* and *look*, RK, a contemporary of the multifaceted and innovative actor Kamal Haasan, emphasises 'style' coupled with comedy and action. Entering the cine industry at a time when people were over-saturated with melodrama, RK was a welcome relief because of the perfect correlation between the anti-hero roles he played and his rather 'villainous look' (which Kamal lacked). His easy-to-imitate gimmicks, popularly called 'style', effectively blended with his 'look' and placed him at the peak as 'super star'.

Notes

1. Unlike English, Thamizh has only one word 'azhagu' for both the male 'handsomeness' and the female 'beautifulness'. The Thamizh culture, it is to be known, reserves 'beauty' for the female and 'valour' for the male.
2. While sharing the same platform with MGR during the Second World Thamizh Conference in Chennai, Annadurai, the then Chief Minister, declared that MGR's definition of poetry as possessing beauty and feelings fits only MGR! See Vijayan (1997: 96).
3. In *Adimai Penn*, however, he acts as a hunch-backed prince; but the way he fights with the ferocious lion offsets the physical defect!
4. MGR, however, was not against 'dying' in the earlier films, such as *En Thangai, Mathurai Veeran* and *Raajaa Daesingu*. But he consciously and consistently avoided such roles, intuitively sensing what his fans crave for, particularly once *Paasam*, an anti-hero subject, which otherwise had all the characteristic MGR masala, flopped at the box-office as he predicted for the sole reason, it was assessed, he dies at the end. The prediction-come-true indeed made MGR the unchallengeable and omniscient craftsman-hero of Thamizh film industry. For a psycho-analytic look into the failure of *Paasam*, see the discussion on 'mother fixation'.
5. In the so-called 'socials' MGR does employ modern weapons like guns and rifles.
6. *Silambam* is a traditional martial art where fencing is done with a staff. *Silambam* is performed during village festivals.
7. While MGR's critics used to ridicule him, saying that he was a 'master of cardboard sword fighting', his devout fans revered him as 'vaaththiyaar' (teacher).
8. Such a sequence has already occurred in *Annaamalai* but with reversal of roles. In *Annaamalai*, released prior to *Paandiyan* in the same year, RK has the 'darshan' of the female body and recites with excitement the same

42 ▪ POPULAR CINEMA AND POLITICS IN SOUTH INDIA

'mantra' of '*kadavulae — kadavulae*'. Because of the overwhelming response of the fans to this sequence, it is added in *Paandiyan*. Incidentally, the same RK–Kushboo pair is involved in both the films.

9. It is true that in RK's films it is rare to find, unless the story warrants, instances of the hero letting the girl entertain amorous fantasies before metamorphosing her into his 'sister'. A noteworthy example for this is *Thampikku Entha Ooru*. In MGR's films, such a situation in most cases will not be an absolute requirement for the development of the main storyline.

4

ON BEING A *MAN's* WOMAN

The presentation of the male body (of the hero), previously discussed, is inextricably bound up with the corresponding presentation of the female body. It is the hero-centricity — *phallo-centricity*, to be precise — that defines the nature and dictates the use of the female body. Accordingly, the female body is depicted as male–dependent and used to actualise and reinforce the male supremacy, being granted at the same time certain degree of 'licence to be female' (as distinct from the male) insofar as the 'licence' does not pose a threat to male centrality.

Compared to MGR, RK 'contemporarises' the presentation of his women by echoing the emerging feminist perspectives within his patriarchal discourse. Thus, MGR's women in general are flat, two-dimensional characters, whereas RK's women incorporate aspects of modernity. In *Padaiyappaa*, for example, RK's daughters can 'freak out' in jeans and have a birthday party, but only as long as they are 'father's daughters'. In spite of the subtle differences, there is a remarkable agreement between MGR and RK in portraying women.

Taming of the Shrew

Of particular interest here is the way MGR and RK 'tame the shrew'. There is an amazing agreement between them in this regard, though RK is more consistent and ruthless.

A woman is labeled 'haughty' when she does not conform to the patriarchal norms and dares to defy the phallo-centric authority. Such a woman is seriously dealt with in a heavy-handed manner. Table 4.1 lists the core characteristics of the 'haughty' woman, and the behavioural manifestations of each of these characteristics.

44 ◖ POPULAR CINEMA AND POLITICS IN SOUTH INDIA

Table 4.1
Haughty Woman

Core Characteristics	*Behavioural Manifestations*
Proud-hearted	Short-tempered, condescending
Educated	Talkative, argumentative, English-speaking
Rich	Status-conscious, egoistic, carefree
Employed, enterprising, talented	Autocratic, obstinate, aggressive, disrespectful
Bold	Venturing alone, risk taking
Modern	Immodest in dress, driving car, etc.
Licentious	Drinking, smoking, etc.
Beautiful, young and attractive	Sensuous, exhibiting beauty

MGR and RK take care to give the reasons why a woman should not be 'haughty'. The consequences of being haughty, as their reasoning goes, can range from sexual provocation of the 'innocent' young men to social ostracism. The oft-cited consequences are:

- Against Thamizh culture
- Incites and spoils young men
- No one will marry
- Prone to sexual assault
- Spoils the family name
- Self-destructive
- Does not go with motherhood

Strangely enough, both RK and MGR take recourse to Thamizh culture to condemn women and justify their anti-women behaviour. In fact, the majority of the references to Thamizh culture pertain to something related to women. Though both of them appeal to culture as a defence mechanism, they significantly differ in the way they 'tame the shrew'. Table 4.2 highlights the salient features of their respective approaches.

If we can think of a continuum between 'gentle' and 'aggressive' poles, MGR's approach will be more towards the 'gentle' end and RK's towards the aggressive end. The impression of being gentle is given through the 'deference technique' — MGR masquerades as another

Table 4.2
Comparative Approaches to the Shrew

MGR's Approach	RK's Approach
Shifts locus	Intimidates
Masquerades	Coerces
Defers conflict	Precipitates conflict
Wins over	Defeats
Provides room for fantasy	Provides room to express
Girl also wins	Girl surrenders

(usually rich) man and makes the girl fall in love with him (without knowing that the man in disguise is the same MGR); by this, he defers the issue of taming, until at the climax she is cowed down. Added to this is the 'locus-shifting technique', whereby he shifts the locus of confrontation from the personal level to the social level; thus a conflict between him and the heroine will be interpreted as one between the poor and the rich, and the 'haughtiness' of the girl will be given anti-poor contours (*Kumari Koattam*, for example). This, we could say, is an original invention of MGR.

RK on the contrary comes down heavily on the 'haughty' girl and precipitates the crisis towards the climax. The 'precipitation technique' involves verbal and physical assaults, startlingly *mutual*, as in *Mannan*, for instance. The physical assault is something unimaginable in MGR, for whom the physical touch is always for romance, more often than not in heroine's fantasies. The ruthless and spiteful manner in which RK retorts amounts to a kind of 'castration' or 'genital mutilation', a point to be further elaborated in the next chapter. The precipitation technique does not give much room for fantasy.[1] But it does provide ample space for the girl to express her sexuality, though against heavy odds. In the case of MGR, however, thanks to the deference technique, the 'haughty' girl, just like the 'normal' girl, entertains romantic fantasies.

Another important difference between MGR and RK is that MGR wins over the girl without really defeating her, whereas RK is bent on defeating her. In the case of MGR, he wins and the girl also has the satisfaction of having won nothing less than MGR himself! In the case of RK, neither he nor she is the real winner — RK defeats her, and the girl surrenders.

Typology of Female Body

Based on the insights drawn from a perceptive look at the extensive repertoire of MGR and RK films, we shall outline the following typology of how the female body is viewed by the protagonist[2] (and by his fans).

Sacred Body of the Mother

The male look at the body of the mother is marked by reverence, obedience, and protection. The mother is placed on an elevated pedestal, always next to god, or as god herself. She is 'the god who stands in front and talks to you'. As Auvai's *Kondrai Vaenthan* (38) says, 'No temple is holier than one's own mother'. Both MGR and RK reduce the mother image to a *totem*, an object of reverential fear. There are at least three models of mother:

- *The Caring Mother* — like the proverbial Madonna, is tender and loving. She is the source of life. She cares and protects; she inculcates values and morals; she is forgiving and her love is universal and unconditional.
- *The Brave Mother* — like the Mother *Kali*, is a destroyer of evil. She cultivates valour and manliness in her son, and wishes her son always to be the winner. She is the motivating force behind his crusade against the evil villain.
- *The Suffering Mother* — like the Pieta, suffers and sacrifices her life for the well-being of her children. More often than not, the suffering mother is used as a device, as seen in the case of *Mannan*, to bear witness to the enormity of the sacrifices of her son.

The filmic depiction of the mother, however, often transcends the clear-cut categories, and used for reasons other than emphasising the value of mother. She is also frequently used, for example, as a justification for the 'deviant' behaviour of the son, such as stealing. MGR transcends, as will be seen later, even the very concept of motherhood.

Tantalising Body of the Fiancée

The fiancée is presented as a 'tantalising' site of contestation in the phallo-centric fight between the hero and the villain, and the body becomes the possession of the ultimate victor. The hero's claim over her body will be justified from the beginning by presenting the love to be mutual or by making the fiancée take the initiative. Invariably all the films of MGR and RK follow the same pattern, though in MGR films the initiative always comes from the woman.[3] RK does not mind taking the initiative himself, but marries the one he likes, who need not necessarily be the one who has fallen in love with him — a blatant contradiction of his clichéd advice that it is best for the man to marry the woman who loves him, and not the woman whom he loves! Interestingly, he will marry his daughters or sisters to those whom they are in love with.

Daunting Body of the 'Seducer'

If the body of the fiancée is glamorous and resilient, the body of the 'seducer' is fatally attractive — she is the *femme fatale*. Frequently, the heroine is portrayed as daunting, not merely tantalising, and threatening, not merely fascinating. Such a body, resisting or defying the male-as-norm discourses, needs to be handled carefully and boldly; otherwise the male faces the danger of risking his 'manliness'. She is, therefore, first 'clipped off', mainly through intimidation and coercion, to 'fall' in line with the patriarchal norms. Once she is 'reformed', she becomes a charming fiancée, and the subjugation continues through scintillating romance to 'house-wifery'. There is a difference between MGR and RK in the way they 'clip off' — RK is rather ruthless and does not hesitate to unleash physical violence, when he thinks necessary. MGR on the other hand, whisks off the threat and moves over to some other conflict, as in *Kumari Koattam*. He does not, under any circumstance, resort to physical assault such as slapping.

Docile Body of the Wife

The tantalising body of the fiancée becomes, after marriage, a 'docile' body, available to the husband to be used at his will. The wife surrenders her right over her body to its rightful owner, the husband. All the films with a marriage sequence either at the end or in between the narrative invariably have a scene of the male taking or carrying the female body to the bed, reducing, thus, the meaning of marriage to sex. Once she is reduced to a sex object, the wife can no more re-claim her

48 ■ POPULAR CINEMA AND POLITICS IN SOUTH INDIA

right to deny access to her body; the surrender is irreversible. Any sign of resentment is construed as 'abnormal' or a health hazard, and the wife will be 'treated' accordingly, as in *Mannan*. The wife, however, is provided with certain 'free space' within the patriarchal universe to recall and reminisce the 'tantalising' time she has had with the hero.

Endearing Body of the Sister

The body of the sister is always beautiful, and 'sacred', if she is elder to the hero, or 'tantalising', if younger. The sister is the object of fraternal affection, and quite often the affectionate body is fossilised. The body is temporarily owned by the brother with whom lies the responsibility to find the best possible groom. To justify this 'ownership' the hero will be shown as the only male in the family. The fraternal 'endearment' frequently acquires contours of incest, which is manifest in lover–like reciprocal body-touching and physical description.[4] While RK stops here, MGR extends the meaning of 'sister' to include any young girl other than the heroine, and, as noted earlier, encourages them to be incestuous.[5]

Extended Body of the Daughter

The body of the daughter is considered, in a patriarchal system, as an extension of the father, who, therefore, is more than the owner. Conflict arises when the daughter affirms her right over her body by falling in love with a person of her choice. Such conflicts are often dramatised with an overdose of sentiment in RK films. For example, in *Nallavanukku Nallavan*, when the daughter falls in love with his rival's son against his wish, he sings: 'A feather has sprouted to my darling sparrow…'. Interestingly, in none of his films, MGR, who is conscious of his age, has a grown-up daughter.

Disposable Body of the 'Prostitute'

The term 'prostitute' is comprehensive and includes the female sex-workers of various kinds, concubines and villains' female aides who may not by profession be prostitutes. In the films of MGR and RK we occasionally come across such characters, which are treated as 'disposables'. Though they may appear only briefly in the narrative, they are the worst-treated lot. Their bodies are treated with hardcore contempt and scantiest possible respect. They are torn asunder between the contesting parties — the villains who exercise complete control over their bodies (because they are the pay-masters) and the heroes who eliminate them as obstacles to their mission.[6]

Defiled Body of the Widow

The body of the widow is the most ignored and ostracised. It is a defiled body. MGR, for example, keeps a safe distance from the widow, even if he has to live with her under the same roof. *Oli Vilakku* is a case in point. MGR takes care of the widow almost like a husband, but he maintains his 'purity' by not taking possession of the defiled body through marriage. He does own that body by making her his elder 'sister', which gives him simultaneously enough space to remain unpolluted. While subscribing to the belief that the widow's body is defiled, RK does not mind accepting the widow as his wife, and thus getting polluted.

Notes

1. Though in *Mannan* the heroine indulges in sado-masochistic fantasies of whipping and getting whipped by the hero. The same sado-masochist tendency is manifested when she, in an attempt to convince RK's mother and gain her consent to marry him, asserts self-righteously, 'I don't like lying; I am very short-tempered; I am strict in my duty; if I see something wrong I condemn it, if not corrected, I punish it; some don't like it, but I cannot do anything about it…', but cuts her hand with a knife as a proof of her love for RK! On the female viewers' response to such sequences, see the analysis of 'space' towards the end of this section.
2. For the villain, the female body in general is something to be raped, to be abducted (to be later exchanged for money/wealth) or to be enjoyed (on payment).
3. A noteworthy exception is *Raaman Thaediya Seethai*. After learning the six 'virtues' of a good family woman, MGR starts dreaming of his ideal woman. This obviously is a rarity, if not an oddity, in MGR films. However, this has deep cultural implications: MGR dreams of an ideal woman, not any

50 ▪ POPULAR CINEMA AND POLITICS IN SOUTH INDIA

woman. In fact, the narrative presents this ideal woman as a sacrificing mother. Similarly in *Ulagam Sutrum Vaalipan*, MGR marries the dancer mostly out of pity and to avoid woman's beauty and youth interfering with his duty (strange!). In *Ithaya Kani* he marries the estate worker in order to avoid the scandal.

4. For example, RK sings in *Tharma Yuththam*: 'The god-given gift of my sister is like the golden yellow full moon seated in a golden car'.

5. In MGR's *Adimai Penn* where the heroine's look-alike falls in love with him, and describes his physical beauty employing a sensuous language. She maintains a love–hate relationship with him till the end, when he declares her to be his sister. What is ingenious here is the usage of the same actor (Jayalalithaa) to play the double roles of his lover and his 'sister'. Incidentally, according to the story the twin characters are sisters.

6. It is good to remind us in this context that MGR and RK tacitly approve of the misogynist patriarchal cultural practices, some of which have already been shed by patriarchy itself. Such practices include: (*a*)*Concubinage* (variously called *chinnaveedu, vappaatti* or *kooththiyaa*, having one or more concubines is considered a male privilege; sometimes it may even be a sign of one's higher social status.); (*b*)*Bigamy*, and (*c*) Multiple marital alliances for *strategic* reasons (very frequent in MGR films, for example, *Naadoadi Mannan, Mathuraiyai Meetta Sunthara Paandiyan*). Even child marriage gets MGR's indirect approval (as in *Kumari Koattam*). But both MGR and RK are silent on crucial issues such as dowry (except for a passing reference or two, as in RK's *Baatshaa*).

5

PSYCHO-CULTURAL MAPPING OF BODY

Cultural Tetrad

Though some of the features of the typology of female body as elucidated in the previous chapter could be universal, they have their roots entrenched in the Thamizh culture. Figure 5.1 highlights from a cultural–anthropological perspective the relative positioning of women according to their social status and developmental stage.

The tetrad consists of four quadrangles formed of two intersecting horizontal and vertical lines. The horizontal line is the continuum with 'sacrificing female' at one end and 'subversive female' at the other. The vertical line is another continuum with 'terrifying female' at one end and 'protective female' at the other. The resultant quadrangles are:

1. **Destructive Quadrangle of the Virgin,** with terrifying and subversive characteristics. The virgin is dreaded as a 'threat'.
2. **Constructive Quadrangle of the Wife,** with protective and subversive characteristics. The wife is treated as a 'devotee' of the husband.
3. **Barren Quadrangle of the Barren,** with terrifying and sacrificing characteristics. The barren (woman) is feared as a 'curse'.
4. **Fertile Quadrangle of the Mother,** with sacrificing and protective characteristics. The mother is revered as a 'god'.

The 'child', the prepubescent 'girl', the 'widow', the 'concubine', and the 'prostitute' are relatively placed on the 'terrifying-protective' continuum. Puberty marks the passage from 'girl' to 'virgin', marriage marks the transition from 'virgin' to 'wife', and child-birth makes the

Figure 5.1
Women — A Cultural Tetrad

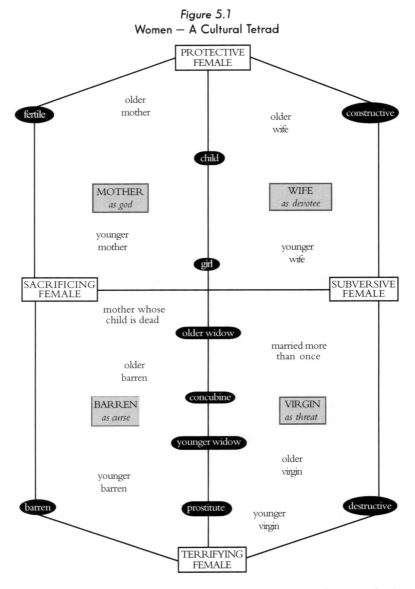

'wife' attain the status of 'mother'. When the 'wife' fails to be a 'mother', she is 'barren'. The widow, the concubine and the prostitute are both a threat and a curse. However, they could on marriage/remarriage, pass over to 'wife'. (None of the socio-cultural sanctions associated with these states like 'inauspicious' and 'defiling' are applicable to the hero's mother!)

The mapping, obviously, is phallo-centric, and a woman cannot pass from one stage to another without the male. Figure 5.2 illustrates the dynamics of male–female inter-relationship. The virgin is a storehouse of energy that needs to be channelised, failing which the energy will turn destructive particularly against the male. Depending on the hereditary and socio-environmental factors, the virgin may be the most terrifying-cum-subversive (the 'seducer' in the eight-fold typology) or the least terrifying-cum-subversive (the 'fiancée' in the typology). It takes a 'valorous male' ('bachelor') to subdue the virgin, and make her a wife. The 'subduing' can range from violent and inhuman 'clitoral mutilation' to gentle persuasion. On subduing the virgin, the valorous male emerges as god, and the wife becomes his devotee.

Figure 5.2
Male–Female Inter-Relationship

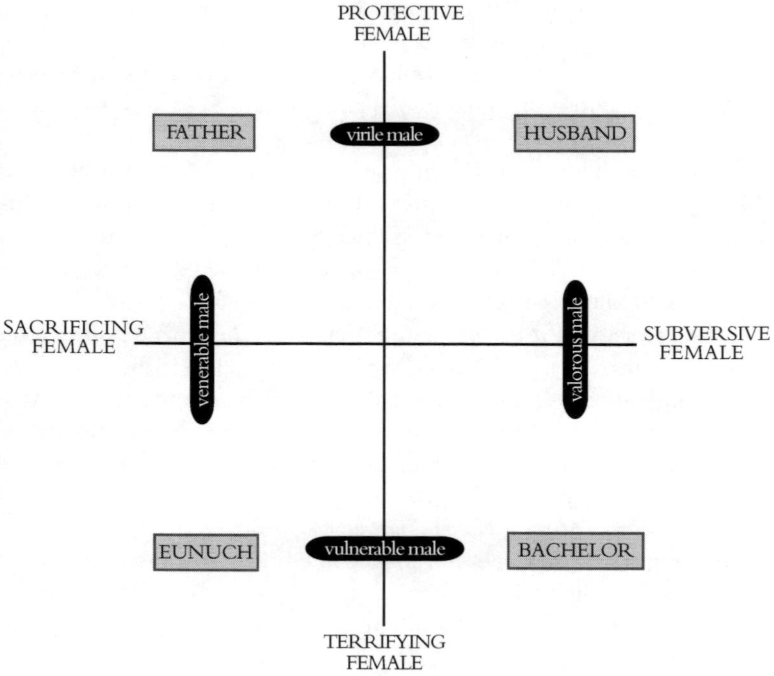

54 ■ POPULAR CINEMA AND POLITICS IN SOUTH INDIA

But even after becoming a wife, the woman continues to be subversive and is capable of making the husband a 'eunuch' (and she the 'barren') by exposing his impotency, causing in him an 'exposure anxiety'. Besides, she is a liability because the villain might rape her any time; for this reason the husband is also suspicious of his wife and might even test her fidelity. The husband overcomes the anxiety and suspicion by exhibiting his 'virility', that is, making the wife conceive and give birth to a child. Simultaneously, he plays god and demands undivided attention of his wife to him. Once the husband proves that he is not a *pottai* ('eunuch') by impregnating his wife, he acquires the 'venerable' status of the 'father'. The fatherhood entails him of greater social esteem (he is eligible to be the 'elder'). That is why the conception is celebrated as a social event. The terrific and terrifying energy of the virgin is, thus, fully and properly channelised when she becomes a 'mother', worthy of worship as god.

What is peculiar is the state of 'barren' vis-à-vis the state of 'eunuch'. Though 'bachelor' who fails to win over the virgin (compare the 'castration anxiety' of psycho-analysis below) becomes a *pottai* ('eunuch'), that state is not considered a curse. It is because the blame for being 'barren' is always on the woman, not on the man. The 'eunuch' is vulnerable (because his wife could not give birth to a child) yet venerable (because he is magnanimous enough to accept and live with a barren woman).

Applying these cultural–anthropological insights to the films of MGR and RK we could find that MGR pays almost exclusive attention to the valorous man, whereas RK often goes beyond the valorous to emphasise the virile man. That explains why MGR exhibits more castration anxiety and RK, more exposure anxiety.

The diversity of roles RK assumes vis-à-vis the female body makes RK somewhat unconventional, which nevertheless is in conformity with his *enfant terrible* and 'anti-hero' image. While he focuses on making the virgin a mother, with an emphasis on the virility dimension, he moves across all the quadrangles as, for example, getting married to a widow (*Thalapathy*), his wife being (made) barren (*Ejamaan*), and marrying a 'prostitute' (*Thappu Thaalangal*).

By contrast, MGR does not dabble like RK by daring to go against the cultural script, or the 'collective unconscious', though occasionally he might deviate a bit. Therefore, he will not try out any of the things

PSYCHO-CULTURAL MAPPING OF BODY **55**

that RK has done. He will not, for example, have a wife who is barren; though many women might love him, he will love only one woman whom he is going to marry. On the contrary, in order to make his image culturally synchronous, he will be ready to let his incorrigible haughty wife get killed (*Panam Padaiththavan*); he will allow the widow to die (*Oli Vilakku*); he will encourage inter-caste marriage, but only too mildly (*Panam Padaiththavan*). Given the fact that the image of MGR consists primarily of valour and romance, and that in real life he had no children (though he married thrice), one could understand why he confined himself to the male action in the virgin–wife quadrangles (where he does not need to prove his virility). All these are, it could be seen, in conformity with his 'affable darling' and 'action hero' image.

Literary Roots: *Aham* and *Puram*

The Thamizh culture, as defined in the earliest grammar book *Tholkaappiam* (Part III: *Porulathikaaram*), makes a clear distinction between 'private' or 'domestic' sphere (*aham*) and 'public' sphere (*puram*). The domestic sphere of 'home-making' is reserved for the female, whereas the public sphere of 'earning', for the male. The domestic sphere consists of *kalavu* (premarital love) and *karpu* (marital fidelity). *Tholkaappiam* further assigns honour (*perumai*) and valour (*uran*) to masculine gender, whereas fear (*achcham*), shyness (*naanam*), ignorance (*madamai*), and disgust (*payirpu*) to feminine gender. *Kurunthohai* from the corpus of *Sangam* literature states that valorous action is the life for men, and for the women of the home, their life is the men (*vinaiyae aadavarku uyirae — manaiyurai mahalirku aadavar uyir*).

Both MGR and RK faithfully adhere to the traditional distinction between aham and puram, and barring an exception or two, they make a lengthy and attractive display of *kalavu*, while upholding *karpu*.

The display of *kalavu* invariably involves description of the female physical beauty. Even in the early *Sangam* literature we could find the tendency to see the female in terms of isolated bodily organs. When a poem, for example, addresses a male (*aadoo munnilai*), it refers to the broad chest or shoulder (implying valour). But when a poem is addressed to a female (*mahadoo munnilai*), every organ from hair to feet (not excluding vagina) is addressed. Later epics such as Kambar's *Ramayanam* delight in lasciviously describing the female beauty from

56 ■ POPULAR CINEMA AND POLITICS IN SOUTH INDIA

'hair on head to foot' (*kaesaathi paatham*) or from 'foot to hair on head' (*paathaathi kaesam*) — a trend that has survived to this day.

Another cultural aspect which persists till date, which MGR and RK faithfully adhere to, is 'double deprivation' of women. Thamizh culture which deifies 'mother', deifies also the 'husband'. In a dramatic reversal, the male, reigning supreme in the public sphere as 'husband', occupies the central place in the domestic sphere as 'husband god', and the 'mother god' is elevated to the public sphere. The woman is thus twice deprived — she is first deprived of any access to the public life, and then deprived of her primacy in the domestic life. The justification for this double deprivation could be found in *Thirukkural* (55) itself:

> One who does not worship god,
>   (but) worships (only) the husband as she wakes up
> If she commands rain, it will rain.

Mother Fixation

One of the most outstanding features common to MGR and RK is their 'mother fixation'. The 'mother sentiment' permeates all their films, even if a film does not have a mother character.[1] The attachment is obviously oedipal, psychoanalytically speaking.

When it comes to his attachment to the mother, MGR is seen to regress from genital stage to oral stage (Figure 5.3). In *Neethikku Thalai Vanangu*, for example, the young MGR is being fed by his mother and later he himself plays the mother to the heroine. The mother even sings a lullaby to put him to sleep. That such a regression is frequent implies that he as an affable child is attached to his affectionate mother. The castration anxiety caused by the 'villain' father is sublimated into a moral anger directed against the 'evil' villain, who by substitution takes the place of the father. When the villain (the father figure) is eliminated, he takes complete possession of the mother. The possession, however, is transferred to a spiritual realm by elevating the mother to the status of god whom he protects, worships and obeys. The oedipal attachment thus gets fossilised forever within the safe spiritual realm.

The other side of the oedipal attachment is the mutual dealing between him and the heroine. Most of MGR's heroines are 'docile'

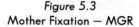

Figure 5.3
Mother Fixation — MGR

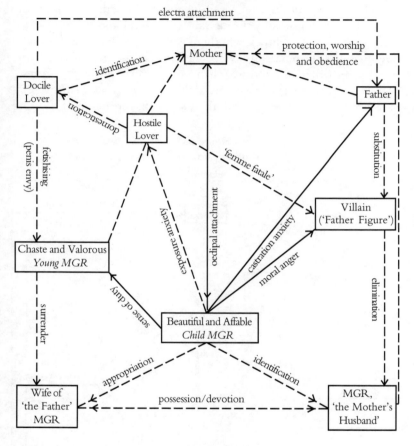

lovers, who respond to the chaste and valorous MGR by fetishising him. This they do through romantic dreams, and finally take possession of the object of their desire by surrendering themselves. They overcome the penis envy by identifying themselves with his mother by first reducing the chaste and valorous MGR to the beautiful and affable child, and then by making themselves the wives of the MGR who has become the 'father' by eliminating the father figure. Occasionally MGR deals also with 'hostile' lovers, in whose presence, as we have seen in our

58 ■ POPULAR CINEMA AND POLITICS IN SOUTH INDIA

discussion earlier, he undergoes 'exposure anxiety.' MGR overcomes this by quickly converting the 'hostile' lovers into 'docile' lovers.

RK radically differs from MGR, as Figure 5.4 indicates, in that he presents himself primarily through his villainous looks as an *enfant terrible*. In most of his films where there is a mother character, we could see his *longing* to be 'oedipally attached' to the mother, or already he will be the 'father'. On the other hand, there will frequently be a strong 'hostile' lover (or a hostile woman, as the mother-in-law in *Maappillai*), a *femme fatale*, who confronts him as a villain, threatening to expose

Figure 5.4
Mother Fixation — RK

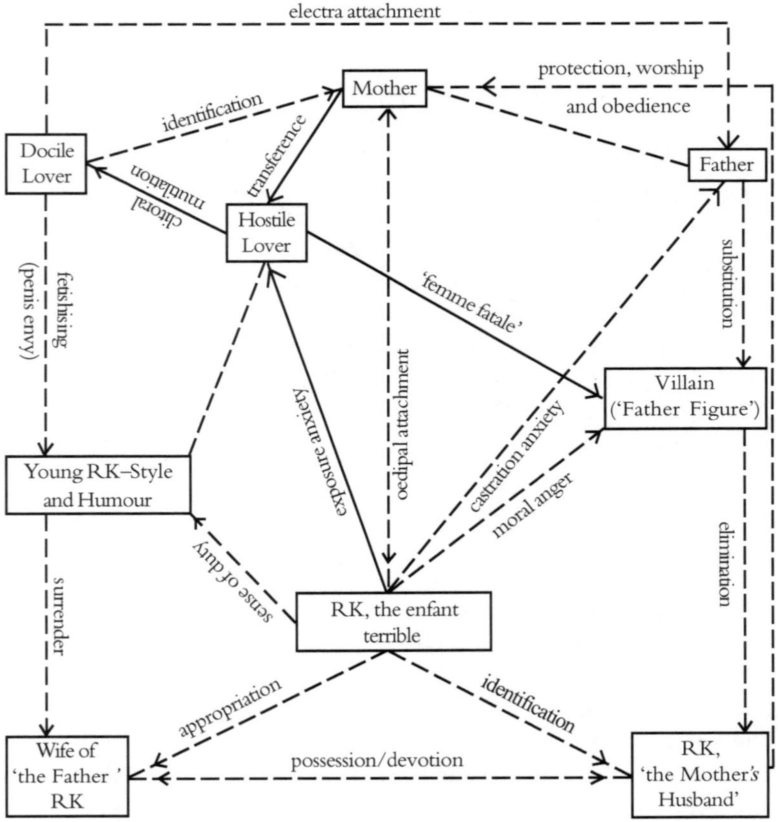

his impotency. RK overcomes this exposure anxiety by subjecting the *femme fatale* to clitoral mutilation and forcing her to identify herself with his mother. The girl in turn fetishises his 'style' and humour and eventually becomes his 'mother'. The initial longing he has had to be attached to his mother is satisfied in the subdued *femme fatale* — she who had first refused any access to her, now 'abandons' herself into his hands. His insistence on making the girl a mother, when seen in this context, is an attempt to perpetuate the oedipal attachment at the physiological level.[2]

It is not out of place to relate the foregoing discussion to the real life experiences of MGR and RK. MGR lost his father when he was two-and-a-half years old, and his mother, it is said, used to scold him as 'mudikaalan' (meaning, the god of death who took away the crown of the family).[3] Driven by poverty and forced to work at the tender age of seven, he was naturally attached to his mother. But he was probably angry with his father who made him a 'mudikaalan' by his death. Strikingly, the same attitudes are reflected also in the analysis of his films. The anger he had against his father who is no more is directed against the film-villains.[4] The oedipal attachment he had with his mother in real life was concealed under the mask of 'devotion'. But his affairs with women[5] show that the 'devotional attachment' to his mother had only led him to repress his sexual desires. It is quite probable that he was trying to see his mother-image in the women with whom he had intimate relationship — an attempt to experience the real oedipal attachment outside of the spiritual realm.

RK on the contrary lost his mother when he was seven. His childhood is marked by no particular attachment to his mother. Probably he was even angry with his mother because he did not get enough attention. The struggle he experienced as a child reflected in his behaviour, and was considered a problem child, an *enfant terrible*. He went to the prostitutes, it is said, at an age of seven, and he indulged in eve-teasing.[6] That he treats the 'hostile' lover as the villain, and is bent on 'mutilating' her could be better understood in the light of his own real-life relationship with his mother. The hostility he had against his mother is projected in the film version to the 'hostile' lover, and he forces her, often violently so, to become his mother with whom he can safely get attached.

That there are subtle yet crucial differences between MGR and RK in the way they approach the female body explains why MGR has enjoyed so great a fan following among women, whereas RK's fans are predominantly the male youth.

Notes

1. Titles of MGR films such as *Thaai Sollai Thattaathae*, *Thaayai Kaaththa Thanayan*, and *Thaayin Madiyil*, popularly known as the 'thaa' series, explicitly refer to 'mother' or maternal instinct. In fact, MGR's 'thaa' series was a response to Sivaji's 'pa' series (like *Paalum Pazhamum*, *Paava Mannippu* and *Paasamalar*). While the 'thaa' series exploited the mother sentiment, the 'pa' series sentimentalised the family-based fraternal, filial and paternal love. In the case of RK, films with 'mother' in the titles are rather rare (such as *Thaai Meethu Saththiyam*, and *Annai Oar Aalayam*), though in many films mother plays an important role.
2. RK, however, does make a god of his mother. But his attitude vastly differs from that of MGR. For MGR his mother is god, and probably the only god he believed and *regularly worshipped* in real life. RK's view of god is very fluid-like, a point to be discussed in a subsequent chapter.
3. See Editorial Board of Manimekalai Pirasuram (1994: 8).
4. It is pertinent in this context to probe into the failure of *Paasam*. The commonly attributed reason for the film's failure is the final death of MGR and the negative role he plays. However, an equally important reason from the psychoanalytical point of view is the way oedipal attachment is (mis)handled. The *enfant terrible* (not the 'affable darling') MGR first eliminates the father figure by murdering the man who plans to remarry. But, as a consequence, instead of uniting with his mother, he is permanently separated from her by being put in prison. So, the Oedipal attachment is not fully reconciled. That is why, once released, he is again after the blood of his (real) father. Unfortunately, he kills his mother, and not his father. Eventually he dies, without gratifying the need to be united with his mother. In the whole film he is obsessed with his father, the villain, and not fixated with his mother.
5. MGR was deprived of normal marital pleasures when he was a youth: Though he married when he was 21, his first wife died very soon; his second wife was bed-ridden for many years; he had to illegally and with

PSYCHO-CULTURAL MAPPING OF BODY ◼ 61

guilt live with another woman for over a decade, before she could be legally married after the death of his second wife in 1962. This is a kind of 'coitus interruptus' — interrupted because physically unfit or associated with guilt. All these have had a profound impact on his perception of women. His real-life exploits with women coincide with that on the screen.

6. RK was even handed over to the police once for his rude behaviour with a girl. See Mathrubootheswaran (1999: 31).

6

DOUBLE-BODIED MIGRANTCY

The (hero's) male body, perceived thus vis-à-vis the female body, is both 'personal' and 'social'. While the 'personal body' remains the core, the 'social body' gives it the form. The personal and the social bodies are *inseparable*, and together they constitute the 'body of the hero' MGR or RK. In fact, the 'personal body' exists *only as* the 'social body', and vice versa. The resultant 'body of the hero' acquires certain *transcendental* dimensions in the socio-economic, moral and political realms through the *narratively* constructed phenomenon of 'double-bodied migrantcy' in a universified multiverse.

Universe and Multi-verse

The social and political universe in which MGR and RK traverse is hierarchically and unequally divided between the haves and the have-nots, the good and the bad, the law-abiding and the delinquent, the powerful and the powerless, the educated and the illiterate, the industrial owners and the workers, the urban and the rural, the rulers and the ruled, the hungry and the obese, the landlords and the agricultural labourers, the moneylenders and the beggars, the high-caste and the low-caste,[1] the religious and the secular, the family and the country, the personal and the social, the male and the female, and so on. It is these contradictions that *collaterally* constitute the warp and weft of the 'social fabric'. Thus, the conflict is all-pervasive, injustice ubiquitous, and authority scattered.

This complex socio-political 'multi-verse' is cinematically woven into a '*uni*-verse,' by making the hero 'autonomous' — he is accorded a 'transcendental' narrative status, which confers on him the authority to *flout* (or 'transcend') all norms — an action which will otherwise be labelled immoral or illegal (Figure 6.1).

Figure 6.1
Universification of Multiverse

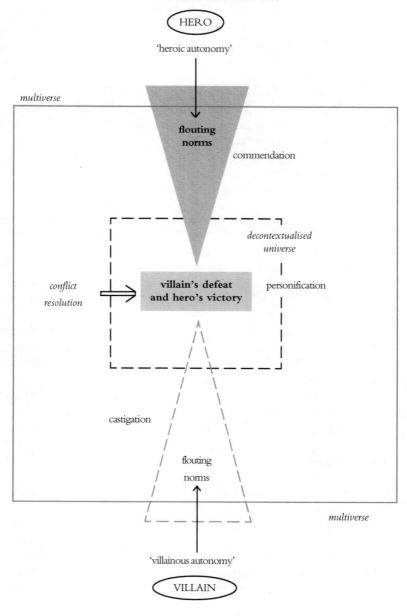

The 'heroic autonomy' (as opposed to the 'villainous autonomy', which is denied to the villain by constant castigation and condemnation) entitles him to meander in the labyrinth of the asymmetrical 'universe', sometimes denouncing, sometimes romanticising the selectively appropriated features. The features thus selected, coalesce into a sharply focused *single conflict* between him, the hero, and the villain. As a result, the issue at stake gets *decontextualised, but personified*. With the defeat or elimination of the villain the issue is *closed as resolved*.

Thus, when the single conflict is 'solved away' with the elimination of the villain, the viewers, who mostly come from the periphery, are given the vicarious satisfaction of having tasted the pleasures of the centre, though momentarily. But their real-life asymmetrical 'multiverse' continues to remain unaltered.

Twin Migration

It is in this fictionally universified multiverse occurs the phenomenon of 'double-bodied migrantcy'. It involves, as illustrated in Figure 6.2, projecting the hero as the 'embodiment' of the subaltern masses living in the periphery of the society, while simultaneously lifting him up from the periphery to migrate to the centre by 'disembodying' the very same people he purports to have embodied.

When the hero migrates affirmatively towards the 'peripheral embodiment', he in effect selectively 'embezzles' the 'riches' of the periphery; when he migrates subversively towards the 'central disembodiment', he judiciously 'usurps' the authority of the centre, by which he distinguishes himself as different from the periphery, now bereft of its 'riches'. The ensuing body of the hero, the 'double-bodied migrant', is both 'embodied' and 'estranged', both 'subalternised' and 'elitised'.

Liminal Spurts

Strikingly, the embezzlement of the signs of the subaltern class is 'fused' with the usurpation of the signs of the dominant class in unique occurrences of 'spasmodic liminal spurts'. These are sudden, sporadic spurts of liminality appearing through the narrative at *irregular* intervals. Such spurts are usually acts of *defiance* of or *affront* to the dominant authority and cultural practices. Defiant acts such as sitting cross-legged on a chair and puffing a *beedi* or a pipe in the presence of the rich are frequently

Figure 6.2
Double-Bodied Migrantcy

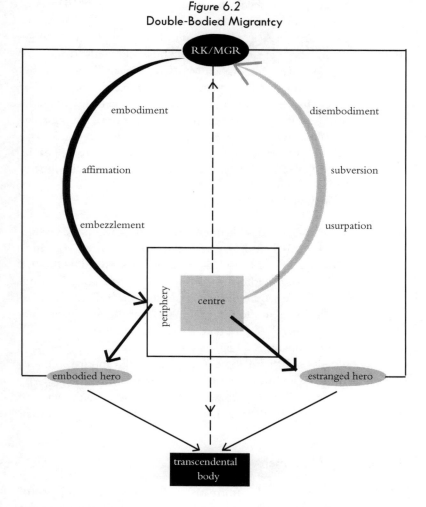

seen in the films of MGR and RK. Instances of affront to the dominant culture also abound in MGR and RK films. In *Enga Veettu Pillai*, for instance, the subaltern MGR sits at the dining table of a rich man and eats sloppily, violating all etiquettes. In *Panakkaaran*, RK conducts a mock 'fashion parade' exhibiting the various items of the 'connoisseurial' attire like trousers, tie, belt and glasses, and commenting on their 'subaltern uses'.

66 ◼ POPULAR CINEMA AND POLITICS IN SOUTH INDIA

The liminal spurts provide the subaltern viewers with flashes of vicarious gratification of their need to defy and insult the oppressors. Interestingly, every instance of liminal spurt is invariably 'equivocal' — the one and the same act is *both* an act of embezzlement and an act of usurpation. Thus, when the orphan MGR in *Meenava Nanpan* dashes into the dining room of the rich man to demand that the poor worker whipped by him for stealing food out of hunger should be seated on the chair, and eat the same food denied to him, he is at once a representative of the subaltern victim (embezzling) and an empowered hero with the authority to confront (usurping). It is this 'equivocal' nature of the liminal spurt that effects the *fusion* of embodiment and disembodiment.

Erasure and Accrual

Intriguingly enough, the double migration — one towards the periphery, the other towards the centre — is 'self-erasing-cum-self-accruing'. The strength of the embodied (subaltern) image erases the disembodied (dominant) image, but without redeeming the signs embezzled from the subalterns. The disembodied image in its turn does the same to the former, but retaining the signs usurped from the dominant elite. This mutual erasure and accrual render the resultant image to be both subaltern and dominant, *and* neither subaltern nor dominant — they are 'neutralised', and 'fused' (at every instance of a liminal spurt) to give rise to the 'synergised' transcendental body. This explains why invariably in every film of MGR and RK, no poor person other than the hero becomes rich at the end, while the rich always remain rich, if not richer.

Embodying Movement

MGR and RK achieve the affirmative 'peripheral embodiment' (or 'subalternising') by adopting one or more of the following narrative milieus:

- they are *born* poor
- they may in fact be heirs to riches/throne, but *by accident* they are reared by 'foster' parents who are poor

DOUBLE-BODIED MIGRANTCY ◀ 67

- if rich, they intentionally *opt* to identify themselves *with/as* the poor
- irrespective of their economic status, they always speak *for* the poor

The hero in a considerable number of films of both MGR and RK is born poor or grows up by mistake in a poor family, which inevitably makes him speak the language of the poor. When the hero is born rich, both MGR and RK frequently resort to 'double act' with one role cast as the rich, and the other, the poor. Interestingly, the role of the poor, illiterate, unassuming person is given an edge over that of the rich person. Even when the 'double act' device is not employed, the hero always identifies himself with the poor, or at least is charitable to the poor, treating them with respect. In any case, the hero is always on the side of the poor and the marginalised, echoing their concerns and aspirations, as the vagabond MGR in *Naadoadi Mannan* tells the minister, 'You (condescendingly) look at the common people from the palace; I observe the palace standing with them'.

MGR and RK take care to behaviourally exhibit their subaltern identity. They do this first of all by showing the hero engaged in a specific action that characterises the occupation. Thus, if MGR is a farmer, he will be seen in the field working as a farmer (for example, *Urimai Kural*), if a rickshaw-puller, he will pull the rickshaw (*Rikshaakaaran*), if a fisherman, he will go fishing (*Meenava Nanpan*), if a cowherd, he will clean the cowshed and milk the cow (*Maattukkaara Vaelan*), if a labourer, he will sweat carrying heavily loaded bags of paddy (*Annamitta Kai*), and so on. The same is true also of RK, who is seen driving an auto (*Baatshaa*), cycling to deliver milk as a milkman (*Annaamalai*), working in uniform as a factory worker (*Mannan*), and so on.

The second way of exhibiting their subaltern identity is through celebration of subalternity. Both MGR and RK romanticise the subaltern masses, more so when the hero himself belongs to such a class. The subaltern people are stereotyped as spontaneous and straight-forward, guileless and innocent, naïve and unassuming, emotional and intuitive, hospitable and generous but poor people, who value relationship more than anything else. They are glorified to such an extent that sometimes they are almost placed at par with the divine. This glorification and

68 ■ POPULAR CINEMA AND POLITICS IN SOUTH INDIA

romanticisation of the subaltern culture and ethos are done normally through the dialogues, and more effectively through the songs.

Another common way of exhibiting the subaltern identity is to manifest the state of deprivation and basic human needs, more specifically the drive of hunger and the need for food, such as MGR devouring food in the hotel in *Enga Veettu Pillai* or RK standing in the queue to receive the *laddu* (a kind of sweet) in *Vaelaikkaaran*. MGR and RK also go a step further to emphasise the *very act of sharing the food of the subalterns with the subalterns*. MGR, for example, joins the workers to share their food in *Annamitta Kai*; RK eats the *ragi* pudding in *Thambikku Entha Ooru*.

Sharing food as a sign of hospitality ('virunthoampal') is an important cultural category. The Thamizh culture, especially the culture of the subalterns, considers food-sharing with guests and even strangers as a supreme virtue. *Thirukkural*, for example, devotes an entire chapter for hospitality (chapter 9, verses 81–90). MGR resorts to this aspect more frequently than RK. Thus, in *Kumari Koattam*, MGR will be hospitable to a thief, who runs away with his hard-earned savings; in *Neethikku Thalai Vanangu*, MGR as a madman will be shown hospitality.[2]

Another aspect of 'subalternising' is to depict the hero to be indulging in 'anti-social' activities, because of the acuteness of the deprivations and the inability to fulfil even the most basic physiological needs. Interestingly, he also partakes of the *helplessness* of the poor. This again is a *stereotype* like glorification, but here it is only reversed. Thus, the subalterns are portrayed as weak and vulnerable, illiterate and susceptible to deceit, passive and submissive, cowardly and unreliable, wretched and despicable, etc. The hero *shares* some of these characteristics also — but only as a *token* — especially through 'double acting'.

The subaltern identity of MGR and RK created on-screen has been strengthened by their real-life experiences — they themselves having come from similar subaltern backgrounds. They have grown up amidst poverty, deprivation, and in the case of RK, also depravity. Their subaltern identity, therefore, is not only 'cinematic' but also 'authentic'. It is this 'authentic' subalternity that is made *total* by the *won consent* of the subalterns, who are shown to be always on the side of the hero. They accept him as their leader, as the one who personifies their collective aspirations. But this is only one side of the picture. The other side involves the subversive migration of the hero towards the 'central disembodiment'.

Disembodying Movement

The hero's migration towards disembodying (or 'elitising') takes place simultaneously with his 'subalternising', enabling him to stand out from the rest of the subalterns. Table 6.1 highlights, for comparative purposes, the corresponding characteristics, i.e., embodying vis-à-vis disembodying. The 'magic' of this estrangement is worked out in one or more of the following narrative milieus:

- the hero is *born* rich
- if not, he grows up (as a foster child) in a rich family by *accident*
- he *masquerades* as a rich man
- he is loved by/*married* to a rich woman

Though the films in which the hero is a subaltern far outnumber those in which he is an elite, both MGR and RK do have a significant number of films to their credit in which the hero remains *rich throughout*.

In some films, he is an orphan (or orphaned by the villain), adopted by a rich, good-hearted man. Sometimes the hero disguises himself as the rich for the sake of teaching a lesson or two to the proud-hearted villain — a device more frequently used by MGR than RK. With hardly a few exceptions, a rich woman falls in love with the hero, and eventually marries him. Thus, he becomes rich through marital alliance.

Table 6.1
Aspects of Embodying and Disembodying

Narrative Milieus	
Embodying	*Disembodying*
Poor by birth	Rich by birth
Poor by accident	Rich by accident
Poor by option	Rich by marriage
Behavioural Manifestations	
Embodying	*Disembodying*
Engagement in characteristic action	Dress and other paraphernalia
Celebration of subalternity	Access to education
Deprivation and food-sharing	Access to wealth and women
Helplessness and victim-hood	Heroism and redemptive action

70 POPULAR CINEMA AND POLITICS IN SOUTH INDIA

At the behavioural realm, the most striking manifestation of 'elitising' is in the *dress* and other costumes of the hero. The hero in general is dressed like a 'non-subaltern', for example, MGR as a rickshaw-puller and RK as a milkman will be seen in well-ironed pants and shirt. This, obviously, is an oddity, because such a sophisticated — even moderately decent — manner of dressing is clearly a sign of the dominant elite. It is precisely by adopting signs of the dominant class, while appropriating the signs of the subordinated, MGR and RK offset themselves from the subalterns. The narrative device of 'double acting' is malleable to this ploy — one will be elegantly dressed and the other, poorly so. But even here the poor man will stand out as different from other poor people. Another innovation in this regard is the poor hero masquerading as a rich man (*Periya Idaththu Penn*, for example).

Next significant sign of the elite is *education*. MGR and RK deliberately distance themselves from the subalterns by having easy access to education, which is denied to the vast majority of the people with whom they 'totally' identify themselves. Compared to RK, however, this aspect of estrangement through education is one of the most basic ingredients of the 'MGR formula'. The poor illiterate MGR in *Enga Veettu Pillai*, for example, takes pains to learn, even while romancing with his fiancée. MGR, as the illiterate cowherd in *Maattukkaara Vaelan* and the yet-to-be socialised prince in *Adimai Penn*, makes concerted efforts to become literate. In *Sangae Muzhangu*, the falsely accused MGR studies night and day with the determination to become a police inspector.

Frequently, the subaltern hero will already be educated. In *Thani Piravi*, for example, the blacksmith MGR is a degree holder; in *Rikshaakaaran*, the rickshaw-puller MGR astounds the judge by quoting Shakespeare ('if you have tears, better to shed them now') and says, 'An occupation can earn respect and honour, only if it combines both physical labour and knowledge'; in *Kumari Koattam*, the MGR doing the boot-polishing amazes his clients by giving the accurate dates of the Jalian Walabagh Massacre and Sepoy Mutiny, and advocates the educational philosophy of 'earning while studying'; in *Panakkaara Kudumpam*, he opines, 'Man needs education to satiate his intellectual hunger and food to satisfy the physical hunger'.

Whether educated or not, RK does *not* in general attach much value to formal education. Thus, in *Murattukkaalai*, both RK and his three brothers remain uneducated, and without any qualms about it. There is a marked difference, however, between his attitude towards *his* education and that of *others* entrusted to his care, such as brothers and sisters. On the one hand, he accepts his illiterate status as 'given' and unavoidable, and only very rarely he expresses the feeling, as in *Panakkaaran*, that he as a child has been deprived of the opportunity to get educated. In *Mullum Malarum*, for example, a humble RK accepts that he is uneducated, and so, he adds, he does not know double-speak. More often than not, he is, in fact, proud of being uneducated, and revels in *undervaluing* formal education through his occasional sarcastic comments such as, 'the more one studies, the less intelligent one becomes' (*Panakkaaran*). On the other hand, the illiterate RK, as a responsible brother, works very hard to provide formal education to his brothers and sisters (*Padikkaathavan*, *Baatshaa*, *Thee*, *Tharma Thurai*, etc.).

Whatever be the case, the illiterate RK does not fail to prove his mettle when required. In *Mannan*, for example, he will demonstrate that he is a cut above the rest of the formally educated by *redefining*, in erudite English, the very concept of education:

> I am mechanic by vocation... I have lots of compassion towards my fellow human beings and brothers... If you people think that only literates are educated, then I am not educated. If you people accept one who is cultured as really educated then I am definitely more - more - educated than you all.

RK usurps education, therefore, through *stipulative redefinition* of education, while MGR does it through *systemic acquisition*.

Another crucial sign adopted from the dominant class is in the economic realm. The 'subalternised' hero is 'privileged' to access wealth and women. Both are, surprisingly, easily 'available' to him! In the *moral* realm, the 'clean image' comes in handy to distance him from the subalterns. MGR and RK, irrespective of their 'moral philosophy', are portrayed as persons who follow the dictates of their 'conscience', a 'conscience' that is ultimately acceptable to both the subaltern and the dominant classes. The final sign that distinguishes MGR and RK from the subalterns is their *heroism*. They are men of action, strong and valorous, who cannot tolerate any form of injustice. There is, however, a striking difference, as noted in an earlier chapter, between MGR and RK. Though both of them are subaltern heroes and the *contents* of their 'heroic deeds' are much the same (the hero assaulting the villain, for example), they differ from each other significantly in the *context* in which they exhibit their heroism and the *manner* (or style) with which they execute their 'heroic deeds'.

Coincidentally, these aspects are also personally significant to MGR and RK. Given their childhood marked by appalling misery and abject poverty, owning up signs of the dominant class does them good in two ways: within the context of the narrative, their subaltern status (rendered authentic and credible by their real past) justifies the adoption of the signs of the dominant class as only natural; in the off-screen context, the fact that these once poor persons are now millionaires is justified as a 'natural' growth of hard-working men. Amazingly, the very past that makes the 'embodying' credible and natural, does the same also to the 'disembodying'.

Notes

1. MGR and RK are very cautious about caste, since it is a sensitive, pervasive and volatile subject, which could, if mishandled, adversely affect the immediate box-office returns and eventually ruin their career prospects. Therefore, they normally avoid entertaining caste conflict in their stories (neither as a subject matter nor as a background) and as a rule they will not have any caste identity; whereas they freely and frequently deal with economic conflicts, and they feel comfortable with their economic status, be it high or low.
2. It should be acknowledged, however, that though food-sharing is considered a supreme virtue, it is rigorously *regulated* by the norms of the hierarchically and rigidly structured *caste* society. Thus, a person belonging to a lower caste cannot share food with a high-caste person, though a high-caste person may occasionally condescend, as a sign of his magnanimity, to share the food of a low-caste person. Hospitality, therefore, is practised only *within* equal-ranking castes. With regard to pilgrims, travellers and beggars, the 'hospitality' recommended implies nothing more than charity. Food will be served to them *outside* the house, and they may rest a while in the *thinnai*, a kind of mud or stone bench adjoining the outer wall but outside the house. But the practice of building houses with the provision for *thinnai* is nothing more than *nostalgia* even in villages. For a eulogy on 'village hospitality', listen to the 'Ballaelakkaa' song in RK's *Sivaji*.

7

WEALTH OF POVERTY

Conflicts ensuing the possession or dispossession of wealth are a staple of the films of MGR and RK. Their attitudes towards wealth are manifest through what they say and what they do, and what catches our attention is that these two forms are more often than not at odds with each other.

Verbal Declarations

Gleaning especially from the *dialogues*, the views of MGR and RK on wealth could be clustered into the following five binaries:

Wealth versus Peace

Wealth beyond a limit can become a burden, and it spoils the peace of mind. It is addictive, and it enslaves you. Though MGR expresses this opinion rather *feebly* and only very rarely in films like *Siriththu Vaazha Vaendum*, it is RK who underscores this through a number of films including *Annaamalai, Muththu, Panakkaaran,* and *Arunaachalam.* 'If wealth is within limits, it will protect you; if it exceeds, you will have to protect it', holds RK. Hence he advocates that money be spent and enjoyed, instead of hoarding it. 'The one who hoards wealth is a fool', says RK in *Arunaachalam*, and continues, 'Once you get saturated, you will not go after it'.

Maanam versus Wealth

Both RK and MGR hold the view that *maanam* (meaning, self-respect or ego), is more important than wealth (for example, RK's

Naan Adimai Illai; MGR's *Thaayin Madiyil* and *Kaavalkaaran*). MGR, however, gives greater importance to *maanam* than RK. 'I am not the one to sell my self-respect (*maanam*) for the sake of money; for me, *maanam* is greater', asserts MGR in *Thaayin Madiyil*. He further affirms in *Raaman Thaediya Seethai*, 'One's social status is not in money, but in character'. It may be mentioned here that the Thamizh culture attaches great value to *maanam*, and MGR by placing *maanam* over wealth syncs with the cultural ethos.

Persons versus Wealth

People and human relationships are more important than wealth, according to MGR and RK. In *Maattukkaara Vaelan*, for example, MGR is categorical that no money on earth can buy one a mother. RK repeatedly stresses that true wealth consists of good parents, wife, children and friends (*Veeraa, Panakkaaran* and *Arunaachalam*). He subordinates material wealth to good physical and mental health, which in his opinion is the true wealth that the parents could leave behind for their wards to inherit (*Paandiyan*).

Inheritance versus Earning

RK is very firm that the wealth inherited from parents cannot really be called one's own. On the contrary, the duty of a son is to earn on his own and support his parents with his earnings (*Arunaachalam*). MGR is not so articulate like RK on this. For him, 'However great may be a person's wealth, if he does not have an occupation of his own, he is like an orphan' (*Sangae Muzhangu*). Both MGR and RK believe that hard work can bring in or increase one's wealth.

'Punyam' versus Wealth

MGR and RK are aware of the impermanency of wealth, and advocate putting it to proper use. It is to be used to help the poor and to generate employment by investing it in industries. RK goes a step further and states that the impermanent wealth (*Veeraa* and *Muththu*) given by god as a gift (*Athisaya Piravi*) is to be spent in earning the *punyam* (deeds meritorious in the presence of god). MGR does not give this religious colouring to spending wealth. For him, wealth must be shared with those who are deprived of it.

WEALTH OF POVERTY ◀ 75

Thus, from what they *verbally* state, it looks that, if MGR and RK are to choose between wealth and peace, wealth and *maanam* or wealth and human relations, they would *not* apparently prefer wealth. It appears that they would opt for own earning instead of sitting and enjoying the wealth inherited. They also seem to believe that wealth should be spent on 'meritorious deeds' (religious or secular or both). But their behaviour with reference to wealth shows otherwise.

In Concrete Action

A keener look into what MGR and RK *do* as heroes with regard to wealth unveils the vast difference in their behaviour depending on their economic status, the kind of villain they are faced with, and the economic status of other key characters with noteworthy bearings on the heroes. Figure 7.1 highlights the behavioural pattern.

The socio-economic status of the hero vis-à-vis that of others results in three sets of combinations, namely, hero versus villain, hero vis-à-vis heroine, and hero vis-à-vis aides.

Hero versus Villain

The hero can either be rich or poor but the villain as a norm is always rich, though his wealth can either be legal or illegal. This gives rise to four possible combinations as explained below.

Rich Hero versus Rich Villain (Legal): When the rich hero confronts a rich villain, whose wealth has been acquired through legal / moral means, such as family inheritance, the wealth of both the hero and the villain are protected at the end. The hero implicitly justifies the retention of his wealth because he is the legal owner. The wealth of the villain remains with himself for the same legal reason, the only change being that he will now be a changed person. The villain, however, is *always* cast in a bad light, as rapacious, immoral and dishonest in spite of being rich (or because they are blinded by their wealth). Therefore, while the wealth may be justified, he is *always* punished on moral and legal grounds for 'being a villain'. Even the elimination of the villain is not infrequent, as in RK's *Murattukkaalai* or MGR's *Adimai Penn*.

Poor Hero versus Rich Villain (Legal): When the hero is poor and is faced with a rich villain, whose wealth is not illegally acquired, often enough the poor hero becomes rich through sheer hard work

Figure 7.1
Attitude Towards Wealth — General Pattern

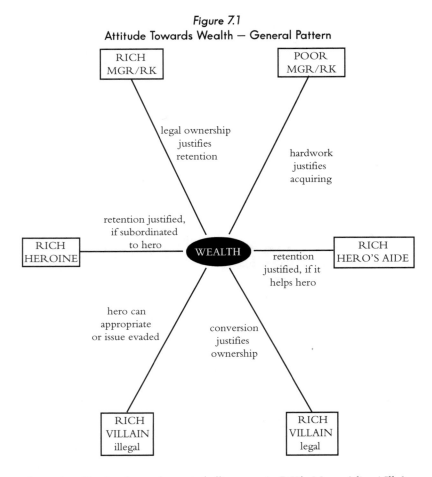

(occasionally also through marital alliance as in RK's *Naan Adimai Illai*). If the hero remains poor till the end, it will be because he deliberately renounces wealth (MGR's *Aayiraththil Oruvan*). The rich, proud-hearted villain normally humiliates the poor hero, who in turn takes it as a challenge to equal him in wealth, if not surpass him (often he does surpass). The rich villain is treated very much like in the previous case — he is punished just enough to make him repent, or the law takes its course, if he is involved in other crimes, but his wealth is spared.

Rich Hero versus Rich Villain (Illegal): If the rich hero faces a rich villain, who has amassed wealth through illegal means, the villain is

WEALTH OF POVERTY ◀ **77**

severely punished often with death. Regarding the villain's wealth, it will return to its legal owner from whom the villain usurped. The legal owner will often be the hero, as in MGR's *Raaman Thaediya Seethai*. If the villain's victim cannot be identified, the question of wealth is closed with the elimination of the villain, as in RK's *Tharma Yuththam*.

Poor Hero vis-à-vis Rich Villain (Illegal): Poor hero confronting a rich villain, who is a depraved anti-social, is very common in MGR and RK films. Interestingly, the hero also will often be an anti-social, but a do-gooder, fashioned after Robin Hood (for example, MGR's *Malai Kallan* and *Oli Vilakku*, and RK's *Thalapathy* and *Baatshaa*). The hero will be 'privileged' to loot and burgle the wealth of the villain and distribute it to the poor and the needy. Invariably the hero will be vindicated, and the villain punished. Sometimes, as in the previous instance, the hero will be the rightful owner of wealth, from whose parents the villain has appropriated it by deceit. In such a case, the wealth will return to the hero.

Hero vis-à-vis Heroine

The hero and the heroine can either be rich or poor. The four possible hero–heroine combinations accruing from this are diagrammatically shown in Figure 7.2.

Rich Hero vis-à-vis Rich Heroine: Usually the rich heroine is associated with haughtiness and arrogance. She is educated, bold, and even enterprising. But exceptions are not uncommon. The combination of rich hero and rich heroine is rare compared to other combinations. In MGR's *Maattukkaara Vaelan*, a rich heroine falls in love with the rich hero MGR, but she has already been 'domesticated' by the poor MGR. In *Enga Veettu Pillai*, the rich heroine is not a shrew, whereas she is, in RK's *Thampikku Entha Ooru* and *Padaiyappaa* (where she is a villain). With the marriage of the heroine her wealth also goes, by implication, to the hero.

Poor Hero vis-à-vis Rich Heroine: The poor hero–rich heroine combination goes often with the typical taming of the shrew, as in MGR's *Periya Idaththu Penn* and *Kumari Koattam*, and RK's *Mannan*. A variant to this occurs, as a clichéd formula particularly in MGR films, in the form of the poor hero resorting to 'pretending' to be rich initially for the sake of taming the shrew. While wealth and haughtiness go together, exceptions are also not unknown. In MGR's *Meenava Nanpan*, the

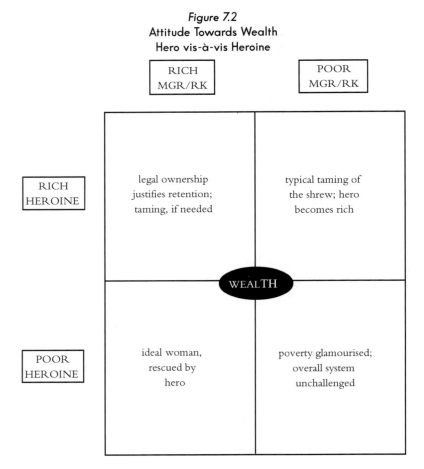

Figure 7.2
Attitude Towards Wealth
Hero vis-à-vis Heroine

educated, rich heroine is so sensible and balanced that she becomes the spokesperson of the poor (and the hero). When the hero meets with a rich heroine, he 'domesticates' (or 'mutilates') her, if she is arrogant, or finishes his 'duty' first, and then gets married to her. Thus, the hero, barring very few exceptions, becomes rich at the end; even in exceptions, he does become rich by virtue of his marriage to a rich woman.

Rich Hero vis-à-vis Poor Heroine: Another popular combination involves a rich hero but a poor heroine. The heroine in this case will always be self-effacing, modest and sacrificing — an *ideal* woman like the mythological *Lakshmi* or *Seetha*. MGR's *Panam Padaiththavan, Adimai Penn, Ithaya Kani, Ulagam Sutrum Vaalipan,* and *Raaman Thaediya Seethai* portray such an ideal woman. Quite frequently, she will be a victim of some sort, and will wait for the hero to rescue her. Sometimes, she is contrasted with the haughty woman, as in RK's *Padaiyappaa* and *Mannan*. At the end, the heroine will no more be poor, and the hero remains richer because of his ideal wife.

Poor Hero vis-à-vis Poor Heroine: Quite understandably, instances of both the hero and the heroine being poor are very rare. Rarer still are the instances of both of them remaining poor till the end, as in MGR's *Thirudaathae* and RK's *Mullum Malarum*. In such films, the poor are glamourised, and stereotyped as representing all that is pristine and traditional. The overall socio-economic system, which has made them poor, is unchallenged. Within the system, however, the hero will be 'richer' in terms of his moral uprightness.

Hero vis-à-vis Aide

Irrespective of the fact whether the hero is rich or not, the rich hero's aide is good and generous, or transformed thus by the hero. He helps the hero achieve his mission, in the process of which, the hero, if poor, is very likely to become rich, as in RK's *Annaamalai*. Occasionally, the aide would be won over by the hero from the villain's camp to his side, or the hero would have rescued him from some danger, as in MGR's *Kumari Koattam*, and RK's *Mannan*. Whatever be the case, so long as the aide helps the hero, he is justified in retaining his wealth (if he does not help the hero, he turns into a villain, and will be treated accordingly). Surprisingly, the poor aides of the hero continue to remain poor till the end, while the hero jumps several steps up in the socio-economic ladder.

The above classification points to three important traits characterising the approach of MGR and RK to wealth, as concretely manifested in their action, irrespective of what they verbally state:

(a) MGR and RK as a rule become rich, or retain their wealth.
(b) They never challenge the overall socio-economic system.
(c) If they remain poor, *they choose* to be so, for greater moral or political gains.

8

DISPENSATION OF JUSTICE

Victim and Custodian

As dispensers of justice in a cinematically universified multiverse, MGR and RK display a delicately complex and subtly intricate behaviour. While they embezzle and usurp the subaltern and the elite signs, they constantly switch their operation between the *contesting yet commingling* moral and legal terrains. Consequently, they exhibit variant responses to the same 'act of violation', depending on whether they assume the role of the *victim* or that of the *custodian*.

MGR and RK share, as noted in the discussion on the double-bodied migrantcy, the helplessness of the subalterns. Quite often they themselves are the direct victims of the unjust socio-political system, which is personified as an evil incarnate villain or a group of villains. The migration towards elitising involves assuming the status of being the custodians of moral values and conformity to law. Besides, the frequently played role of a police officer also reinforces their status as the authoritative and *legitimate* custodians. While both MGR and RK *take the law into their hands* and presume the authority to dispense justice, the way they exercise their authority greatly varies — they contest and even *pre-empt* the legal course, if they are victims; they uphold the sovereignty of law, if they are custodians. Their 'moral economy' is, therefore, marked by an apparent contrast between the moral 'right-ness' and the legal 'correctness', the *sathyam* or *unmai* (the Truth) and the *sattam* (the Law). The contrast becomes very focussed when they are either personally victimised by the villains or they are the police officers themselves.

What is striking in their moral economy is the way violence is portrayed. Both the heroes and the villains resort to violence in both the moral and the legal terrains. The violence employed by the villains is of course condemned outright. But the violence of the heroes, often unleashed to gruesome and heinous levels, is justified in the moral terrain as necessary to *redress* the damage they as victims have suffered, and in the legal terrain, as a *procedural* necessity for them as custodians to 'appropriately' handle the villains to make them confess the truth.

The moral terrain of the victim is characterised by appeal to *subjective conscience* as distinct from the *objective evidence*, which is an absolute requirement in the legal terrain of the custodian. Enigmatically, when MGR and RK are victims, they *presume* certain *epistemological privilege* over the law, and when they are custodians, they *assume* the same privilege over the moral. Often these two 'privileges' are 'combined' (by the victim playing the custodian or the custodian playing the victim), resulting in MGR's and RK's own versions of justice.

Epistemological Privilege

As custodians, MGR and RK assume the epistemological privilege over the moral primarily on grounds of *entitlement* — they are in a super-ordinate position because they are legally or socially entitled to be so. As the ones victimised for no fault of theirs, they presume the privilege on grounds of *entrustment* — they consider them to have been 'entrusted' with the moral responsibility of avenging the wrong and championing the cause of the subalterns. Since it is they as heroes who are the prime victims, the entrustment more often than not amounts to *self*-entrustment.

The self-entrustment that goes to justify the anti-social, amoral and illegal activities of MGR and RK by presuming the epistemological privilege has the following aspects:

The Primordial War

The most frequently cited justification is that MGR and RK as heroes are personally wronged by the villains — they are deprived of their parents (one or both), parental affection and childhood; they are separated from their family and pushed into poverty and misery; they are tricked into anti-social activities, and so on. Once it dawns on them that they have been wronged against, they set out to avenge the wrong by taking revenge on the villains. But this is not to be construed as a

82 POPULAR CINEMA AND POLITICS IN SOUTH INDIA

personal vendetta. They are engaged in the noblest 'duty' of avenging, the duty of waging a 'holy war' between *dharma* (or *aram*) and *adharma*. In this 'primordial' war, naturally, the *sattam* has to be subordinated to the *sathyam*.

The Last Resort

That MGR and RK indulge in illegal and amoral activities only as the 'last resort' is yet another justification. Driven by acute hunger and insurmountable poverty, and confronted with a social system 'infested' with unjust and unkind persons, their very subsistence is depicted to be at stake. In such a gruesome and hopeless circumstance, the indulgence in amoral and illegal activities is not their free choice, but they are forced into it. Even while they try hard to reintegrate themselves with the society after realising their mistake, the shadow lingers on, the past hovers over, and social ostracism persists. They are caught up in a vicious circle. Therefore, it is not the poor MGR and RK who are to be blamed, but the dishonest and uncharitable persons who corrupt the social system.

The Interim Evil

That MGR and RK as heroes are good people, often pursuing a respectable profession, but forced by circumstances to indulge temporarily in illegal activities is another justification. Left to themselves, they will not indulge in such things, but at the given moment they do not have any other go. They yield against their conscience to the evil design of the villain, not out of poverty as in the previous case, but for the sake of a *greater* cause. When they muster enough strength and the time is ripe to overcome the villainy, their involvement in anti-social activities ceases to exist and they go back to their original profession.

The Good End

The rich and the powerful amass and hoard wealth, usurp and misuse power. They are too powerful to be challenged, and too ruthless to be persuaded either. The heroes, committed as they are to the victimised, hoodwink the egoistic, unwilling and unyielding rich and powerful people by engaging in looting and robbing their wealth, which in any case is only due to the poor. Theirs is the typical Robin Hood-styled policy of the (good) end justifying the (bad) means.

The Spokesmanship

This is the more positive and braver front of the Robin-Hoodism mentioned above. The heroes here are the representatives of the marginalised and they boldly confront the oppressors. In the course of championing the cause of the vulnerable and voiceless poor, they resort to means that may be branded illegal by those who monopolise and 'devour' the legal system in connivance with powerful politicians and top police officials.

The Principled Illegality

The most intriguing aspect is that MGR and RK are 'ethical' and 'principled' even in their amoral and illegal activities. They take just what is required. They do not hoard. They do not enjoy life's luxuries by depriving the rich of the same. Oddly enough, they are faithful to their 'boss' and do not betray him as long as they remain with him or until they realise that it is their boss who has caused their misfortune.

Acts of Violation

The 'acts of violation' can be grouped, as Figures 8.1 and 8.2 indicate, into three categories based on the kind of impact they have on the prevailing social order. The *first* category consists of the socially disapproved 'bad habits' such as smoking and drinking, which do not disturb the social order in any significant manner, though culturally they may be considered an offence. Given the cultural context of Thamizh Nadu, however, this attitude is typical of the middle class. For the elite, smoking and drinking are part and parcel of their life-style. While these habits may impinge on the economic condition of the family and often produce health hazards, the subalterns do not normally attach a moral value[1] to them.

The *second* category consists of 'minor offences' including small-time stealing, lying and creating public nuisance. Though an *anti-establishment* and defiant streak is discernible beneath these acts, these may not cause any grave damage to the social order. These are legally

84 ◗ POPULAR CINEMA AND POLITICS IN SOUTH INDIA

punishable, however. It could be seen that most of these offences are linked to poverty and stereo typically attributed to the subalterns. The *third* category consists of 'serious crimes' such as physical assaults, murders, rapes and robberies, which are *disruptive* of the social order, and frequently indicative of a state of *anomie*. The crimes of this nature are usually associated with villains and anti-heroes. The response of MGR and RK to each of these categories reveals their uniqueness.

The 'Bad' Habits

MGR eschews any bad habit and thus consistently projects himself as a man without any 'blemish'. He cannot, in general, be seen smoking.[2] Barring the sole exception of *Oli Vilakku*, he is a teetotaller, though he occasionally 'pretends' to drink for the sake of teaching a lesson to others (for example, *Naan Aanaiyittaal, Panakkaara Kudumpam, Kumari Koattam, Kanni Thaai*). Even in *Oli Vilakku* he is first made semi-conscious by the villain and induced by his fiancée to drink against his will; later his personified conscience reprimands him for his 'animal-like' behaviour and asks him, through a song, if he is a human being.

Insofar as the 'bad habits' of others are concerned, MGR very firmly disapproves. He always comes out as a moralist, frequently combining his roles as the victim and the custodian. Thus, in *Naan Aanaiyittal*, for example, the prisoner MGR insists that his co-prisoner stops smoking in jail. In *Siriththu Vaazha Vaendum*, MGR comes straight from prison to the hotel, takes a seat opposite the villain, warns him to count his days from the next day, then gets up and goes near him, starts saying, 'Besides, there is another important matter…' and pulling the cigarette from his mouth, he continues, 'It is not good to smoke while eating'. Through this, MGR is able to communicate the message to the villain how easy it is to handle him, and the message to the *viewer* how serious it is to smoke. Similarly, he asserts in *Oli Vilakku* that he 'hates the very sight of drunkards and avoids their company'. In *Panam Padaiththavan*, he scolds his alcoholic brother to give up his habit because 'drinking spoils one's body, mind, money and eventually life'. MGR abhors not only drinking and smoking but any activity that is discordant with the culture. In the same film *Panam Padaiththavan* he discourages the woman who is in love with him not to visit discothèque because 'it is not our culture'. In effect, MGR emerges as the embodiment and the custodian of the moral values of the middle-class.

DISPENSATION OF JUSTICE ◼ 85

Figure 8.1
Justice — MGR's Version

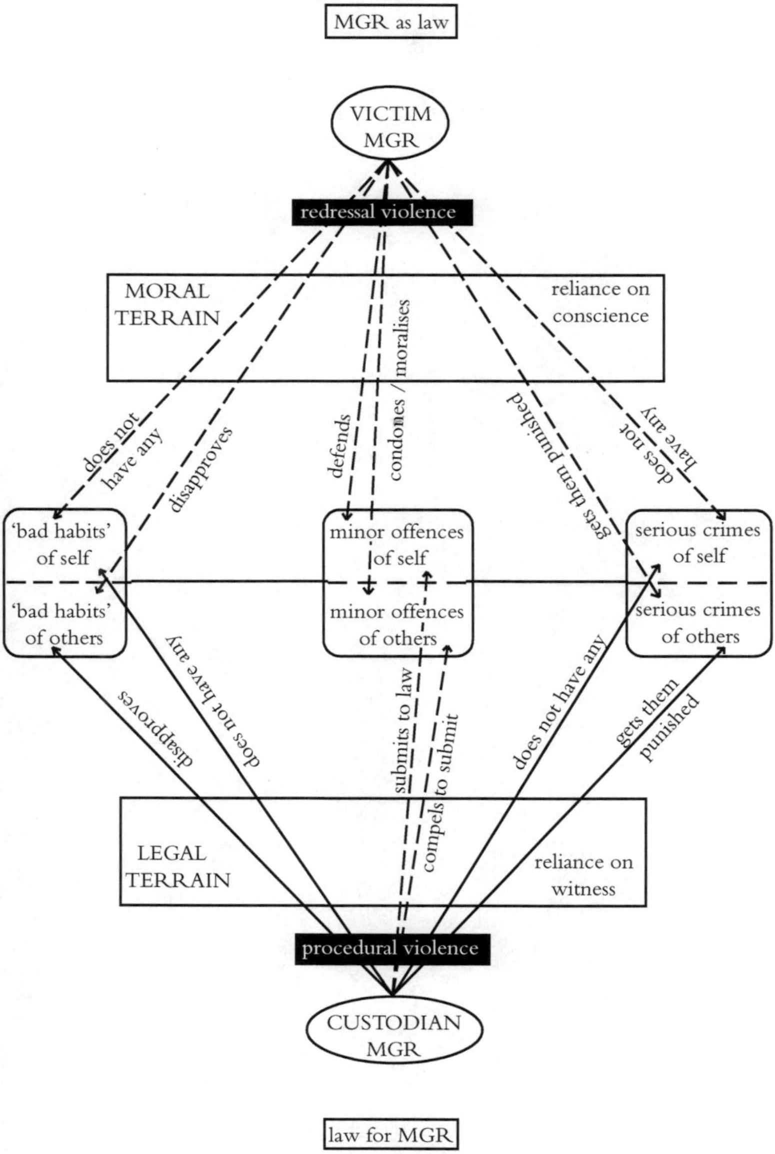

MGR as law

VICTIM MGR

redressal violence

MORAL TERRAIN — reliance on conscience

does not have any / disapproves — defends / condones / moralises — gets them punished — does not have any

'bad habits' of self / 'bad habits' of others — minor offences of self / minor offences of others — serious crimes of self / serious crimes of others

disapproves / does not have any — submits to law / compels to submit — does not have any / gets them punished

LEGAL TERRAIN — reliance on witness

procedural violence

CUSTODIAN MGR

law for MGR

86 ■ POPULAR CINEMA AND POLITICS IN SOUTH INDIA

Figure 8.2
Justice — RK's Version

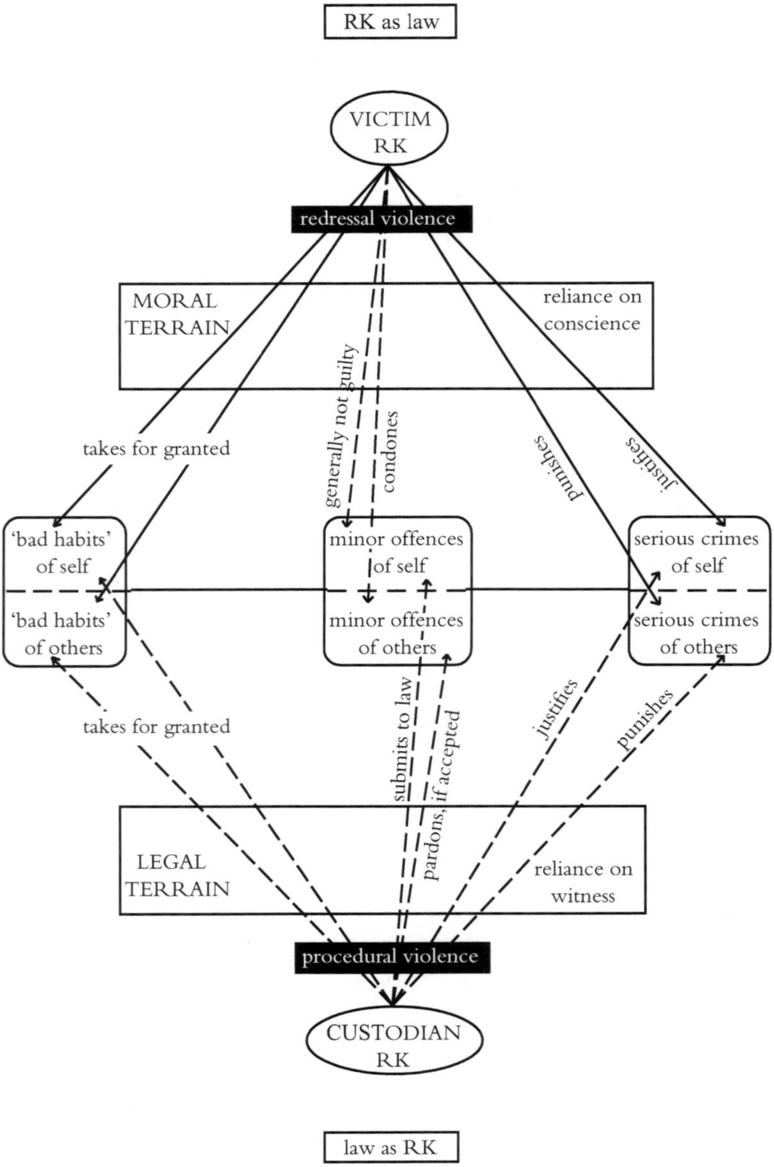

RK as law

VICTIM
RK

redressal violence

MORAL
TERRAIN

reliance on
conscience

generally not guilty

condones

takes for granted

punishes

justifies

'bad habits'
of self

minor offences
of self

serious crimes
of self

'bad habits'
of others

minor offences
of others

serious crimes
of others

takes for granted

submits to law

pardons, if accepted

justifies

punishes

LEGAL
TERRAIN

reliance on
witness

procedural violence

CUSTODIAN
RK

law as RK

DISPENSATION OF JUSTICE   **87**

RK, on the contrary, takes the 'bad habits' for granted. He smokes, in keeping with his high or low status, from pipe to cigarette to *beedi*. In fact, he invents a fascinating *new function* (other than smoking) to cigarette by integrating it with his characteristic 'style'. He is not, when it comes to drinking, a teetotaller either. He is frequently seen to relish drinking, though he is a bit more cautious in later films like *Maappillai* (his friend induces him to drink) and *Padaiyappaa* (he exchanges glasses by accident). His subaltern morality occasionally acquires contours of being subcultural, as in *Moonru Mugam* where he returns from the States as a hippie.

RK in general treats others' 'bad habits' just the way he treats his. He does not attach any moral significance to them, though on very rare occasions he advises the youth through songs not to smoke (*Raajaa Chinna Roajaa*) and not to drink (*Tharmaththin Thalaivan*). In the case of women, however, he is rather categorical that they should not drink because, he reasons in *Naan AdimaiIllai*, 'they are going to be mothers tomorrow and breast-feed children'. Ironically, in the later part of the same film *he* becomes an alcoholic. It could be summed up, therefore, that RK by and large embodies the subaltern morality, except in the case of women towards whom he betrays an attitude remarkably similar to that of MGR.

Minor Offences

Surprisingly, MGR, the custodian of the middle class ethics and culture, *defends* the minor offences, which he as the victim happens to have committed, and condones or moralises such offences of the subaltern victims. As the custodian, he takes an unexpected turn to *surrender* himself to the law, and compels other subalterns to do the same. The victim MGR employs an unambiguous *subaltern* moral language, privileging conscience-based moral 'rightness' over the witness-based legal 'correctness', whereas the custodian MGR speaks the *elite* legal language, to which the subaltern language is eventually deferred.

The dynamics of defence–deference is, for example, obvious in *Thirudaathae*, where MGR, as poverty-stricken Balu, becomes a petty thief in order to feed his hungry mother. He defends his act of stealing based on the 'last resort' rationale, mixing it effectively with 'mother sentiment'. He tells the patron of the orphanage, 'The only person who depends on me in the whole world is my mother. All that I needed to

88 ◾ POPULAR CINEMA AND POLITICS IN SOUTH INDIA

save her was a paltry sum. I searched for a job but to no avail. I could not bear the sight of my mother writhing out of hunger. And so I started stealing against my conscience'.

Yet he is 'principled' in stealing, and donates to the orphanage what is superfluous. That is why when Raju, from whom he has stolen, dies of shock, he conscientiously compensates the loss by giving the stolen money to Raju's mother. He is also in turn 'punished' with the death of his mother — unable to face the truth that her son has been a thief, she dies heart-broken. MGR realises how destructive it is to steal, and starts earning his livelihood by undertaking odd manual jobs like laying the road. While still being 'enghosted' with the thief image, MGR turns out to be a 'street preacher' and through a song advises the kids not to steal, not to be scared of the state of poverty, and not to forget they have talents.

With his 'conversion' and the subsequent reparation, the victim MGR metamorphoses into the custodian MGR. The patron of the orphanage observes, 'All humans commit mistakes. Those who continue to commit mistakes even after knowing are the outcastes (*chandaalarkal*); those who repent are the virtuous (*uththamarkal*)', and certifies that MGR is an 'uththamar'. But the police suspect him to be the one who has robbed the bank (because the money stolen from Raju belongs to the bank). Surprisingly, the custodian MGR evades the police in a kind of 'strategic deferral', utilises the time thus bought to identify the real culprit, and finally submits himself to the law. The court awards life imprisonment to the villain, the notorious thief escaped from Burma. The victim MGR is also sentenced to a three-month imprisonment for petty crimes. However, for helping the police to catch the dreaded criminal, the custodian MGR is 'crowned' with a cash award, which he donates to the orphanage. The victim-turned-custodian MGR accepts the punishment 'as a rare opportunity to become a better person', reminds the child of his advice not to steal, and bids farewell to the viewers.

How the custodian MGR compels others indulging in petty crimes to submit to the law comes out strongly in a film like *Thani Piravi*. When MGR comes to know that his blacksmith father has helped anti-social gangsters break their handcuffs after having escaped from prison, he insists that he submits himself to the police. He tells his mother that he is ashamed of being the son of a criminal and warns his father that he will not enter the house until he surrenders. When his father hesitates

DISPENSATION OF JUSTICE   89

to surrender, he comments, 'There are some who harm the society merely by getting scared of the police. In fact, it is they who must be punished'. On another occasion he advises the public, 'It is the duty of the public to cooperate with the police wherever something against law and society takes place'.

Though RK may submit himself to the law and get punished as a routine, he does not, in general, feel guilty about his petty crimes; neither does he attach guilt to others indulging in such activities. In *Poakkiri Raajaa*, for example, he is put in prison for stealing but he does not seem to feel sorry for having committed an illegal act. In *Moonru Mugam*, the thug RK gets drunk, damages the furniture in the hotel, and revels in creating public nuisance. For the sake of money he impersonates and deceives the court. In *Guru Sishyan*, when the jailer advises RK not to visit the jail again, he retorts, 'If those outside (in the society) are good, why should we have to come inside (the jail)?' Similarly, while coming out of prison after serving the term, RK sings in *Manithan*: 'All those inside are not criminals; neither are those outside a Buddha or a Gandhi…'

Thus, RK is depicted to *take for granted* that minor offences are a part of daily living. In fact, he as a victim treats offences like eve-teasing, street-fighting and even stealing almost on par with favourite 'hobbies'. He does not hesitate to join company with other such offenders. Only when he is personally affected, he takes cognisance of the offensive act, and depending on the gravity of the offence he either condones or punishes.

A striking difference between MGR and RK to be noted here refers to how each of them resorts to 'conscience'. As the victim MGR indulges in minor criminal activities such as stealing *always against his conscience* (as in *Thirudaathae*), and as the custodian he entertains the same *in accordance with his conscience* (as in *Rikshaakaaran*, where he argues in the court that he has followed the dictates of his conscience in smashing the rowdies). While dissociating the conscience from the act of violation justifies the act on moral grounds ('it is after all the last resort') and enables the victim MGR preserve his moral integrity ('he does not really involve'), listening to the conscience does the same to the custodian MGR ('his conscience is clear after all').

In sharp contrast to MGR's dual approach to conscience, RK keeps his conscience off any trace of guilt and *does not regret* his acts of violation, including failing in his duty. *Mullum Malarum*, a 1978 RK starrer,

90 ▪ POPULAR CINEMA AND POLITICS IN SOUTH INDIA

for example, opens with the boy RK breaking the headlight of a car for ridiculing his sister. As a grown up man, he does the same to the car of a rich man who refuses to pay the porter for causing a minor scratch to the car. As a kind-hearted trolley operator in the railways, he allows the villagers to use the trolley, because they have to walk a long distance otherwise. When the engineer tells him that it is against rules, he defends his action, saying, 'This is after all a human to human help…what are we going to carry when we go up (meaning, dying)?' When the engineer sternly warns him, he 'punishes' him by stopping the trolley on the way, saying that it is under repair, and makes the engineer walk the rest of the distance. He commits a series of blunders and continuously fails in duty, but when he is suspended, he blames the engineer of unjustly punishing him.

Whenever RK is personally affected, he impulsively resorts to physical violence to subdue his opponents. The cruelty of the assaults is often disproportionate to the magnitude of the harm done. When he comes to know, for instance, that the clerk has maligned his name by maliciously misinforming the engineer, he beats up the clerk in the street. When his friend refuses to marry his sister, he manhandles him and makes him consent. Throughout the film RK remains 'a thorn and a flower,' an angry young man with a kind heart, but not even once does he accept that he has ever committed a mistake.

Serious Crimes

Strikingly, though MGR may frequently be falsely accused of serious crimes, he does not intentionally commit any. Just as he is free of 'bad habits', he is free of violations disruptive of the social order. When he happens to commit such an act only *unintentionally*, he is only too willing to submit himself to the law as soon as he realises that he is the culprit.

This could be best illustrated with *Neethikku Thalai Vanangu*, in which MGR plays the role of college-going Vijay, the son of a rich businessman. While participating in a race, MGR tries to avoid dashing against some school children. He manages to save the children but in the split-second trauma he does not realise that his car has knocked down two villagers, killing one and blinding another. When the police start the enquiry, MGR's mother pleads with their driver to accept responsibility for the accident, which the driver obliges for the sake of the love he has for his *chinna ejamaan* (junior master). MGR comes to

DISPENSATION OF JUSTICE ▰ 91

know of this later, and decides to submit himself to the police because, he states, 'the culprit should not go scot-free'. But his mother is not emotionally ready to 'part with him' and threatens to die, if he surrenders. Surprisingly, MGR accepts his mother's decision, and tries to compensate for the harm with monetary help to the victims. The same MGR, loved immensely by his mother, decides to leave the house when his father reprimands him. Once he leaves the house, there is no reason why he should not immediately surrender to the police; yet he does not. Paradoxically, his mother is strong enough to bear the physical separation, and for the most part of the film she lives without her son.

The story takes different turns and twists, during which MGR comes into contact with the victims. He works very hard to help them, manages to restore the sight of Chinnaiyan, the person blinded in the accident, and presents himself as the culprit before Chinnaiyan so that he could avenge the murder of his brother. While Chinnaiyan tries to beat him, MGR notices the villain abducting his fiancée and rushes to rescue her, because, he declares, 'It is my duty to protect women's dignity (*maanam*)'. Unable to find Chinnaiyan when he returns, he decides to surrender himself to the police.

Two significant points deserve to be underscored here: First of all, the strategic deferral of submitting him to the law gives him ample scope to make adequate retribution in the moral terrain. He identifies himself with the victims,[3] protects them, and makes enormous sacrifices for them. So much so that the driver's sister, who knows that he is her *chinna ejamaan*, praises him, saying, 'Your heart is always on the side of the poor'. Ironically, the victim Chinnaiyan who does not know the background of MGR and who cannot see, idolises him, saying, 'You are the god whom my eyes have witnessed!' Second, though MGR keeps his promise of providing an opportunity for Chinnaiyan to have his revenge, it is *not* Chinnaiyan who punishes him — he is not there when MGR returns. That is, while in the moral terrain MGR concedes the right of the victim to punish the victimiser, he *transfers* the right to the 'institutionalised representative' of the victim, i.e., the judiciary.

The story ends with adulations[4] galore. Everyone, including Chinnaiyan, thanks MGR for his sacrifices, his father is proud of him, and the court on its part acquits him appreciating his outstanding 'character of bowing before justice'.

While MGR is free of serious crimes or proved innocent when he is accused, RK does commit serious crimes, indulges in anti-social

92 ■ POPULAR CINEMA AND POLITICS IN SOUTH INDIA

and illegal activities, and justifies his actions on grounds mentioned earlier. In *Billaa*, for example, RK is an underworld don, who is a great challenge to the police. He ruthlessly kills people, even his own henchmen, if they desert him or if he suspects them of betrayal. He challenges the DGP, saying, 'Even god cannot catch him'. He eventually chooses death rather than surrender. But the story is not over. RK in his double role, as naïve itinerant dancer Raajappaa aides the police to contain the menace of the criminal activities, by consenting to *act as* Billaa. The police arrest all the notorious international criminals at the end, thanks to Raajappaa, and the social order initially portrayed as anomic is restored.

Two aspects need to be highlighted: First, the society is in a state of anomie, the law and order situation is jeopardised by uncontrollable criminal activities, and the police force is so vulnerable that the criminals are able to infiltrate its rank and file. By contrast, the criminals form their own underground network with international connections. Second, in a disordered and lawless society the criminal RK is neither condemned nor vindicated. Apparently, there is no 'law' to do it either. He is the *law unto himself* and that is why he remains guilt-free till he chooses to die. By contrast, the aide RK manages almost single-handedly and restores social order. It is RK who ultimately 'saves' the law. Coincidentally, both Billaa and Raajappaa are shown to be orphans — the victims of an unkind social (dis)order.

More profoundly manifest is this dynamics in *Thalapathy* where RK plays the role of Surya, a slum dada, who is brutal yet kind. While he is loved and respected by the slum people, the feeling that he is an illegitimate child, deserted as an infant by his unwed mother, haunts him. He remains a trustworthy lieutenant to the gang leader, and 'treats friendship on par with chastity'. When he perceives something as unjust, he plunges into action — he ruthlessly attacks the unjust persons, be they his professional rivals or the police. He beats the money-lender to death, chops the hand of a police inspector in public, burns his rivals in broad day light, dares to enter the police station to assault the police officer, and so on. The intervention of his mother and the consequent realisation that he is no more an orphan and that the collector is his step-brother make him say no to the gang leader, who commissions him to eliminate the collector. Instead, he persuades his leader to surrender. But before they could legally surrender, the collector is transferred and his leader is shot dead by the rival gang leader. RK destroys the rival gang, and reunites with his family. While his collector step-brother leaves for Chennai, his mother decides to stay with RK in Mumbai.

What is noteworthy here is that RK never feels sorry for his actions. Even his decision to surrender is never fully executed. It is pre-empted by the killing of the leader, curiously, by another gang leader. This brings to light the self-regulatory nature of the underworld, an aspect further reinforced by the final showdown of the criminal RK on the rival criminal gang. As a corollary, if at all the restoration of the law and order situation is accomplished, it is because of RK and not because of the collector, who ceases to be the legitimate authority once transferred.

The three-fold categorisation of the acts of violence could be seen from another perspective as well. The 'bad habits' are in the cultural realm and predominantly applicable to the middle class, which is considered to be the guardian of tradition, morality and cultural heritage. MGR reiterates the values of the middle (class) culture, whereas RK rejects them almost *in toto* (except the ones concerning women). The minor crimes (mostly stealing) belong to the economic realm, with an emphasis on subaltern ethics. MGR addresses these crimes both as a subaltern and a non-subaltern, converts what is basically economic into moral-legal, transfers the victim-centred justice to institutionalised justice, and in the process effectively *neutralises* the minor offences as well as the moral rights of the subalterns. RK *naturalises* them by making the minor crimes as a part of the 'day-to-day economics'. The category of serious crimes is essentially political, and involves not only law enforcing but also law-making. In the case of MGR, it is one of 'law *for* MGR'; in the case of RK, it is one of 'law *as* RK'.

'Law For' vis-à-vis 'Law As'

The difference between MGR and RK in their attitude to 'politicisation of justice' could be better understood by comparing films in which they play the *legitimate* custodian role. The most striking difference lies in the relative-positioning of themselves in the overall social order. While MGR places himself above the law but *within* the system, RK places himself above the law but *outside* the system.

In *Siriththu Vaazha Vaendum*, for example, the police inspector MGR, now out of uniform after being punished by law for 'accepting'

94 ■ POPULAR CINEMA AND POLITICS IN SOUTH INDIA

a bribe, gathers evidence to bring the real culprit to book. He discovers in the process that the same villain is the one who has made him an orphan by killing his parents, and warns the villain, 'You have so far been a foe to the law; from now on you are my personal enemy'. He kills the villain in self-defence and the inspector congratulates him for this great feat, for which MGR responds, 'A person fighting for justice, even if he fights a lonely battle, musters the strength of a thousand men; but a man of unjust rule, even if he has a thousand men, will be isolated at the end'. With the elimination of the villain, MGR is back in the uniform. In *Sangae Muzhangu*, the reverse happens. Here the orphan MGR adopted by an international diamond merchant is accused of murder, and to prove that he is not the culprit, he becomes a police officer.

RK presents an interesting reversal of MGR. In *Moonru Mugam*, RK is shown to be an ideal police inspector who 'respects his duty more than his mother, loves it more than his fiancée, affectionate to it more than his son'. He is honest and never accepts a bribe because, he says, 'I am the one who protects the law, not rape it'. His duty consciousness is dramatised — as he gets ready to have sex with his wife, there is a call from the station, and he leaves immediately; when his wife wants him to stay with her in the hospital on the night of delivery, there is a call, and he promptly leaves. He is bold, and even aggressive. Referring to the red colour of the cap and the walls of the police station painted in red, he interprets the red to signify the policemen's readiness to shed blood. He does indeed shed blood. The liquor baron murders him and throws him into the sea waters. His two sons (both played by RK) — one is a US-returned, rich, hippie-turned-businessman; the other is an illiterate, unemployed, poor, reckless rowdy — attempt to avenge his murder. But the son who accomplishes the duty of 'killing the villain the same way as he murdered his father' is, ironically, the callous anti-social.

In *Paandiyan*, the irresponsible, problematic and fearless RK becomes an IPS officer, and on realising vulnerability of the legal system, he throws away his uniform to go back to his real self, characterised by anger, energy, ruthlessness and fearlessness. He uses his muscle power to produce the culprits in front of the judge, and secures the legal release of his sister, another IPS officer imprisoned based on false evidence. Some interesting observations are pertinent here. (*a*) While the angry young man becoming a police officer is kept secret for a long time, the return of the police officer to the angry young man is highly sensationalised, imploring him to 'blow the trumpets of victory', to 'simmer like the Bengal Sea', and to 'wage a war'. RK is seen in black uniform with a white badge carrying a 'right' mark, signifying he is right. (*b*) When RK's sister, a justice-conscious police officer who has not spared even her brother from law, is made a victim of the legal system she upheld, she 'instigates' RK, now the guardian of law, to go anti-legal. In fact, it is she who plucks off the medals from his uniform. (*c*) RK takes on the challenge of the white-shirt-clad politician, who arrogantly declares, 'Law is a kite severed from the thread; court of law is a stage of debate; the khaki shirt is always a slave to this white shirt...' Once RK defeats the politician-police-lawyer combine, he appears in *white* shirt, with tick mark ('right') as the badge. Thus, though RK follows the legal course to get his sister released, he stands outside the law, with the power of the legislator (the politician), who is 'right'.

What is striking is that being in or out of uniform serves not merely a moral purpose but primarily a political purpose. It is no more a question of legal or natural justice; it is a question of appropriating the political authority to dispense justice. MGR appropriates such authority within the prevailing system, by placing him as the 'ideal law' to be emulated by the law itself. On the one hand, he is the law, in the sense of taking the law into his hands; on the other, the law is for MGR, because law becomes so malleable at the hands of MGR that it bends itself to vindicate him and place him as the *supreme law*. RK on the contrary appropriates the political authority to dispense justice by positioning himself as *supra-legal*. The moral-legal system is so corrupted and rendered powerless that it needs 'the right RK' (who defies it) to overhaul and redeem it. In the new dispensation the law is RK.

This observation is further reinforced by the taken-for-granted ritualised closure of the films. MGR fights with the villain, often brutally smashing him, but only to *make him surrender* to the legitimate authority to punish. What MGR does, therefore, is *not dispensing instant justice*, but applying 'procedural' violence to 'facilitate' the villain to acquiesce to the legal course of action to be pursued after submission. The protracted strategic deferral in conjunction with the ritualised arrival of the police at the end to arrest the villain is enough to show that justice is not administered instantly. Justice for MGR is always systemic, not

96 ▄ POPULAR CINEMA AND POLITICS IN SOUTH INDIA

instant.[5] RK, on the other hand, usurps the place of the legitimate authority and 'punishes' the villains. The police arrive at the end only to ratify his action. The way he ridicules the conventional closure of film (that is, the police arriving at the end to arrest) is tantamount to saying that the law does not have any role because he has pre-empted it. The fact that in quite a few of his films the police do not come at all further bolsters up the point that RK's version of justice pre-empts legal justice.

An important point with paramount image-politiking repercussions is the way the moral economy of MGR and RK embraces or excludes certain sections of the people. MGR's moral economy extends to *all* socio-economic classes, more specifically the subaltern and middle classes. RK's moral economy encompasses predominantly the subalterns, especially those with subcultural inclinations, with little or no room for the middle class.

The subaltern slant exhibited by both MGR and RK is, however, partly vitiated by the 'blaring' yet taken-for-granted phenomenon of 'writing off' of the numerous henchmen of the villain. The hero can dispose of the henchmen at will; even a mere stroke of the hero can kill them in 'bunches'. Surprisingly, the question of conscience or guilt never figures at all. This kind of callous treatment meted out to them gives one the inevitable impression that they are, after all, the 'lumpen elements' meant to be eliminated that way. Another related phenomenon that could be observed particularly in RK films is 'scapegoating' — the root cause of villainy is condoned, while the second-level villain or the hireling is condemned to death. In films like *Mister Bhaarath* and *Annaamalai*, RK spares those who are the real cause because they are 'closely-related' to him, and kills only those who are hired by them, ironically, to murder him. The 'scapegoating', in opposition to 'writing off', helps RK assuage the fear of the rich (relatives of his) that his 'subaltern slant' really means eliminating only the hardcore lumpen elements, and is not to be construed as a threat to them, provided they 'adjust' themselves to fall within the universe of his moral economy.

Paradoxically, both for the 'super-legal' MGR and the 'supra-legal' RK the moral-legal system as such is good but it is only swamped by criminals from whose hands it needs to be redeemed. Interestingly, there are always some good people, besides the hero, within the corrupt system. In *Paandiyan*, where the angry and defiant RK throws away his uniform, for example, there is an honest judge who obliges to reopen the case in the face of fresh evidence, and ultimately the legal system is justified. The 'purificatory process' invariably involves the 'sacrifice' of the villains on the 'altar' of justice as interpreted within the parameters laid down by the *hero-centric* moral economy. The conflict between 'conscience' and 'witness' is resolved with the establishment of a legal *system with conscience* through the agency of MGR or RK. As could be predicted, it is MGR and RK who are the conscience in this 'purified' and 'salvaged' system. The 'conscience MGR' remains within as the *paradigm*, constantly inviting the system to *emulate* him, but the system, however, continually falls short of reaching the ideal, and thus stands in perpetual need of MGR's saving hand. The 'conscience RK', on the other hand, performs the function of *surveillance* by remaining outside and demands unqualified *compliance* with him. The system, however, faces the danger of being appropriated by corrupt elements, and to pre-empt any such move his ever-vigilant presence needs to be perpetuated. Remarkably, the same 'emulation-compliance' distinction is seen to be at work in the complex dynamics of fans' identification with their heroes, a crucial point to be elaborated in the next chapter.

Exercise of Power

The exercise of power as depicted in the films of MGR and RK is essentially patriarchal and ubiquitous but concentrated or accumulated in isolated and scattered pockets. While power may accrue to a person by wealth, position or character, everyone in every possible context incessantly attempts to retain or regain power. In effect, the human relationship, be it in familial–social, economic or moral–political realm, becomes a site of contestation marked by the struggle for balancing the unequal power equations between those who have it and those who are deprived of or aspiring for it.

The power struggle, however, is oversimplified by cinematic universification: the villain normally usurps it for personal aggrandise-ment through illegal and immoral means, whereas the hero as the sole representative of the powerless tilts the balance in his favour through his heroic action. Thus, the conflict between the powerless and the powerful, which is in the political terrain, is *switched* to the moral terrain as the conflict between the good and the evil. In the decontextualised universe, the hero and the villain are personified as the good and the evil respectively through the process of 'metaphorical symbolisation', as Figure 8.3 illustrates.[6]

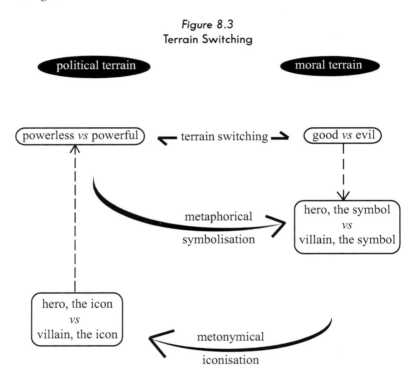

Figure 8.3
Terrain Switching

Accentuated and further strengthened by the viewer's, more specifically the fan's, 'identification' with the hero, the metaphorical symbols acquire the ramifications of icons, i.e., the metaphor of 'the good versus the evil' loses its symbolic value and becomes the metonymical extension of 'the hero versus the villain', which in turn is identified with 'MGR (or RK) versus the villain'. Thus, the clash of symbols turns out to be a clash of icons. As a result, the climactic triumph of the hero is metonymically iconised as the eventual emancipation of the powerless. As the narrative ends with the reversal of the initial power equation now in favour of the hero, the process of iconisation gives the viewer the gratification of having been emancipated.

While the metaphoric–metonymic dynamics is equally applicable to MGR and RK, there are remarkable similarities and amazing differences between them, especially so when it comes to the state power, be it monarchical or democratic. Both MGR and RK acknowledge and accept the necessity and the inevitability of the state power, and its exercise through the 'established structures' of the government machinery, which in itself is good. Power is meant for service, and is to be exercised with benevolence. However, wrong persons appropriate it and abuse it to promote their own interests at the cost of the welfare of the common people. The oppressed lots are helpless and await the arrival of someone who could liberate them. At that juncture, MGR and RK plunge into action as the representative of the voiceless people. Ironically, what triggers off their 'moral wrath' against the oppressor is frequently not the injustice meted out to the common people, but *personal* injustice suffered by them. This element of personal victimisation paves the way for a smooth and credible *terrain switching* from the political to the moral by making the oppressor their personal enemy. What is noteworthy, however, is that they effectively use the double-bodied migrantcy to continue to maintain their role as the spokesmen of the powerless subaltern victims.

The most striking difference between MGR and RK comes in what they have to promise as an alternative to the corrupt and self-centred politics of the villains. MGR promises a utopia that has already come in his person by 'covering up' the inequalities through declarations. In *Thirudaathae*, he prophetically sings that the time to give is fast approaching, when there will not be any need to take. In *Thaayin Madiyil*, he declares that for him the owner and the worker are equal. In *Panam Padaiththavan*, he asserts that the caste and religious divisions have already disappeared. He sternly warns the landlord who prohibited the poor to enter the temple and announces in *Periya Idaththu Penn*, 'Rights, justice and worship are common to all'. In *Raaman Thaediya Seethai*, he proclaims, 'In the upcoming new society the poor and the rich are equal'. In *Meenava Nanpan* he merrily sings, 'This is the time when the crowned king and the military soldier have become equal'. Thus, MGR conveys through the declarations that the ideal rule has already been established and it awaits only a formal inauguration.

The enthusiastic anticipation and the hope-filled 'future that has already become the present' are to a great extent absent in the films of RK. However, RK proposes a parallel government, as he defends his action, in *Nallavanukku Nallavan* for example, of looting a shop where the essential commodities are hoarded, 'What I run is a unique, human government. In my government I am the MLA, I am the MP, I am the minister. None has the guts to challenge me'. He as the underworld *dada* echoes similar sentiments in *Thalapathy*, 'People have faith in us. They come to us because the government is incapable'. But he believes, paradoxically, that politics is 'holy', even while he unleashes, in films such as *Annaamalai* and *Valli*, disparaging and contemptuous comments against the prevailing practice of politics. The 'parallel' government that RK promises, therefore, does not mean any radical rupture with the system, but only a change of government. Quite frequently he presents himself as the most eligible candidate to head the 'changed government' (for example in *Arunaachalam* he affirms, 'If I win, I won't merely talk but act'), when changed. Thus, what RK offers through his films is the foretaste of what he has in store for the people. 'It's only the trailer', as he proclaims in *Padaiyappaa*, 'the main picture is yet to come'.

Another obvious difference between MGR and RK is whether or not they have allegiance to a political party. Almost from the start of his film career as a hero, especially after he officially joined the DMK in 1953, MGR as an actor has been identified with the DMK, and later when he floated his own party, with the ADMK. Thus, his films by and large carry a clear political message. RK, on the other hand, conveys only a general criticism of politics, except for a brief period after *Baatshaa* to *Baba* marked by more precise attacks on Jayalalithaa. That RK does not have a party to belong to is his strength and limitation as well, a point to be elaborated further in the next part.

Notes

1. However, the non-subaltern classes try to impose the middle-class moral values on the subalterns, citing alcoholism as a major reason for their poverty. For a subaltern interpretation of drinking, see the discussion on 'the theology of intoxication' in my book *Thamizh Iraiyiyal Kalangal*. See Rajanayagam (2000d).

2. One, probably only one, noteworthy exception is *Malai Kallan*, in which MGR as a rich Muslim is seen to smoke the 'traditional pipe'. It should be remembered, however, that this kind of smoking is still a part of the North Indian culture. Besides, it should be noted that when *Malai Kallan* was released in 1954, MGR was still evolving his unique formula.
3. Interestingly, when the rich MGR in the bungalow helps the victims, it is always through the mediation of Sathya, an orphan brought up by MGR's father. The poor MGR does away with any mediation, and helps the victims directly.
4. But the silences in the narrative are louder than the praises. The most important instance of silence concerns the unsubstantiated strategic deferral — the narrative does not give any valid and comparable reason for postponing the surrender. There is obviously certain arbitrariness in deciding the why, when and how of the surrender.
5. It is true, however, one gets the impression of instant justice. It is because of the cinematic language of *ellipses*, which skips or condenses chronological progression by wipes, fades and montages to close the narrative on a 'kairological' note.
6. Recall also our earlier discussion on universification of multiverse.

Part III: Politics of Imaging Politics

9

IMAGE AND IMAGINING

Carnival Dreama

A very significant dimension of cinema as a popular medium — still the most popular medium in the context of Thamizh Nadu[1] — is the unique cine-viewing context, intrinsic to the very nature of cine-technology, which metamorphoses the flow and the impact of the narrative content.

Liminal Experience

Cinema demands a darkened surrounding for viewing and the only thing that is lit is the projected image on the screen.[2] The theatrical darkness gives the touch of other-worldliness to the viewing ambience. Film viewing, thus, becomes akin to a 'religious' experience in aliminal zone where *this-world* of reality, the real world of temporal experience, and the *other-world* simulated by the 'pre-recorded' fantasy meet (Figure 9.1). Besides being the combination of realism and fantasy, the theatrical liminality is an amalgam of other psycho-cultural categories including the normal and off-the-normal (in terms of orientation), the time bound and the timeless (in terms of duration), at the periphery and at the centre (in terms of positioning), and subordination and super-ordination (in terms of power relations).

The uniqueness of the theatrical liminality rests on the fact that cinema as an audio-visual technology offers an amazingly magnificent spectacle, especially with its bigger screen, larger-than-life close-ups, and near-tactile quality of the images. By exploiting the physiologically-given persistence of vision to create the illusion of life-like movement, cinema appeals to almost all the senses and provides the viewer with an experience of *sensorial wholeness*. In effect, the cinematic 'realism' renders

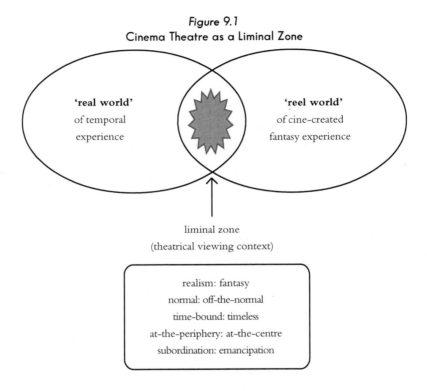

Figure 9.1
Cinema Theatre as a Liminal Zone

illusion more realistic (and attractively believable) than reality itself, and in the process, the little narratives are '*trance*-lated' into a '*dream*-atic' web of a grand narrative. It may be recalled that the very first screening of film in India in 1896, publicised as 'the marvel of the century, the wonder of the world', in fact consisted of footages reproducing reality such as 'the arrival of a train' and 'the workers leaving a factory'.

The theatrical context that could comfortably accommodate hundreds of persons at a time makes cine-viewing a communal affair, somewhat resembling the typical village *thiruvizhaa* (carnival). This is particularly so for the fans because they consciously make it that way.[3] Another technology-related feature that has a bearing on the communal dimension of theatrical liminality is the film projection technique that integrates the audience within the process itself — the viewers are 'sandwiched' between the projector and the screen.[4] Thus, the space for the viewers is well defined, and their movement confined. Added to this, the viewers are assigned a fixed seat. But the very constriction makes the viewers, who may not know each other, become aware of the *unity of purpose* — they are there for the sake of viewing. The fact that every viewer is aware of the presence of other such viewers facilitates 'double voyeuring' — while the viewer has the screened activities (of the star or any character) as the primary object of his/her gaze, the peculiar theatrical screening with a provision for interval and the relative anonymity of the viewers enable the individual viewer to have other viewers as yet another object of his/her gaze. The 'double voyeuring' interestingly results in 'triple gratification' — the one accruing from the para-social identification with the star (or any character), the vicarious pleasure derived from the clandestine gazing at other viewers, and the third drawn from the awareness of the possibility of 'exhibiting' oneself for others to voyeur. Cine-viewing, therefore, very effectively intermingles individual and communal aspects of entertainment and celebration. It is a personalised communal experience.

One of the most outstanding socio-cultural outcomes of the communal nature of cine-viewing concerns the emergence of cinema as a great *social equaliser*, particularly so, given the fact that the majority of the cine-dependent cine-goers are from the lower strata of the caste and class-ridden hierarchical Thamizh society.[5] The cinema theatre, whether permanent or touring, provides a safe haven for the viewer, who is otherwise stifled and bogged down by the monotonous and harsh daily routine, to escape temporarily into the luxury of freedom, fraternity and fantasy. This marvellous 'reversal' is made possible at the social level by the 'secularised' business nature of the functioning of the 'theatre system' wherein any viewer irrespective of his/her caste and social class can buy his/her 'class' of seat within the theatre. That is, a person's 'status' (within the theatre) is decided (in theory)[6] on the basis of his/her 'purchasing capacity', a phenomenon that is unimaginable in a *thiruvizhaa*. The feeling of equality is further reinforced, when it comes to films of stars, by the animated presence of the fans in large numbers. It may be observed that the fans, in any given show, form the majority of the viewers attending it. Interestingly (and disturbingly so for the non-fans), the fans get *physically active* and by their unruly and noisy revelry take control of the show. The 'reversal' is effected at the psychological level by the (externally) unhindered and (internally) uninhibited access to the 'pre-imagined' dream world projected on the screen.

Circles of Thiruvizhaa

Seen from the point of view of the fans, the *thiruvizhaa* atmosphere is not confined to cine-viewing context alone. It also encompasses the realms of the star-centred fan club and political activities, giving rise to 'circles of thiruvizhaa' as shown in Figure 9.2. The three inter-related and mutually reinforcing circles could be collectively labelled as the 'cinemenon' ('cine-phenomenon' as manifested in and through the fan clubs).

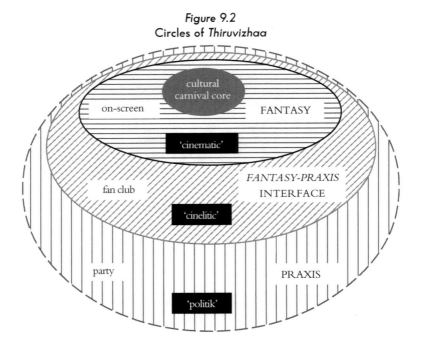

Figure 9.2
Circles of *Thiruvizhaa*

The 'cultural carnival core' refers to the experience of the *thiruvizhaa* proper as traditionally practised by people especially in rural areas. The *thiruvizhaa* is an elaborate process consisting of three phases: (*a*) *preparation*, both remote and immediate, both religious and material; (*b*) the *climactic celebrations*, usually lasting for a few days; and (*c*) the *concluding* ceremonies. The multifarious liminal activities that mark the festive occasion could be grouped into religious worship, socialising and entertainment. While the religious rites are performed with careful adherence

IMAGE AND IMAGINING 109

to customs, the secular activities take place in an atmosphere of liminal freedom characterised by relaxing and flouting the customary code of conduct. Folk forms, especially *koothtthu*, are performed as a part of the festivities. Video screening of feature films has become normative in many places these days. In some places such screening has even replaced the traditional forms of entertainment. It is also not uncommon that on the festival day quite a few go to the theatre, if accessible.

It is important to note here that the *thiruvizhaa* is governed by caste norms. Often each caste has its own *thiruvizhaa*, and, if in some places a common village-level *thiruvizhaa* is held, the caste hierarchy is replicated in the manner of celebrating. Even the 'radical and subversive' potential of *koothtthu* performance varies according to the caste community that celebrates the *thiruvizhaa* — in the performances by/for the lower caste communities, the protest against the atrocities of the higher castes often takes on the form of *ridicule* and *insult* of caste men and caste practices, whereas in the performances by/for middle and higher caste communities there is only general socio-political criticism, if any.

The 'cinemenon' is a modernised re-creation of the carnival drama, fun and free-play. The dream-real interface of the carnival is shifted more towards dream in 'cinemenon', which could therefore be aptly described as the 'carnival *dreama*'. The dynamics of the 'dreama' could be exemplified by an analysis of the functioning of a typical fan club. The club gets activated as soon as the star announces his new film. Fanzines, websites, pages and blogs sprout following the announcement and keep feeding the fans with 'information' on the progress of the production. As the day of the release nears (which usually coincides with a major festival like Deepaavali or Pongal), the club undertakes a fund raising campaign to mobilise money for erecting huge cut-outs of the star, decorating the theatre venue, etc. Fan club rivalries are very common — a club of a star trying to outdo another of the rival star, and not infrequently of the same star too. When the booking opens, the club books *en block* for the first few days. When the film does open, the first day is usually reserved for the fans.[7] Those who are able to get a ticket, walk into the theatre with a sense of pride and achievement. And they are there with their hero in the fantastic world of fantasy — having the first *darshan* of the hero and themselves feeling as the hero. After a week or two, the *thiruvizhaa* spirit wanes and lies low for some time, but it gets revitalised by the occasions of *vetrivizhaa* (literally, 'victory function') marking the 100th day or the Silver Jubilee (25 weeks) of the

110 ◼ POPULAR CINEMA AND POLITICS IN SOUTH INDIA

film's running. Meanwhile, the star would have announced the production of another film. That sets in motion another cycle of *thiruvizhaa*.

The third circle of *thiruvizhaa* concerns the star's ability to extend the carnival spirit to the realm of party-based real politiking. It is evident that not all the stars could succeed in this endeavour. For example, MGR was *consistently* successful but RK was not, a point to be further elucidated in the subsequent chapters.

The following features related to the 'cinemenon' need to be emphasised: First, the release of the film coinciding with a popular festival like Pongal tends to double the carnival spirit of the fans. Second, the release of films at regular intervals constantly revives the slackening carnival spirit. Third, the on-going nature of 'cinemenon' is likely to give certain permanency to the feeling of the fans that they are *superior* to other non-fans, particularly the elites, who in real life treat the fans with condescension and contempt.

Fan-Centred Politiking

The fan-based 'cinemenon' invests the fan clubs with an incredible political potential, which could, if the stars concerned are capable of tapping it with ingenuity, turn the fan clubs into effective political agents.

Psycho-Political Mapping

The comprehensive psycho-political mapping (Figure 9.3) illustrates how an individual (subaltern, to be precise) becomes a fan, how the hero emerges as the saviour, how the fan clubs acquire legitimacy and get institutionalised, and how the media other than cinema contribute to reinforce the screen image.

The individual as a member of the society has needs ranging from the basic physiological level to the higher order needs including security, love, social esteem, aesthetic experience and self-actualisation. There are also deep-seated instincts, specifically *eros* ('love' instinct) and *thanatos* ('death' instinct). These instincts and needs are compounded by issues and problems caused primarily by the misuse of state power by the ruling elite in general and the ruling party in particular. When the individual seeks for outlets to gratify the needs and solve (or escape) the problems encountered at the personal, familial and social levels, s/he is faced with media sources or non-media sources or often both. If

IMAGE AND IMAGINING 111

Figure 9.3
Psycho-Political Mapping of Cinemenon

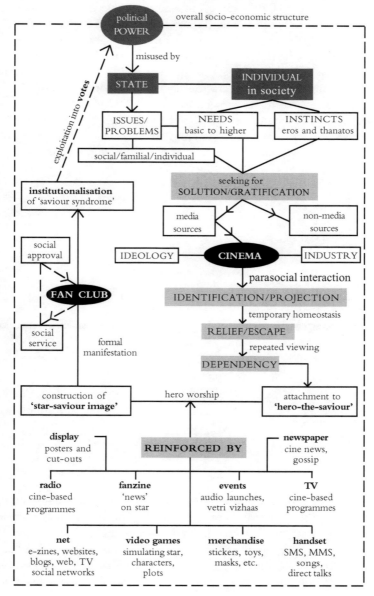

s/he opts for the media, cinema comes in handy as the easily available, most popular, probably the cheapest, and a highly rewarding source.

When the individual chooses cinema, s/he undergoes an experience similar to the 'rite of passage' (Figure 9.4). As s/he enters the projection hall, the 'rite of separation' is performed. S/he with the status as a subaltern buys the ticket and enters into the 'marginal state of dreama' where s/he is without any status (or the status as a 'viewer'). During the screening, the viewer para-socially interacts with the hero (or any other character) through projection and/oridentification, and temporarily reaches a state of *homeostasis*. The intensity of the relief and the necessity of the escape make her/him cine-dependent, and the initial subaltern status eventually changes over to the status as a fan.

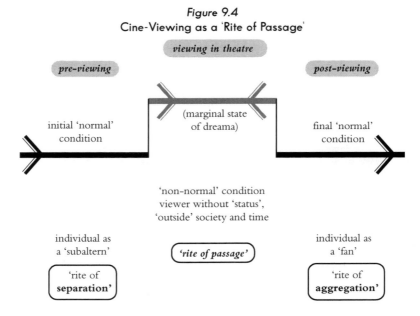

Figure 9.4
Cine-Viewing as a 'Rite of Passage'

The formal manifestation of hero worship is the fan club, which is often called 'narpani mandram' (for instance, *Rajinikanth rasigar narpani mandram*). True to the name, many *mandram*s engage in some sort of 'narpani' (literally, 'good service') ranging from organising blood and eye donation camps and free medical check-ups to free distribution of books and notebooks to school children, sari and dhoti to the deserted, and meal to the deserving on important days such as the star's birthday. Through these acts of 'service' the clubs win the public support to a certain extent and in turn get legitimatised. Leading stars (of the past and the present) have institutionalised their respective images by networking the clubs into an 'anaiththu inthiya' (All-India) or 'anaiththu ulaka' (All-World) association. A few of the *politically-motivated stars* have succeeded in varying degrees in exploiting their institutionalised images to acquire political power.

Concurrently, the *attachment* to the hero gets solidified into hero 'worship', which is further reinforced by the host of mass media — film music, star interviews, etc. on radio; films, clippings (song-dance, comedy, stunt, etc.), interviews, promos, functions, etc. on TV; cine-related news and reviews, gossips, etc. in the mainstream newspapers and magazines; popular biographies and exclusive fanzines with blow-ups and pin-ups of the stars concerned; publicity materials such as posters, hoardings and cut-outs; e-zines, websites and pages on films and stars, social networks, and blogs on the net; SMSs and MMSs on the handset; and special events such as star nights, star cricket matches, audio release functions, etc., which are very often also telecast on TV channels as special programmes to mark special occasions such as Pongal and Deepaavali.

Simulated Worlds

It should be reiterated that the hero worship, however, is not exclusive to the 'cinemenon'. It is, in fact, universal and multifaceted as evidenced around the world in the ever-proliferating 'cults' centred on pop stars, sports stars, and stunningly not excluding 'militants' (or 'the freedom fighters' as the case may be). Figure 9.5 illustrates the dynamics of hero worship.

Cycle 1 is the most desirable, constructive and transformative approach to resolving the complex web of issues and problems, and unfulfilled needs and wants. A genuine search for appropriate and lasting solutions and gratifications lead the individual to look for inspiring models within the realm of reality. If a committed leader is available, s/he tries to emulate the leader resulting in collective social action or at least meaningful action at the personal level. Cycle 2 shows how a leadership *vacuum* in real life could lead the individual astray and force her/him to search for alternatives outside the realm of reality. Cycle 3

Figure 9.5
Psycho-Political Dynamics of Hero Worship

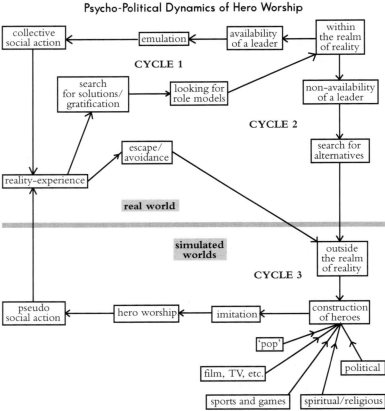

highlights how a person probably lacking the guts and the means to face the reality tries to avoid or escape from it by turning towards models outside the realm of reality. Depending on each one's disposition, s/he gets attached to 'models' from the worlds of pop, politics, religion, sports, cinema, TV, etc. Heroes are constructed at the gut level, while their mannerisms are imitated at the superficial level. The individual's emotional and blind identification with the hero and the total loss of self–identity make her/him effectively *dysfunctional* and lost in the worlds of simulations.

It needs to be cautioned that the real–life experience is more complex than the neatly drawn out 'Cycles'. First of all, it could be observed that the three cycles often co-exist in an individual, though in varying degrees. Thus, an individual, for example, may readily face an issue or a need and try to find a solution within the realm of reality, whereas the same individual may try to escape some other issue and take refuge in the simulated worlds. Second, the same 'models' representing various fields may either be encountered as 'leaders' motivating the individual to engage in constructive action or be worshipped as 'heroes'. Third, the phenomenon of hero worship is most prevalent among the youth, who are by and large unemployed or underemployed with a vast majority of them coming from 'poorer' socio-economic backgrounds. It is reasonable to surmise, therefore, that the youth faced with the apparently insurmountable socio-political problems tend to find in hero worship a welcome relief because it opens up endless and glamorous possibilities of diverting their energy and heroic spirit. Such possibilities occasionally include 'pseudo' social action, mainly charitable in nature, which could in fact bring social recognition to those involved.

Nadukal Politics

The roots of the phenomenon of hero worship in Thamizh Nadu could be traced back to the age-old cultural practice of 'nadukal worship'. The *Nadukal* (literally, a stone erected) is a war memorial erected in honour of the soldiers who exhibited *veeram* and *maanam* by embracing death in the battlefield. Whenever a war was declared, the soldiers gathered around the *nadukal*, and the poets sang the praises of the 'heroes', earlier martyred in order to motivate them. The practice has survived to this day, after having gone through several transmutations, in the form of the worship of folk heroes still prevalent in rural communities. The 'nadukal politics' rests on the philosophy that absolutises and celebrates death by its over-emphasis on dying, not living, for a cause. The same philosophy also underlies the worship of folk heroes, as evidenced by the fact that invariably all the folk heroes now elevated as deities have been, as the legends inform, killed in battles or caste clashes.

While granting that some forms of *nadukal* worship had existed in all primitive cultures, in the context of Thamizh Nadu, however, its originary political dimension got revived with the 'rediscovery' of the Thamizh 'nationalist' heritage and the concomitant linguistic chauvinism in the second quarter of the 20th century, thanks primarily to the DK. The DMK carried it forward reaping rich political harvests.

116 POPULAR CINEMA AND POLITICS IN SOUTH INDIA

Strikingly, both the DK and the DMK fabricated a political scenario simulating a battlefield by setting Thamizh against Hindi. The leaders gave a clarion call to all those Thamizhs with *veeram* and *maanam* to jump into the war. Anyone who got killed in the anti-Hindi agitations was idolised as a martyr. *Nadukal*s were erected in a variety of forms including building memorial pillars, putting up statues, unveiling portraits, and naming buildings. *Ex gratia* payments were distributed in grand public functions. The DMK, however, swiftly shifted[8] the emphasis from dying for a cause to dying for the leaders. It was possible because the leaders were seen in the forefront of the anti-Hindi agitations and they put their rhetorical skills to maximum use to project them as the saviours of the Thamizhs.

The DMK leaders in fact meticulously cultivated the 'leadership cult' and hardcore members with suicidal tendencies coupled with low self-esteem and craving for some social recognition easily fell prey to this cult. MGR, with his added charisma and a clever overlapping of screen and politics, took the leadership cult to its pinnacle. This phenomenon, however, is not confined to the leaders of the DMK and the ADMK. Many of the gifted and charismatic political leaders cutting across parties have emerged as cult figures, with their hardcore followers ready to die for them. When Indira Gandhi was murdered in 1984, for example, 'Thamizh Nadu re-enacted its method of expressing agony with a record number of self-immolations'.[9] When the Supreme Court verdict in 2001 unseated the then chief minister Jayalalithaa, as many as 19 persons died.[10] Over 150 persons either died of shock or self-immolated following the debacle of the ADMK in 2006 May Assembly elections.

The above discussion on *nadukal* worship makes it clear that it will be erroneous to treat the phenomenon of hero worship as exclusively applicable to film stars. In fact, the hero worship has manifested itself in its fullest intensity in the realm of politics, and *not* in that of cinema. Besides, with the advent of satellite TV channels and the live telecasts of sports and games, even television celebrities[11] and sports personalities have emerged as cult figures, some of whom could wield certain political influence. MGR, however, stands as an exceptional cult figure because in him the political 'leadership cult' and the cinematic 'star cult' had fused into one.

Identi-fiction vis-à-vis Identif-action

Given the cultural-anthropological and psycho-political background of the *star-centred* hero worship and the *fan-centred* politiking by the star concerned, it is appropriate here to compare how the fans of MGR and RK identify themselves with their heroes and learn from them.

The image of MGR, constructed on-screen and constantly reinforced off-screen, is one of 'do-gooder action hero', who is at the apex of the moral–legal system as the paradigm to be emulated. From the point of view of the fans, such an image, first of all, is a utopia, and they constantly fall short of meeting the demands. His is a *too perfect* an image to be imitated behaviourally in real life. Second, the very fair complexion of MGR, the exact opposite of most of his fans, alienates them and makes the identification more difficult. Third, outside the screen realm, especially in his public appearances, MGR was always 'shrouded in mystery' — he deliberately mystified his personality by selectively hiding his personality behind the mask, particularly of the fur cap and dark glasses and at the same time by selectively exposing his personality in 'acts of affection' such as hugging (the old), patting (the young) and kissing (the children), besides other acts of solidarity and munificence. Therefore, even if some of his fans got the opportunity to have a glimpse of him — they could only have *a glimpse* in the literal sense of the term — they could never know who he really was, and their feeling[12] had invariably been one of awe, wonder and reverence, much in the fashion of the experience of *mysterium tremendum et fascinans* by deeply religious persons. Identification with MGR, therefore, could be only at the fantasy level, at the level of 'identi-*fiction*'. The experience of his fans at the behavioural realm could be stated as 'I wish I am like him', while in the fantasy realm it is 'I am him'.

RK's image, on the contrary, is one of the 'go-getter angry hero', who is outside the moral-legal system demanding unqualified compliance with him. However, he is a 'style king' and very much resembles his fans in complexion. Most of his 'styles' — except, probably, the recent computer-generated visual gimmicks — could be imitated after some practice. Thus, his fans' identification with him does not stop with fantasy but is smoothly carried over to the behavioural realm. It is indeed 'identif-*action*'. The feasibility of imitating him in real life context and the similarity of complexion make his fans feel 'He is like me'.

118 ■ POPULAR CINEMA AND POLITICS IN SOUTH INDIA

This feeling of his fans is further augmented by his off-screen image, which, in contrast to MGR's, is *transparent*[13] and, more significantly, corresponds to his on-screen image.

When it comes to actual learning from cinema, various factors[14] come into play, as Figure 9.6 explicates. The cine portrayed *acterance* (action+utterance) could be any behavioural act, utterance or character trait depicted in the film being viewed. For example, in the case of MGR, it could be his characteristic stunt and dance, mannerism and presentation style (particularly makeup, costume and hair style), Robin Hood-ist activities, protecting women's *karpu*, usurping signs of authority, subordinating romance to duty, attachment to mother, etc. In the case of RK, it could be his 'style' (including his hair style, costume, walking, delivery and punch dialogue), comedy, stunt, romancing, eve-teasing and subduing the haughty women, attachment to mother, subcultural and defiant behaviour, etc.

The probability of the fan (of MGR or RK) learning the acterance depends on various factors concerning content, arousal, viewing experience and awareness of purpose. The 'content factors' include: the type of role the hero assumes (whether it is true to life or super-human), the degree to which the acterance blends with the personality of the character, the relative positioning of the acterance in the narrative structure, believability and complexity of the acterance, the prominence given to the acterance in terms of time, the frequency of the acterance, the practicality (whether it is easy or difficult to imitate), the response of other characters to this acterance, and the kind of consequence portrayed (whether rewarded or punished). Many of the acterances listed above as examples for MGR and RK would be more on the positive side here, i.e., more likely to be learnt by the fan.

The 'arousal factors', however, greatly modify this. These factors include: whether the acterance is psychologically salient or unimportant, whether it is appealing or insipid, whether the fan is favourably disposed or not, whether the fan actively involves himself or not, whether the fan's prior expectations are satisfied or not, whether the fan's earlier attempts have been successful or not, whether it is relevant to real life or not, and whether the immediate viewing environment is constrained or free (for example, if the fan has come alone or with peers, s/he would feel freer or relatively less constrained than when s/he has come with the family). The probability of learning the acterance

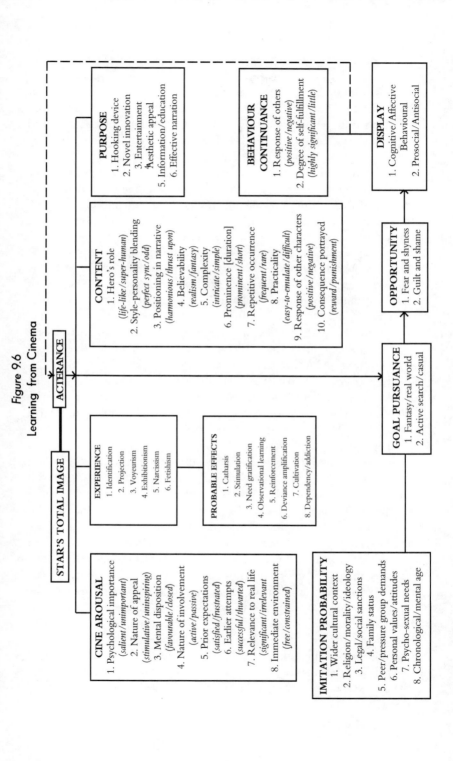

Figure 9.6
Learning from Cinema

is further limited or facilitated by the 'experience factors', which refer to the kind of viewing experience the fan has. Normally, it is a mixture of identification and projection, voyeurism, exhibitionism, narcissism and fetishism. Interestingly, the viewing experience itself is greatly conditioned by the probable 'effects factors' such as catharsis, stimulation, need-gratification, observational learning, reinforcement, deviance amplification, cultivation, and dependency. What pertains here is the degree of satisfaction the fan is able to derive in viewing. If the overall satisfaction is very high, it is less likely that s/he will take time to learn the acterance; instead s/he would prefer to see the film again.

The awareness of the purpose of the acterance being placed in the film ('awareness factors') still more modifies the likelihood of learning. The purpose, from the point of view of the *star*, could be one or more of the following: a hooking device, a novel innovation, better entertainment, aesthetic appeal, information/education and effective narration. It is quite possible that the purpose of the acterance as perceived by the fan may not be the same as the one intended by the star. The cumulative interplay of all these factors decides whether the fan is likely to pursue the goal of learning the acterance. Curiously, the goal could be pursued either in the world of fantasy (which would take the fan back to the theatre) or in the real world (which would lead the fan to action). The pursuance could be *active* or *casual*.

Any effort to pursue the goal is conditioned by 'imitation probability factors', which include: wider cultural context, fan's religious, moral and ideological beliefs, legal or social sanctions associated with the acterance, fan's family status, demands of peer and pressure groups on the fan, the fan's own personal values and attitudes, his/her psycho sexual needs, and chronological vis-à-vis mental age of the fan. When the fan actively pursues the goal in the realm of reality, s/he has to get the right opportunity to actualise it. Psycho-social factors such as fear, shyness, shame and guilt come into play at this stage. The actual display of behaviour that results may either be pro-social or anti-social. The positive or negative response of others, especially the significant others, to the behaviour thus displayed, and the degree of self-fulfillment experienced in the act of display may encourage or discourage the continuance of the behaviour. It is to be noted that the 'anti-social' behaviour need not always meet with disapproval. For example, what the parents disapprove may in fact be approved and appreciated by the peers.

When the combined effect of all these factors is taken into account, the 'style' of RK is seen to emerge as the most prominent 'acterance' that is widely emulated in the *behavioural* realm, whereas the *moral values* of MGR tend to remain at the *cognitive and affective* levels. Some of the easily 'imitate-able' gimmicks of RK have in fact made RK very popular even among children. It could be observed that in many families parents take pride in making their children 'perform like RK' in front of guests. But this difference between MGR and RK cannot be construed as the only decisive index of their impact, particularly on the political behaviour of the fans. The process of identi-*fiction*, involving the 'I-am-he-and-not-he' dynamics, i.e., the feeling of *simultaneous identification* with MGR in the darkness of theatrical liminality and *estrangement* from him in the starkness of real life, has in fact worked in favour of the politician MGR — the identification makes the fans feel that he is their embodiment, and the estrangement places him above them as their fittest leader.[15]

Notes

1. Many of the Thamizh channels have one or more additional film-based channels. The first 'full-length' film-based channel is KTV (started in October 2001) with the slogan 'Non-stop *Kondaattam*' (non-stop celebration) by Sun Network. When started, KTV was indeed a tribute to cinema with its film-exclusive programme package, including three feature films a day. The channel was an instant hit. Sun Network has subsequently come up with film-based music channel (Sun Music) and film-based comedy channel (Adithya). The network has recently added on their DTH service a channel for action movies (Sun Action), and another one (Sun Life) supposedly for lifestyle but telecasting mainly old cine-songs. Other leading networks also have established their film-based channels — Isaiaruvi, Sirippoli and Murasu of Kalaignar TV, Raj Digital Plus and Raj Musix of Raj TV, and Jaya Max and Jaya Movie of Jaya TV, to name a few. This not only shows the popularity of films but also the inevitability of films for the survival of television.
2. TV on the contrary needs to be watched in light and the whole surrounding is either fully or partially lit. However, it is not rare that people switch off the lights, especially while watching films on TV, in order to simulate the theatrical ambience.

122 ■ POPULAR CINEMA AND POLITICS IN SOUTH INDIA

3. The non-fans also often tend to visit theatres as a group of friends, family members, etc. TV, unlike cinema, involves family or private viewing.

4. In the case of TV, the audience is kept off the process: images are beamed from the tube behind the screen. For a comparative study of the three major screens, i.e., cinema, television and internet, see Rajanayagam (2003).

5. The same could be said of the pan-Indian society in general. In any given region in India, majority of the *cine-dependent* cine-goers are from the lower strata of the caste and class hierarchy.

6. 'In theory', because, we must hasten to add, that things are not always as rosy as this statement might imply. In areas where one's caste could be identified, lower caste persons are only 'tolerated' and even a trivial matter could flare up the caste conflict. What happened in Chunduru village in Andhra Pradesh in 1991 is a case in point. The brutal massacre of at least eight persons belonging to a Scheduled Caste (*Mala*) by the higher caste (*Reddy*) community was triggered off by the incident that took place inside the cinema hall, when an SC youth put his leg on the seat in front where a non-SC youth was seated. For more information on this incident, see http://en.wikipedia.org/wiki/Chundur_Massacre (accessed 6 November 2011). Almost two decades after Chunduru, on 7 August 2010, the cosmopolitan Chennai witnessed a blatant act of discrimination when a multiplex in the city refused entry (after buying ticket) into the auditorium to a group of gypsies, because in the words of a victim, 'They said we're not civilised because we're not dressed in pants and shirts. They said only those who wear pants and shirts will be allowed inside'. See http://www.ndtv.com/article/cities/gypsies-face-discrimination-at-chennai-multiplex-42792 (accessed 8 August 2010).

7. Or special screenings are arranged for the fans outside the usual timings. It may be mentioned that some established stars issue in advance some free ('complimentary') tickets to select fan clubs for the 'fan show', a practice that adds to the *thiruvizhaa* spirit.

8. This was very evident in the events that followed the arrest of the DMK president M. Karunanidhi on 30 June 2001. Unable to bear the shock, 67 persons died, including some cases of self-immolation. In the procession organised by the DMK on 12 August 2001 in Chennai to condemn the high-handedness of the police in arresting Karunanidhi, there was a police firing, killing four and injuring many. Instead of being taken to the hospital, some of the injured were taken to the public meeting addressed by Karunanidhi, where they were literally 'exhibited' on the stage for the public to witness the police atrocity. This was also telecast on Sun TV. For an emotional recounting by MK of his arrest after over a decade, see *Nenjukku Neethi*, Part VI, free supplement to *Murasoli*, 30 September 2012. It is not an accident that a boxed highlight (on page 7) describes the death

of 67 'party comrades' as 'suicide' (though many died of 'shock'). For a vivid account of the procession-cum-public meeting, see the supplement to *Murasoli*, 7 October 2012.'Dying for a cause', however, seems to have resurrected particularly in the context of Eezham struggle in Sri Lanka. For a recent example of this, see *The Hindu*, 2013, 'Self-immolation for *twin cause* of Sri Lankan Tamils, corruption' (emphasis added), 5 March, http://www.thehindu.com/news/national/tamil-nadu/selfimmolation-for-twin-cause-of-sri-lankan-tamils-corruption/article4476179.ece (accessed 10 August 2014).

9. Mohandas (1992: 103).
10. *Thina Thanthi*, 4 October 2001. Again in 2014, when the special court convicted Jayalalithaa in disproportionate assets case on 27 September, over 30 persons died within the first three days (Visit http://www.dailythanhi.com/News/State/2014/09/30015526/Jayalalithaa-conviction-Death-Toll-reaches-30.vpf [accessed 30 September 2014]), and 66 in the first one week (see *Thina Thanthi*, 5 October 2014).
11. For example, a 'temple' was built for 'Pepsi' Uma who anchored a popular count-down show on Sun TV for a long time till she later moved over to Kalaignar TV in 2007. (Pepsi was the major sponsor of the programme.) See *Thinakaran*, 4 December 2001. However, a temple had already been built for *cine* star Kushboo. Attempt had been made to build one for the 'sexqueen' Mumtaj. See *Cinema Express* (Thamizh), September 2001, vol. 22, no.15, p. 28. As if to glamourise this practice, in the recent film *Soothu Kavvum* (May 2013) a lead character builds a temple for his heart-throb Nayanthara. It will be interesting to study why the male fans are becoming more overtly expressive of '*heroine* worshipping.' It is noteworthy that the only male star in Thamizh Nadu for whom a temple has been built is MGR. In the North, however, a temple has been built for Amitabh Bachchan, surprisingly in Kolkata, the native land of 'new wave' filmmakers Ray and Ghatak. See *The New Indian Express* (Magazine Section 3), 15 July 2001, p. 21.
12. I conducted in-depth interviews with 18 MGR fans, now in their sixties, on different occasions during 1998–2000. Of the 18, 13 of them had got a chance to see MGR in a public meeting. Two of them had the 'life-time experience' of taking a photograph with him. Recalling the 'momentous *darshan*' they had, all the 13 of them were visibly moved and described it using superlatives profusely. Their feeling of awe, wonder and reverence remained very much the same when I met nine of them again in 2010. For a study on how symbolic meanings of hero MGR have shifted over a 20-year period from mid-1980s to mid-2000s, see Dickey (2008).
13. What is noteworthy in RK's public appearances is the 'clean' image he projects by looking 'ugly'. A classic example is the way he looked during

124 ■ POPULAR CINEMA AND POLITICS IN SOUTH INDIA

his historic interview in 1996 — without make-up, with a few days' beard on his face, and head clean shaved (in the USA; 'by accident', he said). Achieving the image of being *genuine* through 'exposing' the real face was diametrically opposed to the 'hiding' tactic of MGR who always appeared in public only with heavy makeup (but he managed to achieve the same image of being genuine through other means). That this apparent transparency of RK could be interpreted as his *mask* is another question.

14. The basic framework for this model is drawn from Comstock, Chaffee, Katzman, McCombs, and Roberts (1978). The factors listed in this flow-chart are based on my interaction with over 100 fans across the state, on different occasions during 1998–2000. The model has been frequently revisited based on field-data during the last one decade, and given the final touch based on interactions with another set of over 100 fans during 2009–11. The list of factors is quite comprehensive, but not exhaustive. The numbers do not necessarily indicate ranking. This is a heuristic model, yet to be tested in an experimental setting.

15. This viewing process of identi-*fiction* (what happens to the fans) and the narrative process of subalternising cum elitising (what MGR does on-screen) reinforce and complement each other, and are two inseparable dimensions of MGR's image politiking.

10

POLITICALLY LOADED OCTA-MOTIFS

The analysis in the previous chapter sufficiently highlights the psycho-cultural underpinnings of image politiking. The degree of success in actual image politiking depends on the star's ability to imaginatively evolve and effectively manipulate certain politically loaded motifs in the fantasy–politics interface, which constitute what could be termed as the 'politiking formula'. In the case of MGR and RK at least eight such motifs — *octa-motifs* — could be identified. These motifs are distinct yet interlaced so as to create a synergetic impact.

The *Thaai Kulam*

One of the most essential, original and creative constituents of MGR's politiking formula, which are also the most fundamental tenets of his political philosophy, is the concept of *thaai kulam*. The term is culture-specific and emotionally loaded. The word 'thaai' means 'mother', and 'kulam' can mean, depending upon the context, 'caste', 'community', 'race', or 'family'. For want of a better term, 'community of mothers' is provisionally used as a translation of *thaai kulam*.

The umbrella concept of *thaai kulam* covers mothers proper, wives, lovers, sisters and daughters, abandoned women (such as beggars, orphans and those deserted by lovers), socially ostracised women (including prostitutes, concubines, call-girls and widows), and all others who do not fall under any of these categories (including 'queer' and psychologically not-so-normal women). MGR makes sure that in his films he has something romantic and spectacular, something vicarious and gratifying, to attract them to him. He is quick to endear women through adopting proxy mothers and proxy sisters. By fetishising the fair

126 ▪ POPULAR CINEMA AND POLITICS IN SOUTH INDIA

skin and fully shaven torso (considered effeminate by male standards), with the occasionally popping up transvestic streak he also caters to the needs of women (and men) with special sexual preferences.[1] More importantly, he arouses the maternal instinct of women and presents himself as the most desirable child or promises them a beautiful child *like him*. It is true that most of the mothers in Thamizh Nadu prefer a male child to a female child, and wish their child be 'beautiful'. MGR gratifies them both as the ideal child himself and as the ideal man fathering an ideal child (like him).[2]

From the beginning RK did not enjoy women fan-following because he did not have much to offer to women's dreams: the women, especially the rural women, in real life suffer at the hands of their husbands, and RK with his anti-hero image and villainous screen presence resembles their cruel and irresponsible husbands. On the contrary MGR offers women a 'dreamatic' relief from real-life sufferings by his action hero image and enchanting screen presence. His fair complexion is his greatest asset — it offsets the little traces of real life resemblance that may be there in his screen image and reinforces the ideal young man image, as Figure 10.1 shows.

RK's dark complexion only accentuates the resemblance of his image with the real-life husbands. Besides, he does not provide enough space for fantasy where the women could abandon themselves and give free vent to the repressed desires caused by the rigid patriarchal system. The little space he does provide for them to express their sexuality is more a replica of their real-life struggle against the tyrannical patriarchy to express themselves. Therefore, when RK shows in a film like *Mannan* that the girl is physically attracted to the hero who only tortures and victimises her, the women will not be able to identify themselves with her (unless one has masochistic tendencies).

MGR, on the other hand, creates unrestricted space for unbound fantasies. There is no threat, no intimidation; it is 'me and my ideal man'. MGR thus becomes temporarily the 'surrogate' husband or lover and gratifies the repressed sexual desires of women. That explains the secret of MGR's popularity among women.

The Co-Born

Another original constituent of MGR's politiking formula is the concept of 'co-born'. For MGR, his fans were not mere fans but 'co-borns'

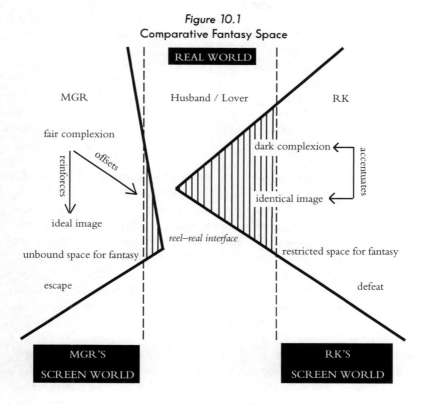

Figure 10.1
Comparative Fantasy Space

(*udan pirappukkal*), related to him 'by blood'. Significantly, the same term has been employed by M. Karunanidhi to denote the party workers.[3] When the rift between MGR and Karunanidhi got widened leading eventually to the formation of the ADMK, MGR qualified the 'co-borns' by adding the adjectival phrase 'en raththaththin raththamaana', which literally means, 'the blood of my blood'. What is innovative here is the metonymical attribute MGR gave to this peculiar metaphor by linking[4] it with the shooting incident that had happened in 1967. When he was hospitalised, he said, he had received blood from many who were unknown to him, and as a gesture of gratitude, he had decided to address all his 'co-borns' as 'en raththaththin raththamaana udan pirappukkal'. Thus by linking what is essentially political with something personal (and tragic), MGR achieved two things: on the one hand, he successfully rendered the phrase credible and genuine; on the

128 ◾ POPULAR CINEMA AND POLITICS IN SOUTH INDIA

other hand, he used it as a ploy to outwit his arch-rival Karunanidhi by exhibiting that he was 'more intimate' with his 'co-borns' than MK was with his 'co-borns'.

MGR not only employed this phrase in his speeches and writings — it was customary for him to commence his speech with addressing the *thaai kulam* and the 'blood-of-my-blood co-borns' and end it with tributes to Anna ('Anna naamam vaazhha', meaning, 'long live Anna's name') — but also strategically placed it in his films. In *Urimai Kural*, for example, he asserts, 'I can lose anything except the great treasure called *udan pirappu*'.

RK on the contrary prefers to call his fans 'koottam', which means 'crowd'. He, however, qualifies it by contrasting it with the 'crowd' that is brought or allegedly 'bought' by some politicians in order to demonstrate their strength to their opponents. His is the 'crowd that has gathered on its own volition' (*thaanaa saentha koottam*). While the term 'koottam' goes hand in hand with the kind of subcultural anti-hero image of RK, it tends to lumpenise his fans, particularly when compared to MGR's 'udan pirappu', which in fact gives certain dignity and respectability to his subaltern fans.[5] But the 'spontaneous crowd' is not an unruly mob; it has its distinct identity, the identity of RK himself. 'His blood and the blood of his fans', as he sings in *Arunaachalam*, are 'related' (though not the same), and he and they are 'one in complexion and character'. Thus, the identification of RK and his fans is mutual and almost *natural*. MGR on the contrary has to *overcome* the disparity of complexion between him and majority of his fans by interpreting the transfused blood 'running in his body' to be the same as that of his 'co-borns', though externally he looks different from them.

The Subaltern

MGR and RK imaginatively yet calculatedly mould and orchestrate the social dimension of their respective images to sync with the 'existential agony' and 'eschatological hope' of their subaltern targets, without at the same time challenging the overall socio-economic, moral and political system that begets, perpetuates and accentuates societal divisions. At the same time, however, there is a marked difference between them in what constitutes their subalternity. MGR is a 'do-gooder', whereas RK is a 'go-getter'. The very titles of a significant number of their films are indicative of this difference. The titles of RK-starrers display his 'rebellious, delinquent and anti-social' nature[6] ('The Just War', 'My Challenge', 'Wicked Man', 'Uncouth Raja', and 'Good for the Good', to name a few). In the case of MGR, they are more sober, *occupation-oriented* and positive[7] (for example: 'The Boatman', 'The Worker', 'The Hunter', 'The Guard/Policeman', 'The Farmer', and 'The Rickshaw-puller').

Strikingly, many of these titles (of both MGR and RK starrers) refer to the subalterns in the third person *non-honorific* singular (like rikshaakaa*ran* and vaelaikkaa*ran*), which is commonly considered disrespectful, if not derogatory.[8]

Not only the titles but also the type of roles they play in their films highlight that MGR embodies the rural subaltern masses in general with noticeable importance to the agriculturalists, while RK in general embodies the rural and the slum youth, and industrial workers, with special focus on the unemployed and the delinquent youth.

Thus, while both MGR and RK embody the subaltern, RK's image is that of a 'socially deviant', subcultural personality, whereas MGR's is that of a 'socially desirable' subaltern personality. The psychological traits of being an 'enfant terrible' and 'affable darling' go to reinforce their respective images.

The *Thamizhness*

The language of politics, including that of image politiking, is bound up with the politics of language in the context of Thamizh Nadu, a State that takes pride in according a divine status to its language.[9]

It is indeed a paradox that in such a language-sensitive State MGR and RK, both non-Thamizhs by birth, could apparently emerge as great political forces to be reckoned with. They have achieved this status by adopting their own unique *multi-pronged* strategies.

In the case of MGR, placing himself within the Thamizh cultural universe was in a way easy, thanks to the DK/DMK's emphasis on 'thiraavida naadu' (Dravida Nation) till the early sixties. MGR being a Keralite was well within the boundaries of the definition of 'Dravidianness'. He consistently projected him, *both* on-screen (particularly in films scripted by the DMK activists) and off-screen, as a spokesperson of 'thennakam'(Southern Homeland) or 'thiraavida naadu'. MGR's efforts in this were ably complemented by the DMK leaders, especially Anna, who gave MGR a pride of place within the party hierarchy and

130 ■ POPULAR CINEMA AND POLITICS IN SOUTH INDIA

presented him as *the representative* Dravidian. As a result, by the time the DMK gave up its demand for the separate 'thiraavida naadu', MGR had already comfortably located himself within the political map of Thamizh Nadu, using 'thiraavida naadu' as a means.[10]

If MGR used his identification with the DMK to politically position himself within Thamizh Nadu, he made effective use of his films to culturally root himself. To start with, he acted *only* in Thamizh films.[11] Second, he always upheld Thamizh culture, especially *veeram*, *maanam* and *karpu* and projected himself as the guardian and ambassador of Thamizh culture. Third, he tactically associated himself with Thamizh literary works andscholars. Often he himself was described primarily through songs as a great Thamizh poet and scholar, and not infrequently, as Thamizh itself. Fourth, he projected himself as a Thamizh *accepted* by the Thamizhs.

Strikingly, MGR used his genius to 'unbound' himself from the roots he established in the Thamizh political and cultural terrains, curiously by selectively resorting to the Thamizh world view, which could be succinctly stated in the words of Kaniyan Poongundran (*Puranaanooru*, 192): 'Yaathum oorae; Yaavarum kaelir', meaning, 'To us all (places) are hometown; All persons our kin'. Such an attempt, increasingly manifest in the seventies, was his response to Karunanidhi, who indulged in branding him as a Malayalee and hence unfit to be in Thamizh Nadu politics. MGR in fact adopted a multi-directional approach to respond to Karunanidhi. First, he took pains to affirm his *Thamizhness*, sometimes claiming him to be the original Thamizh, and some other times *redefining* being a Thamizh to mean 'anyone speaking Thamizh and/or living in Thamizh Nadu'. Second, the popular biographies traced his genealogical roots to Thamizh Nadu.[12] Third, the ADMK speakers entertained a *counter-campaign* publicising their 'discovery' that Karunanidhi was not a Thamizh but a Telugu.[13] Fourth, MGR made deliberate attempts to transgress and transcend linguistic and national boundaries. In *Ithaya Kani*, for example, he is described as a 'world citizen'; in *Sangae Muzhangu*, his fiancée, though born and brought up in Thamizh Nadu, is born to a Punjabi father and a Bengali mother; in *Ulagam Sutrum Vaalipan*, the Thai girl speaking Thamizh is relished: 'It is so sweet when those who do not know Thamizh speak Thamizh'. Fifth, by encouraging his fans to celebrate his 're-birthday' (the day he recovered after being shot at by M R Radha in 1967) instead

OCTA-MOTIFS ■ 131

of his actual birthday, MGR tried to erase his actual origin outside Thamizh Nadu and to *re-root* him in the Thamizh soil. Finally, MGR was interpreted as a gratuitous *gift* to Thamizh Nadu. The opening song in *Ithaya Kani*, for example, compares him to the river Cauveri, which benefits Thamizh Nadu, though it originates in Karnataka.

RK's multi-pronged strategy of language politiking is distinctly different from that of MGR. The core difference lies in the fact that, if MGR is a gift to Thamizh Nadu, for RK the people of Thamizh Nadu are 'the gods who make him prosper' (*ennai vaazhavaikkum theivangalaakiya Thamizhaha makkal*). This phrase often employed by RK implies that he acknowledges he is an *outsider* and at the same time he is grateful to the people of Thamizh Nadu for what they have done to him. The 'outsider-who-has-immigrated' syndrome is picturesquely described in *Panakkaaran*, when RK declares: 'I like this soil very much. From now onwards, till the end of my life, this body will walk only on this soil; even after death, this soul will relate only with this soil. There is no return from here. I'll settle down here'. RK, thus, adds a special cultural contour to his subaltern image by 'settling himself' in the Thamizh cultural milieu. Once immigrated, RK becomes a *citizen* of Thamizh Nadu, as he affirms in *Naan Adimai Illai*: 'I am a citizen of Thamizh Nadu… And I know how to behave with a woman'.

Other differences between RK and MGR include: First, if MGR manipulated the construct of 'thiraavidam' as a cover to conceal his non-Thamizh roots, RK resorts to 'Indian-ness' as a shield. For example, when asked who he is in *Thampikku Entha Ooru*, RK retorts, 'I am an Indian'. Second, more than MGR, RK appeals to the 'hospitality' of the Thamizhs — *vanthaarai vaazhavaikkum Thamizhaham* (meaning, the Thamizh Nadu which makes anyone who comes there live and prosper) — to justify his immigration to Thamizh Nadu. Third, if MGR used his real life 'rebirth' as a ploy to erase his origins, RK tries through his film stories to convey the message that he becomes a Thamizh by marital alliance. Films like *Nallavanukku Nallavan*, *Muththu* and *Arunaachalam* are typical examples. In all such films, RK as an honest 'immigrant' will get ready to leave as a 'renouncer', leaving behind all that he has earned or what belongs to him. But in none of the films he really leaves. He is pleaded to stay behind, and in films like *Arunaachalam* he is brought back to find the fiancée waiting for him to marry.[14]

132 ◄ POPULAR CINEMA AND POLITICS IN SOUTH INDIA

At the same time, however, RK also resorts to many of the devices employed by MGR. Like MGR, he projects himself as the champion of Thamizh culture, particularly when it comes to the question of subordinating women. When his political intervention received an overload of publicity during 1995–96, he even attempted, like MGR, to redefine 'Thamizhness'. In a televised interview[15] on his birthday in 1995, answering the question, 'Some political leaders have said that only a Thamizh should rule Thamizh Nadu, what is your opinion?' RK said: 'It's welcome. They have rightly said it. After all, they have not said that only a Chettiyaar or a Gounder or a Muthaliyaar or a Thaevar or a Brahmin or a non-Brahmin should rule Thamizh Nadu; they have only said a Thamizh should rule. According to me, *all those who speak Thamizh are Thamizhs*' (emphasis added). He, however, did not pursue the argument, and there was no need for it either, because he did not contest in the elections. Significantly, in a moving speech on the occasion of the jubilee of *Padaiyappaa* (on 28 October 1999), he referred to the 'eeramulla irumpu nenjam' of the Thamizhs (the heart of iron but moist [with flesh]) and observed that it is difficult to get inside but once gone inside it is impossible to come out.

The Orphan

A recurrent feature present in MGR and RK films from the earliest is the 'orphan-hood' of the hero. In majority of their films, they are either 'full orphans' (without both parents and siblings) or 'semi-orphans' (with only one of the parents, mostly mother; sometimes without both parents, but with a sister or a brother). Quite frequently, they appear *in medias res*, without any past. They are 'uprooted' from nowhere as it were, and 'transplanted' in the narrative for the sake of the story. But they always end up 'un-orphaned' either by 'discovering' the parents (often the hero will be the lost child) or establishing the heroine's lineage to have links with that of the hero, or by acquiring new relatives through marital alliance.

The orphan syndrome helps MGR and RK in so many respects, as Figure 10.2 illustrates. First of all, playing orphan elicits a sympathetic response from the viewers, who are able to *feel for* the hero. Emotional appeals such as, 'I am an orphan. There is none to weep for me even if I die' (MGR in *Maattukkaara Vaelan*) are sure to move the hearts

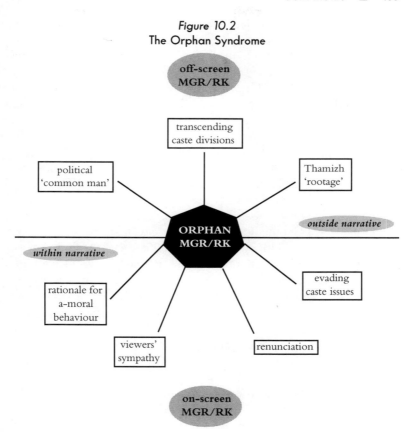

Figure 10.2
The Orphan Syndrome

of the viewers. Once the viewers are attracted thus and initiated into the narrative sentimentally, the hero then proceeds to make them get emotionally involved and *feel with* him as the narrative builds up. Eventually the viewers are led to *feel as* the hero. When the story closes, their hero is no more an orphan — he has married the heroine, and, more importantly, they have accepted him into their fold.

Second, playing orphan helps MGR and RK to easily transcend the caste-class barriers, especially the caste-barrier, both within and outside the narrative. It is true that their fans are vastly rural, but they are not homogeneous with regard to caste (though a huge chunk is from the scheduled and the most-backward castes). The 'pastlessness' of the orphan makes MGR and RK evade any caste colouring to their image,

134 ▌ POPULAR CINEMA AND POLITICS IN SOUTH INDIA

which results in a 'common man' image, acceptable to fans of any caste. This 'common man' image obviously is well-suited for politiking, given the history of caste-based electioneering in Thamizh Nadu. Within the narrative, the hero can, by virtue of his being rootless, conveniently avoid caste identity. Strikingly, barring a few stray references here and there, MGR and RK do not 'meddle' with caste in their films, however burning the issue may be (or precisely because it is a burning issue!).

Third, the orphan-hood provides MGR and RK with a rationale for their ruthless, often violent, manner of handling the villain. The hero is portrayed as a victim of the unjust men and structures, which made him an orphan. The childhood deprivation, in turn, becomes a justification not only for punishing the villain but also for the 'anti-social' activities of the hero. In *Oli Vilakku*, for example, MGR eloquently defends his stealing: 'I am a thief. I lost my parents as a child. I was wandering around as an orphan. Men in the world did not have the heart to ask me who I was and what my needs were; the god above also did not have the time. I had to struggle between my mind and stomach. Finally only the stomach won. To fill my stomach I started stealing. At the age of five I stole'. Thus, the a-moral or immoral behaviour of the hero is brought within the universe of moral economy.

Fourth, playing orphan facilitates MGR and RK to emphasise the renouncer dimension of their images. They achieve this by linking the orphan status with detachment to wealth, power and prestige. Yet another use of the orphan-hood relates to the non-Thamizh roots of MGR and RK. Being orphans, MGR and RK belong to where they are! This, no doubt, is significant, given the language-sensitive nature of the Thamizh audience.

It could be seen, therefore, the 'orphan syndrome' takes MGR and RK a long way in constructing their screen images so as to make them sync with the psychological and moral aspirations of their fans within the socio-cultural and political ethos of the Thamizh audience.

The Renouncer

While MGR and RK are very conscious of the accumulation of 'enormous wealth', they make deliberate attempts to offset this *fact* by projecting, both on-screen and off-screen, a renouncer image. Both of them are strikingly unanimous in justifying the accumulation of wealth, though RK's mode of renouncing wealth is through detachment, whereas for MGR it is through charity. When it comes to appropriation of power, they make it clear that they are aware of the political potential of their huge fan club network, but they choose to remain detached; they merit to be at the helm of affairs, but they condescend, out of their generosity and magnanimity, to leave it to others. They manifest, albeit subtly, the same condescending attitude when others praise them — without disowning the adulations, they would say that they have after all done their 'duty'.

The renouncer in them could be seen when they subordinate love and romance to duty. MGR has been more consistent than RK in this regard. He places duty not only above the lover but also all blood relations, including the mother (for example, *Neethikku Thalai Vanangu*). RK's attitude to blood relations is accompanied by an interesting mix of emotions. In a film like *Mullum Malarum*, for example, RK first asserts his right over his sister, and then he decides to allow her fiancé to marry her. Same attitude he betrays with regard to traditional honour due to him. For example, in *Ejamaan*, when his cousin tries to usurp the honour reserved to him, he first re-claims it and then condescends to give it to his humiliated cousin.

Culturally, renunciation has been considered a supreme spiritual value. MGR and RK appropriate this spiritual value and 'politicise' it to justify their image politiking. It could be seen that the 'renouncer' and the 'orphan' are two different manifestations of one and the same reality (of lack or 'absence') and they both perform same political functions.

The Donor

The 'donor' is yet another aspect related to the 'renouncer' and the 'orphan'. While the renouncer *transcends* everything s/he owns, the donor gives away in acts of munificence and charity *out of* what s/he owns. In Thamizh culture, munificence has been considered as an important virtue of kings, nobles and feudal lords. The *Sangam* literature is replete with incidents of impressive munificence shown to poets. The literary genre 'Aatruppadai' celebrates kings and chiefs who are munificent. The whole corpus of Thamizh literature, in general, holds this virtue of munificence in high esteem. There are innumerable

136 ■ POPULAR CINEMA AND POLITICS IN SOUTH INDIA

references to the tradition of the great 'last seven donors' (*kadai aezhu vallalkal*) like Paari and Kaari.

The most enduring characteristic feature of MGR that is constantly reminisced by those who have encountered him is his munificence. Many of the epithets and titles conferred on him concern his 'selfless and tireless' giving. MGR was able to achieve this status as the *donor par excellence*, thanks to a combination of factors belonging to the realms of screen, politics and personal life.

MGR is indeed extravagant in his on-screen display of munificence. He is charitable to the beggars (*Kanni Thaai*), concerned about the poor and the needy (*Siriththu Vaazha Vaendum* and *Thirudaathae*), redeems the destitute (*Ulagam Sutrum Vaalipan*), and contributes generously to government's war and relief funds (*Malai Kallan* and *Kaavalkaaran*). When he is *rich*, he generously distributes his personal wealth to the poor, and makes the workers shareholders, if need be (*Ithaya Kani*). When he is in a position of power, he readily uses his office for the uplift of the downtrodden (*Naadoadi Mannan*). When he is poor, he does not hesitate to share his meagre resource (*Kumari Koattam*), and works very hard to help others. In the typical Robin Hood style, he frequently indulges in 'anti-social' activities like looting and stealing and gives the booty to the poor and the deserving (*Aayiraththil Oruvan*). Sometimes he participates in competitions in order to mobilise the amount required for a noble cause (*Neethikku Thalai Vanangu*). It is significant that invariably in all his films MGR makes it a point to make at least one character to proclaim his munificence.

In the realm of real politiking, the DMK leadership often *overstated* the munificent nature of MGR with an ulterior motive to keep him in good humour, mainly because he was an important financial source for the party, besides being a crowd-puller. MGR on his part *dramatised* his acts of charity into glittering 'public shows'. He auctioned, for example, the golden sword (110 sovereigns) presented to him on the occasion of the jubilee of *Naadoadi Mannan* in Madurai, to contribute to the Indo-China war fund.[16] More remarkably, whenever the *subalterns* were affected either by fire or by flood, his presence was always there in the form of providing relief. He made it a point at the same time to exploit his acts of munificence to further his political career by getting them *publicised*. MGR, however, convincingly projected him as a person *genuinely concerned* about the poor by linking up the acts of charity with his early deprivation. He also made use of the fact that he did not have children to reinforce the message that all his wealth was indeed meant for the poor.

Though RK has not been publicised for his munificence to the extent of MGR, he does take care to project him as a person sensitive and responsive to the needs of the poor. Particularly after he has started intervening in politics, he is seen to be making calculated and concerted attempts, both in films and public forums, to display his munificence. The most hyped show was the jubilee celebration of *Padaiyappaa* during which he announced his sudden decision to 'give back' the (contro-versial)[17] marriage hall (*kalyaana mandapam*) he owned to the people of Thamizh Nadu (supposedly represented in the Sri Ragavendra Trust he floated for this purpose). In his speech he said,[18] 'I dedicate this prop-erty, which is more than half of what I have earned, to the people of Thamizh Nadu. I have not earned this because of my hard work. This is what *you* have given me by buying five rupee and ten rupee tickets with your hard earned money. I just give that back to you'.

The God

The culmination of renunciation and munificence is the deification of MGR and RK. While there are differences between MGR and RK in the kind of belief systems they have, there are very striking similarities in the way they acquire the divine status.

MGR had been a member of a political party, which initially claimed to profess atheism but later modified its atheism to a sort of humanism as expressed in its oft-repeated slogans, 'Onrae Kulam — Oruvanae Thaevan' (One Community — One God) and 'Aezhaiyin sirippil Iraivan' (God in the smile of the poor). Intriguingly, MGR had never been an atheist in the true sense of the term. Time and again he had clarified that he was not anon-believer but a believer who disapproved the superstitious religious practices and exploiting the people in the name of religion. Though as a rule he did not act[19] in roles in which he had to worship god, quite a few of his films had other characters worshipping god. In real life too, he never interfered with the belief of others, and in fact most of the people who worked with him were staunch believers.[20] He had a profound veneration for his mother, and had the habit of worshipping her as the god. At the same time, however, he had personal devotion to the deity at Mookambika.

RK claims himself to be a believer, and is free from the inconsistencies that could be detected in MGR. His interest in religion and spirituality could be seen from his rather bold decision to play the role of Sri Ragavendra — a role that is totally discordant with his anti-hero image — in his 100th film. In *Baba* (2002), he plays, though not to the liking of his fans, the role of an *avatar* of a mythological sage called Baba.

Like MGR, RK also gives in his films a divine status to mother; but unlike MGR, he places mother only *next* to god. As a believer, he has also exhorted his fans on several occasions to spend a few minutes every day in prayer.

Irrespective of the differences in their belief systems, both MGR and RK are seen to systematically cultivate a divine image for them. This is where the 'politicisation of god' and the 'deification of politicians' meet. On-screen, MGR/RK will have characters deifying him, at least praising him to be godly. Saving women in danger, munificence cum personal sacrifice, and punishing the evil are the frequently recurring justification for making a god out of him. In a perfect correlation to the 'saviour' image, the screen characters who deify him are invariably the subalterns and the women. Off-screen, the fans of MGR/RK indulge in worshipping him as a god. The 'rituals' performed to the cut-outs when a new film is released are more deeply religious than the temple-based rituals. When the screen-constructed divinity is transferred to the realm of fan clubs, MGR/RK is no more a god 'image' or *avatar* but god himself (for the fans).

The Interlace

The octa-motifs as explicated previously are interrelated as Figure 10.3 illustrates. The eight motifs are interlaced with 'hero-centricity' as the all-pervading centric force. The *thaai kulam*, the quality of the *fan-bond* and the *subaltern* with the associated character of the *Thamizhness* form the 'centrifugal triangle'. The *orphan*, the *renouncer* and the *donor* form the 'centripetal triangle' of which the *god* is the culmination. All the eight constitute the 'politiking formula' and pave the way for the appropriation of the 'cumulative authority'.

It is quite probable that the fans encounter 'cognitive dissonance' when the star concerned exercises his politiking formula. The 'dissonance' often results from the perception of obvious discrepancies in the

Figure 10.3
Politically Loaded Octa-Motif Interlace

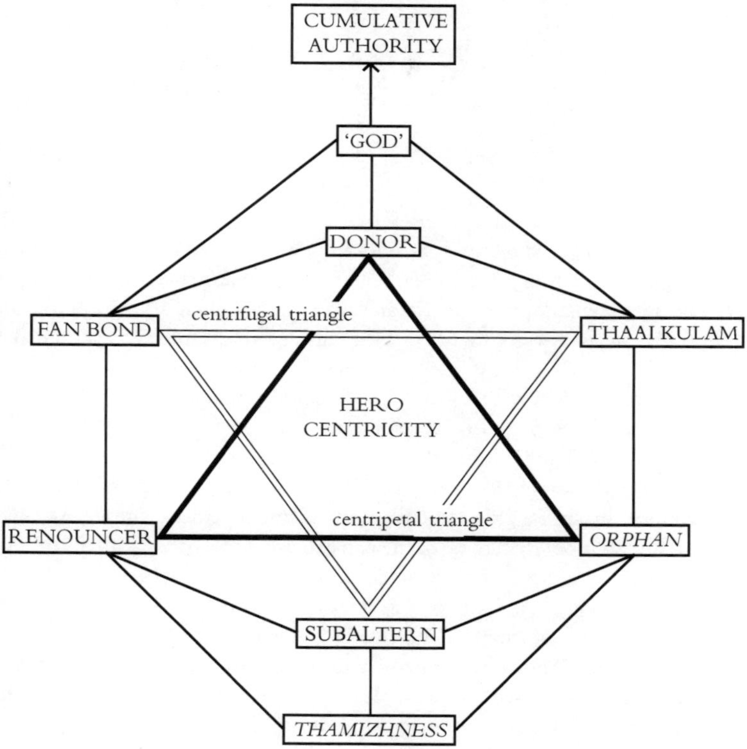

behaviour of the star. When a bit of information leads to dissonance, the fan concerned may indulge in one or more of the following: discrediting the source of the discordant information (as not credible and unreliable), blaming the rival party (as the enemy's evil device to malign the hero's name), proof-texting films in defence, generalising (as everybody is like that, a *man* will be like that, etc.), seeking more information in fanzines and from other fan-friends, and quoting other real-life behaviour of the star that would counter the discordant information (as being charitable, being religious, etc.).

Significantly, while in general the state of dissonance is quickly resolved, it is not rare that the dissonance is never resolved. In such a case, the fan might prefer to continue to live with the dissonance at the cognitive level but at the emotional level s/he hardly gives up membership.

Notes

1. The only category that is consciously avoided by MGR is that of the daughters. That is because, as noted elsewhere also, having a grown-up daughter will make him a 'father', which means that he concedes his critique's remark of his being an 'aged actor'. Even after jumping into politics he was trying hard to 'hide' his age under the fur cap and dark glasses.
2. MGR always prefers a male child, if he has one, whereas RK prefers female children. MGR promises in a song in *Panam Padaiththavan* that his child will be 'exactly like' him.
3. The DMK founder leader Anna addressed the party workers as 'thampikal' (younger brother). This suited his status as 'Anna' (elder brother). Age-wise also he was older than most of the party members. Karunanidhi improvised this and coined the term 'co-born' (brother), a term which conceals any disparity of age (implying one as the elder and the other as the younger) and treats the 'brothers' as equals. It was important for Karunanidhi to resort to such a non-discriminatory term because many of the front-rung leaders and party workers were of his age, and some of them were even older than him. MGR preferred the term 'co-born' to 'thampi' for an exactly opposite reason — if Karunanidhi used the 'co-born' to hide his 'juniority', MGR did the same to hide his 'seniority'.
4. Vijayan (1997: 80).
5. It is interesting to compare MGR and Sivaji in the way they describe the bond with their fans. While MGR calls them 'blood-of-my-blood co-borns', Sivaji calls them 'pillaihal', which generally means 'children', and within the context of family, it means 'sons and daughters'. The tone is clearly paternalistic. See Editorial Board of Manimekalai Pirasuram (1995: 153).
6. From the late 1980s, the delinquent colour in the titles slowly fades out, while more positively heroic colour sets in.
7. The titles of MGR films in fact indicate different emphasis at different times. During the 1950s they are pronouncedly mythological or 'historical' but the contents are overtly political, and the attacks are primarily against the

ruling Congress party. During the 1960s they reveal a noticeable shift in emphasis. The titles of the early 60s are more 'family-oriented' with moral and social connotations. It is noteworthy that the 'mother sentiment' series (the 'thaa' series) predominantly belong to the 1960s. Concomitantly, the subaltern slant also finds a place in the titles through the early 1960s, but it comes to prominence from the mid-1960s through the 1970s. Though titles with political overtones have been a constant phenomenon, they turn explicitly political once again during the 1970s, particularly after the formation of the ADMK. The attacks directed against the Karunanidhi regime are couched, however, in the triumphalistic tone of the titles. For a comprehensive analysis, see our discussion on MGR's way of tactexting, in the next chapter.

8. Unlike English, the last syllable in Thamizh indicates respectability (*thinai*), besides gender, number, tense and place. For example, a simple sentence like 'She came' can have two Thamizh equivalents — 'Aval vanthaal' (disrespectful) and 'Avar vanthaar' (respectful). Sometimes an extra suffix is added to the already respectful form, as in 'Avar*kal* vanthaar*kal*' – an exaggeration commonly employed in political circles.

9. The 'Invocation to *Mother* Thamizh' (*Thamizh Thaai Vaazhththu*), officially translated in English as the 'Invocation to *Goddess* Thamizh' is sung in all government functions in lieu of 'prayer song'.

10. It is to be noted that once the reorganisation of States on linguistic basis came into being during the mid-1950s, the demand for a separate *thiraavida naadu* turned rather feeble and that too was heard only within Thamizh Nadu. From then onwards, 'Thiraavidam' and 'Thamizh' came to be interchangeably used, and in the political parlance meant the same. This worked very much in favour of MGR and enabled a smooth transition from being a 'Dravidian' to being a 'Thamizh'.

11. Except three films dubbed — one each in Hindi, Telugu and Malayalam.

12. For instance, according to one such popular biography, MGR's forefathers originally belonged to the Mandraadiyaar caste from Coimbatore district. They migrated to Kerala, the biography guesses, looking for greener pastures. See Editorial Board of Manimekalai Pirasuram (1994: 6). Somewhat similar is the latest reminiscing of erstwhile popular dialogue writer Aarur Doss. See *Thina Thanthi*, 14 September 2013, p.15.

13. On the controversial debate on genealogy, see Rajadurai and Geetha (2000).

14. Incidentally, in real life also RK is married to a woman from Thamizh Nadu. Ironically, all the three wives of MGR and his intimate lady-friend Jayalalithaa were born outside Thamizh Nadu.

142 ■ POPULAR CINEMA AND POLITICS IN SOUTH INDIA

15. The complete text of this two-part interview was published in *Thina Thanthi*, 13 December 1995 and 14 December 1995.
16. Narayanan (1981: 505).
17. At the time of RK's announcement, there was a legal dispute going on concerning the marriage hall. Some, therefore, interpreted RK's decision to hand it over to a trust as a way of escaping the legal tangle.
18. The whole programme was later telecast on Sun TV. The translation given here is from the telecast version of RK's speech.
19. There are exceptions, however. In *Jenoavaa*, for example, he plays the role of a believer; in *Mathurai Veeran* he plays the role of Veeran who attains divinity at the end.
20. See Vijayan (1997: 78), for one such example.

11

IMAGING BY TACTEXTING

The apparent success of the image politics of MGR and to a certain extent that of RK largely depend on the way they image politics in their films. This is done though the innovative and intricate 'tactexting'[1] (tactical texting) — a narrative technique by which selectively drawn politically loaded acterances are tactically positioned at 'critical joints' of the narrative structure[2] and inseparably meshed with the story so that for the viewer — censors included — such messages look unassumingly neutral or are so innocently spontaneous that they go unnoticed. Even vitriolic political attacks are made unobtrusive and subterraneous by cleverly camouflaging them as integral to the story, and the resultant meta-narrative maintains the semblance of political neutrality. But tactexting is not just that simple! While each film as a grand narrative opens up a *dreamatic* world of fantasy for the fans to temporarily *trancelate* the harsh realities of day-to-day existence, the acterances at the joints inspire (or instigate) a more specific and motivated political reading of the film, offering a 'double-relish' to the fans. Even while the viewing is going on, the ardent fans of MGR and RK, being familiar with the political happenings pertaining to their respective heroes, unravel the acterance at each joint and lapse into 'ecstasy' by the decoding of the 'revelation' of the political stand of the hero. Besides, the decoding of an acterance at one joint leads the viewers to expect more acterances with similar or greater political import to occur with the progression of the story, and the experience of suspense and surprise come into play; not so infrequently, the same expectation leads the viewers to impute political meaning where it is not intended originally. Thus, tactexting makes the narrative at once a parallel political discourse — a delightful one at that — simultaneously with the story's unfolding. The impact of

144 POPULAR CINEMA AND POLITICS IN SOUTH INDIA

tactexting enigmatically does not depend on the number of acterances; rather it depends on the intensity of the star's political involvement and the potency of the text to catapult a forceful big-bang at current politics. That explains why both MGR and RK resort to tactexting as the most common technique to sustain an on-going para-social interaction with their fans even beyond the screen.

Blurring and Blending

Significantly, tactexting involves, as Figure 11.1 shows, three overlapping realms — the more explicitly political 'public realm', the publicly known side of the 'private realm', and the self-reflexive 'screen realm'. The public realm includes any reference that is directly political, such as icons (for example, photograph of a political leader), party symbols (rising sun, twin-leaves, etc.), critical comments, ideological statements and culturally rooted motifs and archetypes. The frequently recurring 'politicisable' references to the private life invariably consist of the past experiences — childhood deprivation, especially poverty, the odd and menial jobs undertaken in the struggle for survival, and some dramatic incidents (MGR being shot at, for instance). The self-reflexive references within the screen realm but laden with the potential to be politicised include repeated usage of honorifics (for example, 'vaaththiyaar, vallal' and 'ponmana chemmal' for MGR; 'super star' for RK), certain motifs (popularly called 'sentiments' — the 'snake sentiment'[3] of RK, for instance), and mere titles of films by the same star (a typical example for this is the 'Kaalai Kaalai' song in RK's *Manithan* which refers to his *Murattu Kaalai, Poakkiri Raajaa, Paayum Puli*, and *Nallavanukku Nallavan* — all box-office hits). This aspect of self-reflexivity activates the memories and subtly re-evokes the previous experiences of the viewers — more specifically of the fans, as they would have seen the films referred to — and enables them derive 'cumulative pleasure' from the present viewing.

Interestingly, the three realms are 'metaleptically' related — their boundaries are intentionally blurred and blended. The public-private, the private-cinematic, and the cinematic-public interfaces are made so nebulous through transgression of boundaries that the public, the private and the screen realms appear to be metonymic extensions of one another or mutually interchangeable. As a result, even seemingly a-political references to the private life of MGR and RK and to their

IMAGING BY TACTEXTING   145

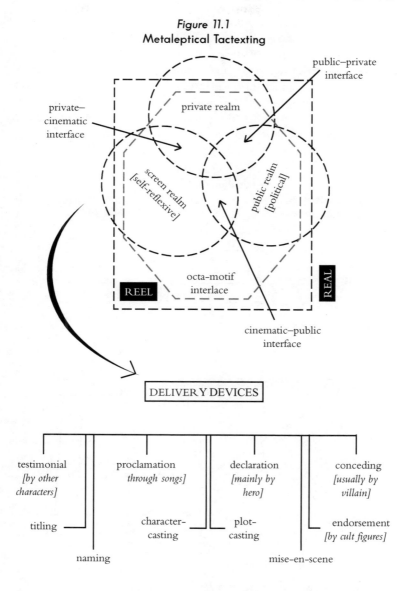

Figure 11.1
Metaleptical Tactexting

films acquire amazing political contours. The harmonious merging of the blurred-and-blended realms with the backdrop of the 'octa-motif interlace' renders the tactexting process effective.

146 ■ POPULAR CINEMA AND POLITICS IN SOUTH INDIA

Consequently, the reel–real interface is also effectively blunted by the metaleptical carrying over of the real-life events into films. Off-screen references to the same real-life events especially of the past and to roles enacted on-screen reinforce the corrosion of the reel–real distinction. Strikingly, the 'actor-character identification,' both on-screen and off-screen, further heightens the corrosion, as delineated in Figure 11.2.

To the subaltern masses, the honorifics, most prominently that of 'vaaththiyaar' for MGR and 'super star' for RK, are not mere titles,

Figure 11.2
Synonymisation and Self-Reflexivity

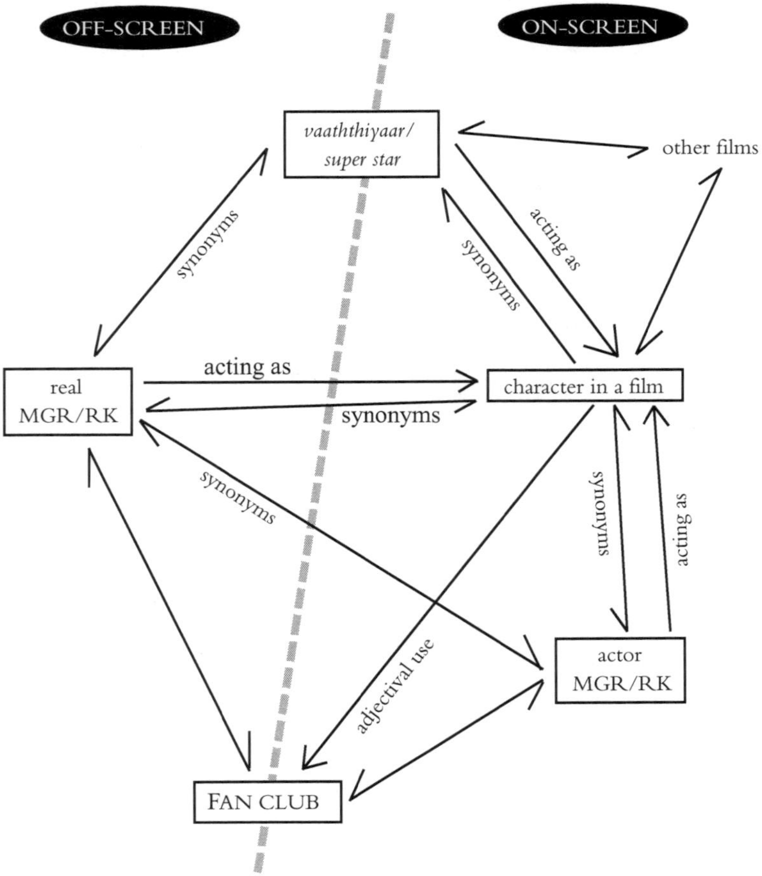

but the *names* of the actors as perceived and received by the fans. Thus, when MGR/RK plays a particular role in a film, the fans perceive it as their 'vaaththiyaar/super star' playing the role. Another aspect of this process of 'synonymisation' is the concomitant identification of MGR/RK with the character played. In RK's *Annaamalai*, for example, the duet 'Kondaiyil Thaazhampoo' refers to the 'super star' acting as 'Annaamalai' as 'Rajini', the real name. Similarly, the song 'Vahuththa Karunguzhalai' in *Raaman Thaediya Seethai* refers to the 'vaaththiyaar' acting as 'Raaman' as 'MGR', the real name. In exceptional cases like *Anpulla Rajinikaanth* RK plays the role of RK himself. Another noteworthy aspect of 'synonymisation' is the extended use of the character's name as an epithet or honorific title to the name of the actor, the most prevalent practice among the fans in naming their clubs (for example, '*Padaiyappaa* Rajini Rasikar Mandram'). Significantly, it is with this practice of the fan clubs in view that in many of the films, particularly of RK, the hero is eponymous or the film titles are phrased as *epithets* to the hero such as *Enga Veettu Pillai* and *Aayiraththil Oruvan* (a common feature in MGR starrers).[4]

The fans of MGR and RK are thus led to believe that the reel and the real are only two interchangeable dimensions of their respective heroes — it is not MGR/RK acting as a character in the story, but MGR/RK acting as MGR/RK. The image politics in essence amounts to the real politics of the real MGR or RK. It is, therefore, no longer image-only politics; it *is* real politics. And every film, in turn, becomes a *political statement*, and every screening session becomes an extraordinary *public meeting* where such a statement is personally issued to individuals.

Delivery Devices

The metaleptically blurred-and-blended acterances embracing the public, private and screen realms are delivered on-screen through one or many of the following devices, which are often a combination of the narrative and technical elements:

- *Proclamation*: The socio-political ideology of the hero is usually proclaimed through songs visually accompanied by dance sequences invariably shot in exotic locations. Frequently, the songs are the 'cinematised' versions of the hero's socio-political manifesto.

148 ■ POPULAR CINEMA AND POLITICS IN SOUTH INDIA

- *Declaration*: If the songs are the 'poetic' versions of the hero's socio-political ideology, the statements, mainly of the hero, are the 'prose' versions of the same. Such declarations are often categorical and assertive, pointed and poignant, positive, and promising. Not infrequently, they crystallise into crisp and succinct punch dialogues. Declaration is one of the devices commonly employed by the hero to subalternise himself.
- *Testimonial:* The noble character of the hero, an aspect intrinsic to the hero's saviour image, is attested to by other characters especially in the form of adulations. Frequently, the victims of villainy 'redeemed' by the hero serve in the narrative as live testimonies to his invincibility and commitment to the subalterns.
- *Conceding:* Another striking device related to the testimonial is the final surrender usually of the villain and his/her aides after the climactic showdown. While the very defeat of the villainy amply testifies to the unconquerability of the hero, the verbalised conceding of the villain further heightens the political significance of the hero.
- *Naming:* Surprisingly, even the naming of the characters, specifically of the hero, can be a political act. The hero is usually given a name that is either culturally and religiously significant or common among the subalterns. Often enough, the so-called 'Tom-Dick-and-Harry' type names like 'Muththu' are given. It is not rare to find, especially in MGR films, conspicuously political names such as 'Uthaya Sooriyan' (literally, 'the rising sun', the DMK party symbol) are being employed.
- *Character-casting:* Casting the characters with resemblances to real-life political figures is also a favourite device resorted to by MGR and RK. The 'resemblance' may be in the form of parody, caricature, metaphor, or sometimes metonymy. While the villain's depiction as a norm resembles real-life political rivals, the hero is portrayed as the real MGR or RK.
- *Plot-casting:* Not only the names and types of characters but also the plot may at times symbolise the current political happenings. Intriguingly, even a 'non-political' or 'family-based' story is structured in a way that certain 'dramatisable' features of the real political confrontation are transported to the narrative realm, as a result of which the story turns out to be 'political-by-proxy'.

IMAGING BY TACTEXTING   149

- *Titling:* One of the most innovative features is using the title itself as a political statement. Ironically, while the story and the title are normally linked thematically, the story and the political message communicated through the title need not necessarily go together.
- *Mise-en-scene:* The 'setting' of a scene, including the props, can occasionally be politically motivated. Politically significant icons (such as portraits and photographs of political, national or religious leaders) and symbols (such as flags and election symbols) are utilised for this purpose. Cultural symbols like the *vael* are also at times politicised.
- *Endorsement:* There are rare incidents of endorsement of the hero by political cult-figures like Anna through audio, visual or verbal 'quotes'. These quotes may sometimes remain at the level of a mere mention of the names of the cult-figures. Interestingly, from the 1980s MGR also has become one of the cult-figures for the politically active actors, including RK.

The narrative contexts in which these devices are utilised include the dialogical, the confrontational, the celebratory, the romantic and the comical. A mix of these narrative contexts, the aforesaid delivery devices, the three overlapping realms of the public, the private and the screen, the interlaced octa-motifs having the capacity to be politicised, and the dialectically linked reel–real spheres constitute together the base for imaging politics. MGR and RK differ in the way they manoeuvre these elements, as explicated in the classified survey of films in the subsequent chapters.

Meta-Texting

While tactexting is employed by the star concerned, there are two other meta-texting devices, i.e., cross-texting and trans-texting, used by others. Meta-texting helps nurture and reinforce the political image built through tactexting.

Cross-texting refers to 'idolised' use of MGR and RK by other junior stars in their films. This is usually done by selectively 'quoting' from the films of MGR/RK certain statements, songs and visual clips. Sometimes MGR/RK's photographs and film posters will be displayed. While such cross-textual use goes to accord MGR/RK with the status of being legendary or semi-mythological figures, the concerned junior star 'elevates' himself to the status of MGR/RK.

Transtexting refers to the occasional use of 'clips' (includes dialogues, and songs, comedy and stunt sequences) by non-movie media sources, especially television and radio, to respond to a contemporary situation. Such situations come years after the release of the films 'quoted', and in most cases not related to the narrative contexts of those films at all. This transtextual use reinforces the star-fan bond(age).

The most popular and sentimental transtexting occurred in 1984, when MGR suddenly fell ill. In every nook and corner of every village in Thamizh Nadu the songs, 'You must be well, if the country is to prosper...' (from MGR's *Ithaya Kani*) and 'God, in your palace there are thousands of lamps...' (from *Oli Vilakku*) were blasted through loud speakers.

Notes

1. It is useful to disinguish tactexting from subtexting. Subtexting refers to the true or deeper level meaning underlying a surface level word or action. The purpose of subtexting is to make the characters life-like by adding a depth dimension, and to make the narrative absorbing. Frequently sexual messages and sometimes political ones are communicated through subtexting. This is usually done through metaphors, innuendos, double entendres, paradies, paralanguage, and the like. In tactexting, the acterances at the joints transform the story itself into a discourse by transporting the plane from narrative fictionality to political *actuality*. Thus, unlike subtexting which enhances the character, tactexting achieves the alchemy of real MGR/RK acting as real MGR/RK, both in reel and real realms!
2. The narrative structure here referred to is the *assemblage* structure delineated in the first part of the book. The assemblage structure accommodates a variety of elements and weaves them all into one whole. Therefore, 'critical joint' need not necessarily be an emotional entanglement or high drama; it can also be a location that is effortlessly glossed over such as a pass-by.
3. RK has a tendency to fetishise snake, ever since he first introduced a successful, cheesy comedy sequence involving a snake in *Thampikku Entha Ooru*. He introduced a similar sequence later in *Annaamalai*, which again became a hit, mainly because of the 'Kadavulae...'context. Similar sequence

IMAGING BY TACTEXTING ■ 151

(without snake) was repeated in *Paandiyan*. In *Muththu* a snake is used to add comical effect to a chasing sequence. In *Arunaachalam* a snake comes as a 'friend' to warn a trouble-maker. In *Padaiyappaa* a snake is introduced to exhibit RK's power and piety. A snake figures in *Chandramukhi* to enhance the mystery and terror surrounding the haunted palace. And in *Enthiran*, one of the killer-forms the robot takes is that of a monsterous anaconda. From the point of view of the fan who has seen all these films as and when they are released and continue to see them repeatedly whenever he gets or creates an opportunity, each encounter with the snake sequence becomes a lot more pleasurable by coalescing the currently evoked emotions with the re-evoked gamut of previously-experienced ones into a kind of 'rainbow experience'. RK's snake sentiment has influenced other actors also, as for example, his son-in-law Dhanush apes RK in *Yaaradi Nee Moahini*.

4. A classic example of the name of a character becoming the name of the actor himself is the use of 'Captain' as an epithet to Vijayakanth or simply as a proper noun instead of Vijayakanth. The word 'Captain' is from *Captain Prabhakaran*, a super-duper hit film of Vijayakanth. The title became very popular partly also because of its reference to the LTTE chief Prabhakaran, and the name of the villain alludes to the 'forest brigand' Veerappan, another popular figure. In TN politics today, 'Captain' could mean only Vijayakanth. Such is the synonymisation. So much so that his TV channel is named 'Captain TV'.

12

MGR: POLITICS AS CO-TEXT

The imaging of MGR's politics consists of three 'phases' and two 'faces'. The first phase approximately covers the 1950s climaxing in *Naadoadi Mannan*. The second phase runs through the 1960s till the formation of the ADMK in 1972. The third phase culminates in *Mathuraiyai Meetta Sunthara Paandiyan*.

The two faces running parallel to each other and spread over all the three phases of the entire film career are epitomised in *Naadoadi Mannan* (NM) and *Enga Veettu Pillai* (EP). The 'NM-face' is the image of MGR-dominant in films that could be classified as the 'historicals' such as *Marma Yoagi*, *Mathurai Veeran*, *Aayiraththil Oruvan*, *Adimai Penn*, and *Mathuraiyai Meetta Sunthara Paandiyan*. The politicality of the narrative ambience of these 'historicals' render the face more 'naturally' political. Tactexting political comments, therefore, becomes spontaneous and convenient. The 'EP-face' is the image of MGR prominently projected in the 'socials' like *Malai Kallan*, *Thirudaathae*, *Oli Vilakku*, *Maattukkaara Vaelan*, *Rikshaakaaran*, and *Meenava Nanpan*. As the narrative setting of the 'socials' lends itself to critique the social evils, EP-face, more often than not, is the 'politicisable', 'social' side of the 'total' MGR face interlaced with the octa-motifs. Strikingly, the NM-face acquires pre-eminence during the first phase, whereas the EP-face stands out during the second phase. A calculated amalgam of both the faces with comparatively greater emphasis on the EP-face dominates the third phase. The 'do-gooder action hero', however, constitutes the substantial core of the two faces. Throughout all three phases, the tactexting is superbly intricate, complex and consistent, making political events and his films as 'co-texts'.

The 'MGR's DMK' Phase

In consonance with the then prevalent political ideology of the DMK, the MGR starrers during the first phase alluded to the conflicts of the North versus the South, the Brahmin/Aryan versus the Dravidian, the United India versus the Dravida Nation, the Congress versus the DMK, Hindi versus Thamizh, theism versus rationalism, subordination versus self-respect, and so on. While these conflicts were presented in the DMK political platforms (off-screen) as well-defined and clearly demarcated binary opposites without any intermediary grey areas, at least till 1956 when the party decided to contest in the general elections the following year, MGR had in fact been very moderate from the very beginning in propagandising the DMK ideology, with some notable exceptions of films scripted by the leading DMK activists like Karunanidhi and Kannadasan. Instead, MGR chose to play on the DMK-emphasised *karpu* (chastity, often equated to virginity), *maanam* (respect and dignity), and *veeram* (valour) as essential aspects of the Thamizh culture. The DMK ideology as propagated through MGR starrers, in effect, amounts to a reading of it by MGR. *Naadoadi Mannan*, 1958, is a quintessence of this reading.

In fact, *Naadoadi Mannan* was in many ways a watershed in MGR's career. First of all, it was the first film directed by MGR himself and produced by his own Emgeeyar Pictures. As the producer, MGR had borrowed money from various sources, and risked his future, as he anxiously used to say during the days of production that he will be a *Mannan* if it wins, and a *Naadoadi* if it flops. The phenomenal success of the film (it ran for 25 weeks), however, proved that he was destined to be the 'king' and not a 'vagrant', as he feared.

Second, the film is a very imaginative MGR-centric mix of all the core elements of MGR's image, tested (and tasted) over the years, and the popular aspects of the DMK ideology hand-picked by MGR. The peculiar mix renders the film the *visual version* of the DMK ideology with MGR as the centre, replacing Anna, the founder-leader of the party. It is indeed the ideology of MGR's DMK, the forerunner of the ADMK. The film, in effect, cogently and persuasively presents MGR as the most desirable leader.

Third, the overwhelming reception especially from the fans that the film received was enough to impress upon the DMK leadership that

154 ◼ POPULAR CINEMA AND POLITICS IN SOUTH INDIA

MGR had established himself as a force to reckon with, and in a swift move, the leadership made the success of the film the party's own by organising 'victory celebrations' (*vetri vizhaa*). Anna spoke of MGR as his 'ithaya kani' and went on to say that he had become 'a model to all the artistes. He did not merely look at the outside world through the balcony of the "home of art"(*kalai veedu*), but jumped into active politics... This act of his is revolutionary'. He observed 'something fundamentally wrong in the approach' of other artistes who claimed to participate in politics. They had entered the DMK, he opined, because MGR, whom they like and trust or whose help they need, had entered it.[1] Karunanidhi on his part conferred on MGR the title 'Revolutionary Actor' and came up with a hyperbolic poem[2] in which he stated that MGR 'devised an action plan to picturise in art the ideology of the Movement (*iyakkam*, implying the DMK), the interpretation of the vision (*latchiyam*), and the means to set ablaze superstition'. The success of the film, then, not merely reinforced the niche MGR had cut out for himself within the DMK, but, more importantly, made the leadership acknowledge that MGR was inevitable to the party and the party would not be the same without him and his massive fan following.

Politically, the success of *Naadoadi Mannan* was primarily due to its 'bi-focal' identity — as a DMK film, it was patronised by the DMK men; as an MGR starrer, it attracted his fans who were also active party workers at the grassroots. As an MGR starrer, the film is a paradigm of hero-centricity, with MGR playing the double roles of the victim and the saviour. He upholds the Thamizh tradition by being the saviour of the hapless women and the protector of *karpu*. On the day of coronation he is accorded a 'messianic' reception accompanied by a song sung in all the four south Indian languages (Telugu, Kannada, Malayalam, and Thamizh) depicting him as 'the emperor blossomed in the Dravidian garden'. He gives away half of his personal wealth for the public cause. He echoes the concerns of the subalterns and promises, 'I am going to enact laws — in common; plans that will do good...'

When he appropriates more power, he does announce to the chagrin of the elite 'new laws' favouring the subalterns. He talks to the queen about the 'other world' of the deprived, and how he, unable to bear the atrocities against the poor, has left the defense and turned a revolutionary. Convinced, the queen prophesies, 'Not only me, this whole nation has to trust you'. As the film ends, he tolls the death-knell

MGR: POLITICS AS CO-TEXT ■ 155

of monarchy, while the masses evince their trust in him by celebrating him as 'the first leader of the country'.

As a DMK film, *Naadoadi Mannan* for the first time showed the DMK flag on the screen albeit only as the emblem of Emgeeyar Pictures. Significantly, the tactexted political message was not only for the then Congress government but for the DMK as well. MGR achieved this, thanks to the duality of identities: while he as the hero symbolised the DMK, he retained his identity as MGR. Further, by overlapping these twin identities, he singled him out from the rest and persuasively projected him as the sole candidate eligible to be 'the first leader'. Thus, the tactexted messages were 'equivocalised' on purpose either as the criticism of the Congress government (MGR as the DMK symbol) or as his personal message to the DMK leadership (MGR as the DMK member). For example, while the vagrant MGR acting as the ad-hoc king tells the minister that he can continue to act provided he gets the powers to enact laws, he remarks: 'You (condescendingly) look at the people from the palace, I watch the palace standing with them'. This could be interpreted as a hit against the Congress, because that was how the DMK described the Congress in its campaigns. But this was also MGR's personal message to other DMK leaders. Similarly, the vagrant MGR, while revealing his identity, tells the queen, 'Ours is not an armed revolution — we don't believe in it either — but a knowledge revolution (*arivu puratchi*)'. This assertion could mean, given the then prevailing socio-political turmoil caused primarily by the 'agitational' strategy adopted by the DMK against the ruling Congress party, particularly on issues related to the imposition of Hindi and *kulak kalvi*[3] plan, that the DMK-sponsored on-going agitations were only steps towards a 'knowledge revolution'. This could also mean, as a personal message of MGR to assuage the public anxiety, that his version of 'revolution', unlike the DMK's agitations often threatening to disrupt the law and order situation, would confine itself only to the realm of 'knowledge'. He assures his followers of his steadfastness and invites them to have faith in him: 'There are many who have ruined themselves without trusting me. There is none who has got ruined after having trusted me'.

Significantly, when reporters asked MGR as he assumed office as the chief minister what his plans were, he promptly replied,[4] 'See my *Naadoadi Mannan*, and you'll get the answer'. Later in 1984 during

156 ◾ POPULAR CINEMA AND POLITICS IN SOUTH INDIA

the platinum jubilee celebrations of Anna at Trichi, MGR specifically referred to *Naadoadi Mannan*, and reiterated that his government was executing what he had promised in that film.[5]

Even as the period under review came to a close, in 1959 MGR met with a near-fatal accident and broke his leg while acting in a stunt sequence in the stage play *Inbak Kanavu* at Sirgali in Tanjore. The only film released this year, *Thaai Magalukku Kattiya Thaali* (story by Anna), was a flop at the box-office. At the same time *Veerapaandiya Kattabomman*, a Sivaji starrer happened to be a hit. Many of MGR's critiques, therefore, predicted his 'end', but he bounced back with three films the very next year, and proved himself inexorable.

The 'MGR-as-DMK' Phase

The first phase of imaging MGR's politics is, as noted above, marked by a calculated pro-DMK slant that simultaneously serves as an ideological kernel of the 'proto-ADMK'. The political response during the second phase takes on an ingenious crafting of the image of MGR through the interlaced octa-motifs. Concomitantly, the NM-face dominant during the first phase recedes to the background, while the EP-face comes to the fore. Even the 'moderate' anti-Congress-cum-pro-DMK ideologically motivated remarks get further diluted to the level of being generalised social criticism, while continuing to give the impression of operating within the DMK universe by blowing up *karpu*, *maanam* and *veeram* propagandised by the DMK as the core of the Thamizh culture. At the same time, MGR's personal response to the political happenings within the DMK — the intensifying resentment to his increasing importance and the power struggle in general — becomes very specific and pointed, particularly after the sudden demise of Anna. The bi-focal identity of MGR and his films is thus carried on in this phase also, and the tactexted messages are directed more towards the DMK than towards the Congress. The second phase, as a result, is characterised by a shift from presenting the DMK as MGR's DMK to subtly manipulating the MGR image so as to *equate* MGR to the DMK.

The dynamics of this phase could be illustrated with *Enga Veettu Pillai* wherein MGR re-enunciates *Naadoadi Mannan* in a 'social' narrative context and reiterates the golden rule already announced there.'Through you let the aspirations of the people be fulfilled', the people greet MGR. He assumes messiahship, and with a whip in his

MGR: POLITICS AS CO-TEXT 157

hands, sings: 'If I legislate, and if that materialises, the poor will not suffer...' He implements 'socialism' by doling out loans and bonuses to the workers. The hard way he acquires education exemplifies how the 'knowledge revolution' propounded in *Naadoadi Mannan* could be implemented. And finally, he is acclaimed on behalf of the people of Thamizh Nadu as 'our household darling'. Remarkably, during the 1967 election campaign, the DMK put the title back to the people and asked them to 'vote for your household darling'.

When *Enga Veettu Pillai* was released, the posters and the cut-outs prominently displayed the MGR with a whip in his hands. It was as if he was out to chastise those who caused him injustice. However, *Aayiraththil Oruvan*, released a few months later, took the whip out of the hands of 'our household darling' by depicting him as the renouncer par excellence, who outrightly condemns rebellion. He is 'the one enthroned in the hearts of the poor' yet he declines the offer to lead the country and prefers to spend his whole life 'in creating a healthy human society'. The king symbolising Anna endorses him as the 'one in a thousand in the whole world'. But MGR's off-screen response is a mixture of contradictions. In August 1965 he writes:[6] 'As a *thondan* who does not deviate from the footsteps of Anna, as a servant who does not violate his strategy, I have dedicated myself to serve the party...' While addressing a public meeting on the occasion of the birthday celebration of the Congress leader Kamaraj in the following month, referring to Kamaraj's decision to revoke the controversial *kulak kalvi* plan imposed by his predecessor and vehemently opposed by the DK and the DMK, MGR said:[7] 'Kamarajar wishes to achieve the goals of the *Kazhakam*. It might be delayed. My leader is Kamarajar; my guide is Anna. I will remain a *thondan* who follows Kamarajar...' The obvious contradiction shows that MGR was 'an enigmatic personality. Sources close to him during the period say that his mind was not fully with the DMK... He was a split personality, and he took to the DMK because it was a growing party and the oratory of its leaders impressed the masses... Though not an intellectual, he developed the art of double-think and double-talk. He saw nothing wrong in the apparent contradictions in himself...'[8]

There were also widespread rumours during this time that he would be joining the Congress. MGR put a definite end to all the rumours in his *Naan Aanaiyittaal* (1966): 'I swear by mother! I swear by Thamizh! Whether I am isolated or slain, I will arrest the evil...'

158 ▪ POPULAR CINEMA AND POLITICS IN SOUTH INDIA

The year 1967 is considered as a milestone in the history of MGR, because of two important events: First, he was shot at by his co-actor. There was overwhelming sympathy spontaneously expressed by his fans. It has been pointed out under the discussion on the 'udan pirappu' motif how this deadly event gave a 'blood' dimension to the star–fan relationship. An unexpected fall-out of being shot at was a certain noticeable slur in MGR's speech, which his fans did not mind, as the success of his subsequent films indicates, to the utter dismay of his opponents who hadonce again predicted the end of his era. Second, the DMK won the elections and formed the first non-Congress government in the State (after Independence). Though MGR was convalescing during the election campaign, the poster showing him with a heavy bandage around his neck contributed immensely for the electoral success of the DMK — a clear instance of metal eptical overlapping of politics and what belonged to the private realm. MGR himself entered the fray and was elected to the legislative assembly. The title of the first film released after these epoch-making events tactextually described the people's mandate as the 'Royal Mandate' (*Arasa Kattalai*). The revelry over the electoral victory, however, was short-lived because MGR was not included in the cabinet of ministers. As a compromise, Anna made him the Vice-Chairman of the Small Savings Scheme with a cabinet rank. Through his next film *Kaavalkaaran*, the disappointed MLA MGR passed on the message to the DMK leadership that he would continue to watch over the government.[9] At the same time, he diplomatically shows the government now headed by Anna in a positive light by, for instance, donating the prize money to the Chief Minister's Relief Fund. In *Oli Vilakku*, through the song of a 'newly-wed' gypsy couple, who have had an 'economical' and 'self-respect wedding' he would laud several pet welfare schemes of Anna such as family planning, *padi arisi*[10] (one measure of rice for a rupee), and huts-to-concrete housing. In the same breath, however, the diplomatic MGR incorporates sequences, which amount to an action-replay of the spontaneous response of his fans when he was shot at the previous year. While trying to save a child from fire, as the story goes, MGR is injured, and the people make collective prayers to Murugan offering to sacrifice their own lives in exchange for his speedy recovery. Once healed, MGR gratefully acknowledges the mass sympathy: 'People's love has healed all my wounds both in the body and in the heart, and cleansed me.'

MGR: POLITICS AS CO-TEXT ▰ 159

The untimely death of Anna in 1969 gave MGR the opportunity to play the king-maker role. MGR supported Karunanidhi in the tussle for the chief-ministership, whereas Karunanidhi, once he became the chief minister, did not include MGR in his cabinet. As a compromise, he was offered the party treasurership instead. With this, the cold war between Karunanidhi and MGR slowly but definitely comes to the fore. The films released after the death of Anna have the following features:

- The tactexted attacks on the DMK leadership and the government headed by Karunanidhi are *more* vocal and pointed. The tone of these on-screen criticisms syncs with his off-screen comments, augmented further by the accusations of rampant corruption by the veteran Congress leader-cum-former chief minister Kamaraj.
- The vacuum created in the off-screen politics by the absence of Anna is filled on-screen by *personifying* the DMK as MGR. Though this dynamics of equating MGR and the DMK is detectable throughout the second phase, it gets more intense and prominent after Anna's demise.
- The revival of Anna's memory becomes an important political motif. It has been earlier pointed out that MGR tried to *replace* Anna while he was alive by projecting him as the most eligible person to lead the DMK. Now that Anna is no more, MGR makes a conscious attempt to appropriate and *own* Anna by quoting and iconising him, and thus he persuasively presents him as the 'legitimate' heir to Anna, if not as an incarnation of Anna.
- Through a well-orchestrated manoeuvring of the octa–motifs, MGR convincingly projects his saviour image *independently of the DMK*, as if saying that even if there were no DMK, he would be the ideally fit person to be the leader of the Thamizhs.

These features are observable in *Adimai Penn*, which, to start with, is very vociferous in attacking the Karunanidhi government. 'The world laughs at you', sings MGR, 'seeing your actions, even your shadow hates you...' The function of panoptic surveillance comes out strongly, when he admonishes Karunanidhi, 'Don't cheat; don't get deceived... Even the darkness has the eyes to see; the walls have ears to hear; and they wait quietly till an opportune moment comes, when they reveal it'.Concurrent to the critical comments is the attempt to present MGR

160 POPULAR CINEMA AND POLITICS IN SOUTH INDIA

as the personification of the DMK. MGR's fiancée who teaches him to worship 'the rising sun, our god', later equates him to the sun: 'You're the one who won over time, you're the one who became the epic… In working tirelessly, *you're the sun…*'

Nam Naadu, the second of the two films released in 1969, is set in a municipal level power struggle, a micro-model of the State-level macro politiking; thus, the film naturally lends itself to critique the Karunanidhi government and paints a parallel MGR government. Echoing the allegations against Karunanidhi now the chief minister and earlier the minister for public works, the villain swindles public money and is ready to kill anyone who is suspected of betraying him. He and his clique are decried as 'selfish tigers, hounding dogs, poisonous viruses, venomous snakes…' and 'to end their atrocities, to challenge all these, for our country to prosper, a genuine peoples' servant is needed'. Even as these words are uttered in a directorial voice over, MGR appears on screen reading a book with portraits of Gandhi and Anna on front and back covers respectively. In a montage of mini-narratives that follows, he smashes a pickpocket, saves a girl from eve-teasers, prevents children from eating unhygienic food sold on the street and gives money to the poor old vendor to do an alternative job, saves an old lady from traffic congestion and makes sure she safely gets into the bus, and demands a rich man to follow the queue to get ration from a shop. As a clerk, the upright MGR chides the chief accountant who gets a bribe, 'You who should be an example to others doing like this… what justice is this?' and warns him that 'getting a bribe is a crime according to law'. At the very outset, therefore, the film contrasts Karunanidhi and MGR, and presents the latter as clean, justice-conscious and concerned of the poor, the qualities which make him the most desirable, most popular leader. Witnessing his commitment and courage, for example, a man exclaims: 'It is enough even if there is one person like him in every village, our country will be okay'. The slum-dwellers plead with him to contest in the election: 'You are doing so much for us from outside (*paadupadureenga*), the same thing why don't you do from inside?' and they are confident, 'Only if you win, our sufferings will come to an end.' When their *vaaththiyaar* is elected, people celebrate that as their victory:

> The sun has risen, darkness has disappeared,
> history is changing; now on, everything will be alright

On his part, the newly-elected MGR instructs his assistant, 'to issue a notice to surrender, with proper accounts, the many lakhs of rupees collected from the people by deceit'. Since he assumed office, 'the time has changed'.

The use of octa-motifs in *Nam Naadu* is noteworthy. MGR is very affectionate to children, and advises them in a song to 'laugh like a flower, and live like *Kural*'. His devotion to Thamizh goes a step further when he entreats them to 'protect our language, considering it like our eyes'. He attributes all such wonderful thoughts to the 'Gandhi of *Thennadu*' (meaning, the Gandhi of South India), an epithet for Anna. The process of subalternising is effectively employed, starting from his identification with the poor to a street coconut vendor from the slum falling in love with him. Synonymisation of cinelitic and on-screen realms is achieved by making the poor, slum people simulate the fans, especially the constant use of the term *vaaththiyaar* to refer to their 'redeemer' whom they venerate as 'god'. Like in any MGR-starrer, his body is fetishised: the girl as soon as she knows that MGR is in love with her, she dances in the rain singing, she is 'fortunate to obtain him', and describes him as 'the beauty having a body like gold'.

The most interesting feature of *Nam Naadu* is the intriguing twist in the plot which interprets the politics of Anna–MGR–Karunanidhi triangular relationship. The person whom MGR's *annaa* (meaning, 'elder brother') keeps in high esteem is in fact a criminal. Unfortunately, *annaa* misunderstands him and sends him out of home because he dared to challenge the villain (whom he respects on par with god). Only when he overhears his plan to hoodwink and trap him, he realises how evil he (Karunanidhi) is and how innocent his *thampi* (MGR) is. The brothers reunite, whereas the villain and his gang are handed over to legal course of action. The message is that MGR is the rightful heir to Anna, and Karunanidhi actually is an outsider — an enemy, in fact — who does not belong to the 'house' of Anna.

The film reveals the political agenda MGR is contemplating, and presages a kind of 'road-map' for his imminent real politiking: he is disenchanted with the Karunanidhi regime, on the one hand, because corruption is rampant, and as the treasurer of the party he is going to ask Karunanidhi for accounts; on the other hand, he is unhappy because basic amenities like drinking water are not available to the poor, evils such as drinking have become a serious social menace, and

162 ▪ POPULAR CINEMA AND POLITICS IN SOUTH INDIA

as an 'aezhai pangaalan' ('partaker of the poor') he is going to voice his concern over these issues. He believes that the people are with him, and is prepared to contest in the elections and stake his claim for the highest office/s.

As if an oracle destined to come true, the intuitive MGR foresees his future: he is sent out of home (= dismissed from the DMK); with the support of the poor he wins the election and comes to power; the schemer Karunanidhi creates insurmountable problems, maligns his name, plays divide-and-rule game, and succeeds in ousting him out of power (= MGR ministry abruptly dismissed by the Centre); but eventually MGR will be the victor. He is, after all, 'the one who accomplishes what he has thought out', as a song in the film goes, he is 'the one who has cultivated boldness in mind'.

In sum, MGR's message in *Nam Naadu* is three-directional: First of all, he sends warning signals to Karunanidhi to mend his ways and not be so arrogant and ungrateful to MGR who in a way connived with him to make him the CM following the demise of Anna. Second, he alleviates the fear and anxiety of his fans who were being subjected to increasing intimidation by the Karunanidhi regime by telling them that if the repressive measures are continued, he would sooner or later take a radical decision in their best interests. Third, he assures the general public that he would voice their issues and concerns and is — like them — painfully aware of the corruption and nepotism that have become the hallmark of the Karunanidhi government.

The DMK swept the polls in March 1971 general elections, and formed the government with a 'brutal' majority. Besides the active State-wide campaign of MGR, the DMK also cashed in on the image of MGR by making Mu Ka Muthu, Karunanidhi's son, act as MGR in the propaganda plays. MGR himself was elected for the second time from the same constituency. The one-and-a-half years that followed the massive victory witnessed unprecedented turbulence within the DMK, and Karunanidhi was accused of corruption and nepotism. Behind the apparently despotic and arrogant Karunanidhi was a Karunanidhi threatened by MGR. So Karunanidhi tried to promote his son Muthu as a hero modelled on MGR. Muthu's resemblance to MGR made the aping easier. Karunanidhi himself scripted and produced *Pillaiyoa Pillai* (Darling Child) for his 'darling child'. As the film was released in July 1972, there was a mushrooming of officially promoted fan clubs, the

'Muththamizh Selvan Mu Ka Muthu Rasigar Mandrams', all over the State. Though the film was a miserable flop at the box-office, official patronage to the Muthu *mandrams* continued, while Karunanidhi took stringent measures to curb the autonomy of the MGR *mandrams*. In some places MGR *mandrams* were dissolved allegedly at the instigation of Karunanidhi. The ardent fans of MGR reacted fiercely, and posters decrying Karunanidhi appeared everywhere with the rhymically worded heading, 'appan adippathu kollaiyoa kollai; makan nadippathu pillaiyoa pillai', meaning, 'The Father Loots — The Son Acts'. All the nine MGR starrers released during this period appropriately reflect and respond to the upheaval.

The 'Anna' DMK Phase

By the time of the split in the DMK, MGR had firmly established himself as the most acceptable alternative to the then DMK leadership by metalepticaly overlapping the screen, private and public realms. The Anna whom he tried to replace during the first phase and to appropriate and own during the second phase is now ceremoniously *re-placed* as the figure-head of his party, the *Anna Thiraavida Munnaetra Kazhakam*. The naming of his party formed in October 1972 as *Anna* DMK (meaning, the DMK of Anna) amounts to saying that the 'DMK' led by MGR is the 'original' DMK founded by Anna, as distinct from the DMK now headed by Karunanidhi. The message thus communicated is that the ADMK is not a new party different from the one founded by Anna, but the same party founded by him, only now liberated from Karunanidhi's illegal possession. MGR's political genius, outwitting all others including Anna, is evident in the way he had engineered the smooth, logically consistent and emotionally convincing metamorphosis of the proto-ADMK (phase-1) to parallel-DMK (phase-2) to Anna-DMK. In a striking correspondence, once MGR was dismissed from the DMK, he constantly referred to the DMK only as 'Karunanidhi katchi' (Karunanidhi's party).[11]

The spontaneous response of the fans of MGR to the dismissal was violent and posed a serious threat to the law and order. In cities like Madurai, even the State machinery was paralysed for a while. The Karunanidhi government came down heavily on the followers of MGR and repressed the agitations. The days that followed witnessed more

164 ■ POPULAR CINEMA AND POLITICS IN SOUTH INDIA

organised processions, rallies and public meetings. It is during these days of agitations MGR's own production *Ulagam Sutrum Vaalipan* was released (May 1973) after a protracted struggle to mobilise sufficient financial resources to produce. The DMK men expected severe criticism of their party in the film and were prepared to disrupt the screenings. A schemer as he was, MGR disappointed them all by ignoring to play their style of politics. Except for a moral or two — 'You should live laughing but don't live in a manner where others laugh at you...'— which might be construed as a mild criticism of Karunanidhi, the film did not reflect the sensational politics of the day. He played his own political cards instead. His was the 'politics of winning by failing to fulfil the expectations' of the foes. With foresight, he addresses cultural-psychologically rooted and politically significant issues.

First, he refutes the allegation that he is aged — therefore, by implication, too old to be popular — by touring around the world in double roles with four young girls. As one of the girls sings, he is the *vaalipan* (young man) 'of golden colour, child's heart, munificent character', 'the divine son who comes as the king'. While the 'vaalipan' MGR feasted the fantasy of women viewers, the 'generous exposure' of the heroines satisfied the male voyeurs. Naturally, the film was a super-hit. Second, he puts a definite full-stop to the controversy over his origins. He comes across not merely as a Thamizh but the saviour of the Thamizhs, especially Thamizh women, and the guardian and ambassador of Thamizh culture and tradition.

Defying speculations that the ADMK would merge with the INC once it weakened the DMK, it contested in and won the by-election for the Dindigul parliamentary constituency in May 1973. Its impressive electoral success in Coimbatore and Pondicherry (February 1974) proved beyond doubt that the ADMK was truly the Anna's DMK. These events are appropriately tactexted, as in *Siriththu Vaazha Vaendum* (November 1974), a victim of the villain extols MGR: 'The might of your ideology (*kolhai*) is greater than the strength of their office (*pathavi*)'. In a song in *Naetru Indru Naalai*, released in the same year, MGR hits at the nepotism of Karunanidhi: 'They talk of people's (*makkal*) welfare, but mean only their sons' (*than makkal*) welfare'. In *Ithaya Kani* the ADMK flag's colours are black and red, and the election symbol twin-leaves are prominently featured. The film starts with the prefacing of Anna's compliment to MGR (said in 1958): 'There was a

MGR: POLITICS AS CO-TEXT   165

fruit on a tree. I was waiting to see in whose lap it would fall. Fortunately it has fallen right on my lap. I have taken that fruit and kept it safely in my heart'. Though this statement does not have anything directly to do with the narrative, it is included primarily to *rekindle* the memory (besides being a justification for the title, which also is not linked to the story, except in a general way). There are also references to event-shappened in his personal life, such as the 1967 shooting, obviously to induce the viewers to refresh their memories of the days of Anna who gave MGR a privileged treatment. Thus, 'rekindling' is a deliberate attempt to present the ADMK as the original DMK.[12] The tone of the film is triumphalistic, as if to inaugurate MGR rule. People promise, as a song goes, unflinching support to 'Anna's way to prosperity', and a character gleefully declares: 'Now everybody is in Anna's party!' His aide gratefully acknowledges that MGR has 'feasted us with dinner on twin-leaves', and the twin-leaves are 'just administration and success in getting rid of corruption'.

The DMK ministry was dismissed in January 1976, and Sarkaria Commission of Enquiry was appointed by the government to look into the corruption charges. Amidst hectic political activities, MGR came out with *Neethikku Thalai Vanangu* (March 1976). In a song sequence in the film, MGR re-enunciates in a somewhat comical manner the important charges that figured in the memorandum submitted to the Governor and later to the President. In another song sequence he masquerades as a mad man and proclaims: 'I may look like a mad man; but I can give treatment even to your grandfather… The time is nearing for your story to end'. At the same time MGR is depicted as an upright person. He sternly warns those who indulge in malpractice: 'I'll handle you, once the opportune moment comes'. Those who are affected by his uprightness grudgingly concede: 'He does not know how to make money. Neither does he allow us to do it'. The naming of a street after Thaalamuththu is illustrative of MGR's attempt to appropriate all that have been celebrated by the DMK. Thaalamuththu was one of the two youths died in prison during the anti-Hindi agitations in 1938–39, whose names the DMK has entered in its annals as the 'first martyrs' for the cause of Thamizh. The role of the temple priest intertextually echoing the villainous priest of *Paraasakthi* of 1952 could be cited as yet another example for appropriating the wealth of the DMK. It is an irony that MGR tries to usurp the work of his arch-rival Karunanidhi

166 ▪ POPULAR CINEMA AND POLITICS IN SOUTH INDIA

himself! Interestingly, the whole narrative is structured to project MGR as a paradigm for 'bowing before justice' and committing oneself to judicial enquiry, which, by implication, means that Karunanidhi has to emulate MGR.

Following the March 1977 parliamentary elections, assembly elections were held in June 1977. The ADMK won and MGR formed the ministry. *Meenava Nanpan* released during this time presents the government as a 'co-redeemer'. Much like its predecessors, this film also rekindles the memory, especially of Anna and the experience of being shot at. 'Let them come face to face, if they have guts', challenges MGR and assures, 'We'll see only victory in Anna's path'.

If *Naadoadi Mannan* announces the good news that the reign of MGR has come, *Mathuraiyai Meetta Sunthara Paandiyan* officially inaugurates his reign. Based on the original story by Agilan, well-known among the Thamizh literati and a winner of Sahitya Akademi Award, produced and directed by MGR himself, and released months after he assumed office as the chief minister, the film is the sum total of all the honorifics bestowed on him. He is 'the god (*paramaathmaa*) who appears wherever injustice is done'. He is 'the great force which unifies the thoughts of the people'. He is the 'nation's star of faith'. He is 'the ideal *thampi*' of Anna, and when he takes up leadership, it is like 'the *dharma* taking up leadership'. He is 'the revolutionary leader who has come to redeem the people from the flood of sufferings'. Though normally there is only one mother to a person, for him 'there are crores of mothers all over the nation'. He is 'the human-god who shows mercy even to the enemies'. MGR on his part swears by the land, 'I will take revenge on those who massacred thousands of my blood-of-my-blood co-borns' (*udan pirappu*). After dedicating himself to the country and its people, he feels he cannot afford 'to worry about imprisonment and torture'. 'Is there any scheming which I have not faced in politics?' he queries. 'Every place is my native land, everyone my relative', he declares, and affirms, 'It is not I who am enthroned. All are of one caste; all are of one race; all are kings of this country'. Finally he promises: 'You have allowed me to be your ruler. But in my thought and action I will remain your *thondan*'.

The title itself, meaning, 'the beautiful Paandiyan who salvaged Mathurai', signifies that MGR the chief minister (the 'Sunthara Paandiyan') has 'salvaged' (by winning in the elections) the 'Paandiya

Kingdom' (Thamizh Nadu) from the DMK (implied). Ironically, MGR who in his first directorial venture *Naadoadi Mannan* ends monarchy and makes democracy flower forth, in his last directorial venture goes back to the 18th century monarchy, even as he assumes office as the democratically elected leader.

Notes

1. See Vijayan (1997: 94–96).
2. The full poem appears in the souvenir to commemorate the victory of *Naadoadi Mannan*. See Narayanan (1981: 506).
3. When Rajaji became the compromise chief minister following the 1952 elections, he revamped the educational system by introducing a novel plan, which was stigmatised by the DK and the DMK as amounting to imposing the caste system through the back-door. According to the plan, the children would attend the customary classroom sessions in the morning and spend the afternoon in learning the traditional family/caste trade. The plan met with a State-level protest, and eventually had to be dropped. Rajaji himself was forced to resign and K. Kamaraj succeeded him in 1954.
4, Narayanan (1994: 248).
5. See *Ithaya Kani*, September 2001, p. 14.
6. *Ithaya Kani*, September 2001, p. 16.
7. Gopanna (1999: 94).
8. Mohandas (1992: 15–16).
9. The term 'kaavalkaaran' has a wide range of meanings, including policeman, watchman, guard, protector, and supervisor. Thus, when MGR declares, 'I swear that I am a *kaavalkaaran*', he implies that he would be doing the function of *panoptic surveillance*, a point which he would articulate more clearly in later films.
10. Anna's *padi arisi* scheme however met with a premature death. It was Karunanidhi who revived it in 2006. From 2011, Jayalalithaa has taken the scheme further to 'price-less rice'(*vilai-illaa arisi*).
11. Ilamathi (1997: 31).
12. Another striking instance of rekindling occurs in *Pallaandu Vaazhha*. In the Hindi original, the thieves will see the statue of Lord Krishna and repent; in the MGR's version Krishna is replaced by Anna.

13

RK: POLITICS AS CONTEXT

Unlike MGR films which smartly co-text with corresponding political events, the films of RK by and large employ the corrupt political system merely as a 'context' for his filmed narratives. This is so at least till the death of MGR in December 1987. His criticisms of the political system and the politicians appear to be politically motivated from 1988, a year marked by chaotic factionalism and frantic political activities caused primarily by the absence of MGR and the impending elections the following year (1989). RK's comments, however, become deliberately political from 1995, again in the context of elections, this time preceding the one in 1996. His political intervention reaches its definite peak when he openly opposed the Paattaali Makkal Katchi (PMK) in 2004 elections. When that proved fatal, he withdrew from politics for good, though treating it as a context of his later narratives.

The imaging of RK's politics could therefore be seen in four phases: the first extends over the major chunk of his acting career from *Apoorva Raagangal* (1975) to the death of MGR; the second covers the period from *Guru Sishyan* (1988) to *Baatshaa* (1995); the third starts with *Muththu* and extends through *Baba* (2002) to the parliamentary elections in 2004; and the fourth phase starts with *Chandramukhi* (2005) and goes through *Enthiran* to the present (2014).

The 'Outside-Outsider' Phase

Party politics during the first phase is treated as an integral part of the overall socio-political system, which is wilfully challenged, defied, toppled and finally conquered and redeemed by the *supra-legal* RK, who positions himself above but outside the system. He comes out as the angry young man — the go-getter, anti-social, subcultural and rugged saviour — showing up strong anti-establishment tendencies, directing his anger against *the system as a whole*. Evidently, the occasional political remarks are very generalised, lacking specificity and focus. Such a 'generalisation', however, is not accidental, but premeditated. He is forced to show himself to transcend partisan boundaries obviously as a tactic not to antagonise and alienate his fans who cut across parties. Thus, he deliberately and consistently projects him as the 'common hero' to his fans irrespective of their political allegiance. He nurtured at the same time certain 'common identity' among his fans by encouraging them to engage themselves in 'collective acts of solidarity' in the cinelitic realm, where his fans were set against Kamal Haasan fans. The difference resulting from the internecine animosity was the foundation on which the respective unique identities of the fans of RK and Kamal rested.

Remarkably, the first phase saw the swift ascendancy of RK from the status of the villain (to Kamal in most of the early films) to the anti-hero in his own right to the *numero uno*, the 'super star'. By mid-1980s RK emerged as the 'style king' too well aware of his popularity among the subaltern Thamizh masses, particularly among the youth, and the saleability of his 'super star' image. It is noteworthy that the metaleptical tactexting during this phase almost exclusively concerned the private and the self-reflexive screen realms interlaced with the octa-motifs. In *Nallavanukku Nallavan*, for example, RK's employer asks him: 'Have you heard of the one who was initially a bus conductor, but later turned out, because of sheer hard work, to be the "super star"?'

The 'Outside-Insider' Phase

Following the death of MGR, there was an intense and acrimonious struggle for succession, resulting in the imposition of the President's rule in the State for a year. The AIADMK eventually split into two major factions headed by Janaki (MGR's wife) and Jayalalithaa. In another development Sivaji left the INC and floated his own party with the hope that he would be able to fill in the vacuum created by MGR's death. In *Guru Sishyan*, released during this year (1988), RK loathes: 'Our Bharath is a country fighting for the chair. Who is going to listen, if I say?' About him, he merrily announces: 'I am a rowdy, lumpen anti-social, unemployed person, and tube-light (meaning "dull-headed")'.

170 ■ POPULAR CINEMA AND POLITICS IN SOUTH INDIA

But that is not the complete RK. He is proud to belong to *kooth-thaadikal*, as in *Raajaa Chinna Roajaa*, because 'it is the *kooththaadikal* who captured the fort (meaning the Fort St George, where the State Assembly is housed)'. He goes further, and projects the image that he is the personification of all the legendary figures of Thamizh cinema: 'I can sing[1] like Bagavathar; I can wield sword like MGR; I can act like Sivaji; I can speak Thamizh like Kalaignar (MK)...' He is all of these 'legends' rolled into one and emerges the 'super star'. No wonder his fiancée proclaims: 'If you ask who the super star is, even a little child would answer...'

In spite of repeated assertions on-screen that he is destined to be in *koattai* (as in *Athisaya Piravi*) RK did not play any role in the elections held in June 1991. The astounding victory of the ADMK headed by Jayalalithaa, his neighbour in Poes Garden, however, effects significant changes in his strategy. First, while he continues to reinforce the image of the angry (young) outsider, he makes sporadic but scathing attacks on party politics and career politicians a regular feature. Second, he offsets the impression of attacking the ADMK rule by 'idolising' MGR and differentiating the corrupt politicians from the good ones. Third, the intense ego-clash between him and his neighbour-turned-chief-minister Jayalalithaa constantly recurs under various guises. Though the tactexted cues alluding to Jayalalithaa are pointed and convincing, he is unsuccessful, when compared to MGR, in attributing altruistic motives to his criticisms. Fourth, at the level of the fan club activities the traditional rivalry of 'Rajini versus Kamal' acquires a definite political slant by steadily *replacing* Kamal Haasan with Jayalalithaa. Fifth, there is a clear dichotomy in his attitude towards politics as manifested in the cinematic and off-screen realms — on-screen, he evinces keen interest in political power; off-screen, he hesitates and endlessly defers reveal-ing his 'plans'. Sixth, by employing his business acumen, he transforms the very uncertainty and self-doubt into a seemingly imminent direct political involvement, and thus effectively hooking the viewers, more specifically his fans, for repeat viewings. Finally, the effort to keep his fans together by creating an impression of transcending political parties is further strengthened by flattering and romanticising the common subcultural features between them and their 'super star'.

Many of these features are evident as early as June 1992 in *Annaamalai*. RK warns the chief minister Jayalalithaa: 'I mind my own business and keep to my own quiet way; don't drag me into *vampu*. If you do, I'll do what I've said and what I've not said'. As the *supra-legal* guardian, he insists: 'There are thousand ways to make money; do not use the "holy politics" for that'. It should be noted that the Jayalalithaa government was accused of corruption and high handedness from the very first year onwards.

Best remembered for its popular USP, 'If I say once, it is like saying a hundred times', *Baatshaa* (January 1995) is an affirmation of RK's (and his fans') subcultural characteristics: With a 'magnet in his name' (*kaantham*, referring to Rajini '*kanth*'), 'he is the king of the kingdom of (bad) odour and sweat…'

The 'Inside-Insider' Phase

While RK had largely confined his politics to the cinematic realm during the first two phases, he was in a way 'conscripted' into direct politics by circumstances. RK willingly yielded to this and apparently liked being in the limelight accruing out of the newly accorded political status of being the 'saviour of TN'. In fact, he not merely liked being in the 'political limelight', but saw the business potential of it, and shrewdly exploited it to market his films by playing 'saviour' during the release-time of his films.

Muththu (October 1995) is a case in point. Foreshadowing its release were a series of sensational events triggered off by RK's challenge to Jayalalithaa (April 1995), and as the general elections due the next year were fast approaching, the excited fans expected him to announce his new party any day. It is in this context *Muththu* was strategically positioned as RK's response. Amidst embraces, kisses and pelvic thrusts in a duet sequence, RK appears much like a career politician in full white for a couple of shots, and reveals the 'answer' to the question tormenting his fans:

> 'What party is our party?'
> 'Our party is the party of *Kaaman* (god of love).'

Tactexting the ego-clash between him and Jayalalithaa is more conspicuous and blatant, especially in the stage-'duel' sequence in which he disparages her as a 'chinna ponnu' (literally, 'small girl') who does not know what she talks. He, on the other hand, is the 'owner of this land', the one destined 'to rule this land'. But he opts to be 'a servant

172 ◼ POPULAR CINEMA AND POLITICS IN SOUTH INDIA

to all, always'. He proves that he is a cut above the rest: 'He is not like us. His route is different'.

If *Muththu* was a pre-election hit, *Arunaachalam* was a post-election success. As predicted, the anti-Jayalalithaa wave that swept the state unseated her. Attributing the humiliating electoral debacle of the ADMK to the 'divinely' intervention of RK and their hard work, RK's fans started feeling that they were not properly honoured and rewarded by the DMK once it came to power. *Arunaachalam*, released during this time (April 1997), is an attempt to rejuvenate the spirit of his fans, and to pass on the message that he cannot be taken for a ride because now he knows the nitty-gritty of politiking.

Meanwhile, India had to face another round of general elections in 1998 (March). In the thick of the moment he left for Singapore and on his return he gave an interview on Sun TV (February), assuring the people that M. Karunanidhi would step down from the chief-ministership on his own, if the bomb blasts were to continue.[2] The results, however, came as a rude shock to RK and the DMK alliance, with the ADMK alliance absolutely sweeping the polls.

Padaiyappaa (meaning, 'the one who has an army'), released during this time (1999 April) could be said to be the fictionalised program-matic statement of RK, presenting a summary of the rivalry between him and Jayalalithaa, and asserting that he still has the 'army' (of fans) intact (even after the humiliating defeat in 1998).With the oft-repeated, 'My way is a unique way; don't provoke me' as the USP and, 'There is no history of a man excessively ambitious and a woman excessively angry having lived well' as the central message, *Padaiyappaa* is the culmination of RK's version of gender politics manifested in films such as *Maappillai* and *Mannan*. There are pointed cues which enable the viewers identify the villain Neelaampari with Jayalalithaa. The most obvious one is the scene of RK going to meet Neelaampari in her house. Before he comes, she gets all the chairs except the one on which she is seated removed, thus forcing RK to stand in her presence (while she is seated). This scene is clearly a cinematised replay of the phenomenon frequently observable in public functions and meetings, particularly of the ADMK, in which Jayalalithaa (as the chief minister) would take part. Regarding his political entry, if a song pleads with him to 'take a decision', yet another song gives a romantic twist to the much-awaited political decision: 'In the election of love, with cot as the election symbol, may you win and live long!'

The most spectacular gain RK has made during this 'inside-insider' phase concerns the huge profits he reaped by brilliantly positioning his films across his political interventions stretched over five years, making them super hits. So much so he had to float exclusive 'trusts' for films such as *Arunaachalam* and *Padaiyappaa* to avoid income tax problems.

It is a different story with *Baba*. The very timing of the announcement about the film in the thick of a sensationalised political climate thanks to Andipatti by-election, coupled with the news that RK himself has scripted it gave rise to the expectation that he was going to 'reveal his mind'. But the film, released amidst fanfare and hype, controversies and legal disputes turned out finally to be a 'film for ladies and children'[3] because of a curious mix of spirituality and politics peculiar to 'Bhagwan Rajini',[4] though, paradoxically, it had everything typical of RK.

In many respects *Baba* is the culmination of RK's version of the politicisation of spiritualism or the spiritualisation of politics. His fans, ironically, have rejected outright his way of mixing politics and spiritualism — both on and off-screen.[5] The reason is two-fold. On the one hand, the super star's fans would like 'their god' to change the system by his own power, not through the agency of some extraneous power sources like black magic! As a corollary, RK has probably failed to take cognisance of the fact that his own 'economy of salvation' does not (or need not) sync with that of his fans. Afterall, what is meaningful to RK the multi-millionaire need not make any sense to the fans struggling to make both ends meet!

Regarding his political involvement, RK evinces for the first time 'withdrawal symptoms' when he dispassionately states: 'It is not necessary that we should directly come to power and do good to the people; it is enough if through us some good person comes to power'.

It is noteworthy that RK's tactexting strategy in this phase, pertaining particularly to *Padaiyappaa* and *Baba*, is that all his political references concern the recent, not the current, happenings.[6] This kind of 'lagged tactexting' helps RK in two ways. First, by evoking certain curiosity in the fans as to the 'hidden' political 'message' of their super star, it makes the film 'a much-talked-about' one,[7] and, thanks to the discussions in the cinelitic realm, the entertainment becomes more engaging. Second, by confining the criticism to the *previous* regime, RK makes sure that he does not earn the wrath of the ruling party, if not enjoy its protection. But in the realm of real politiking, the lagged tactexting only ends up in putting the fans in a dilemma as to whom they should

174 ■ POPULAR CINEMA AND POLITICS IN SOUTH INDIA

identify themselves with: the general public who by and large are critical of the incumbent or their super star who is critical of the former ruling but presently the opposition party, and by doing thus remain out of sync with the predominant mood of the public.

The 'Inside-Outsider' Phase

While people rejected *Baba* (and its politics), they received *Chandramukhi* well. A typical 'masala' film, it relies more heavily on RK's comedy than action, with RK pairing with the popular comedian Vadivel; and Jothika's performance as Chandramukhi[8] is also critically acclaimed as a great asset to the film.

Though apparently with a-political contents and strategy, somewhat echoing MGR's *Ulagam Sutrum Vaalipan*, *Chandramukhi* does in fact have some key politically-loaded motifs and techniques of an RK starrer: RK is an orphan; he returns from the US (the outsider); he is a professional psychiatrist (appropriating education); he successfully solves the problem (the saviour); though he is obviously rich, he gets married to the servant's daughter (who is also a house-maid), and probably settles down in Thamizh Nadu.

The astounding success of *Chandramukhi* immediately after the 2004 political debacle makes it clear that though people have rejected RK's way of dabbling into politics they still accept him as a super star. Realising this, RK self-silenced his 'voice' during 2006 assembly elections under the pretext of being busy with shooting. His next film, a typical Shankar film[9] with a narrative style resembling his *Mudhalvan*, was designed ingeniously to capitalise on the huge image of RK. The film was deliberately baptised *Sivaji*, an eponymous title but it could also mean the thespian actor Sivaji or the great Sivaji of Maharashtra (RK has his roots in Maharashtra) or RK himself (his original name is Sivaji). Further still, the protagonist Sivaji poses in the second half as M G R (avishankar), implying that RK 'contains' both Sivaji and MGR!

But for media hype, the film was very much reminiscent of the 1980s role of RK, i.e., 'the angry young man', with a run-of-the-mill story line of the 'victim-turned-villain-turned-victor'. Politically, in consonance with the film's business that is global, the film speaks the language of the neo-Indian IT/corporates generation, employing concepts characteristic of this class, such as, NRI, the US-returned, software systems architect, education as a corporate endeavour, corrupt system unfavourable to corporate climate, black money, Swiss bank, etc.[10] In the same breath it also accommodates the Thamizh sentiments, from giving pure Thamizh names such as Thamizh Chelvi, Chezhiyan and Arivu to RK looking for a chaste, tradition-bound but fair-complexioned and beautiful[11] girl with a social status, as per male norms, below his (but not poor). It is noteworthy how RK tries to win over the 'traditional' girl and her conservative parents through 'non-traditional', typically Western, ways, such as the sequence of 'vaanga pazhakalaam' ('come, let us get acquainted'). This precisely exemplifies the double standards and the schizophrenic streaks of the neo–Indian IT class who expect their 'dream girls' to be moulded on the values of Thamizh/Indian culture and tradition but on their part would adopt a typical American/Western life-style without any prick of conscience.

While RK typifies the values of the 'yuppies', the very narrative structure of the film, however, lends itself to make a delicate balance between the rural, rustic fans eating *mann soaru*[12] as a *vaenduthal* (promise) to gods to make 'their God's' film a hit and the neo-globalised post-modern fans who visit multiplexes as one among many weekend activities to satiate their obsession with thrill and variety. The balance is somewhat upset in his next film *Kuselan* by the way the fans are differentially portrayed privileging one class over another.

Kuselan, the story of the relationship between a famous hero and his childhood friend who is poor, is an adaptation of a Malayalam film, but avariciously redesigned to exploit the refurbished super star image of RK and the now expanded global market. Thus, if in the original version the 'hero' only plays a cameo role, in the Thamizh version RK is everything, so much so that the film was promoted as the 'real' story of RK. In fact, almost everything of RK finds a place in the film, starting with adulations bordering on fetishising him: the whole country knows that 'it is the super star's breath that is blissful'. He is 'a man of simplicity and that simplicity is his strength'. The fan behaviour perceived by the general public as a social nuisance is sanctified through a song: 'When the super star appears on screen, whistle sound tears the sky off; the fan crowd will shower milk and honey over the banner and sing his praises'. 'The army of Padaiyappaa is lined up all over the world', the song continues, 'He is the only king who rules over the hearts of people'.

176 ■ POPULAR CINEMA AND POLITICS IN SOUTH INDIA

It may be true that RK 'rules over the hearts' but it is not a sufficient condition to ensure the success of a film. The most pivotal question the fans ask is: what place *does he give* for them in his heart? The following observations could be made in this regard:

First, the fans of any star normally adore him, as we have discussed earlier under psycho-political mapping of cinemen on, because they see themselves in him on screen. In *Kuselan*, interestingly, they themselves are on screen besides their hero, and this unique storyline greatly modifies the viewing experience. A carefully crafted screenplay could have offered the fans a doubly pleasurable viewing by enabling them to parasocially interact with the hero, while identifying themselves with them as portrayed on-screen. Unfortunately in *Kuselan*, while RK has a distinct identity of a 'super god' placed at an inaccessible distance (the whole shooting area is cordoned off and RK is given a high 'z-category' police protection), the fans thronging to have a *darshan* of him are seen as a nuisance and constantly pushed out of the fence. The separation is made legal, and any violation is viewed as a legally punishable trespassing. Such an on-screen depiction of the discordant, alienating star–fan relationship obviously cannot facilitate the fan-viewers to identify themselves with RK; rather they would spontaneously identify with the fans portrayed.

Second, the fans have every reason to disapprove how they are callously and casually lumpenised with scant respect for their human dignity. For most fans, their life-time ambition after all is to have a glimpse of their super star, and if possible to meet him directly and have a photograph[13] with him. Attempts to realise this rather naive, ardent desire are not only made arduous and hazardous but also interpreted as a law-and-order problem created by an unruly mob, and repeatedly lathi-charged. Fans who dare to sneak into the security zone are manhandled by the police, while their god does not do anything to reach out to them, to save them from the brutal police force; instead, sadly, he only 'pities' them. In the process, RK betrays that his view of fans, ironically, is no different from the elites' stereotyping. As a result, viewing *Kuselan* becomes a humiliating and bitter rather than a pleasurable experience.

Third, the fans are very demanding and in as much as the star is everything, including god, to them, they expect him to accord them a prime place in his personal universe as well. But *Kuselan* discriminates fans into two opposing categories, viz., the fair-skinned, foreign fans who 'fly down to meet him' and the dark-skinned (the very complexion of RK himself), local/Thamizh fans who are a nuisance and a threat to his security, and privileges the former over the latter. In sharp contrast to the Japanese fans who are accorded a red carpet welcome and shown excessive hospitality, only a few representatives of the local fans are let in, that too after a prolonged struggle. It is indeed very revealing that gypsy fans are chosen for this purpose. Their representatives give him a memorandum stating that no big star has donned a gypsy role after MGR, and since RK has fans all over the world, the whole world will respect them, if he acts as a gypsy. Through this sequence *Kuselan* affirms two things: that RK's fandom is spread world-wide, and that RK is the heir to MGR.

Conversely, the realistic and vivid portrayal of fandom and the overall narrative context in which the fans are placed in *Kuselan*, in fact amounts to an unintentional deconstruction of the fan behaviour rather than glamourising it. The fan witnesses on the larger-than-life-size screen an authentic mirroring of the humiliating treatment meted out to him, paradoxically by his own god who practises double standards: singing as praiseworthy of the fan behaviour in theatre premises (where only his image is present) but letting the police beat them up when their behaviour amounts to interference with his work at the shooting spot (where he is physically present)![14] The contrast is too stark to swallow, and the film is destined to be a flop. Obviously, it is too presumptuous to expect the fans to pay for watching how they are insulted right under the nose of their saviour!

Physically having crossed 60, politically having hit the rock bottom, and professionally having given a mega flop, RK was in a critical juncture to prove himself the super star; he did prove it, though with the backing of many big names,[15] as demonstrated in the production of his high-profile *Enthiran*.

A poor Kodambakkam imitation of Hollywood science fiction, half-baked by Shankar who is enamoured of VFX, *Enthiran* alluded not only to RK's popular punch dialogues and films but also to the hits of Aishwarya Rai and Shankar.[16]

Set in a sophisticated pan-Indian, sanskritised cultural milieu, and speaking the language of the global, neo-Indian audience akin to *Sivaji*'s, *Enthiran* in effect is a grand narrative that feels comfortable

178 ▪ POPULAR CINEMA AND POLITICS IN SOUTH INDIA

with references to Kargil war (the robot itself is made to be used in the military), Carnatic music, Seetha of Ramayana, and the Rig Veda but is intolerant of little narratives. A striking example is RK's bizarre reaction to the noisy celebration of the *Amman* festival in a slum — he gets so angry that he runs hysterically to break the mic sets! It is indeed an irony that the subaltern culture celebrated by 'RK-the-*aatoakaaran*' is now condemned by 'RK-the-Vaseekaran'![17]

The innovation in *Enthiran*, however, is the introduction of the android robot who turns into a villain (the 'villainesque'[18]) as a buffer between the positive protagonist (who is patriotic and committed to his research and country's security) and the antagonist (who is ready to betray his country), and RK playing double roles of the hero and the 'villainesque'. But unlike his earlier films, the system's RK (the hero) finally triumphs over the anti-system's, 'villainesque' RK whose misdemeanours the hero condones by passing the blame to humans ('you have learnt to violate the law only from human beings...') and thus making the story also politically correct.[19]

Enthiran, in short, tries to capitalise on the image of Rajini built over the years thanks to his subaltern fans by doing a world-wide business,[20] but it fails, in the kind of story it tells, to give any worthwhile status and satisfaction to the very subaltern fans, and by dismantling the *Enthiran* RK, any traces of commonality between RK and his fans are erased for good.

The process of distancing RK's fans from RK reaches its pinnacle in his next film *Koachadaiyaan*. Hyped up ad nauseam because it is a debut directorial venture of RK's daughter, the pathetically amateurish 'motion capture' technology which, though fetched her an award for technical innovation[21] even before the film could hit the screens, took away the very life and soul of Rajini from 'Rajini image', reducing its appeal in effect to a degree far lesser than that of a conventional cartoon character. The historical setting of the narrative and the archaic style of spoken language further alienated the fans, though the storyline in fact had sufficient scope to be shaped into a typical RK starrer, had it been a live-action film. Desperate to salvage his image and revive the spirit of his heartbroken fans, RK swiftly announced his next project *Lingaa*, and since then he has been in the news, partly because of the BJP's move to persuade him to embrace its banner, and partly because of media's over-indulgence.

Even as the 'inside-outsider' phase moves towards the denouement (or yet to reach the climax?) one feature that stands out is the fact that RK has definitely lost interest in playing god in Thamizh Nadu politics or he has got convinced that he would not be able to effectively play god in politics, and his sole preoccupation has been with profitably selling himself as an actor before the industry labels him 'too old' or 'too sickly'. Being aware that in an era of globalisation, marketing cinema also has to go global, RK has started addressing a global/overseas audience; consequently, his fan base has shifted from the rural, illiterate to the urban, elite; and the more global he goes in marketing, the greater is the alienation from his original fans. To put it differently, till the global market expands enough to make the 'local' Thamizh Nadu market insignificant, RK would continue to keep his 'old school' fans in good humour.[22] That is the attitude he betrayed in the function on 13 December 2012 to mark his birthday: even as he sentimentalised the religious sacrifices of his fans for his recovery when he was sick, the shouting of an ardent *devotee*, 'neenga vaanga thalaivaa' (you come, leader) — as a spontaneous intervention to RK's sympathising with the political leaders, who cannot do any good even if they want, said RK, because 'the system is such' — went unheeded, nay unnoticed, by his 'god'. Quite understandably so.

Notes

1. In fact, in *Mannan* RK tried his hand in singing. The song 'Adikkithu Kuliru' was sung by him.
2. *India Today* (Thamizh), dated 4 March 1998, p. 35.
3. That was the comment of a fan as we were coming out of the cinema hall after seeing the film on the second day of its release in Theatre Albert, Chennai. Most of the fans across the state felt the same way, and as a consequence, promotional attempts were made to reposition the film as meant for men as well. For example, in the advertisement in *Thina Thanthi*, dated 26 August 2002, it is said, 'not only women but all the men also should see the film'.
4. That is the headline to a story in *Outlook* published during the time of release of *Baba*. See http://www.outlookindia.com/article/Bhagwan-Rajni/216985 (accessed 9 September 2014).

180 ■ POPULAR CINEMA AND POLITICS IN SOUTH INDIA

5. That the on-screen politics-spiritualism mix was rejected by the fans is evidenced by the box-office failure of *Baba*; the rejection of the 'off-screen mix' is obvious from the disheartening response to RK's 'voice' in 2004 parliamentary elections.

6. This is where MGR markedly differs from RK. Unlike RK's, MGR's tactexting, as seen earlier, is a response to live, current politics, making each of his films a political statement. MGR was able to achieve this because he made sure that his screen presence remained ever fresh and up-to-date, without too long a time gap between his films.

7. The general public also is dragged into this puzzle-solving game by the publicity given by the news-starved media, particularly the biweeklies and the weeklies. The resultant excessive hype and the 'engagement' may not always work in favour: in *Padaiyappaa*, they did; in *Baba*, they failed.

8. In fact, the most talked about acting was Jothika's, not RK's. Her acting, particularly the 'laka laka laka' sequence, was imitated by Sathyaraj dressed up like Chandramukhi in the film *Englishkaaran*. Jothika's superb acting does indeed justify her being the eponymous heroine.

9. 'The whole credit goes to Shankar and AVM — I am only an actor', confessed RK in the interview to *Times Now* on the eve of the release of *Sivaji*. 'AVM' referred to by RK was the company that initially produced *Sivaji*; but in the final stages the production 'was made to switch over' to Sun Pictures, a part of Kalanidhi Maran's Sun empire. The Sun empire then wielded enormous power over the entire Thamizh film industry — production, distribution, exhibition, and publicity—because of its unrestrained political influence during the DMK rule. The monopoly reached its zenith in the second half of the DMK regime and remained unchallenge-able till the end of the DMK reign. The suppressed resentment and the simmering anger prevailing in the film industry found a timely outlet when in the 2011 elections the DMK was overthrown. Many filmmakers heaved a sigh of great relief and some openly celebrated the defeat by firing crackers.

10. Anyone who is familiar with Anna Hazare and his team can easily notice that the language of *Sivaji* is like a precursor to Hazare's. It is noteworthy that Shankar's earlier film *Anniyan* also propagates Hazare-style justice based on legendary Manu's jurisprudence. Curiously, many film personalities in Chennai, allegedly indulged in tax evasion and black money, were openly supporting Hazare's fast in August 2011. RK went a step further and lent his wedding hall for Hazare supporters to hold their protest fast on 28 December 2011; senior TNCC leader EVKS Elangovan criticised RK for doing this and alleged that the very wedding hall was built with black money. See all Thamizh newspapers including *Thina Thanthi, Thina Malar* and *Thina Mani* dated 29.12.2011.

RK: POLITICS AS CONTEXT　181

11. In as much as the film accommodates the Thamizh sentiments it *offends* the same as well. For example, it ridicules Angavai and Sangavai (daughters of the legendary donor Pari) by depicting them over-dark, obese and unattractive; they are so 'ugly' that RK runs away in aversion. Worse still, the episode involves Solomon Pappaiya, a much-televised debater and a Thamizh scholar, as the comedian father of the girls.

12. There are several masochistic religious practices such as eating *mann soaru* (eating the food placed on the bare ground), climbing up temple steps on knees, and taking *kaavadi* (carrying the offering to god; there are several types and ways to carry, ranging from the harmless to the gory), which the fans undertake to ensure the success of their hero's films. In the context of *Sivaji*, some RK fans indulged in eating *mann soaru*; when in the interview on *Times Now* (uploaded to *You Tube* on 30 June 2007) RK was asked about this, he replied, 'They are so innocently showering their love on me... It touches me'.

13. Taking a photograph with the star is like a primordial experience because the climactic moment of being with the star is frozen for ever into a relic. For the ramifications of photographing, see Rajanayagam (2004d).

14. As RK becomes more and more global, and withdrawn from politics, the demarcation of boundaries of various realms gets more pronounced, and the metaleptical overlapping keeps shrinking in real life, though in the realm of reel he deliberately blunts and blends boundaries. In real life, for example, the Poes Garden residence is strictly reserved for family, and select friends who are big shots; the farm house on the ECR is so exclusively private, it is said, that even family members cannot have free access; the fan club head-office (housed in the *kalyana mandapam*, itself a commercial enterprise) is cinema–politics interface where RK holds his press-meets, and meets fan club office-bearers and influential fans; shooting spot, especially outdoor, is an interface between private and public realms, where fans are tolerated only as spectators so long as they do not obstruct his duty; theatre premise is the only place open to unrestrained and uninhibited fan activities.

15. *Enthiran*, in fact, involved a whole contingent of top-ranking personalities, including Shankar, A. R. Rahman, erstwhile 'Miss World' Aishwarya Rai, Kalanidhi Maran, Thamizh science fiction writer Sujatha (whose sudden demise when the production was underway also served as an added publicity), many-time award winning lyricist Vairamuthu, cinematographer Rathnavel, art director Sabu Cyril, and editor Antony. With so many 'celebrities' in the cast and crew, the film could have been a success even without RK, though the turnover might not have been to this magnitude.

16. That is another indication that RK is not the sole auteur, and there are other heavyweights as well who are indispensable to price the film so high.

182 ∎ POPULAR CINEMA AND POLITICS IN SOUTH INDIA

The USP is not RK but a 'mega combo of mega banners'. Strikingly, even adulations to RK are very sparse in *Enthiran* unlike a typical RK-starrer.

17. The 'nuisance scene' described in *Enthiran* is not so different from RK's dance in public places for songs such as 'naan aatoakaaran' and 'vanthaendaa paalkaran'. In *Enthiran* no subaltern element is positively highlighted. Sadly, there is no poor at all in the film's universe of discourse. Concerning the process of the double-bodied migrantcy, only elitising happens, not subalternising.

18. 'Villainesque' is a term used here to denote 'the villain played by the hero'. Unlike the anti-hero who is against the unjust system, 'villainesque' plays the villain or plays into the hands of the main villain perpetrating injustice. The negative features of the 'enthiran RK' are a replica of the 1970s' 'villain RK'. It is note-worthy that on the occasion of his birthday celebrations in Chennai on 13 December 2012, RK referred to the popularity his negative roles — Vaettayan in *Chandramukhi*, 'Mottai Boss' in *Sivaji* ('villain-to-villain' role, said RK) and robot Chitti in *Enthiran* — have over the positive ones. In the same line, he said, he had plans to play the 'ultimate villain' in *Raanaa*, a mega project dropped due to his ill-health.

19. Ever since his confrontation with the PMK miscarried, RK has become very conscious of projecting a politically correct image in both real and reel lives. Such an image is a prerequisite to successful global film business today. It would, therefore, be too much to expect RK to risk playing totally negative roles. It might be possible, however, with young stars and newcomers without any political agenda, as for example, Ajith's recent hit *Mangaaththaa*, and debut director Nalan's *Soothu Kavvum* which extol values condemned as evil by mainstream society. Thamizh cinema has indeed come a long way, from 'all-good epic hero' to 'anti-hero' to 'villainesque hero' to 'villain-as-hero'!

20. It is true that the film's transactions involved huge amounts, creating probably a national record, but not all the parties in the deal equitably profited, and, alas, some also met with a loss. The truth came to the fore once the government changed over to the ADMK in May 2011. For example, the Tamil Nadu Theatre Owners' Association dared to lodge a complaint against Sun Pictures, in which they said 'theatre owners had incurred a huge loss after screening *Enthiran* and that many had demanded their deposits back'. See *Times of India*, dated 9 July 2011.

21. The director of the film RK's daughter Soundarya won the NDTV 'Indian of the Year' award for 'technical innovation in film'. See http://movies.ndtv.com/bollywood/ndtv-indian-of-the-year-soundarya-rajinikanth-honoured-for-technical-innovation-in-film-638972 (accessed 11 September 2014).

22. The music video *First Day, First Show* released online as a promo to *Koachadaiyaan* is a case in point. While the lyrics glamourise the hysterical activities of 'classical' fans (such as shouting, whistling, breaking coconut, and firing crackers), the visuals present well-choreographed, stylised dance movements performed for the camera by pretty-looking, urban, sophisticated boys and girls — a depiction that misses the spontaneity, impulsive raw-ness, vitality, the sweat and the dirt of the genuine fans. The video could not become viral; neither did it attract the fans to the theatre to watch *Koachadaiyaan*.

14

CINELATING POLITIKING

Twin Centre Politiking

The foregoing analysis demonstrates that though both MGR and RK have resorted to tactexting, MGR has done it consistently and effectively by identifying himself with a party and treating politics and films as *co-texts*, whereas RK has continued to maintain the image of being an 'outsider' to politics by not openly belonging to any party and reducing politics to be the *context* of his films. This difference between MGR and RK, having far reaching consequences in influencing the voting behaviour by mobilising the electorate in their favour, could be further illustrated by comparing the 'twin-centre' political manoeuvrings of MGR and RK vis-à-vis their respective fans.

Revolving Twin Centre

All the films of MGR/RK are invariably hero-centric, and the same hero-centricity continues also in the cinelitic realm where the fan clubs function as potential political agents. Though both MGR and RK solely depend on the strength of their fan following, MGR has judiciously *actualised* the 'politicisable' potential of the fan clubs, whereas RK's success has not been constant in this regard, as manifested in the lack of enthusiastic response to his political interventions, culminating in his own eventual withdrawal. The single most decisive factor could be traced to the concurrence (or the lack of it) of their respective political identities as projected on-screen with the ones as manifested in the realm of real politiking.

It is true that MGR openly identified himself as a Congress sympathiser till his early thirties, but that was the time when he was struggling in the film industry for survival, playing very minor roles. The scenario changed when he started associating with artistes who were DMK activists or sympathisers. He was seen playing the lead roles, and concomitantly, he definitively gravitated towards the DMK, leading to his joining the party as a member in 1953. From then on, he took pains to show himself, both on-screen and off-screen, as a staunch DMK man, and later when he formed his own party, as the true heir to Anna's DMK. What is amazing is his strategic maintenance of 'revolving twin centres' all through his association with the DMK. The phase-wise observations made made earlier in the book amply illustrate the dynamics of revolving twin-centre politiking of MGR.

During the first phase, he started off at the periphery of the party as a member, and of the film industry as a promising actor. As his fan following grew in size and got institutionalised in the form of a well-knit *mandram* association, he as a smart politician moved towards the centre of the party. By the turn of the 1950s, especially with the run away success of *Naadoadi Mannan*, he was the centre of his own empire at the cinelitic realm, while in the realm of the party politiking he as the 'ithaya kani' of Anna was accorded a central place on par with Anna and M. Karunanidhi. MGR's fan following was very unique in the sense that majority of his male fans were also active DMK grassroots workers, and as such they remained very much at the periphery of the party. Cinematically, he presented his version of the DMK ideology, which in essence amounted to a proto-ADMK ideology, in the universe of which MGR, the embodiment of the subalterns, was the centre.

In the second phase the same phenomenon got strengthened, especially with the overwhelming reception to films such as *Enga Veettu Pillai*. By the end of this phase, MGR had risen to the level of the king-maker within the DMK, and was respected on a par with the chief minister-cum-party president. While the helm of party affairs was marked by an intense rivalry between MGR and Karunanidhi, MGR had taken his fans well-knit as a parallel organisation further away from the DMK headed by Karunanidhi, by his persuasive cinematic presentation of himself as the perfect personification of the DMK. Thus, a superbly laid ground for an impending launch of his party was ready. The logical build-up of these factors resulted in the spectacular third phase. The bifocal identity of MGR maintained through the previous two phases was 'unifocalised' with MGR as the centre of the party affairs while Anna adorned the centre of the party flag, and the

186 ■ POPULAR CINEMA AND POLITICS IN SOUTH INDIA

institutionalised fan clubs kept politically alive thus far got transformed into full-fledged party units.

Two points need to be underscored concerning the twin centre politiking of MGR: First, MGR consistently projected a complex twin identity. In the realm of real politiking, on the one hand, he showed himself to be a committed DMK *thondan*, while demanding and asserting his due share in power; in the cinelitic and cinematic realms, on the other hand, he portrayed himself as the ideal political leader and saviour, while convincing the subaltern viewers that he was just *one among them*. Strangely enough, the MGR, who was always out of sync with the DMK ideology, was not willing to leave the party either. His unwillingness or at least the hesitation to leave the DMK was not only cinematically manifested (as in *Urimai Kural*) but also in real politiking, as evidenced, for example, in the initial *positive* response he gave to the merger initiatives[1] taken by the Janata Party leader Biju Patnaik prior to the parliamentary elections in 1980.

Second, MGR was not a mere 'film actor who *clicked* in politics', as observed by a Thamizh film analyst.[2] He was 'a shrewd politician, socially conscious, who exploited the medium of cinema to drive home his message *to mould* his public, to make them think and change'. In fact, MGR's use of the medium of cinema and politics was highly ingenious. As a *politician who acted in films*, MGR exploited the medium to advance his political career, and his rising political stature guaranteed in turn the success of his films. Not surprisingly, MGR treated politics and cinema on par with each other in the sense that both belonged to 'the world of make-believe'.[3] He maintained, therefore, a delicate and profitable balance between cinema and politics, and when the opportune time came, as sung in one of his films, to 'blow the victory conch', he extended the metaleptical overlapping of both to their virtual merger.

Satellite Twin Centre

The twin centre politiking of RK qualitatively differs from that of MGR. Like MGR, RK enjoys a committed, and to a great extent well organised, fan following centred on him. But unlike MGR, his fans have *yet another centre* when it comes to their political allegiance. Since RK does not explicitly identify himself with any political party — except, may be, his 'hysterical' political stand during 2004 general elections opposing the PMK and supporting the BJP — his fans have to necessarily cut across various parties, both national and regional. This gives rise to 'satellite twin centres' for his fans: RK as one centre in the cinelitic realm, and each fan's political leadership as another centre in the realm of politiking, where RK does not apparently have any role to play. There is, therefore, a clear dichotomy between these two centres. Significantly, though most of RK fans follow different political courses, they remain, as in the case of MGR fans, at the peripheries of their respective parties.

While the enormity of the fan clubs ensures RK comparably huge returns at the box-office, when it comes to real politiking, however, the fans are put in a dilemma as to whom they owe greater allegiance — to RK or to their respective party leaderships. RK himself has been aware of this, and he has always had, as observed in the previous chapter, his eyes intently focused on the box-office, even as his political interventions have been sensationalised by the media.

Models of Cinelation

The difference between MGR and RK could be better explained with the notion of *cinelation*. Cinelation is a process that involves simulating cine constructed archetypes in the realms of fan club (cinelitic) and real politiking, and feeding the cinematic realm back from the politik and the cinelitic. The process, thus, is multi-directional with different degrees of correlation of archetypes among realms. Through metaphorical symbolisation and metonymical iconisation in the screen realm, the archetype of *the good versus the evil* is personified as *the hero versus the villain*, which in turn is 'synonymised' as MGR/RK versus the villain. In the cinelitic realm, the archetypal binary is transferred to the inter-fan-club rivalry centred on the respective stars. In the realm of the real politiking, the cinematically constructed archetype and/or the cinelitic rivalry are/is transferred further as metonymical extensions to the real political personalities at loggerhead with MGR/RK, and further still to the institutional level of the political parties. The degree of political success of MGR/RK depends on the 'degree of correspondence' among the manifold cinelations. When there is a perfect isomorphic correspondence, the political impact also is seen to be the maximum.

Given the peculiar context of Thamizh Nadu where intermingling of cinema and politics has become the norm, at least five models of cinelation could be identified: (*a*) the politician-cum-actor model of

MGR; (*b*) the actor-turned-politician model of Sivaji; (*c*) the star-intervening-politics model of RK; (*d*) the value-added-star model of actors such as Sarath Kumar, Napoleon, Ramarajan, and T. Rajendar; and (*e*) the star-as-campaign-attraction model, most commonly employed by almost all political parties during electioneering.

Isomorphic Cinelation

The MGR model of cinelation is an ideal example for *isomorphism* because of the smoothness of the transference of the archetypal *the good* (hero MGR) *versus the evil* (villain) from one realm to the other. In the cinematic realm, the emotional content of the binary of MGR versus the villain snowballs from film after film by iconising the characters — casting the same actor Nambiar repeatedly in the role of the villain, while MGR always plays MGR. When transferred to the cinelitic realm, the binary takes on the form of the hero MGR versus the 'villain' Sivaji, a binary that is at once political because of the opposing political identities of MGR (DMK) and Sivaji (Congress). The mutual opposition between the DMK and the Congress in the realm of real politiking flows back into the cinelitic inter-*mandram* rivalry, reinforcing and accentuating it. The real politiking is further taken to the cinematic realm in the form of tactexting, and thus rendering the villain a political metaphor. This in turn is transferred to the cinelitic and political realms. The dynamics of cinelation is, therefore, cyclical, with the binary at one realm radicalising and strengthening the other.[4]

But MGR's way of cinelation does not stop with this. He simultaneously extends the cinematic archetype to intra-party rivalry between him and other leaders, particularly Karunanidhi, and expertly sustains a twin-centre politics. The cold war comes to the open after Anna's death and the tactexting increasingly focuses on the intra-party affairs. Consequently, the cinelitic rivalry between MGR and Sivaji mellows down, culminating in the effective replacement of Sivaji by Mu Ka Muthu, officially promoted (by his father-cum-chief minister Karunanidhi). This forms the crucial interface between the DMK versus the Congress and the ADMK versus the DMK. The cumulative effect of the binaries involving personalities such as MGR versus Muthu (cinelitic) and MGR versus Karunanidhi (politik) results in the justification of the institutionalised binary of the ADMK versus the DMK.

CINELATING POLITIKING   189

Though not to the degree of MGR, Vijaykanth could be seen as a contemporary example for (limited) isomorphic cinelation. In the cinematic realm, he has consistently been the angry young man who challenges the corrupt establishment, much in the fashion of RK. In the cinelitic realm his fans had no specific villain, though they were occasionally playing opposite to RK's. In the real politiking Vijayakanth was identified as a pro-DMK hero. The timing of his floating the party when the ADMK was in power, gelled with his anti-establishment, pro-DMK image, and in fact there were speculations that he would ally with the DMK in the election soon to come. When Vijayakanth was steadfast in projecting his party as being an alternative to the well-entrenched ('Dravidian') parties who have been alternately playing the protagonist and the antagonist, the anti-establishment image bolstered his polemics but the pro-DMK image was seen to be haunting. That is where the process of cinelation faltered. There is no concrete personification of a single villain in any of the three realms, and the fuzzy 'anti-establishment' image was not strong enough to subdue two strong villains (Jayalalithaa and Karunanidhi) in real politiking. Now that he has allied with one villain to defeat the 'more evil' villain, 'isomorphism' has got stuck and the future course of action would decide the type of cinelation.

Scrambled Cinelation

The Sivaji model of cinelation is an example for the 'scrambled' cinelation. While in the cinelitic realm Sivaji has a concrete villain in the person of MGR, in the cinematic realm he does not consistently play the positive hero. On the contrary, his roles are variegated, from action hero to anti-hero to sentimentalised family hero. Thus, there is a *lacuna* in personifying the archetype of *the hero versus the villain*. More striking is the 'scramble' characterising the real politiking. As a DMK artiste he shared the same platform with MGR and Anna, whereas as a Congress artiste he was set against them. At the same time, unlike MGR, Sivaji did not project himself as a competitor to other party leaders for positions within the party hierarchy or outside of it (like MLA and MP); thus, unlike MGR, he was not the centre in the political realm. Though he employed his *mandram* as an auxiliary organ of the party, he kept his *mandram* activities, at least till late 1970s, mostly confined to the cinelitic realm. While an incessant and internecine fight

190 POPULAR CINEMA AND POLITICS IN SOUTH INDIA

between his and MGR's *mandrams* kept them politically alive, the real politiking forced him to change colours frequently. He not only traversed through the DMK, the INC, the Congress (O), the unified INC (after Kamaraj's death), the *Thamizhaka Munnaetra Munnani* (TMM), the party which he floated, and Janata Party to political oblivion, but he also had to share the platform, depending on the alliance partners, with foes-turned-friends and criticise friends-turned-foes.

In a curious move, taking the cue from the astounding political success of MGR, Sivaji in fact evinced interest in direct politics and attempted to project him as a political centre. When MGR met with an election debacle in the parliamentary elections in 1980, Sivaji *mandram* jumped into anti-MGR campaign, projecting Sivaji as an alternative to MGR.[5] Within the Congress also, he tried during the early 1980s to present him as the most eligible candidate for the presidentship of the Thamizh Nadu Congress Committee (TNCC), challenging G. Karuppiah Moopanar. The inner-party bickering reached such a height that the *mandram* was planning to unilaterally declare Sivaji as the president. 'The two-day jamboree of his fans... proved the fairly substantial sway he held over the party's mass base. Moreover, the presence of bigwigs like R. Venkataraman, Gundu Rao and R. V. Swaminathan made it appear that they had found a "Trojan horse" to wage their war against Karuppiah Moopanar'.[6] A compromise was struck by making Sivaji a Rajya Sabha MP in 1982.

Sivaji made a more daring attempt during 1988–89, when he, embittered with the party leadership for appointing Moopanar as the TNCC president, broke away from the INC. He floated his own political party, the TMM, hoping to fill in the vacuum created by the death of MGR.[7] He even came up with the propaganda film *En Thamizh En Makkal*, in which he played the role of freedom fighter Vinayagam, the leader of *Engal Thaesa Katchi* ('Our Nation Party'). According to the story, when his party comes to power, he makes his foster son Gandhi Raman (allusion to Rajiv Gandhi, the prime minister) the chief minister. But his son is corrupt, and so the patriotic, 'nationalist' freedom fighter, paradoxically, starts a regional party, the *Thamizh Thaesa Katchi* ('Thamizh Nation Party'). Obviously, the corrupt villain is Rajiv Gandhi, and the patriotic Sivaji is 'worried because the party is going to be torn to pieces in the hands of small boys'. The film also underscores the yeomen service rendered to the INC by his fans: 'When there was none to stick posters for the party, I sent thousands of "my *pillaihal*" (children, i.e., his fans) with paste and bucket in hand'.

The film miserably failed at the box-office; so was the fate of his TMM. He formed an electoral alliance with the Janaki faction of the ADMK. Both the TMM and the ADMK (JR) were thoroughly routed, and the TMM lost deposit in all the constituencies it contested. Heart-broken, Sivaji dissolved his party, joined the Janata Party and remained for a while its president at the state level before he quit active politics.

A perceptive look into the politiking of Sivaji vis-à-vis that of MGR brings to light that MGR's successful, even enviable, political career has served as a paradigm for Sivaji, whose political course takes three different but interrelated directions depending on the then prevailing overall political climate — to compete with MGR, to emulate MGR, and to appropriate MGR. His attempts to compete with MGR were manifested in his open anti-MGR campaign in 1980. At the end of the campaign, he could, however, come nowhere near MGR, as the results of the subsequent assembly election showed. Sivaji could not be MGR's competitor because, by then, MGR had metamorphosed himself as the 'revolutionary leader' and full-fledged politician, whereas Sivaji was seen primarily as an actor in support of the INC.

Incidentally, the whole of the seventies prior to the formation of the INC-DMK alliance in 1979 witnessed a hand in glove political manoeuvrings of the INC and the ADMK. During this time Sivaji as a Congress (O) activist had opposed the DMK and the ADMK, had opposed, joined hands with and then merged with the INC; as an INC activist, he had shared platforms with the ADMK, and later with the DMK. Thus, Sivaji did not have a credible political standing to rise to the level of an alternative to MGR. Significantly, MGR himself ignored Sivaji (already from the late 1960s onwards) at the cinelitic and cinematic realms and focussed exclusively on Karunanidhi and his son.

Just as the MGR-factor did not work out in the 1980 parliamentary election, publicised as a contest between the 'national' victim Indira Gandhi (victimised by the Janata Party-led government at the Centre) who only could provide a stable government and the coalition of 'vil-lains' who could not rule for a full term, the Sivaji-factor receded to the background as insignificant in the subsequent assembly election, picturised as a struggle between the 'state-level' victim MGR (whose government was dismissed by Indira Gandhi as the prime minister) and the 'villains' Karunanidhi (who induced the Centre to dismiss the MGR government) and the INC (of which Sivaji was a member).

192 ◼ POPULAR CINEMA AND POLITICS IN SOUTH INDIA

Realising that his versatile acting alone would not suffice to subsume all other stronger and deep-rooted political forces, Sivaji turned his attention to the intra-party politiking, trying to assert his eligibility over others for the TNCC presidentship. In this, he attempted to emulate MGR, but there were (and are) too many factions, and the contestants for the post were indeed too numerous. Besides, persons like Moopanar were too influential with the party high-command, and the 'uproar' Sivaji made through his *mandram* was effectively silenced by master tacticians, solacing him in return with an MP post, however.

Following the death of MGR and the consequent split in the ADMK, Sivaji dramatically walked out of the INC, much in the fashion of MGR who left the DMK, to float his own party. He earnestly believed that he could 'appropriate' the MGR legacy, because he was also, like MGR, an *actor*. The election outcome proved that all his calculations were wrong.

First of all, Sivaji made the strategic mistake of aligning with the wrong faction of the ADMK. The election scenario was marked by utter chaos within the ADMK with at least three different groups pitted against one another claiming the MGR legacy — the Jayalalithaa faction, the Janaki faction, and the one led by Nedunchezhiyan, the number two in MGR's cabinet — and none of them was allowed by the election commission to contest on the twin-leaves symbol. Of the three faction leaders, Jayalalithaa, however, was widely acknowledged as the 'charismatic' political 'heir' to MGR because of her role as the propaganda secretary of the party while MGR was alive. Janaki, who had remained a 'housewife' till MGR's death, was suddenly dragged into the seat of chief-ministership in an attempt to pre-empt Jayalalithaa. While Jayalalithaa was trying to woo the INC to be an alliance partner, Janaki in a bizarre move approached the DMK itself to strike a deal, which the DMK promptly turned down. Only after the DMK closed its doors, Janaki and Sivaji could arrive at an electoral understanding.

Second, the TNCC under the leadership of Moopanar renewed its slogan, 'let us live with *maanam*', meaning, that the INC would contest on its own strength, and the then prime minister-cum-party president Rajiv Gandhi, made thirteen visits to Thamizh Nadu. The TNCC with its promise of 'the return of the golden rule of Kamaraj' temporarily transcended the factionalism that used to plaque the party, and emerged as a strong competitor to the DMK. The contest in effect was among Karunanidhi, Moopanar and Jayalalithaa, and all the others were in fact fighting a losing battle. The maximum Sivaji could achieve in this election was to eat a bit into the votes of the INC, and thus contributing in some constituencies to a nominal increase in the margin of victory for the DMK.

Third, Sivaji's leaving the INC was ill-timed. By the time of this election, most of his fans, being in their forties and fifties, had already 'settled' in life and many of his 'pillaihal' had become 'thaaththaa-s' (grandpas)! Besides, a few of them in fact had the opportunity to savour political power as MLAs and MPs. The younger generation on the contrary had their younger stars like RK and Kamal Haasan, and Sivaji himself had by then started *co-starring* with them. Thus, when Sivaji launched his party banking on the strength of his *mandram*, his *mandram* was bereft of the youth and the vigour — 'the *pillaihal* with paste and bucket in hand' — necessary for a new party to take roots and spread wings.

Finally, Sivaji failed to name the correct enemy. In his propaganda film he named Rajiv Gandhi as his enemy, whereas all along he was leading a crusade against Moopanar. Given the fact that when it comes to voting, the people of Thamizh Nadu consistently apply, as will be evident in the chapter to follow, two different sets of norms, one for the parliament and another for the assembly, depicting Rajiv Gandhi as the villain was indeed inappropriate; no wonder then that the film flopped. But for this single overtly propaganda film, none of his regular films during this period tactexted even faintly the concurrent political happenings. MGR in a striking contrast had never made any separate propaganda film but made all his regular films as *his* propaganda films.[8]

Isolated Cinelation

The RK's 'star-intervening-politics' model is an example for partially effective *isolated* cinelation. The impact is only partial because the inter-connectivity of the realms is imperfect. During the 'outside-outsider' phase there is a harmonious link between the cinematic and the cinelitic realms, but the political realm remains isolated (or only indirectly linked) by not naming the 'villain'. As in the case of MGR, RK also iconises the archetypal binary of the hero versus villain as RK versus the villain by making Radha Ravi or Raguvaran repeatedly play the villain against RK. In the cinelitic realm the binary takes on the

194 ■ POPULAR CINEMA AND POLITICS IN SOUTH INDIA

form of RK versus the 'villain' Kamal. It is to be emphasised that this phase marks the transition of RK from villain to anti-hero, the angry young man, who is out to take revenge on the unjust persons and set the system right.

In the cinematic realm during the second 'outside-insider' phase, the anti-establishment focus continues, while he depicts himself as the most appropriate political alternative. This phase has a concrete political villain in the person of the chief minister Jayalalithaa, and there is a correspondence between the cinematic and the political realms. But the cinelitic realm hangs isolated, because his rival Kamal, much like RK, has kept himself off from any party politiking. The rivalry between the fan clubs of RK and Kamal becomes less and less pronounced as RK resorts more and more to tactextual attacks on Jayalalithaa. Significantly, the villain on-screen frequently includes a 'haughty' woman, and in films like *Mannan*, she is the sole villain.

During the third 'inside-insider' phase when RK is 'conscripted' into politics, the cinematic anti-establishment focus stands him in good stead because of smooth corroboration between the cinematic villain and the political villain Jayalalithaa, who represents the establishment by virtue of her office as the chief minister. Ironically, the hero at the realm of politiking is *not* RK, or the hero remains ambiguous, to say the least. The real hero is Karunanidhi because, when it comes to whom the people are going to vote for, the choice is between Karunanidhi of the DMK–TMC combine and Jayalalithaa of the ADMK–INC combine, and not between RK and Jayalalithaa. However, the anti-establishment, 'outsider' image of RK blended with other factors, the combined effect of which led to the 'wave' of anti-incumbency.

When RK supported the same DMK–TMC alliance in the subsequent parliamentary elections held after the DMK had come to power (1998 and 1999), his 'outsider' image did not click because such an action was clearly incongruous. Similar incongruous and inconsistent political stand in 2004 cost him dear. In this respect, RK could be compared to Amitabh Bachchan, the 'angry young man' of the Hindi filmdom, whose entry into direct party politics ended up in a fiasco.[9] There is an important difference between RK and Bachchan, however. In spite of the calculated tactexting especially in the third phase that he was ideally cut out for political leadership, which was also reiterated by the parties determined to oust Jayalalithaa, the 'supra-legal' RK deliberately kept himself off politiking by endlessly deferring the starting of his own party, by forbidding his interested and capable fans to contest in the elections to local bodies, by refusing to contest himself, and to crown it all, by taking an ill-informed electoral decision (in 2004) that misfired. Many of his ardent fans found him disconcertingly enigmatic,[10] and quite a few of them lost heart and moved over to other younger stars like Vijay and Ajith; and the fans who have been nurturing political ambitions found a 'way out' in Vijayakanth, when he boldly started his party.

Many lapses in the process of cinelation could be identified in the fourth phase. In the cinematic realm, the hero RK is there but he fights with villains who cannot be iconised because of changing nature of their identity from film to film — incidentally, there were only five films in twelve years after *Baba* — and in *Kuselan* strictly speaking there is no villain at all! More importantly, these films offered little scope for the fans to get into the narrative milieu. In the cinelitic realm, the villain is totally absent. In the politiking realm, the hero himself is absent! This has to be so, especially at a time when his two erstwhile villains (Jayalalithaa and Karunanidhi) 'happen to be his friends'![11] As of now, RK survives not by his image but the 'after-glow' trailing his image.

Tangential Cinelation

Though the next two models concern the political use of cine-popularity, they do not in fact involve the process of cinelation in any significant manner. Of these, the value–added-star model is an example of the *tangential* cinelation, wherein the inter-connectivity of realms in terms of the archetypal binaries is only nominal or remote. It involves the established political parties inducting cine artistes and fielding them as their candidates in elections. The DMK, for example, has used actors such as Sarath Kumar, Napoleon and T. Rajendar, and the ADMK, Ramarajan and Radha Ravi. Even here, the parties do not treat the 'star value' as an over-riding factor. It is only one of the criteria employed, and other crucial factors, more importantly caste, are duly considered. Sarath Kumar and Ramarajan, for instance, were fielded in constituencies where their own caste people are strong, while T. Rajendar and Napoleon were fielded in a traditional DMK strong-hold. Interestingly, not all the stars contesting on party tickets were elected — Sarath Kumar (1998) and T. Rajendar (2001) had been

196 ▪ POPULAR CINEMA AND POLITICS IN SOUTH INDIA

defeated. It is remarkable that in the recent history of Thamizh Nadu no actor contesting as an independent candidate relying solely on his popularity has got elected. More remarkable is the fact that,except MGR, all actors, including Sivaji and T. Rajendar, who floated their own party and contested in the elections, were thoroughly trounced and humbled.

The *PS Study 2001*[12] amply illustrates the extent of the electoral reception the stars could have vis-à-vis other factors such as the voters' political affiliation and caste. According to the *pre-alliance* survey, while 87.3 per cent respondents *like* some actor or the other, only 31.5 per cent like the actors to get into direct politics. However, if their favourite actor contests in their constituency on *their party* ticket, as many as 74.8 per cent say that they would vote for him/her (will not vote = 21.9 per cent; not willing to comment = 3.3 per cent), though the chances of his/her winning are only 40.6 per cent (no chance = 16.3 per cent, not sure = 43.1 per cent). The response is dramatically reversed, if he/she contests as the *opposition* candidate. 76.8 per cent say that they would not vote for him/her (would still vote = 19.7 per cent; not willing to comment = 3.5 per cent). 22.5 per cent are confident that he/she would win and 23.9 per cent think otherwise. But majority (53.6 per cent) is not sure of the outcome. If the favourite actor contests against another of their *own caste*, the opinion is equally divided with 46.5 per cent in favour of the actor and the same per cent in favour of the caste candidate (not willing to comment = 7 per cent). The above responses clearly indicate the voting pattern of the people — on the one hand, they are *strongly attached* to their political parties, and the 'star factor' can have only a marginal influence over them; on the other, they are more ready, when compared to their political allegiance, to *transcend their caste* in favour of their favourite star. In other words, the popularity of an actor alone does not suffice to overcome the firmness of political and caste allegiances.

Peripheral Cinelation

The *peripheral* cinelation refers to the strategy of political parties to employ cine stars as 'star' attractions during the election campaigns. The practice has almost become a norm. During the 1996 elections, for example, the DMK-led alliance had the 'super star' on its side, while the ADMK had the popular comedian Manorama to criticise RK. In the next assembly elections (May 2001) the campaign was indeed star-studded. The DMK alliance had Sarath Kumar, Radhika and Napoleon, while the ADMK alliance had Radha, Ambika, S. S. Chandran, and Radha Ravi. In the recent assembly elections (April 2011), the 'star value' of the DMK alliance (with Kushboo and comedian Vadivael) far outweighed the competitors, though the actual election outcome turned out to be ruinous for the DMK alliance.

Though the presence of the multitude of these stars might have served as a crowd-puller, the impact on the voting behaviour of the people has surprisingly been negligible as the *PS Study 2001* indicates. The *post-election* survey shows that only 12 per cent of the respondents have attended the meetings addressed by the stars, though they are aware that one or more stars have visited their place. Even of this 12 per cent, as many as 39.6 per cent have said that they went out of curiosity to see the stars, and 27.6 per cent, because they represented their parties. Only 9.7 per cent have said that the stars were persuasive enough. According to the *pre-alliance* survey, majority of the respondents (57.5 per cent) have replied that they will not be influenced by the speech of their own favourite actors. 29.3 per cent have said that they will favourably respond to their favourite stars, provided the stars campaign for their own party. Only 13.2 per cent have said that they would vote for the candidate supported by their favourite actor, even if the candidate does not belong to their party. The *mid-campaign* survey highlights the steady waning of the star attraction as the polling day fast approached: Only 28.6 per cent favour the idea of cine stars indulging in campaign, as against 66.5 per cent who do not favour it (4.9 per cent are indifferent). However, when the actors do come for campaigning, 77 per cent assert that they will not be in any way influenced by them. 15.5 per cent state that they would oblige the actor, only if he/she supports their party candidates. Only a meagre 7.5 per cent are ready to desert their parties for the sake of the actors and support the candidates of the opposite alliance. This once again proves that the 'star attraction' can at the most reinforce the already existing affiliation to one's party, rather than making any worthwhile inroad into the opposition camp.[13]

198 ■ POPULAR CINEMA AND POLITICS IN SOUTH INDIA

Notes

1. Biju Patnaik proposed that MGR would continue as the chief minister while Karunanidhi would be the party president. For Karunanidhi's version of this initiative and the conditions he put for the merger, see *The Hindu*, 2009. See also, Mohandas (1992: 24–25, 47); and Ilamathi (1998a: 159–60).
2. See Guy (1990: 154). Guy goes on to compare MGR's use of the movie screen to Rousseau's pen and Karl Marx's *Das Kapital*. Elsewhere in the same article he asserts: 'In fact MGR would have made it in politics and public services even if he had never seen a movie camera or heard anyone yelling *cut!*' (ibid.: 151). Thandavan is more moderate in his assessment: '... although MGR came to prominence through the cinema, the film alone was not responsible for his political achievements' (Thandavan, 1987: 111).
3. Mohandas (1992: 4).
4. The DMK profited a great deal in the 1967 elections by 'cinelating' the shooting of MGR. By exhibiting posters of MGR with a bandage, the DMK transferred the hero versus the villain (cinematic) to the hero-turned-victim MGR versus the villain M. R. Radha (real-life–private) to the DMK representing the 'victims' of the repressive Congress regime versus the Congress (political).
5. Mohandas (1992: 50).
6. Mohandas (ibid.: 86).
7. Editorial Board of Manimekalai Pirasuram (1995: 169).
8. In 1980, it is said, MGR was planning to produce a propaganda film with the intention of using it during the election campaign. He had to drop the plan because the elections were suddenly announced and there was not enough time to undertake such a venture (Narayanan, 1981: 684). In 1984, when MGR was away in the US, R. M. Veerappan made a special documentary, *Vetri Thirumagan* (The Victorious Venerable Son) and extensively used it during the election campaign (Mohandas, 1992: 50).
9. Das Gupta (1991: 234–47).
10. Recalling the mental depression he underwent during the late 1970s, *Naveena Netrikkan*, a popular investigative magazine, interpreted the 'un-understandable' behaviour of RK as the relapse of the depression. The front cover of the issue featured RK with the caption 'Something has happened to Rajini' (*Rajinikku ennamoa aayiduchchu*). See *Naveena Netrikkan* (2001).
11. See RK's interview to NDTV on the eve of the release of *Sivaji*. (Uploaded on *You Tube* on 30 June 2007). When reporters asked him why he invites politicians like Jayalalithaa and Karunanidhi for the preview of his films, he said, they were his 'friends who happen to be politicians!' In 2012, during the public function on 13 December 2012 to mark his birthday, a

CINELATING POLITIKING ◀ 199

happy RK said that the stage was adorned by 'Poes Garden' (Jayalalithaa's residence)) and 'Gopalapuram' (Karunanidhi's official residence), and he was a friend to all.

12. *PS Study 2001* is the massive survey I carried out in the context of 2001 assembly elections. It was done in three phases: the *pre-alliance* phase conducted well before the formation of alliances (13–20 January 2001, with 2250 samples), the *mid-campaign* phase (26 April–2 May, with 2468 samples), and the *post-election* phase (19 May–10 June, with 2630 samples). The samples were spread over all the 30 districts of Thamizh Nadu.

13. The stars who campaign, however, are amply rewarded both monetarily and politically. Immediately after the 2001 elections, for example, Sarath Kumar and S. S. Chandran were made Rajya Sabha MPs by their respective parties.

15

POLITICS BEYOND POLITICS:
TRANS-IMAGE VOTING

Contrary to the popular belief that the Thamizhs are carried away by the screen image, the foregoing discussion points to the fact that, when it comes to exercising their franchise, they are 'image discriminative', that is, they are able to make a clear distinction between the screen-constructed popularity and the socio-political considerations pertaining to real politiking. The extraordinary political success of MGR lies precisely in his *intuitive awareness* of the fact that the people are image-discriminative. It is only based on this profound insight that MGR with his political acumen built up his political empire — he creatively turned his films into effective propaganda tools through tactexting, skilfully chiselled his action hero image, ingeniously devised the twin-centre dynamics, shrewdly appropriated the DMK, and ultimately emerged as the sole political centre of Thamizh Nadu.

The media scholars, overwhelmed by the prevalence of cinema and the popularity of cine stars, have been too quick to conclude that the screen image exerts a sweeping influence also over the voting behaviour of the people. The examples cited from such an *image-deterministic* point of view in the context of Thamizh Nadu include Anna, Karunanidhi, MGR, Janaki, Jayalalithaa, and of late RK and Vijayakanth because they are all in some way or the other related to the cinema industry. While these examples may be right, the conclusions are disputable because of two reasons: First, the presumed cause-and-effect relationship between the popular reception to stars and the people's voting is unwarranted and unsupported.[1] Second, the studies have not addressed the vital question of *what better choice people could have made*, given the political options available to them in the electoral contests. An in-depth analysis of the people's voting pattern based on the available election results testifies to the fact that the people have been image discriminative and have always chosen the best option possible.

To begin with, though the DMK did not participate in the 1952 first general elections in the independent India, it decided to support candidates who were ready to commit in writing that they would speak on its behalf in the assembly and the parliament, if elected. Eight for the parliament and 42 for the assembly were elected with the support of the DMK.[2] But most of those elected thus for the assembly crossed over to the INC, which managed to win only 152 seats in the 375-member assembly.[3] The DMK expressed its displeasure by organising demonstrations showing black flags to those who violated the electoral contract. After toying with the idea of directly contesting the elections for a while, a formal decision in the affirmative was taken in 1956.

For the purposes of the analysis the elections from 1957 till 2014 could be divided into five 'eras' — the era of radicalism-turned-rhetoric (1957–71), the era of promise-turned-pathos (1977–84), the era of gender politiking (1989–96), the era of minor parties (1998–2004), and the era of alternative-turned-ally (2006–14). The rationale for such a periodisation would become evident in the course of the discussion below.

Era of Radicalism-turned-Rhetoric

The results of the elections held during this period (Table 15.1) highlight the steady decline of the INC and the corresponding rise of the DMK. When the DMK entered the fray in 1957, the Congress leadership in fact did not take it seriously. But to the dismay of the Congress the DMK won as many as 13 seats and proudly walked into the assembly and, in a matter of 10 years, it successfully unseated the INC. The DMK's growth graph is best evident in the progressively dwindling number of seats for which it forfeited the deposit: In 1957, it contested 100 seats but forfeited its deposit for 39. In 1962, it contested 149 seats, and lost the deposit only for 11. In 1967 and 1971 it did not lose its deposit at all, while securing 138 (out of 173 contested) and 184 (out of 203 contested) seats respectively.

202 ■ POPULAR CINEMA AND POLITICS IN SOUTH INDIA

Table 15.1
Era of Radicalism-turned-Rhetoric — Electoral Performance: 1957–71

		Assembly		Parliament
Year	Party	Vote Share (in %)	Seats	Seats
1957	DMK	12.79	13	1
	INC	45.34	151	31
	Others	41.87	41	9
1962	DMK	27.10	50	7
	INC	46.14	139	31
	Others	26.76	17	3
1967	DMK	40.59	138	25
	INC	41.38	50	3
	Others	18.03	46	11
1971	DMK	48.58	184	23(35.19%)
	Cong (O)	34.99	15	1(30.55%)
	INC	–	–	9(12.49%)
	Others	16.43	35	6

This impressively ascending electoral performance was possible because of the following reasons:

First, by publicising the EVR's late-marriage being at odds with his own rationalist principles as the main cause for the split, by playing the sentimentalised political game of declaring the DMK president's chair to be vacant till EVR filled it, and by proclaiming to profess the same *Dravida Kazhakam*. Ideology of rationalism, self-respect and social reform, the DMK convincingly projected itself as the 'progressive' champion of the Dravidian cause. Over the years, EVR himself became a 'cultural superfluity' by his self-contradictory political stance, as for example, his decision to campaign in 1957 for a Brahmin against a non-Brahmin stalwart because he belonged to the same Congress to which Kamaraj, a 'pachchai Thamizhar' (pure Thamizh), also belonged.[4]

Second, by adopting an *agitational strategy* involving the youth, especially the college students, in large numbers, the DMK indeed thrived on the well-orchestrated *cycle of agitations* — the State machinery's repressive measures often resulted in lathi-charges, firings and arrests, which in turn triggered off another round of agitations. In 1953, for example, the DMK's 'three-pronged struggle' (*mum-munai poaraattam*) — to oppose the *kulak kalvi* plan of Rajaji, to condemn Nehru for calling

POLITICS BEYOND POLITICS ▟ 203

the DMK-led agitations as 'nonsense', and to demand that the name Dalmiyapuram be changed to Kallakudi — led to a series of arrests. The agitation in 1965 against the imposition of Hindi, spearheaded by the students, turned so violent that 33 were shot dead on the first two days.[5]

Third, the DMK was too quick to make diplomatic, if not opportunistic, compromises. The party started as a movement fashioned after its parent movement *Dravida Kazhakam*, turned into an election-based political party by 1956 because, it was said, the legislature was an ideal forum to emphasise its demands, which included, ironically, the demand for the 'Dravidian Nation'. Soon the very demands were dropped from its agenda fearing that the Centre would ban the party. Even the notion of 'Dravida' underwent a sea change. Though theoretically it encompassed all the four southern states, Karnataka and Kerala were by and large outside its ambit from the beginning. For instance, during the first state-level conference of the DMK in 1951, only Thamizh and Telugu plays were staged.[6] Once the Madras Presidency was reorganised on linguistic basis, the word 'Dravida' completely lost its 'South Indian' face because it had no takers outside TN and for all practical purposes it became a synonym of 'Thamizh'.

Fourth, the DMK leaders, particularly Anna, carefully projected a subaltern image, while setting them apart from the same subalterns. This dynamics of the 'double-bodied migrantcy' of simultaneous subalternising and elitising enabled them with the charisma that at once appealed to the illiterate masses and the educated urbanites. Anna, for example, repeatedly emphasised that he came from a humble background, while he was always addressed as 'arignar' (the learned).

Fifth, all the DMK public meetings and conferences were patterned on carnival. Surprisingly, even the agitations were very much 'carnivalesque' in experience. The conferences were elaborately organised: decorative arches and party flags adorned the venue; posters and portraits of leaders were prominently displayed; huge stages and sets were specially erected. Amidst the celebration of real camaraderie, the party artistes performed propaganda plays, while the leaders took important political decisions. What is appreciable is that the DMK continues to this day this pompous, carnival mode. Recent examples include the 'fill-the-jail' agitation against the ADMK government staged on 4 July 2012 during which as many as 2,00,000 exuberant cadres courted arrest

204 ▪ POPULAR CINEMA AND POLITICS IN SOUTH INDIA

(but the unprepared ADMK government released them all in the evening on the same day). As a preparation, a chain of meetings were held throughout the State for about a month preceeding this event. The tacit message from the party high command that only those who get arrested would be considered for future party posts came as an incentive to get arrested and many in fact came well prepared to spend an indefinite number of days in jail. Another recent example is the conference convened in Chennai on 12 August 2012 by the Thamizh Eezham Supporters Organisation (TESO) headed by M. Karunanidhi. Preceding the conference, the organisers, particularly Karunanidhi, held frequent press meets and the party media carried stories and promos for a number of days. On the conference day, while in the morning the 'Eezham Thamizhs Rights Protection Conclave' was held in a hotel for invited delegates from India and abroad wherein the delegates deliberated on the topic and passed 14 resolutions, in the afternoon a public meeting (*maanaadu*) was held for the grassroots party cadres during which the resolutions were read out for 'ratification' by the cadres. Besides these special occasions, even routine annual functions are always *mupperum* ('three-big') or *aimperum* ('five-big') *vizhaas* such as the *mupperum vizhaa* in Vizhuppuram on 15 September 2012, commemorating the birthday of Anna, the birthday of Periyar and the anniversary of launching of the DMK. In this, the ADMK outdoes everyone by making what is supposed to be the everyday affair of a party leader, namely, the (occasional) visit of Jayalalithaa to their party headquarters, a great event to be celebrated (with banners displayed from her residence to the party office, causing frequent traffic jams).

Sixth, the DMK leaders were multi-faceted personalities and skilled in the manipulation of the *media*. Many of them were effective and persuasive orators, each with his/her own style. Their speeches were replete with alliterations (*ethukai* and *moanai*), often tinged with inflammatory anti-Hindi, anti-North and anti-Congress rhetoric. Equally powerful was their writing in their party newspapers, especially in *Murasoli*. They also held sway over the cinema industry not only as dialogue writers but also as producers and actors. Quite a few of them, including Anna and Karunanidhi, were also good stage artistes. The DMK in fact made extensive use of the medium of drama both to propagandise the ideology and to raise funds. The media skills of the DMK leaders were, however, put at the service of the changing ideological positions, and

POLITICS BEYOND POLITICS ▄ 205

by the end of the period under study what remained was a mere media rhetoric devoid of any radical content of the initial years.

Further, the DMK leadership was sharp to learn fast the intricacies of political diplomacy and soon after the 1957 elections it realised the importance of mobilising the anti-Congress forces by forming an extensive and elaborate alliance. In this, the DMK was ready to sacrifice its own vision and shed its own principles. Thus, in 1962 elections the DMK struck an electoral deal strangely with the Swatantra Party, headed by its erstwhile arch-enemy, the *kulak kalvi*-fame Rajaji, who as the chief minister during 1952–53 was determined to 'crush the DMK like a bug'. A more extensive and strategic alliance was forged in 1967 with the Swatantra Party, CPM, Muslim League, Thamizharasu Kazhakam, Forward Bloc and a few other minor parties. During the 1971 elections, the Congress faction led by the then Prime Minister Indira Gandhi (later recognised as the INC) joined hands with the DMK.

Finally, by the time the DMK jumped into direct politics, the people had started getting disenchanted with the performance of the Congress governments both at the Centre and in the state because none of the promises given to the people during Independence was converted fully into concrete action. The grandiose developmental projects of the government could only meet with partial successes profiting a section of the society. By the mid-1960s the feeling of having been betrayed was so intense that the people were desperately looking for an alternative to the Congress. Very early did the DMK perceive this aspect of public disillusionment and articulated it, complementing it with the rediscovery and affirmation of Thamizh culture, and in the course of time it emerged as the champion of the Thamizhs. Over the years the DMK had also brought a sizable communist vote bank into its fold by its effective use of the simplified, easy-to-understand 'communist lingo'. That explains why Thamizh Nadu is one of the first few states to overthrow the Congress rule, and the only State where the Congress, once out of power, could never stage a comeback but has to permanently depend on one of the two Dravidian parties even for its own survival.

Given the background as summarised here, the voting pattern during this period is self-explanatory. In 1957 the DMK was a new entrant whose front-rung leaders except Anna, MGR and a few others were in their thirties, while a sizable number of the members were in

206 ■ POPULAR CINEMA AND POLITICS IN SOUTH INDIA

their twenties. The DMK itself contested only 100 seats. By 1962, the DMK as an organisation had grown but not without the intra-party squabbles. Just prior to the elections one of the founder leaders E. V. K. Sampath caused a near-vertical split in the party and floated his own party. It took some time for the DMK to come out of the rather chaotic situation that ensued. Meanwhile the DMK had to face the elections, with one founder leader within and another outside the DMK. The results show that while the people were better disposed to the DMK, they did not consider it strong and stable enough to rule the state — while 50 DMK candidates got elected, Anna was defeated in his own native constituency of Kanjeepuram.[7]

The next five years witnessed a plethora of agitations organised by the DMK on issues close to the public such as price rise and scarcity of essential commodities. But the most sensational agitations concerned the imposition of Hindi. While the Communists were busy during this time quarrelling over ideological issues, which finally ended up in two factions, the CPI and the CPI (M) in 1964, the DMK emerged as the prominent political voice of the Thamizhs, strong enough to challenge the Congress. In the 1967 elections, the DMK polled 40.59 per cent votes as against 41.38 per cent of the Congress.[8] The number of seats secured, however, present a paradox: the DMK secured 138 seats out of 173 it contested, whereas the Congress secured only 50 out of 234 seats it contested. The success of the DMK owes a great deal to the extensive alliance that its leadership was able to forge. The DMK had over the years consolidated its position and had become politically more mature and wiser, while the Congress was able to retain its vote bank, may be with minor bruises.

The Congress, however, underwent a split in 1969 with the 'moderates' staying with Congress (O) and the 'radicals' following the leadership of Indira Gandhi. The split in Thamizh Nadu was not very favourable to Indira Gandhi, with majority of the Congress members staying with K. Kamaraj, though at the all-India level the INC was rejuvenated under the leadership of Indira Gandhi, with the induction of more and more young persons into the party fold. The Communists continued their ideological debates, giving rise to a proliferation of new splinter groups, the most noteworthy among them was the CPI (ML) formed in 1969. The DMK during this time lost its founder leader Anna (February 1969), and Karunanidhi had just taken the reigns into his hands. Meanwhile, the assembly was dissolved in January 1971 and fresh elections were announced. The DMK had stayed in power for hardly four years (approximately two years each for Anna and Karunanidhi), and the people felt, as reflected in the 1971 elections, the party was not given enough time to prove its mettle. They overwhelmingly preferred the DMK led by Karunanidhi to Congress (O) led by Kamaraj. The DMK won 184 seats polling 48.58 per cent votes, while the Congress (O) could get only 15 seats, though it polled 34.99 per cent votes. Curiously, the DMK aligned with the very same INC, which had abruptly dissolved the assembly, effectively dividing the Congress votes.

The role of MGR in the electoral politics of the DMK during this period was two-fold — he was one of the main sources of finance for the party,[9] and a charismatic campaigner. While he was conscious that the party needed him, he had been using his films with an agenda of his own, as elaborated in the previous chapters, to project the DMK as the 'proto-ADMK' and later to present him as the personification of the DMK. He had been simultaneously concentrating on building his fan clubs and swiftly networked them into a politically 'hot' organisation. Significantly, the formation of fan clubs almost co-originated with the formation of the party units of the DMK. When the first fan club was formed in 1953, the year MGR joined the DMK, the party itself was in its initial stages, the leaders making concerted efforts to take the nascent party to the grassroots and start new units. The fan club association, the supreme index of MGR's might, therefore, grew with but parallel to the party, and 'there was a time when the DMK's six lakh membership included three lakhs of those who were members of MGR *mandrams*'.[10] In fact, in most of the rural areas the *mandrams* were functioning as the de facto party units. And in some places, the DMK itself got introduced to the people only through and as the MGR fan club!

In another clever move, MGR was determined to go directly to the people, especially after Anna had 'persuaded' him to resign the MLC post, to prove to other full-time, career politicians critical of him that he was on a par with them. He did contest in 1967 and 1971 elections, and won both the times.

MGR was a man endowed with an intuitive knowledge of the 'mass psychology', and he habitually employed 'psycho-political tactics' to be the centre of attraction, whenever he took part in the public meetings of the DMK. Irrespective of the leaders (including Anna) on the dais and irrespective of the purpose of the meeting, he not merely 'showed his face' to pull the crowd, he also spoke to the people as an ideal

208 ■ POPULAR CINEMA AND POLITICS IN SOUTH INDIA

representative of the subaltern masses, employing their lingo, and succeeding in the very act in informing the leaders on the dais that he was the empowered conscience of the subalterns. Above all, he turned every DMK meeting he addressed into a show[11] of *his* munificence by generously announcing donations to the party and to other public causes.

It is noteworthy that MGR was not the only star who campaigned for the DMK. During the 1962 elections, for instance, the DMK engaged the stars like 'Kalaivaanar' N. S. Krishnan and S. S. Rajendran, besides MGR. Learning from the DMK, in the 1967 elections the Congress used, besides Sivaji, artistes including Gemini, Savithri, Padmini, Major Sundarrajan, and Srikanth.

Era of Promise-turned-Pathos

The elections held in 1977, 1980 and 1984 bear testimony to how promise and pathos could be converted literally into electoral waves 'sweeping' a person to victory (Table 15.2). While in 1977 the ADMK cashed on the promise of a stable government in the Centre and a corruption-free government in the state, it won the other two elections because of pathos. To interpret the electoral performance of the ADMK during this period in a proper perspective, an understanding of the interplay of various forces from 1971 becomes necessary.

Table 15.2
Era of Promise-turned-Pathos — Electoral Performance: 1977–84

Year	Party	Assembly		Parliament	
		Vote Share (in %)	*Seats Won*	*Seats Won (in %)*	*Contested*
1977	AIADMK	30.37	130	18(30.59)	20
	DMK	24.89	48	1(18.06)	19
	INC	17.51	27	14(22.27)	15
	Others	27.23	29	6	
1980	AIADMK	38.74	129	2(25.38)	24
	DMK	22.54	38	16(23.01)	16
	INC	20.48	30	20(31.62)	22
	Others	18.24	37	1	
1984	AIADMK	37.09	133	12(18.36)	12
	DMK	29.49	24	2(25.90)	27
	INC	16.46	62	25(40.51)	26
	Others	16.96	25	0	

POLITICS BEYOND POLITICS   ◼   209

Getting overconfident with himself by the unexpectedly huge victory of the DMK in the 1971 elections, and holding the twin offices of being the chief minister and party president, Karunanidhi was seen to have become very autocratic. He, however, perceived in MGR a great, constant and immediate threat to his supremacy; MGR, on his part, started sensing that his future in the DMK was rather bleak. Thus, the dramatic birth of the ADMK was the result of the inevitable political necessities both of Karunanidhi to dismiss MGR from the DMK and of MGR to leave the DMK. The issues over which the split occurred include: (*a*) In the realm of politics, MGR felt he was not given his rightful place because Karunanidhi denied him a place in the cabinet. In fact, from 1967 MGR had been nurturing the feeling that his services to the party were not being *comparably* rewarded. It intensified when Karunanidhi who had become the chief minister because of his mediatory role tried to ignore him. (*b*) The acute feeling of being sidelined in politics got compounded when Karunanidhi interfered with the functioning of the MGR *mandram*s. To keep MGR under check, Karunanidhi dared to suck in the very life-blood of MGR by insisting that the *mandram*s be registered with the head office — an attempt to convert them into official party units. In another shrewd move, Karunanidhi not only schemed to oust MGR from the filmdom by projecting his son Muthu, the MGR look-alike actor, as 'young MGR' in contrast to the (real) aged MGR, but also officially promoted the fan clubs of his son as a rival to MGR *mandram*s. It was alleged that Karunanidhi resorted to unethical means to buy up MGR *mandram* office-bearers and instigated them to dissolve the *mandram*s. He even went out of his way to lend his tacit support to Sivaji. (*c*) In his personal life, MGR was undergoing a severe financial crisis because of the production of *Ulagam Sutrum Vaalipan*. There were also enquiries from the Income Tax Department. Neither as the friend nor as the chief minister was Karunanidhi willing to help MGR to resolve the crisis. MGR was particularly hurt by Karunanidhi's refusal to negotiate with the Centre to settle the issue of income tax arrears.

Politically sidelined, financially broke, intimidated by the Centre, and his *mandram*s repressed, MGR was feeling indeed as a hapless victim, but he was the 'do-gooder action hero' all the same, and he bounced back in response in his own unique way by covering his bitterness and frustration under the carpet of two other issues which were in consonance with his image. First, the 'do-gooder' MGR projected himself

210 POPULAR CINEMA AND POLITICS IN SOUTH INDIA

as the champion of the public welfare by opposing the decision of the Karunanidhi government to lift the prohibition of liquor.[12] Second, the 'action hero' MGR projected himself as the crusader against injustice by focussing on the allegations that the DMK government indulged in corruption and nepotism, allegations proved true in the concretely visible, disproportionately huge wealth amassed by many of the DMK legislators and party officials at various levels. MGR's interpretation of the governmental decision to lift prohibition converged on corruption by attributing the ulterior motive that it was not to fill the state exchequer but to fill the pockets of the party-men. Taking up both these issues reinforced and further enhanced the image of MGR because he had the credibility — in his personal life he was a teetotaller, and in the party he was the treasurer, entitled to demand from the party office-bearers financial accountability and transparency.

The overconfident and apparently irritated Karunanidhi dismissed MGR in a haste because of his miscalculation that MGR's opposition would soon fizzle out, just like what had happened to E. V. K. Sampath in the early 1960s. But MGR was not to be another Sampath because of the following reasons: First of all, even before MGR started the ADMK, the party 'structure' had already existed as the *mandram* association, and he just had to rechristen it. That explains how it was possible for the ADMK to form 6000 units with over 10 lakhs enrolled as members within 15 days of its birth.[13] Second, the very birth of the ADMK took place amidst the 'big bang' of spontaneous outburst of MGR fans, creating a challenge to law and order in many parts of the state. The repressive measures of the Karunanidhi government only added fuel to the fire. The sensationalised manner in which MGR's crusade against corruption was spearheaded was reminiscent of the 1965 anti-Hindi agitations of the DMK. But as a skilled organiser, he smoothly channelised the energies of his fans within the organisational framework of the political party. Third, as a determined politician, he sustained his concerted efforts by strategically making the crusade collaborative. He rallied all the anti-DMK and non-DMK forces round him — as soon as he formed the party he made a courtesy visit to Rajaji; the Congress led by Indira Gandhi actively supported him; the CPI threw its lot with him; even Kamaraj indirectly helped him by his strong criticism of the DMK government. Thus, MGR was able to successfully usurp the anti-DMK vote bank, especially of the Congress (O).[14]

POLITICS BEYOND POLITICS　211

The diplomatic acumen with which MGR handled the first by-election to the Dindigul parliamentary constituency in 1973 kept even his foes wonder-struck. He outwitted not only the DMK (by not playing the game of getting the ADMK merged with the INC as expected by Karunanidhi) but also the INC (by contesting in the election, which was totally unexpected by the INC leadership). Besides, he exhibited his political sagacity by fielding as the ADMK candidate a person from the majority caste (Thevar) of the constituency. Thus, it is clear that MGR did not want to risk his political career by wholly relying on his charisma. As the combined result of all the factors enumerated above, the ADMK won the seat with 52.55 per cent of valid votes polled, followed by the Congress (O) with 23.97 per cent and the DMK with 18.83 per cent, and the Congress (R) trailing far behind with 2.3 per cent.

That the elections are fought on a set of rules different from the 'rules of cinema' is evident from the subsequent by-elections in Coimbatore (1974) for a seat each for the assembly and the parliament. Feeling deceived by the ADMK in the Dindigul by-election, the Congress (R) had an electoral understanding with the Congress (O) and put up a common candidate. As a result, the ADMK just scraped through with a thin margin of only 306 votes (ADMK = 37.12 per cent, Congress (O) = 36.67 per cent, and DMK = 23.71 per cent) in the assembly seat, and the CPI, the ADMK alliance partner, won the parliamentary seat. Similarly, in the Pondicherry assembly elections held at the same time, the Congress alliance (consisting of both the factions) won 12 seats equalling that of the ADMK. The lone parliamentary seat in Pondicherry went to the ADMK but with a reduced margin (ADMK = 38.26 per cent, Congress (O) = 33.15 per cent, and DMK = 21.68 per cent).

The popular mandate in the crucial by-elections vindicated MGR's crusade and sustained its momentum, and the crusade, having acquired a definitive political dimension, projected MGR as the credible and promising political leader, surpassing Karunanidhi and Kamaraj. The by-election results indicate that the DMK had been relegated to the third position, after the ADMK and its close rival the Congress (combined). Meanwhile, the Congress itself got unified. The Centre (ruled by the INC) dismissed the DMK ministry and appointed an enquiry commission to look into the corruption charges. This obviously came

212　POPULAR CINEMA AND POLITICS IN SOUTH INDIA

as a morale booster for MGR, whose unrelenting crusade against Karunanidhi was further vindicated. But the INC, realising that it could no more entertain the dream of coming back to power in the state, was prepared to support either of the two regional parties (ADMK or DMK) at the state-level, provided it was able to get greater mileage with regard to the parliamentary elections. Given the corruption charges against the DMK, the INC naturally decided to align with the ADMK together with the CPI in the 1977 (March) parliamentary elections. The results were as expected — the ADMK won 18 seats and the INC 14, with the DMK managing to get only one. But the INC failed to get the required majority to form the government in the Centre. As a result, a coalition government led by the Janata Party was formed.

The ADMK and the INC parted ways in the assembly elections held in June 1977. There was a four-cornered contest with the ADMK, DMK, INC and the Janata Party in the fray. The ADMK romped home with 130 seats (MGR was elected from the Aruppukkottai constituency) in a 234-member assembly, inaugurating the rule of the 'revolutionary leader'. In terms of percentage, however, the ADMK had faced a steady decline from its first by-election. It could poll only 30.37 per cent, followed by the DMK with 24.89 per cent. While the ruling Janata Party (in the Centre) could secure only 10 out of 233 seats it contested (it forfeited the deposit in as many as 122 seats), the INC secured 27 seats polling 17.51 per cent. It is noteworthy that after the merger of the Congress (O), which used to maintain the second place in the by-elections, with the Congress (R), the unified Congress was relegated to the third position because the group of ardent followers of Kamaraj led by P. Ramachandran opposed the merger and chose to remain outside the fold of the unified Congress. However, the probability that the DMK could have come to power had it aligned with the INC made it clear to the ADMK and the DMK that they needed the INC if they had to have a comfortable victory in the assembly elections. This realisation made both the Dravidian parties clamour for the INC's friendship, as would be evident in the subsequent elections.

Being a four-cornered contest with four major parties (ADMK, DMK, INC, and Janata Party) contesting on their own strength, the 1977 assembly election results clearly demonstrate the preference of the people. Of the four contenders for the chair, the INC and the Janata Party did not have any widely accepted and credible person as the chief

POLITICS BEYOND POLITICS ■ 213

ministerial candidate. The election, therefore, amounted to the fight between Karunanidhi and MGR. Of these two, Karunanidhi had all along been accused of corruption even by the Congress. MGR then was the only choice left, with a reasonable credibility, assiduously built over the years by his determined crusade against corruption.

Elections during 1980 witnessed a different scenario, but the pattern of the people's verdict followed the same 'meta-rational' logic.[15] The election scenario was different mainly because of the political turmoil at the Centre during the Janata Party rule. The former Prime Minister Indira Gandhi was expelled from the parliament and sentenced to imprisonment, which in fact worked in her favour by creating widespread public sympathy. MGR took the course of *non-confrontation* with the Centre, because of which he was reluctant to the idea of Indira Gandhi contesting in the by-election for Thanjavur parliamentary constituency. While she eventually contested from Chikmagalur (Karnataka), MGR went out of his way to assuage her hurt feelings by strategically campaigning for the INC candidate in Thanjavur. He even 'financially supported Indira Gandhi, though she did not acknowledge it with grace'.[16] To make things worse, when Morarji Desai resigned from his Prime Ministership, MGR joined the coalition government led by Charan Singh, and the ADMK had two ministers in the Centre. When the Charan Singh ministry fell, elections were announced for the parliament. In a surprise move, the DMK moved the coins diplomatically and struck a deal with the INC, in spite of the fact that the very same DMK had made an attempt to assault Indira Gandhi herself hardly two years earlier. 'At Madurai, hysterical and stone-throwing crowds surrounded Indira Gandhi's car, severely injuring her and also her companions Maragatham Chandrasekhar and G K Moopanar. Cars were damaged beyond recognition and but for the strong intervention of the police, the scene would have turned similar to the one at Sriperumbudur in May 1991 — if not in the modern technique used for Rajiv Gandhi's assassination, at least in its cumulative effect'.[17] Even while the gory incident had not faded away from the memory of the people, the INC–DMK alliance was finalised, and MGR was left with no other option except to align with the Janata Party, which had no base at the grassroots. While the DMK publicised the slogan, 'Welcome Nehru's Daughter — Give us a Stable Government' (*Nehruvin makalae varuka — Nilaiyaana aatchi tharuka*), the Janata–ADMK combine could

214 ■ POPULAR CINEMA AND POLITICS IN SOUTH INDIA

not even face the electorate. The INC's campaign that the elections were caused because of internal squabbling in the Janata-led front, that no party other than the INC could give a stable government, and that Indira Gandhi had been harassed and victimised by the Janata leaders appealed to the electorate. The Congress came back to power with a nation-wide landslide victory; in Thamizh Nadu, the INC–DMK combine won 36 out of 39 seats, and the ADMK had to be content with just two.

The results got stunningly reversed in the assembly election held in June 1980 — in a matter of just over five months. The election itself was thrust upon the people of Thamizh Nadu by the INC, which prematurely dismissed the ADMK government in February, within a month after it captured power at the Centre. The same DMK–INC alliance continued also in the assembly elections. Boosted by the unexpected victory in the parliamentary elections, the DMK's campaign was marked by jubilation and triumph, as though it had already captured power. But MGR stuck to a single-point agenda for his campaign. He harped on the fact that his government had been dismissed within two-and-a-half years against the verdict of the people. He presented him as the one 'unjustly punished' by the INC at the instigation of the DMK. Significantly, the fact that he had made sincere attempts to give a corruption-free government during his chief ministership added further strength to his pathos-filled campaign. As a result, the ADMK was voted back to power with 129 seats (an increase of 8.37 per cent over the votes polled in 1977), while the DMK got 10 seats less than what it had in the previous assembly.

The results of the elections during 1977 and 1980, when compared, clearly demonstrate the uniqueness of the Thamizh Nadu voters. The sole criterion applied for the choice in the two parliamentary elections was stability at the Centre. For example, when all other states exhibited in 1977 at least some degree of displeasure with the INC because of the alleged excesses during the internal emergency, the Thamizh voters, oddly enough, overwhelmingly supported the INC. But this 'oddity' was proved to be the right assessment by the mere fact that the Janata-led government was unable to manage hardly beyond two and a half years. For the very same reason of 'stability' the Thamizh voters in 1980 were able to transcend MGR's 'charisma' and vote for Indira Gandhi. Incidentally, the Thamizh voters have always evinced a 'soft corner' for the Nehru family; in all the elections in which the INC contested

POLITICS BEYOND POLITICS ■ 215

under the leadership of Nehru, Indira Gandhi and Rajiv Gandhi the INC-led alliance has won the majority of seats.[18]

When it comes to the assembly, the Thamizh voters keep the state in mind and intuitively reason out and choose the best option available. The dramatic reversal of results in the 1980 assembly elections is a case in point. Karunanidhi with all his political shrewdness failed to understand that the victory in the preceding parliamentary elections was a vote for stability, which, under the prevailing circumstances, only Indira Gandhi could promise. When all his political manoeuvrings based on this wrong reading of the psychology of the Thamizh voters proved only futile, the disappointed Karunanidhi lamented, 'The people have not become mature yet'.[19]

The 1984 elections also prove the same point. The elections for the parliament and the assembly this year were held simultaneously and under tragic circumstances — Indira Gandhi had been assassinated and MGR had fallen seriously ill. When Rajiv Gandhi who had just taken over the reins of prime ministership wanted to seek a fresh mandate, MGR also decided to prematurely dissolve the assembly and seek a fresh mandate. The ADMK and the INC formed an alliance, and the DMK was perplexed as to how an appropriate election strategy could be worked out. The DMK in its campaign assured the people that it would hand over the chief ministership to MGR, if and when he came back safe and sound, and till then Karunanidhi would occupy the chair.[20] The poll promise was ambiguous enough that it indirectly amounted to a campaign for MGR and the ADMK. The ADMK mass circulated a video showing MGR 'safe and sound' in a US hospital. Besides, the Nutritious Noon Meal Scheme introduced in 1982 had brought especially the rural people to the side of MGR because it was for them a tangible proof that the government was for them. The ADMK–INC combine swept the polls and the people's mandate was clear — MGR to continue as the chief minister for another term and Rajiv Gandhi to be the Prime Minister. The results could not be otherwise — the DMK fighting a lonely battle did not have a prime ministerial candidate, and there was no convincing reason why the people should prefer Karunanidhi to MGR.

Concerning the three assembly elections MGR had faced as the leader of the ADMK, two features stand out as salient: First, though MGR managed in all the three elections to get the majority to form

216 ▪ POPULAR CINEMA AND POLITICS IN SOUTH INDIA

the government, the party's share in the valid votes polled was less than one-third (when it contested on its own in 1977) and slightly higher than one-third (in 1980 and 1984). That means, at least over 60 per cent of the voters have consciously and consistently voted against him (or preferred someone else to MGR).[21] This is fair enough an evidence to show that any sweeping statement that the Thamizhs are carried away by cine stars is unsubstantiated. Second, in the last two assembly elections (1980 and 1984) it was *not* the hero MGR but the *victim* MGR who was voted to power.[22]

Era of Gender Politiking

The next three pairs of elections (Table 15.3) could be described as the 'era of gender politiking' because all the election issues in one way or the other were linked up with the question of gender. In all these elections, Jayalalithaa had been the key figure playing varied roles — some assumed, others attributed — of the fighter, the victim, the saviour, and the villain.[23]

Table 15.3
Era of Gender Politiking — Electoral Performance: 1989–96

Year	Party	Assembly		Parliament
		Vote Share (in %)	*Seats*	*Seats*
1989	AIADMK			
	(JL)	21.90	29	11
	(JR)	9.13	1	
	DMK	33.34	151	0
	INC	20.19	26	27
	Others	15.44	27	1
1991	AIADMK	44.39	164	11
	DMK	22.46	2	0
	INC	15.40	61	28
	Others	17.75	7	0
1996	AIADMK	21.47	4	0
	DMK	42.07	173	17
	INC	5.63	0	0
	TMC (M)	9.30	39	20
	Others	21.53	18	2

POLITICS BEYOND POLITICS ▰ 217

In a striking correspondence, the elections held during this period also witness the same meta-rational logic in the voting pattern. There was a three-cornered contest in the 1989 assembly election (the first one after the death of MGR) and the people had no better choice than Karunanidhi. The ADMK, being haunted by MGR's ghost, was undergoing a deep *identity crisis* by getting split into ADMK (JL) led by Jayalalithaa and ADMK (JR) led by Janaki, and its vote-bank as a consequence was shattered. The fact that the twin-leaves symbol was frozen by the Election Commission also added to the woes of the ADMK. The INC was equally afflicted with inner party bickering and had a similar split spearheaded by the actor Sivaji. Given the chaotic circumstances, it was natural for the *neutral* voters to swing towards the DMK, which emerged with a thumping majority. The election outcome had its impact on the factions — Janaki withdrew from politics for good, and Sivaji merged his with the Janata. When the parliamentary elections were held in November that year, the crisis-ridden political scenario had changed, and the (unified) ADMK and the INC joined hands to form an alliance. The DMK joined the National Front. The Thamizh Nadu electorate preferred the *single* leader Rajiv Gandhi (from the Nehru family) to a *group* of National Front leaders, and the DMK drew a blank for the first time. Though the National Front eventually formed the government at the Centre, the coalition was wrought with contradictions, which led to its ultimate downfall.

The DMK ministry in the state, however, was short-lived. The gruesome murder of 16 persons of the EPRLF including its leaders Padmanaba and Kirubakaran in Chennai (June 1990) intensified the allegations that the DMK was harbouring the Sri Lankan Thamizh extremists and the law and order mechanism in the state had failed. Consequently, the DMK ministry was dismissed and fresh elections were held together with the parliamentary elections in 1991. The ADMK–INC alliance continued in this election too. Having firmly established as the undisputed leader of the ADMK, Jayalalithaa in her campaign persuasively appealed to the women voters, the *thaai kulam* of MGR. The *thaai kulam*, on the one hand, perceived in Jayalalithaa their *representative*; on the other hand, they sympathised with her when she repeatedly interpreted the attempted attack on her in the legislative assembly during the first budget session (on 25 March 1989) as a blatant misogynist act. Meanwhile, the murder of Rajiv Gandhi at the

218　POPULAR CINEMA AND POLITICS IN SOUTH INDIA

thick of the campaign came as a severe blow to the DMK because it became a *justification* for the dismissal of the DMK government. The DMK as a result lost its face, and the ADMK came to power with the highest percentage of vote share in its history (44.39 per cent). In the parliamentary elections the ADMK–INC combine won all the 39 seats.

When the ADMK government completed its five-year term (the first one to complete the full term since 1967!), the ADMK leadership was facing all the accusations that were, ironically, once levelled against the DMK by MGR — amassing disproportionate wealth by a blatant misuse of power, rampant corruption, intolerance to criticism, repression of any dissent, etc. The attacks on the ADMK government became very virulent, scathing and widespread from mid-1995: the state governor permitted Subramanian Swami and others to file cases against the chief minister Jayalalithaa, and the Central government's Enforcement Department filed cases against the family of Sasikala, the closest friend of Jayalalithaa, for foreign exchange violations; the bomb explosions at film director Mani Ratnam's house and the RSS office in Chennai were publicised as evidence for a deteriorating law and order situation; attacks on T. N. Seshan, the Chief Election Commissioner, lawyers Vijayan and Alandur Bharathi, IAS official Chandraleka and Central minister P. Chidambaram were cited as instances of the ADMK's high handed manner of dealing with criticism; the extravagant wedding of the chief minister's foster son in September 1995 came as a climax.

While all these events helped the anti-ADMK forces, more specifically the anti-Jayalalithaa forces, get mobilised, within the party Jayalalithaa had alienated, antagonised and sidelined the 'devotees' of MGR. It was alleged that she deliberately attempted to erase the memory of MGR by projecting her as the only 'revolutionary leader' (*puratchi thalaivi*). Naming government buildings and organisations — from the transport corporations to the Film City — after her name was interpreted as a sign of arrogance and haughtiness. Feeling not duly and properly respected, the MGR fans-turned-politicians gathered around R. M. Veerappan and formed a federation of MGR *mandrams* (MGR Munnani). Initially RK supported the MGR Munnani because he was feeling guilty that R. M. Veerappan had been sacked by Jayalalithaa because of him. But as the elections came closer RK withdrew his support because he felt that R. M. Veerappan was 'misusing' his name. Meanwhile, RK made a few futile attempts to persuade the INC

POLITICS BEYOND POLITICS ◾ 219

president not to align with the ADMK. Later R. M. Veerappan floated his own political party called MGR Kazhakam and aligned with the DMK–TMC combine, which RK supported.

Even as the anti-Jayalalithaa forces were gathering momentum, the differences of opinions within the INC on the issue of electoral alliance led to the dramatic birth of the TMC a few weeks prior to the elections. All the INC members opposed to aligning with the ADMK left the party under the leadership of G. K. Moopanar in *defiance* of the party high-command. The daring act of Moopanar to break away[24] from the INC (ruling in the Centre) against joining the ADMK (ruling in the State) projected the TMC as a credible, justice-conscious, radical party. Moopanar's own personal simplicity and the presence of 'intellectual' politicians like P. Chidambaram added to the party's credibility.

Meanwhile, the DMK was making concerted efforts to bring together all the anti-Jayalalithaa, anti-ADMK and anti-INC forces. It went to the extent of telecasting on Sun TV an interview with the outlawed 'sandalwood' Veerappan, who severely criticised the ADMK and its leadership. When the TMC was floated, the DMK went out of its way to strike a deal with it by accommodating all its demands. Thus, the winning DMK–TMC combine was born, and the much-publicised support of RK came as an added strength to the combine. Given these circumstances, the contest in the assembly elections was between Karunanidhi and Jayalalithaa, the *persona non grata*. The neutral voters, obviously, had no other choice than to lean towards Karunanidhi. The results were a near-reversal of that of the 1991 elections. Stunningly, the TMC winning 39 assembly and 20 parliamentary seats effectively replaced the INC, which drew a blank in both. With regard to the parliamentary elections, in the absence of a worthwhile charismatic leader in the INC and the existing leadership tainted with allegations of horse-trading and bribing, the people of Thamizh Nadu rightly foresaw, as the subsequent elections testified, that the time was ripe for the end of the rule of a single party, be it the INC or the BJP or something else.

Significantly, if the victory of Jayalalithaa (and the ADMK) in 1991 is attributed to the popularity of her screen image (particularly her image as MGR's co-star), then her very defeat in her constituency (besides the ADMK being routed) in 1996 goes to demythologise the same. Incidentally, of the 137 films Jayalalithaa had acted from 1964, only in 28 films she had co-starred with MGR.

Regarding the political intervention of RK in the 1996 elections, certain observations are in order. First, RK not merely remained outside the realm of party politics, but he operated exclusively from within the cinema industry. All his political interventions have been from a film-related platform, be it the function to honour actor Sivaji or the *vetri vizhaa* of his films or the award functions, outside of which he never addressed any public meeting. His contact with the publics was only through the media, mainly press releases. Second, there was a great enthusiasm, even jubilation, among his fans because they expected him to float a party.[25] Apparently, many of them were *wrongly motivated* by the example of the established politicians, treating politics as a shortcut to earn quick money and fame. Third, he seemed to be too naïve and crude in his approach to politics, lacking the 'diplomacy' to tackle the intricate, cut-throat political manoeuvres. While this might be his strong point, its weakness was manifest in his endless hesitation to take a firm decision.[26] Fourth, he came across as a person who was hurt and excessively obsessed with 'punishing' Jayalalithaa. As a result, his political criticisms lacked the *social* dimension. Fifth, he was preoccupied with the self-doubt of whether he would be able to win, if he started a party. He was so conscious of his screen-constructed 'super star' image that he was afraid of facing any failure.

Based on the available data, it could be surmised that, had he started a party, its success would have been very doubtful, if not catastrophic.[27] The hardcore members of the ADMK and the DMK have always stood solidly behind their leadership. Even under the most adverse situations, at least one-fifth of the people of Thamizh Nadu have remained faithful[28] to each of these parties, as for example, when the performance of the ADMK was at its worst, it polled 21.47 per cent (1996), and for the DMK it was 22.4 per cent (2011). Other parties too have their faithful hardcore, however small it might be. Thus, if RK were to start a party, it would almost be impossible for him to lure the faithfuls of other parties away to switch allegiance in his favour to a magnitude that befits his larger-than-life screen image. He had to necessarily align with other parties, in which case he would cease to be the sole 'supralegal super-star'.[29]

Finally, RK's style of political intervention in 1996 apparently clicked because the cinelation of the RK-versus-the-villain archetype to the political realm as RK-versus-Jayalalithaa coincided with the devastating anti-Jayalalithaa, anti-incumbency wave of the day.[30]

POLITICS BEYOND POLITICS ■ 221

Even if it were to be conceded that Jayalalithaa was defeated solely[31] because of RK, the subsequent elections proved that the people were able to decisively transcend the hold of RK's screen-constructed image, and thus falsifying the popular belief that the screen image wields over-riding power over the masses.

Era of Minor Parties

The outcome of the two successive parliamentary elections in 1998 and 1999 shows that the people have been getting increasingly convinced of the suitability of a coalition government at the Centre in which the regional parties assumed a greater role. The regional parties in turn have started increasingly depending on significant minor parties, mostly confined to certain pockets or sections within the state.[32] The same trend has come to prevail in the making of the state government as well, where the two main players are the ADMK and the DMK, and, curiously, all the 'national' parties including the INC and the BJP are reduced to the status of 'minor' parties.[33] The pattern of seat-sharing among the alliance partners is symptomatic of this trend.

In the 1998 parliamentary elections the ADMK formed an alliance with the MDMK and PMK,[34] besides BJP, Subramanian Swami's JP and erstwhile Congressman Vazhappadi Ramamurthy's Thamizhaga Rajiv Congress;[35] whereas the DMK alliance had the same 1996 partners, i.e., DMK, TMC and CPI. The CPI(M) tried to join the DMK alliance and when that failed, it decided to contest on its own in two seats where it believed to have a strong presence and support the DMK alliance in the rest. The INC, MGR–ADMK[36] and United Communist Party of India formed a separate front. In the final outcome, the number of seats won corresponded to the cumulative strengths of the alliance partners (Table 15.4). The ensuing BJP-led coalition government formed in the Centre was so vulnerable and at the mercy of 'all-and-sundry' parties that it eventually collapsed in a matter of months for want of a single vote in a confidence motion and a fresh mandate had to be sought. The 1999 elections also witnessed a scenario not so different from that of the previous year with the minor parties wielding enormous bargaining power at the negotiating table. There was of course a realignment of parties, and the electoral field witnessed a few new entrants with clear caste identities like Viduthalai Chiruthaigal Katchi (SC — Paraiyars) and Puthiya Thamizhagam (SC — Pallars or Devendra Kula Vellalars);

222 ■ POPULAR CINEMA AND POLITICS IN SOUTH INDIA

Table 15.4
Era of Minor Parties — Electoral Performance: 1998-2004

Party	1998	1999	2001	2004
AIADMK	18	10	132 (31.4%)	0
DMK	5	12	31 (30.9%)	16[1]
INC	0	2	7 (2.5%)	10[2]
TMC (M)	3	0	23 (6.7%)	
BJP	3	4	4 (3.2%)	0
PMK	4	5	20 (5.6%)	5[3]
MDMK	3	4	0 (4.7%)	4
CPI(M)	0	1	6 (1.7%)	2
CPI	1	0	5 (1.6%)	2
Others	2	1	6	0

1998 JP – 1; TRC (as independent) – 1
MADMK: 1999 – 1 parliament; 2001 – 2 assembly

Note 1: The Muslim League candidate contested in the DMK symbol, and so counted as a part of the DMK.
Note 2: Before this election the TMC had merged with its mother party, i.e., the INC.
Note 3: The lone Pondicherry seat also was won by the PMK.

but the results once again demonstrated that the cumulative strength of an alliance's partners and the number of seats won neatly corresponded.

Preceding and surrounding the 2001 assembly elections, there was a mushrooming of minor parties with definite caste and geographical affinities, such as *Makkal Thamizh Desam Katchi* (*Yadhavars*), *Puthiya Needhi Katchi* (*Mudhaliyars*), *Kongunadu Makkal Katchi* (*Vellala Goundars*), *Thamizh Nadu Mutharaiyar Sangam* (*Mutharaiyars*), All India Forward Block (*Mukkulam*), and John Pandian's *Thamizhaga Makkal Katchi* (SC — *Pallars*). All these parties contested in the assembly elections, mainly as part of the DMK camp. Other tiny parties which were accorded 'partner' status by either of the State supremos include: *MGR Kazhagam* (R. M. Veerappan), *Thamizhar Bhoomi* (Ku.Pa. Krishnan), *Congress Jananayaka Peravai* (P. Chidambaram), *Indian Uzhavar Uzhaippalar Katchi* ('Vettavalam' Manikandan), and *Thondar Congress* (Kumari Ananthan). The relatively bigger parties after the ADMK and DMK in the electoral fray included: all the parties that had contested in 1999 elections (TMC, INC, MDMK, PMK, BJP, CPI, CPI[M], VCK, PD, MGR-ADMK, etc.) and three muslim factions, i.e., *Thamizhaga Muslim Iykkya Jamaat* (J.M. Haroon), Indian Union Muslim League (Khader Mohideen), Indian National League (M. Abdul Latheef).

POLITICS BEYOND POLITICS ◄ **223**

With so many parties vying with one another for seats, and the DMK and ADMK trying hard to accommodate as many as possible, no wonder there was a strong feeling among the alliance partners particularly of the ADMK that the state was heading towards a coalition government, and the predominant opinion was that such a coalition government would be led by the ADMK. The TMC leader Moopanar went a step ahead and insisted, at least initially, that the next government *should be* a coalition one.[37] The fact that the ADMK contested only in 141 seats[38] (the DMK contested in 183 seats) leaving the rest for its partners (TMC and PMK were the major partners) indicates that the ADMK leadership was prepared for a coalition government, if such a situation arose.

That the people were getting ready for a coalition government in the state was highlighted in the *PS Study* 2001 (pre-alliance phase). According to the survey, 60.8 per cent of the respondents said there would be a coalition government (headed by either the DMK or the ADMK) in the State. Interestingly, such an expectation was equally prevalent among those who said they would vote for the DMK (as many as 57.8 per cent of them said it would be a coalition government; of those who said they would vote for the ADMK, the percentage is 61.6 per cent). In consonance with the party leader Moopanar's demand, only 4.3 per cent (of those who said they would vote for the TMC) said the DMK would form the government on its own (none expected the ADMK to form the government on its own). The strategic alliance that Jayalalithaa was able to work out (with both the Communist parties, both the Congress parties and the strongest caste-based party PMK as the constituents) significantly altered the electoral outcome in terms of the seats won. In terms of votes polled by individual parties, however, there is only a slender margin between the DMK (30.9 per cent) and the ADMK (31.4 per cent), which, incidentally, is the lowest margin ever.[39] These calculations apart, from the point of view of the people, there was no convincing reason why they should not prefer Jayalalithaa to MK— the DMK also was facing the same allegations it had levelled against the ADMK (specifically corruption and nepotism) in 1996, and during the five-year rule of the DMK Jayalalithaa had been subjected to the legal course[40] for the alleged excesses committed during her regime.

The euphoria over the caste-based new entrants to 2001 elections started fading away already during the campaign itself[41] and the election

224 ▪ POPULAR CINEMA AND POLITICS IN SOUTH INDIA

results revealed that the people were not as casteistic as the leaders of the caste parties believed their respective caste people to be or at least would have liked them to be. As a result, by 2004 many of these caste-based parties exited the electoral contest for good and some of the other minor parties merged with bigger ones, like TMC merging with the INC, and MGR–ADMK with the BJP. Thus, in the 2004 electoral fray, besides the supremos (ADMK and DMK) and the 'national' parties (INC, BJP, CPI and CPI[M]), the smaller parties contesting got reduced to PMK and MDMK in the DMK alliance, and Makkal Thamizh Desam Katchi, Puthiya Thamizhagam, and Viduthalai Chiruthaigal Katchi in 'People's Alliance' led by JD(U). The results once again demonstrated the enormous power wielded by the regional and minor parties in the formation of the Central government.

The ground reality being thus, RK's political interventions during this period could be assessed better. In 1998, RK gave a televised interview[42] against Jayalalithaa and assured the people that the Karunanidhi government would take strong measures to curb bomb explosions, but the people voted in favour of the ADMK alliance. This was because of the glaring contradiction in RK's image and the isolated nature of cinelation. In contrast to 1996 assembly elections in which the actual electoral combat between Karunanidhi and Jayalalithaa had been popularly projected as the war between RK and Jayalalithaa, the 1998 parliamentary election was not understood by the people as a battle primarily between Karunanidhi and Jayalalithaa. Factors such as serial bomb blasts[43] foreshadowing the elections, the incapability of the United Front government at the Centre to survive for a full term, the image of Vajpayee as a moderate BJP leader, and the extensive and strategic alliance forged by the ADMK far outweighed the RK image. In the absence of a prime ministerial candidate on the side of the INC and the United Front having lost its credibility, Vajpayee was the only worthwhile choice left. Added to this, the corruption charges against Jayalalithaa had been partly vitiated by the fact that Subramanian Swami, one of the first persons to indulge in vituperative attacks on her preceding the 1996 elections, aligned with her in 1998.

Given this background, RK's criticism of Jayalalithaa and his support for Karunanidhi looked jarringly inconsistent with the real-life happenings. His assurance to the people that Karunanidhi would resign his chief ministership, if another bomb were to explode was in direct

POLITICS BEYOND POLITICS ◄ 225

contrast to his vociferous attack on the ADMK government not too long ago for not containing the 'bomb culture'. This indeed was a dramatic reversal. His defence of the Karunanidhi government militated against his anti-establishment tendency, the hallmark of his image, and as a consequence, RK lost his credibility and became irrelevant.

The 1999 parliamentary election scenario was marked by an almost *en masse* migration of the ADMK partners of 1998 to the DMK fold. The former major partners of the ADMK including the BJP, the MDMK and the PMK moved over to the DMK camp, the ADMK aligned with the INC, now rejuvenated by the entry of Sonia Gandhi, wife of the late Rajiv Gandhi, and the TMC broke away from the DMK alliance and headed a third front. The BJP publicised its successes at Pokran (nuclear tests) and Kargil (war with Pakistan) and pleaded for a clear mandate. The INC projected Sonia Gandhi as the new hope of the country and the symbol of a stable government. Thoroughly browbeaten by the humiliating rout of the DMK alliance in 1998, RK was a bit more cautious this time, and issued only a press statement exhorting the people to punish those who had caused this election. But the people perceived the issue at stake differently — it was not punishing a regional party but choosing between the Vajpayee-led BJP and the Sonia Gandhi-led INC, one which would form a stable coalition government. Though the BJP alliance criticised Sonia Gandhi as a foreigner, the legacy of the Nehru family was revived, and, as the results showed, the people of Thamizh Nadu were comparatively more inclined to the INC in this election than in 1998. Thus, in spite of the extensive alliance and the support of the super star RK to the DMK alliance, the ADMK won as many as 10 seats, falling short of the DMK's by just two.[44] The decent scoring of the ADMK again indicated that the people did not punish it as RK had exhorted them.[45]

In the 2001 assembly election neither the Vajpayee-factor nor the Sonia Gandhi-factor had any noticeable impact, though the overall policies and the agenda of their respective parties within the state affected the outcome. It was essentially a contest between Karunanidhi of the DMK alliance and Jayalalithaa of the ADMK alliance. According to the changed nature of the contest, the alliance partners also changed: the TMC, together with its parent INC, joined the ADMK, a decision negating the *raison-d'être* of its very birth;[46] parting company with the DMK, the PMK came back to the ADMK, while the MDMK went

226 ■ POPULAR CINEMA AND POLITICS IN SOUTH INDIA

on its own; recently floated caste-based parties joined the DMK; both the Communist parties became allies of the ADMK. RK, unable to understand the voting pattern of the people and disillusioned by the 'unprincipled' alliances, kept himself off the election.[47] During the civic polls in October 2001 he ordered that none of his fans should contest in the elections, not even as independent candidates.[48] In an interview later, he categorically asserted,[49] 'Cinema is my world; I will not come to politics'. But the story was not to stop there.[50]

Hardly a few months later during the by-election to Andipatti assembly seat for which the chief ministerial candidate Jayalalithaa contested, the opposition parties were seriously contemplating whether or not to field a strong common candidate against her; some[51] even proposed that RK should take up this challenge and contest in the election. In fact, that the voters of Andipatti were somewhat ready to consider RK as a serious contender if only he contested was brought to light by the *PS Study 2002*.[52] According to the first round of the study (pre-campaign phase), the star candidate Jayalalithaa got 46.7 per cent, and her rival DMK candidate Vaigai Sekar 33.4 per cent. But if RK were to contest, 47 per cent said they would go for him, whereas the chief ministerial candidate got only 29.8 per cent, and the DMK candidate a paltry 11.9 per cent. However, instead of RK, if someone with RK's support were to contest, s/he would get only 28.1 per cent but Jayalalithaa, 42.7 per cent. It is noteworthy, at the same time, 27 per cent of the ADMK voters, i.e., those who had said would vote for ADMK, said they would not vote for ADMK if the chief-ministerial candidate Jayalalithaa were not to be in the fray. In a dramatic reversal, immediately after Jayalalithaa's campaign, the second round study conducted showed a deep slide in RK's popularity[53] — he would get only 31 per cent whereas Jayalalithaa's share soared to 50.1 per cent. The candidate with RK's support would fare much poorer with only 20.6 per cent but Jayalalithaa, 52.7 per cent. Without the hypothetical candidature of RK, 56.9 per cent would vote for Jayalalithaa, and 34.4 per cent for Vaigai Sekar. While there might be a change in RK's fortune because of the intervention of Jayalalithaa's campaign, he still remained the second relegating the DMK candidate to the third place.

When all eyes were focused on RK to know his response, he announced to the merriment of his fans, instead of his candidature, his next film project *Baba* for which he was the script writer. By doing so, on the one hand he effectively evaded the issue whether he was

POLITICS BEYOND POLITICS ■ 227

ready to contest opposite Jayalalithaa, his sworn enemy once, and prove that he was the real super star superior to Jayalalithaa; on the other, he cleverly hooked his fans and generated fresh excitement among them by giving room for the expectation that the answer to the question of his entering politics or not would be answered in the forthcoming film. And when the film *Baba* was about to be released, 'I am very contented with cinema', said RK in a function held in Malaysia, 'and to get into politics depends on god's mandate'.[54] Thus RK made an about-turn in a matter of a year, from saying 'cinema was his world' to saying 'he was contended with cinema'. But when *Baba* was released in August 2002 amidst much media hype, controversy regarding reference to E. V. R. Periyar in lyrics and confrontation with the PMK which, objecting to excessive drinking and smoking scenes, went to the extent of disrupting screenings in a few theatres, the film failed to satisfy any and performed miserably at the box office.[55] After the rude shock from *Baba*, RK had to reassure for himself and prove again for others that his fans were still with him, and the issue of sharing Cauveri waters between Karnataka and Thamizh Nadu came as timely in October 2002. While the Thamizh Nadu Cine Artistes Association held a protest rally in Neyveli headed by filmmaker Bharathiraja to warn Karnataka that electricity supplied to them from Neyveli would be cut off, if they did not release waters as per court orders, RK held an independent nine-hour fast in Chennai the very next day, placing his own demand for linking all the rivers of India and announcing that he would donate ₹ 1 crore to the then prime minister Vajpayee, if the project took off. After this he went into hiding, busying himself probably with his next film project.

When the 2004 parliamentary elections were drawing near, RK was again in the limelight. This time though his intervention was definite and unambiguous like the one in 1996, and he straight named the 'villain' to be opposed and the 'hero' to be supported. In the press statement[56] RK issued in this context which was inflammatory and emotionally charged with very caustic remarks against the PMK leader Ramadoss, he endorsed his fans' decision to work against the PMK in all the six constituencies the party fielded candidates (five in Thamizh Nadu and one in Pondicherry), and directed his fans to vote for the ADMK and the BJP because these parties 'would provide protection to his fans' against the attacks of the PMK cadres. In the second part of the same press statement RK favoured Vajpayee for prime-ministership

228 ■ POPULAR CINEMA AND POLITICS IN SOUTH INDIA

and declared he would vote for the BJP because their election manifesto mentioned interlinking of all the rivers of India. He further appealed not only to those in Thamizh Nadu but 'all the people living in India' to think (like him) and vote (like him). The results should have been nightmarish to RK because the people neither thought like him nor voted to his liking! The PMK won in all the six constituencies with significant margins. Not only that. In Delhi Ramadoss was accorded the status of a 'prince' (the king/maker was Karunanidhi), with ministerial berth for his son Anbumani who did not even contest in the elections! And in the Centre, the rather 'unknown' Congressman Manmohan Singh, not Vajpayee, became the Prime Minister, without contesting in the elections!

On closer scrutiny of RK's involvement in this election, the following points stand out:

First, RK seemed to have sincerely believed that his film *Baba* flopped at the box-office because of the disruption of screenings by the PMK cadres at the instigation of their leader Ramadoss. RK's reading of the *Baba* fiasco, however, was incomplete, if not entirely wrong, because the public reading of the same differed vastly from his, and made clear that the reasons for the failure of *Baba* were to be seen mainly in the film itself. According to the *PS Study 2004* (mid-campaign phase),[57] of the top five reasons for the failure of *Baba*, three responses (constituting 65.8 per cent of total) concerned the narrative aspects (the story was not appealing to the public — 36.4 per cent, the character did not suit RK's image — 21.3 per cent, disappointment with the film because there was nothing spectacular in the story comparable to the excessive publicity — 8.1 per cent), one concerned the adverse role of media (unfavourable reviews on TV and newspapers –27.8 per cent), and the last in the list concerned the role of the PMK[58] (disruption of screening by PMK in some places — a meagre 6.4 per cent). This shows that RK did not see the complete picture of the whole *Baba* episode. Moreover, he also committed another mistake by stretching this issue too far, as if it were the most important national issue that should decide one's electoral choice — that too after a lapse of almost two years since it had taken place. Granted, this might be a grave enough issue for his fans, but it would not be fair to assume that the same weightage would be given also by the public. This obviously was too narrow and too personal an issue to be on the national-level election agenda, and in fact, people of Thamizh Nadu had really more pressing things to consider in this election as the subsequent discussion would delineate.

POLITICS BEYOND POLITICS ■ 229

Second, RK chose a weak enemy, if not a wrong enemy, in the person of Ramadoss because the image of Ramadoss as the leader of a party that is largely confined[59] geographically to a few northern districts of Thamizh Nadu and *caste-wise* to the *Vanniar* community predominant in those districts was not on par with RK's 'super-star' image. Even in terms of outcome, since this being a parliamentary election which normally[60] would not have any major repercussion on the affairs of the State, the impact of defeating RD would only be very limited — it would not in any significantly visible or tangible manner alter the status[61] of neither the fans nor RK, except, might be, making them feel proud that they had established themselves as a force to reckon with in the subsequent elections.

Third, there were too many lacunas in cinelating from the realms of cinematic to cinelitic to politik. In the cinematic realm, the tactexting in *Padaiyappaa* targetted Jayalalithaa, while in *Baba* the target shifted to a male politician, probably alluding to Karunanidhi. The fans were at a loss as to which 'stand' of RK was to be privileged — the *Padaiyappaa* stand or the *Baba* stand — since *Padaiyappaa* was such a massive hit and the tactexted message, reinforced by the series of subsequent *vetri vizhaa*s, continued to loom large among the fans even after the release of *Baba*. The target in the cinelitic realm was Ramadoss and the PMK in the *Baba* episode when all RK fans all over the statewere fully engaged. However, this lasted only for a brief period till the confrontation took on a direct political dimension. In the realm of politik, the battle-lines were not clearly drawn as it was obvious from the wavering in the 2004 press statement. While naming Ramadoss as the enemy to be opposed was clear, the positioning of Ramadoss in the overall electoral milieu was highly misleading. Statements such as, 'If they win, it does not mean we have lost; if they lose, it does not mean we have won', only showed his diffidence and self-doubt. To cap it all, in conclusion of his tirades against Ramadoss came the statement, 'You have taken refuge in the house of my friends', referring to Ramadoss's alliance with the DMK whose chief Karunanidhi was supposed to be RK's friend; and ironically, Jayalalithaa, though not yet a friend of RK, was not to be his enemy either, because of her alliance with the BJP, whose leader Vajpayee RK supported. In terms of concrete action in the electoral field, majority of his fans were 'jobless'. The fans in the six constituencies all situated in the northern part of Thamizh Nadu and the adjacent Pondicherry had a reason to be active also in the political

230 ◾ POPULAR CINEMA AND POLITICS IN SOUTH INDIA

realm, but the fans in the other 34 constituencies did not have much activity because there was no 'villain' to be opposed — in these areas the PMK itself was practically non-existent. The whole scenario which only vitiated the anti-establishment, *supra-legal* image of RK, failed to catch the imagination of his ardent fans who legitimately wanted their *thalaivar* to be the king or at least the king-maker.[62] Many were in fact disappointed and withdrew, and that explains the debacle RK met with in the elections. The *PS Study 2004* (mid-campaign phase) amply supports this observation. According to the study, only a little above one-tenth of Thamizh Nadu voters (10.7 per cent) endorsed the view that opposing the PMK was the right strategy to prove RK's strength. Majority of the respondents (41.2 per cent) expressed the opinion that RK should have kept quiet in this election. Around one-fourth (24.5 per cent) thought that RK should have handled the conflict with Ramadoss at the personal level without having resorted to politicising it. Other responses included: RK should have started a new party (13.8 per cent), he should have fielded his own fans as candidates without supporting any party (9.8 per cent).

Fourth, RK picked up a utopian dream of sorts that was not uppermost in the electoral agenda of the people of Thamizh Nadu, viz., interlinking rivers, as the deciding issue — in fact, the only issue — for the election. Regarding his claim that he supported the BJP *because* it was for linking rivers, only 13.0 per cent thought, according to *PS Study 2004* (mid-campaign phase), that this was a well-informed decision taken after carefully reading and reflecting on the manifestos of all the parties, whereas almost double that percentage (25.5 per cent) thought he had already decided to support the BJP, and he gave this apparently unconvincing, superficial reason only to justify his stand already taken. The strongest response (30.9 per cent) was that RK failed to see the more important issues that plague the nation, and an equally strong response (30.6 per cent) was that we did not have to attach much importance since this was his personal view.

Fifth, RK's reading of the election dynamics and the voters' mind was probably misinformed and clearly out of sync with the general voters, though he might have emotionally echoed the sentiments of his hardcore fans. According to *PS Study 2004* (mid-campaign phase), majority (58.1 per cent) foresaw a coalition government at the centre led by the INC, and only about one-third (35.0 per cent) expected the BJP alliance to form the government. In terms of voting, according

POLITICS BEYOND POLITICS ◾ 231

to the study, the 'pro–DMK wave' apparently swept the State, with the DMK alliance having a definite lead with 62.1 per cent, and the ADMK alliance with only half of it (31.7 per cent). In terms of seats, the study noted, all except two were found to be highly favourable to the DMK alliance (as per actual results, the alliance bagged all the seats). Regarding the next PM, Sonia Gandhi was ahead of Vajpayee by 10 points (Sonia — 72.0, Vajpayee — 62.1).[63] While this was the mood of the voters, RK asserted in his press statement (on 11 April 2004) that while he 'went around many States in India', one thing was 'directly evident' to him, i.e., 'in this election it is the NDA government under Vajpayee's leadership that is going to be seated at the Centre'. Like a hardcore BJP party cadre RK declared categorically that this was 'confirmed', ironically when the BJP itself had started realising its poll campaign strategy pitching on the 'feel-good' factor was not all that good and even attempted in some places to shift the focus from 'India Shining' to local issues.[64]

Sixth, ever since the ADMK came to power in 2001, there had been an emotional upheaval rocking the State with too many and too frequent traumatic happenings. Starting with the sensational midnight arrest of the DMK chief Karunanidhi and Union Minister Murasoli Maran that jolted the State, the insensitive and ill-timed anti-conversion act which created quite a stir among the minorities, the banning of animal sacrifices in temples, a time-honoured socio-cultural 'little tradition' practice, not merely a religious ritual, which antagonised the rural masses, the retrenchment of about 10,000 road workers by abolishing the post of 'gang mazdoor' on the grounds of economy, the non-bailable arrests of Pazha. Nedumaran and the MDMK leader Vaiko under POTA (Prevention of Terrorist Activities Act) for supporting the LTTE, and the general anti-LTTE, anti-Thamizh Eezham stand taken by the Jayalalithaa government, which enraged the Thamizh nationalists, the issues that added up to the turmoil were indeed too many. The severest of them all that undid whatever good the government had done was the unprecedented en masse dismissal of over two-lakh government employees and the related events including midnight arrests, forced eviction of families from government quarters, and other forms of harassments. The DMK garnered and precipitated the anti-incumbency feelings of various quarters and, effectively combining it with sympathy for Karunanidhi, cleverly changed the very nature of the electoral game from the Centre-field to the State-field, where the

232 ■ POPULAR CINEMA AND POLITICS IN SOUTH INDIA

contest was between Karunanidhi and Jayalalithaa.[65] That people also had taken this election as a referendum on the ADMK regime was more than evident in the *PS Study 2004* (post-election phase), according to which a significant 38.9 per cent understood the astounding victory of the DMK alliance as a judgement against the ADMK rule, and another 17.2 per cent interpreted it as a mandate in favour of the DMK leadership; though the INC alliance eventually formed the government at the Centre, only 15.5 per cent thought the voting was for that alliance, and a meagre 11.4 per cent thought it was against the BJP rule.[66] RK on the contrary apparently failed to take cognisance of this mood of the voters, including his fans in as much as they were a part of the state. On the one hand, he had been keeping an unexplained silence over the burning issues of the state; on the other, he voluntarily joined the ADMK–BJP bandwagon and gave his 'voice' in support of the pan-Indian 'India Shining' chorus, which had little relevance to the people writhing under a repressive regime — at least as per the scenario then sketched out by the DMK.

Seventh, though RK was directly and emotionally involved in this election, his media visibility particularly on TV was negligible when compared to a similar situation in 1996. Sun TV, enjoying a viewership share[67] of over 70 per cent, which had earlier projected RK to be the super star 'redeemer' of Thamizh Nadu politics by the repeated telecast of his brief interview in 1996, not only now sidelined him by and large, because he happened to be in the camp opposite the DMK, the party the channel was identified with,[68] but also played havoc by the sensationalised vividness of depiction of all the crucial and critical issues over which RK had been tight-lipped. What Sun TV did in this context was not a mere 're-presenting', i.e., a reportage of past events, with the view to evoke the feeling of nostalgia; neither was it an overtly propagandist act of deliberate mis- or dis- information. Curiously, it had all these aspects and excess dimensions as well, thanks to the innovation in re-designing the footages of disparate, scattered, even unrelated past events into a coherent single story, not chronological but dramatic in structure. It is a kind of 're-presencing' the past events as a paradigmatic nonlinear montage assembled with a not-that-easily-visible ulterior motive and an embedded pre-decided sense — 'pre-sense' — giving a certain 'immediacy' to the past events as if they happened 'just yesterday'. A new collective reality is constructed by painting the present with all the traumatic past in one stroke, picturising the longitudinal happenings into a cross-sectional dramatic depiction. This amounts to a 'reverse palimpsest' technique (i.e., covering the present with the past, instead of doing the reverse), privileging the past as the foreground while the present recedes as the background. The past thus acquires a new meaning against the backdrop of the present, and it also becomes a statement on the present, rendering the present with a new meaning. The newly-designed, synergised action-replay is so incredibly credible and awesomely real that it elicits a terrific cumulative response of willing abandonment to an emotional hijack which in an electoral context metamorphoses into the behaviour against the incumbency.[69]

Further, RK's political intervention, though very strong this time, was not only ill-conceived[70] but also *ill-timed*, particularly when his super star image was at its lowest ebb after having suffered serious, multiple setbacks in politics and cinema. In the political front, his 'voice' in the previous two parliamentary elections had met with a lukewarm response, and in the last assembly election he deliberately avoided any 'voice' (but his silence was conspicuous, though) for fear of getting rejected. Moreover, he exposed his fear of failure when he chose to miss out on the golden opportunity to play hero–versus–villain with Jayalalithaa on a one–on–one basis in Andipatti. In the cine career front, the film *Baba* cost him very dear financially, and as an inevitable consequence his image as the 'selling hero' was shattered. According to the *PS Study 2004* (mid-campaign phase), only 12.8 per cent supported the view that this was the most opportune time[71] for RK to enter politics, and another 12.1 per cent thought that this might be the right time but there was no clarity in his political stand, while 14.4 per cent thought he should have waited till the next assembly elections. The majority opinion (60.7 per cent) was that he was unfit for politics, and he should confine himself only to acting.

Ninth, while it is true that there are hardcore fans ready even to die for RK, a vast majority of his fans and the general public as well like him as an actor, but not so much as a political leader: it is one thing to imitate his 'style', it is another to follow his dictates, especially when he himself is not the key player in the actual field. The reasons people cited for the voice of RK not being effective in 2004 elections augment this point. According to the *PS Study 2004* (post-election phase), over one-third (35.1 per cent) thought RK's voice was not effective

234 ■ POPULAR CINEMA AND POLITICS IN SOUTH INDIA

because he did not enjoy an adequate fan base, and another one-fourth (24.5 per cent) were of the opinion that his own fans had rejected his appeal. Around one-fifth (20.1 per cent) concluded that RK did not know politics, and an equal number (20.3 per cent) feared that by indulging in politics he had spoiled[72] his acting career. To the question whether RK would come to politics again, only 24.3 per cent answered in the affirmative, 36.7 per cent said he would not come, and majority response (39.0 per cent) was that even if he came people's support would not be there. When the same question was repeated in the *PS Study 2004* (November), only 12.3 per cent said he would come to politics, whereas 36.4 per cent replied in the negative and almost half the respondents (49.6 per cent) said there might not be support even if he came.[73] That RK was not effective as a political leader was again confirmed by the kind of interpretation given by the people to the silence of RK following the 2004 election results. According to the *PS Study 2004* (post-election phase), RK was keeping silence because, to go by the majority opinion (42.5 per cent), he had realised that his voice was not effective. As many as 30.3 per cent understood his silence as 'his usual style', and only 7.3 per cent thought he was getting ready for the forthcoming assembly elections.

While the foregoing analysis demonstrates that for majority of the people RK was a political misfit, regarding his future course of action as an actor, the opinions were so divided and varied according to the *PS Study 2004* (November),[74] ranging from guessing that he would continue to act (17.6 per cent) to recommending retirement from acting (19.9 per cent); while some expressed the doubt whether he would come up with another film (17.2 per cent), and whether he would be able to attract the younger generation because of his age (15.1 per cent), some others suggested that he could continue acting in roles that befitted his age (16.4 per cent). That was the predicament of RK at the close of the era: people perceived in general a rather bleak future, politically pulverised, and as an actor, stranded. On the part of RK, he had to prove: (*a*) after the box-office failure of *Baba* that he was still a selling super star and had his fans solidly behind him; and (*b*) after the humiliating defeat in the election that his voice still had an impact. The former in fact he achieved with *Chandramukhi*, and the latter he continued to evade, as we would see in the next section.

POLITICS BEYOND POLITICS ◀ 235

Era of Alternative-turned-Ally

With the formation of the political party called Daesiya Murpoakku Dravida Kazhakam (DMDK) by the actor-turned-politician Vijayakanth in September 2005, the cartography of Thamizh Nadu politics has got irreversibly changed and so the period spread over the last two assembly and two parliamentary elections could be termed as the era of the DMDK. Though the party was flagged off with tall claims to be the alternative[75] to the ADMK and the DMK — often derisively referred to as the 'Dravidian parties' — it had to come to terms in a short span of nine years and four elections with the fact that it could survive only as an ally to one of the very same 'Dravidian parties' it had sought to replace. In the first ever election faced by the DMDK in 2006, with all the hype comparing Vijayakanth's political entry to MGR's and N.T. Rama Rao's styles and fielding candidates in all the constituencies, it got only one seat won by the founder–leader Vijayakanth, but it came as a definite warning to other parties by the percentage of votes it could poll on its own — it had a clear edge over other minor parties such as the PMK, MDMK, CPI, CPI(M), and VCK, and equalled the INC in terms of vote share (Table 15.5).

Table 15.5
Era of Alternative-turned-Ally — Electoral Performance: 2006–14

	2006		2009		2011		2014	
Party	Seats	Vote %	Seats	Vote %	Seats	Vote %	Seats	Vote %
AIADMK	61	32.6	9	22.9	150	38.4	37	44.3
DMK	96	26.5	18	25.1	23	22.4	0	23.6
INC	34	8.4	8	15.0	5	9.3	0	4.3
PMK	18	5.7	0	6.4	3	5.2	1	4.4
MDMK	6	6.0	1	3.7	–	–	0	3.5
CPI(M)	9	2.7	1	2.2	10	2.4	0	0.5
CPI	6	1.6	1	2.8	9	2.0	0	0.5
VCK	2	1.3	1	2.4	0	1.5	0	1.5
BJP	0	2.0	0	2.3	0	2.2	1	5.5
DMDK	1	8.4	0	10.3	29	7.9	0	5.1

In the 2009 parliamentary elections given the Thamizh Nadu voters' psychology of applying different sets of norms for assembly and parliamentary elections, many of the DMDK cadres wished to align with

236 ■ POPULAR CINEMA AND POLITICS IN SOUTH INDIA

a national party, preferably the BJP, but Vijayakanth stubbornly stuck to his guns reiterating that his alliance was 'with god and the people'. Unfortunately, both his 'god and the people' forsook him, and the party was routed in all the constituencies. However, it improved its vote share from 8.4 per cent in 2006 to 10.3 per cent in 2009, vying with the INC for the third place. The electoral outcomes of these two elections revealed the size of more or less stable vote bank the DMDK had come to enjoy and its relative status among the parties. Realising that to have any significant presence in the assembly or in the parliament he had to align with one of the two major players, i.e., the ADMK or the DMK, Vijayakanth finally relented and made the strategic decision to align with the ADMK in 2011 assembly election, and, as could be expected, the alliance had a clean sweep, the DMDK winning 29 out of 41 seats contested, raising Vijayakanth to the status of the leader of the opposition in the assembly.[76] But the DMDK's alliance with the BJP in the subsequent 2014 parliamentary election led its vote share slip down to 5.1 per cent, winning no seat, while probably helping the BJP more than double its vote share to 5.5 per cent (from 2.2 per cent in 2011). Thus, Vijayakanth's limited success as an ally is at the same time a failure to be the alternative force in Thamizh Nadu.

This era also witnessed the formation of political parties by other film stars. Actor Sarath kumar who had been switching camps from the DMK to the ADMK finally followed suit after Vijayakanth by floating Akila Indhiya Samathuva Makkal Katchi; actor Karthick, after a short stint with the All India Forward Block, floated Naadaazhum Makkal Katchi; T. Rajendar, who had earlier left the DMK to start a party and after a while got it merged with the DMK, again left the DMK and floated Latchiya DMK. Interestingly, these actors' parties also have specific caste groups[77] as major, if not exclusive, supporters, as, for example, Sarathkumar's has significant support among the *Nadars* and Karthick's among the *Mukkulam*, both communities concentrated in the southern districts.

Starting parties during this period was not confined to cine stars alone. The *Kongu Vellala Gounder* community widespread in the north-western districts (known as *kongu nadu*) re-emerged with greater strength and by contesting 2009 parliamentary elections asserted itself as a force to reckon with in the *kongu nadu*. There was also realignment among the minority Muslims resulting in the formation of one more party with a secular face called Manithaneya Makkal Katchi which by 2011

POLITICS BEYOND POLITICS   **237**

emerged as an important representative of the Muslim community. Indhiya Jananayaga Katchi started prior to 2011 assembly election by educationist turned politician[78] Pachamuthu of SRM University targeting the votes of *Parkavakulam*[79] joined the fray as the latest addition.

Against the background as outlined above, let us now turn to the key factors that impacted on the three elections held during this era. The 2006 election scenario was not only hemmed in by several of the unresolved issues[80] that had caused the decimation of the ADMK alliance in 2004 election but also got compounded by newer issues such as the arrest of Kanchi Sankaracharya in connection with a murder case which antagonised the caste Hindus,[81] and the official participation of the ADMK cadres in the *kar seva* of the BJP organised as an attempt to build the Ram temple at Ayodhya which further alienated the religious minorities from the ADMK. At the same time, following the defeat in 2004, Jayalalithaa tried on the one hand to assuage the feelings of the people by revoking the controversial legislations and soft-pedalling many issues, and on the other hand she implemented many welfare schemes to woo the voters.[82] The DMK on its part formed a strong alliance with the INC, PMK and the Left, whereas the ADMK had only MDMK and VCK as partners. Besides, the DMK came up with a manifesto promising several welfare schemes including a free colour TV set to every home. Though many were sceptical about the practicality of these schemes, the DMK manifesto received such a rousing public welcome that the ADMK also was forced to imitate it.[83] The cumulative effect of all these factors resulted for the first time in a fractured verdict, with no party enjoying an absolute majority, though the DMK emerged as the single largest party and formed the government which was throughout its term of the next five years disparagingly referred to as 'minority government' by Jayalalithaa.

In the context of 2009 election, people had no great complaints against the DMK government in the state and the INC-led government at the centre, and have learnt to tolerate the frequent current cuts and escalating prices as inevitable;[84] only the worsening condition of the Thamizhs in Sri Lanka during this time was becoming a thorn in the flesh of the DMK-INC combine.[85] As the war in Sri Lanka intensified killing the innocent Thamizh civilians in thousands, people in Thamizh Nadu were so enraged, and the youth spontaneously took to the streets, triggered off by the suicide of Muthukumar.[86] By January 2009, the whole state was simmering with anger[87] and *all*[88] the parties with

238 ◾ POPULAR CINEMA AND POLITICS IN SOUTH INDIA

election in mind were devising strategies to capitalise on this. When majority of the people accused the INC-led government for actively supporting the Sri Lankan war crimes, the DMK claiming to be the champion of the 'world Thamizhs' and VCK another party known for the commitment of its leader Thirumavalavan to the cause of the Sri Lankan Thamizhs were not willing to break ties with the INC and, much worse, shared the same dais with Sonia Gandhi and other Congress leaders during electioneering. While remaining staunch allies of the INC, the DMK and the VCK in the same breadth were placing demands on the INC to stop the war against the Thamizhs in Sri Lanka — the DMK chief and chief minister of the State Karunanidhi went to the extent of going on a hunger strike[89] regarding this. In the other camp, Jayalalithaa who had all along vehemently opposed the LTTE became a surprise champion of the Sri Lankan Thamizhs fighting against the Sinhalese government. In another dramatic move, the PMK who had been clinging on to power at the Centre till the last moment severed its ties with the INC all of a sudden citing INC's apathy towards Thamizhs' cause as the reason and joined hands with the ADMK. Because of contradictory statements and behaviours of the politicians such an intensely emotional issue became profoundly de-focussed and thoroughly directionless, and failed as a result to get precipitated as the rallying point neither against the ruling combine nor in favour of the opposition.[90] Given this general climate of all-pervasive anguish, in an otherwise issueless election, the only thing that was widely talked about was the 'Alagiri Formula' or the 'Thirumangalam Formula'[91] which in a way 'repressed' the 'collective anguish' and induced a mood of celebration of a 'national festival'.[92] Moreover, the alternatives[93] to the INC-led alliance available at the national and constituency levels were no better, and the people therefore voted more in favour of the DMK alliance, though half-heartedly.[94]

In the 2011 assembly elections, however, the Thamizh Nadu voters got greater scope to give a somewhat free vent to their emotions. Four factors which played an important role in this election could be highlighted. First, the continued support of the INC-led government to Rajapaksa government even when many countries accused it of war crimes with substantial evidence telecast on Channel 4 of the UK forced the ardent Thamizh voters conclude that the Centre did not bother to respect their feelings and it was time to teach the INC a hard

POLITICS BEYOND POLITICS ◀ 239

lesson. These anti-Congress sentiments were further augmented by the aggressive anti-Congress campaign by Thamizh activist movements such as *Naam Thamizhar Katchi* of cine actor-cum-director-turned activist Seemaan who was becoming increasingly popular among the Thamizh enthusiasts, particularly the youth.[95] Second, whether the 2G scam involving the DMK became a serious election issue or not, the massiveness of the wealth allegedly amassed by the DMK — it was so common during the election campaign to quiz about the number of zeros in the scam amount — certainly created a climate for the voters to demand as a matter of right a share in the booty! The opposition parties also campaigned to that effect 'advising' the people to get the money but vote for them, though the Election Commission on its part was running a counter campaign asking the people to vote but refrain from accepting money for voting.[96] All these contributed to effective neutralisation of the Alagiri Formula, and led to a voter turn-out which was considered unprecedentedly high. Third, in spite of fulfilling several of the election promises, the DMK managed to earn a bad name because of the excessive involvement of Karunanidhi's families in government affairs, and the undue importance given to the wards of Karunanidhi in public and government functions.[97] Fourth, the DMDK which had been insisting on being the alternative and contesting on its own, relaxed its position and aligned with the ADMK; thus the ADMK alliance emerged stronger than the DMK's.

Thamizh Nadu witnessed a peculiar scenario in 2014 parliamentary elections. First, once Vijayakanth parted ways with the ADMK, other parties openly expressed their eagerness to align with the DMDK in the 2014 elections. Ultimately the BJP prevailed upon Vijayakanth and formed a relatively 'mega' alliance with DMDK, its rival PMK, MDMK, and three others as partners. While the ADMK closed doors for others, the DMK severed its ties with the INC just prior to the elections and managed to bring a few others to its fold. Finally it turned out to be a multi-cornered contest with at least five major players (ADMK, DMK, INC, BJP and the Left), each (except the BJP) almost contesting on its own strength. Second, while the 'Modi wave' was sweeping across the North India, Thamizh Nadu experienced a 'pro-ammaa' wave thanks to the ADMK's convincing campaign that Jayalalithaa would have a chance to be the next PM or at least she would play a decisive role in the centre. Third, the BJP alliance tried to project itself as the

240 ■ POPULAR CINEMA AND POLITICS IN SOUTH INDIA

most credible to champion the cause of Eezham Thamizhs (because it had MDMK and PMK as partners), and most suited to be the alternative to the Dravidian and the Congress parties. Fourth, realising that the charisma of Vijayakanth or the Thamizh sentiments of Vaiko and Ramadoss would not suffice to increase its support base the BJP tried to woo other leading cine stars: At the thick of his whirlwind campaign, the BJP prime ministerial candidate Modi made a 'courtesy' visit to RK at his residence on 13 April, obviously embarrassing Ramadoss and Vijayakanth; and three days later 'ilaya thalapathi' Vijay went to Coimbatore to pay a 'courtesy' visit to Modi (24 April was the polling day in Thamizh Nadu). Fifth, the Election Commission took stringent measures to curb the cash flow: For the first time in election history it clamped Section 144 of CrPC for 36 hours from the time the campaign ended, which the opposition parties criticised as a move to facilitate the ruling ADMK to surreptitiously distribute cash to voters. The results came as a pleasant surprise to the ADMK, winning 37 seats, far higher than the polsters' predictions. The BJP and PMK won one seat each but in terms of vote share the BJP emerged as the third largest, while the PMK, DMDK and MDMK registered a decrease.

The role of RK in these four elections was insignificant, though during this period he hit the headlines a few times, but mostly film-related. After the devastating blow he received in 2004 parliamentary elections, RK lay low and got busy with his film *Chandramukhi*. More than his political image, RK was in fact worried about his success in the film world, and was keen on a comeback after the *Baba*-blow. With the 2006 assembly election round the corner, RK indeed regained his super-stardom in cinema[98] with the run-away success of *Chandramukhi*, though he carefully avoided any role in the election by saying that he had already got busy with his next mega film project *Sivaji* with Shankar, one of the costliest directors in the country. The real star attraction in this election was 'puratchi kalaignar' 'captain' Vijayakanth with another new political title '*karuppu* MGR' (Dark MGR).[99]

That the people also were not expecting RK to lend his 'voice' was clear from the *PS Study 2006 April*. To the question, whom RK might support in the forthcoming assembly election, more than half (52.2 per cent) said he might not openly support anyone as he was currently busy with his *Sivaji* shooting; that he might support the ADMK was another significant response (18.9 per cent). When asked what the response would be, just in case RK openly announced his support to a party, around one-third (32 per cent) guessed there might not be any impact, as was the case in the preceding parliamentary election; an almost equally strong response (29.2 per cent) was that his own fans were not in a mood to listen to him; only a small percentage (16.4 per cent) expressed the opinion that the party RK supported would win majority of seats.

Of all the events during the year that preceded the 2009 general elections, three significant events concerning RK's politics need to be mentioned here. First, in April 2008, together with other film personalities RK criticised the Karnataka government for objecting to the Thamizh Nadu's Hogenekkal drinking water project. But he soon (in July) retreated and apologised *in Kannada* to the people of Karnataka, and pleaded with them to allow the release of his film *Kuselan* in Karnataka.[100] This episode shows that RK was more concerned about his film business rather than his commitment to the welfare of the Thamizhs. Second, when a group of overenthusiastic fans were ready with the name, flag, and logo for a party in RK's name in October 2008, he issued a press statement severely warning them not to start any party in his name, and ended his press release stating, 'Finally and firmly what I want to say is, **"If I have to come to politics, no one can compel me. If I decide thus to come to politics, none can prevent me either."** In that situation, I will welcome my fans to join me'(emphasis original).[101] The reason for making such a decision was that he was 'fully immersed in *Enthiran* which was coming up in gigantic proportions'. So he put a definite full-stop — at least for the time being — to all guesses and made it clear that he would not come to politics and film-acting was his utmost priority. Third, in November 2008 he appeared 'for name's sake' with other film personalities on the Sri Lankan Thamizh issue. His involvement was so nominal and uneventful that it would not in any way affect his film business. And when the parliamentary elections came in 2009 May, he got busy with the shooting of his *Enthiran*, another mega-budget project with director Shankar, slated to be released in 2010.

Nothing politically significant involving RK happened between the 2009 parliamentary and the 2011 assembly elections, except in a function in February 2010 to felicitate the chief minister Karunanidhi, a leading actor Ajith accused the office bearers of artistes' association of coercing

242 ■ POPULAR CINEMA AND POLITICS IN SOUTH INDIA

and intimidating artistes to attend public, political functions. When everyone was stunned and feeling awkward by the speech, RK, who was sharing the dais with Karunanidhi and Amitabh Bachchan, made the situation more awkward because he was the only one to clap — that too standing![102] — thus showing his displeasure with both the DMK-dominated artistes' association and Karunanidhi who had created the impression that he was obsessed with flattery and very fond of functions to honour him. But as if he regretted his action, he hurried to patch up with Karunanidhi by paying a visit to his house to invite him to his daughter's wedding. In 2011 April assembly elections, on the day of polling RK voted for twin-leaves in the morning, and in the evening watched the film *Ponnar Sankar* scripted by Karunanidhi, interestingly with Karunanidhi himself![103] During the elections to local bodies in October 2011, RK did not vote citing health reasons. However, a few days earlier to the polling day he went to Hyderabad to play a cameo role in Shah Rukh Khan's *Ra-One*, and hardly a couple of days after the polling day he travelled 175 kms by road to Thiruppathi.[104] Thus, his political saga[105] came to the sad end[106] whereby the democratic duty of exercising one's franchise was subordinated to one's business interests or personal commitments.

In 2014, RK was busy with his *Koachadaiyaan* and remained invisible in the electoral battlefield, till Modi met him. Interestingly, neither RK fans nor the general voters could ascribe any political significance to this meeting because RK was non-committal in his support — he just wished Modi 'all the best'. Even the BJP which had expected RK to 'give voice' was not able to get any worthwhile mileage out of this.

As an actor, however, RK has (re-)established[107] himself as a selling — probably the highest paid-actor — and with global releases of mega budget blockbusters such as *Sivaji* and *Enthiran* he has emerged as the 'god of Indian cinema'.[108] RK himself has openly acknowledged that 'god has given him an actor's role to play',[109] and his 'capital investment' (*moolathanam*) in the cine field is the speed of his body'.[110] He is confident to assert, 'I will continue to act as long as there is speed in my body'.[111]

Even as the era under scrutiny concludes with the (down)fall of RK as a politician and vanishing into political oblivion, or conversely, with the resurrection of RK as an actor of global proportions, the new era has dawned with the comeback with a bang of Jayalalithaa as the CM and with Vijayakanth as the leader of the opposition with 29 MLAs at his command. As an interesting coincidence, for the first time in the Thamizh Nadu assembly the leaders of both the ruling and the opposition parties have been the front-of-the-camera cine artistes. However, while Jayalalithaa has already gone through enough ordeals to shed off even the traces of cine glamour surrounding her and to emerge as a seasoned politician in her own rights (as *ammaa*), Vijayakanth has been made to become painfully aware in the assembly itself that cinema and politics are different: when Vijayakanth demanded time during the assembly session on 1 February 2012 to discuss issues such as Thane cyclone relief works in Cuddalore district and unexpected hikes in bus fare and milk price, the ADMK MLAs objected to his body language, shouting, 'this is not cinema' (*ithu cinema illa*).[112] Vijayakanth therefore has to *de-cinematise* himself, if he has to survive as a political leader! Incidentally, the performance of the DMDK in the by-elections[113] from Shankarankoil (March 2012) and Pudukottai (June 2012), and the 2014 parliamentary elections is a stark reminder that Vijayakanth the '*karuppu* MGR' has a long way to go, if he has to emerge as the 'captain' for the State.[114]

Notes

1. No empirical study has been done yet to establish cause-and-effect relationship between popular reception to stars and people's voting behaviour. There is no sufficient ground to rule out the possibility that it may be a mere *coincidence* that the people's choice happens to fall on persons related to the cinema industry.
2. Ilamathi (1998b).
3. The results of 1952 elections were as follows: INC 152 (for the assembly) and 35 (for parliament), Communist Party of India 62 and 8, Kisan Mazdoor Praja Party 35 and 6, Tamil Nadu Toilers Party 19 and 4, Krishikar 15, Socialist Party 13 and 2, Commonweal Party 6 and 3, Muslim League 5 and 1, All India Forward Bloc (Marxist Group) 3 and 1, Federation 2, Justice Party 1, and Independents 62 and 15. All the election related data are gathered from the official publications of the Election Commission of India and the Public (Elections) Department, Government of Tamil Nadu, unless explicitly stated otherwise.
4. Rajadurai and Geetha (2000: 559).

244 ■ POPULAR CINEMA AND POLITICS IN SOUTH INDIA

5. Ilamathi (1998b: 196). MGR also was arrested during the anti-Hindi agitations; it is said that he spent five days in jail. See Vijayan (1997: 42–45).

6. Ilamathi (1998b: 96). It may be mentioned here that the politics in the Madras Presidency was heavily dominated by leaders of Telugu origins. The legacy continues to date with Telugu-speaking politicians playing a significant role in Thamizh Nadu politics. The notion of 'Dravida' also has served as a protective cover for them. In fact, 'Dravida' only helped — is helping — the non-Thamizh politicians in Thamizh Nadu to justify themselves. Remember how MGR exploited this. No wonder why 'Thamizh' politicians like S. Ramadoss criticise 'Dravida' as a mirage or a myth (*maayai*).

7. If Annadurai's ascendancy in politics is construed as the result of his links with the cine field, then his defeat in his native constituency is enough to prove that the people are able to transcend the cine-glamour surrounding him. It may be reiterated that Anna was endowed with great political acumen, and was indeed multifaceted with skills such as oratory for which he was primarily known, and writing of which script writing was a part; the people rightly saw him as an 'arignar', and not as a cine personality, though the opposition leaders derided him and his team as 'kooththaadigal'. The real link Anna had with the cinema, from the point of view of the ordinary people, was in the form of his 'owning' MGR as his 'ithaya kani' and MGR conceding him to be his leader.

8. The votes got by a party as an alliance partner is in fact the sum total of the votes of all constituent parties in the constituencies it contests, and so the votes it polls ('vote share') cannot be an accurate measure of its own individual strength ('vote bank').

9. Ilamathi (1998a: 101); also, Thandavan (1987: 49).

10. Thandavan (1987: 51).

11. MGR used to deliberately delay his arrival to the meetings. His late arrival usually disrupted the meeting, which would have already commenced, and thus drawing the attention of all towards him. After Anna's demise, he regularly practiced deliberate late-arrival as a psycho-political tactic. The film *Iruvar* directed by Mani Ratnam has a sequence graphically depicting this attention-drawing mechanism.

12. MGR obviously had his vested interest in opposing the lifting of prohibition. He was afraid that he might lose out a chunk of his film audience, if they started spending their already meagre income on drinking.

13. Editorial Board of Manimekalai Pirasuram (1990: 76).

14. Gopanna (1999: 93).

15. The term 'meta-rational' refers to the kind of 'reasoning with the heart'. Such a reasoning often eludes the grasp of the scholars who tend to think that the thinking is the exclusive prerogative of the 'head'. They tend to

POLITICS BEYOND POLITICS **245**

overlook the fact that the heart, after all, 'has its reasons, which the reason does not know', as the 17th century French philosopher Pascal would say in his posthumous work *Pensees*. The term, however, is used in this study interchangeably with intuitive logic.

16. Mohandas (1992: 45).
17. Ibid.: 27.
18. Except in 1967 when the elections for the parliament and the assembly were simultaneously held. The INC was the ruling party then both at the Centre and the State. As noted earlier, though both the DMK and the INC had a more or less equal percentage of votes, the DMK won mainly because of the extensive alliance. After Rajiv Gandhi, the INC slowly fell out of favour with the Thamizhs. Though the entry of Sonia Gandhi marginally revived the attachment to the Nehru family, as evidenced in the kind of response to the ADMK–INC combine in 1999, it was too late by then — the TNCC had been split in 1996, and the splinter group TMC had emerged stronger. However, after the merger of the TMC with the INC, things again improved for the INC. During 2004 elections the Democratic Progressive Alliance (DPA) headed by the DMK in Thamizh Nadu swept the poll, winning all the 39 seats. Even in the 2009 parliamentary elections, when many thought the going would be very tough for the Congress because of its stand on the sensitive Sri Lankan Thamizh issue, it managed to win eight out of 15 seats it contested. The story is different when it comes to the assembly elections, in which the people of Thamizh Nadu go by the state-level players and issues.
19. Ilamathi (1998a: 161–62).
20. Ibid.: 174.
21. Leave alone his party, MGR's own individual performance also was not the 'ultimate'. In 1977, for example, when he contested in Aruppukottai — that too as the chief-ministerial candidate — he secured around 56 per cent of votes polled (over 31 per cent electors did not vote; that means, MGR's charisma was not strong enough to pull them to the booths!), whereas there were others who had outshone him: ADMK's S. Ramachandran won Panrutti with 59 per cent, FBL's Mookaiah Thevar won Usilampatti with 62 per cent, and JNP's Vijayaraghavan won Killiyur with 79 per cent. See: Election Commission of India's Statistical Report for 1977.
22. Even in 1972 when MGR started his party, he waited to be dismissed from the DMK so that he could cash in on the public sympathy for him as the victim who had raised just questions but was unjustly punished. 'Getting victimised' also served as an emotional justification for starting his party.
23. The worst kind of humiliation Jayalalithaa could ever suffer as a woman concerns Karunanidhi's and other DMK men's frequent male-chauvinistic, sadistic, derogatory references to her past, particularly her living with

246 ■ POPULAR CINEMA AND POLITICS IN SOUTH INDIA

the Telugu romantic hero Sobhan Babu. For example, in 1989 when Karunanidhi was the CM and Jayalalithaa, the leader of the opposition, he made an unwarranted comment on this in the assembly itself (and there was also an attempt to physical assault on her by two DMK ministers), which provoked her to vow that she would enter the assembly only as the CM. Twenty years later, in 2009, when Jayalalithaa referred to the DMK government as 'the minority government' — which is a political statement — Karunanidhi retorted by a personal attack on Jayalalithaa, calling her 'thirumathi' (meaning, Mrs.), implying that she was married to Sobhan Babu, and reprinting in the DMK's official daily *Murasoli* (dated 19.08.2009) Jayalalithaa's old interview to *Kumudham* weekly (in which she talked about her relationship with Sobhan Babu). A few Telugu channels picked this up and made a 'news' story probing into Jayalalithaa–Sobhan Babu affair. For example, see http://www.youtube.com/watch?v =OM-FMumPshs (video uploaded on *You Tube* on 23 August 2009; accessed on 10 May 2012).

24. Looking from another angle, the birth of the TMC in the act of protest makes it the latest incarnation of the 'politics of dissent' spearheaded by Periyar. Quite strikingly, while all the front-rung leaders of the TMC when floated were non-Brahmins, the INC president and the ADMK general secretary happened to be Brahmins. The remnants of the 'anti-North' sentiment of Periyar could be found in the very naming of the party as the *Thamizh Maanila* Congress.

25. Since RK also gave them the hope that he might at any time start his party, the number of fan clubs soared — so much so that Sathyanarayana, the president of the All India Rajinikanth Rasigar Mandram, had to warn them not to open RK *mandrams* in names other than 'Rajinikanth Rasigar Narpani Mandram' (See *Thina Thanthi*, 3 August 1995). On closer scrutiny, it could be discovered that these *mandrams* were purposely started by politicians craving for RK's support as a device to lure him to support them.

26. For example, he was moved with sympathy for R. M. Veerappan and supported his politiking; parties like MDMK were hopeful that he would support them; he tried to block the INC aligning with the ADMK; later he announced no party should use his name or picture; suddenly he left the country; he came back and supported the DMK–TMC alliance.

27. To be fair to RK, two hypothetical instances may be considered. First of all, what if Moopanar, who had the boldness to break away from the Congress but lacked the confidence to face the elections alone, dared to go alone with RK's support or with Moopanar consenting to project RK as the chief ministerial candidate? I am of the opinion that the TMC

could have won in either case, given the fact that people were angry with Jayalalithaa and generally disillusioned with the so-called 'Dravidian' parties. But in either case RK would not be the 'super star'. If Moopanar had become the CM with RK's support, RK would only be the king-maker, not the king himself — a situation not so different from he supporting the DMK–TMC combine. If RK became the CM, Moopanar will be the king-maker, which would certainly undermine RK as the super star of politics. Second, again for the sake of argument, if RK started a party while Moopanar also started his, then, probably the anti-Jayalalithaa votes would have been divided; besides, the Thamizh versus non-Thamizh issue would have been raked up. More importantly, RK would not be in a position to talk of 'alternative' to 'Dravidian' parties, because he himself would need this 'Dravidian cover' to justify his existence in Thamizh Nadu. (Remember how MGR used this effectively to cover his Malayalee origins. This is also applicable to Vijayakanth's politics as well.)

28. A committed party cadre owes great allegiance to his party and is emotionally attached to the party leader — often bordering on fanaticism — just as a devoutly religious person would be to his religion and god. The word 'faithful' with its religious connotations explains this phenomenon better than the word 'loyal'. Recall also our earlier discussion on *nadukal* politics.

29. The *PS Study* 2004 (November) provides a substantial support to this observation. According to the study, the party-wise percentages of *party members* ready to desert their party in favour of RK in the event of his floating his own party are as follows: ADMK — 11.3 per cent, DMK — 10.0 per cent, BJP — 14.6 per cent, INC — 17.4 per cent, Left parties (CPI and CPI[M]) — 16.7 per cent, MDMK — 12.5 per cent, and none in PMK. The corresponding figures for Vijayakanth are: ADMK — 19.5 per cent, DMK — 11.2 per cent, BJP — 14.6 per cent, INC — 8.7 per cent, Left parties — 16.7 per cent, PMK — 9.1 per cent, MDMK — 16.7 per cent. Vijayakanth seems to enjoy a slightly better support than RK. The study also reveals that even RK's fans do not overwhelmingly support RK starting his own party. The percentages of various categories of fans supporting RK are as follows: registered fan club members — 41.7 per cent, ardent fans but not registered members — 39.4 per cent, and admirers (who watch all his films but do not indulge in typical fan club activities) — 26.5 per cent. Surprisingly, there does not seem to be a big difference between fans and the general public in their support to RK starting party: different categories of RK's fans put together — 34.6 per cent; overall total (fans and general) average — 30.1 per cent. At the same time, RK is the most favourite of all actors (topping the top-ten list with 13.0 per cent, while Vijayakanth takes the third place with 10.7 per cent).

248 ■ POPULAR CINEMA AND POLITICS IN SOUTH INDIA

The *PS Study 2004 (November)* was elaborately designed by me (with a sample of 3256 spread over all the districts of Thamizh Nadu) to assess the state of the State, specifically with regard to the interplay of caste, religion, party and cinema. The reports on the findings served as position papers for the research seminar on 'Thamizhagam 2005: Caste-Religion-Party-Cinema: Thamizh Nadu Politics-Culture-History' organised from 3–5 December 2004 by Culture and Communication, Chennai.

30. The fact that RK gave only his voice and remained 'outside' the power race (as saviour/prophet) cinelates well with his image as a *renouncer* — an important motif in his films. He is the rightful owner/heir but magnanimously 'sacrifices' it for the sake of others. (This was also the story of the later mega-flop *Baba*.)

31. It could also be argued whether the apparent impact on voters attributed to RK is due to his brief statement against Jayalalithaa or because of the repeated telecast of that statement especially on Sun TV which then had an unparalleled reach, and was in fact synonymous with the term 'cable TV' by being the 'default channel' (i.e., the channel that is normally seen first as soon as the TV is switched on). Owned by the family of Murasoli Maran a front-rung DMK leader and nephew of Karunanidhi, Sun TV undertook a blatant and well-orchestrated campaign against Jayalalithaa. The campaign package consisted of repeated telecasts of interviews of anyone worth the name, including, as noted earlier, personalities like 'sandalwood' Veerappan; RK's interview synergised with the total campaign, may be as the climax. It is really unfortunate that no study has been made to gauge the extent of the impact of repeated telecasts (of contents such as RK's speech) on the electoral decision-making process of the voters. Even the more general areas such as the role of TV campaigns particularly on channels like Sun TV in the formation of public opinion have not been adequately studied. It should be remembered that RK, unlike MGR, is in the era of insatiably hungry back-to-back TV news channels, and is kept politically 'alive' *by TV* because TV needs many such icons.

32. The reverse process also needs to be simultaneously emphasised. It is true that the national players depend on the regional and minor parties; it is equally true that these minor and regional parties depend on the national ones for their survival. For the voters of Thamizh Nadu, the national parties who could lead the coalition government in the Centre have been narrowed down to the INC and BJP, on which depend the two strongest State level parties, i.e., the ADMK and DMK, for the parliamentary elections. The same reverse dependence is applicable also to the State assembly elections.

33. So much so that the 'national' parties are sometimes ignored, and much worse, considered liabilities at times, by the two State 'supremos' during

POLITICS BEYOND POLITICS ■ 249

the assembly elections particularly when they are not paired with the parliament elections. This is especially true in the case of BJP which always comes only after PMK and MDMK.

34. In 1996, the MDMK and PMK headed their own alliances (MDMK, CPI[M], and Janata Dal as one front; PMK and All India Indira Congress (Tiwari) as another front) but could not win any seat for the parliament, though the PMK won four assembly seats. Only when they aligned with either DMK or ADMK from 1998 had they won any seat for parliament and started enjoying any worthwhile presence in the state assembly. It may be mentioned that the PMK was started by Dr S. Ramadoss in 1989 as the political wing of *Vanniar Sangam* which he founded in 1980. The PMK has been contesting in elections from 1989 onwards, and in 1991 it won its first assembly seat.

35. The Thamizhaga Rajiv Congress (TRC) was formed by Vazhappadi Ramamurthy, who was once the president of the Thamizh Nadu Congress Committee. After leaving the INC, he was, for a while, with the Tiwari Congress in which ticket he contested in 1996. Later TRC merged with the INC, its mother party.

36. The MGR–ADMK was formed by S. Thirunavukkarasar, who had left the ADMK disgruntled, solely based on his popularity in Pudukottai constituency. His popularity cut across caste communities and he remained an undisputed leader, much like a benevolent feudal chieftain. His was a rare example of electoral politics wherein geographical affinities tended to transcend caste affinities. In 2002, however, he merged his party with the BJP.

37. Moopanar however gave up this demand in the later phase of his campaign and spoke of the 'MGR Rule' instead of the 'Kamaraj Rule'.

38. Contesting in just 141 seats cannot be construed as a sign of confidence on the part of the ADMK. During the time of seat-sharing there was apparently no wave as such either against the DMK or in favour of the ADMK, and it was generally thought that the fight would be very tough.

39. It is to be remembered that in a 'first-past-the-post' kind of electoral system as practised in India, even a slight swing in favour of a party can result in an unproportionately high number of seats in its favour.

40. The legal course of action also included arresting Jayalalithaa and remanding her to judicial custody for about two weeks in December 1996 in connection with a scam in the purchase of colour TV sets by her government.

41. At a time when the caste-based parties were blowing their trumpets too loud with the view to have a better bargain in seat sharing, the *PS Study 2001* (pre-alliance phase) observed that around 30 to 40 seats would be decided primarily by caste-based parties and organisations. But once the campaign took off, the *PS Study 2001* (mid-campaign phase) noted

250 ▪ POPULAR CINEMA AND POLITICS IN SOUTH INDIA

the definite change in the mood of the people and observed that these parties would play a significant role only in around 15 to 20 seats where there would be a stiff fight between ADMK and DMK alliances.

42. RK himself was not very convinced of his criticism of Jayalalithaa who was then not in power and his support for Karunanidhi was merely a half-hearted lip service, because, ever since the DMK came to power, the RK fans had been nurturing a feeling that the DMK government was sidelining them, a feeling which RK also shared and in fact effectively tactexted in the film *Arunaachalam* (and much later again in the film *Baba*). 'Sidelining' or 'not respecting' the fans are political euphemisms and meant in practice that they were not given any preference in the recruitment for a wide range and variety of government posts, in the sanctioning of government contracts, and in the implementation of government welfare schemes with them as beneficiaries or as 'mediators'. RK gave the interviews in 1998 and again in 1999 in support of the DMK alliance because he could not but oblige Karunanidhi, the then chief minister. During the birthday function on 13 December 2012, an apologetic RK stated that he supported the DMK alliance (in 1996) in order to prove that he was not a 'coward'; and once 'committed', he continued to support for the next five years because it was 'dharma', 'kadamai' (duty).

43. When the BJP leader L. K. Advani came to Coimbatore for campaigning in February 1998, there was a chain of explosions in 16 places, including the one where he was to address, killing over 50 persons. Already in December 1997 there had been bomb explosions in three trains killing at least 10.

44. The results of 1999 elections made two things obvious. First of all, though many political pundits saw an apparent contradiction in the DMK (claiming to be rationalist) aligning with the BJP (known for the so-called *hindutva*), people were either able to transcend the 'contradiction' for a greater cause and voted for Vajpayee or the DMK's rationalism had been so watered down over the years that they did not perceive its current practice as ideologically opposed to the BJP. Second, the TMC which came as a thunderbolt in 1996 and considered to be the potential alternative to the DMK and ADMK, was thoroughly routed, though it 'increased' its strength by forming an alliance with parties like VCK. This again shows that no party however strong it is can survive without the ADMK or DMK. This would once again be proved later in the case of the DMDK also.

45. However, the BJP-led alliance managed to get the majority to form the coalition government, and promptly reciprocated the services of RK by honouring him with a *Padma Bhushan*.

46. Reacting to this decision of the TMC leadership, P. Chidambaram, a former front-rung Congress leader and a co-founder of the TMC, broke

POLITICS BEYOND POLITICS   ■   251

away from the TMC and floated his own party — Congress Jananayaka Peravai. The party, however, remained a non-starter and served only to expose Chidambaram as a 'political orphan' with no significant following. Eventually he had to beg his way through to merge with the INC in 2004.

47. Though RK enjoyed the patronage of the DMK government through-out the tenure, may be with grumblings here and there by his fans, he kept himself off the election because that was a safer bet. There is reason to believe that he was disenchanted with the DMK, but did not want to come out openly for the fear that in the event of the DMK coming to power again — the initial opinion polls were in favour of the DMK — the consequences could be adverse for him. Thus, contrary to the cinematic boldness, in real life RK was cowardly or, to put it positively, diplomatic. He did the same also in 2011 elections, as we would see later.

48. *Junior Vikatan*, 14 October 2001, p. 30.

49. The interview was published in *Thina Thanthi*, 28 November 2001.

50. Though RK was haunted with self-doubt leading him to choose silence as a safer option in this election, a significant section of the people still had hope in him as the *PS Study 2001* (pre-alliance phase) highlights: Regarding the favourite actor, RK tops with 26.7 per cent, followed by Vijayakanth with 12.9 per cent. If actors start their own political parties, majority say they will not support anyone (56.7 per cent). However, a little above one-fourth (26.4 per cent) say they will consider supporting RK, if *he* starts (it is only 11.1 per cent in the case of Vijayakanth]).

51. For example, film comedian-cum-editor of the Thamizh periodical *Thuglak* Cho Ramaswamy was one such person who 'beseeched RK to join politics and offer "an alternative to the Dravidian parties".' See http://www.outlookindia.com/article/Bhagwan-Rajni/216985 (accessed on 9 September 2014). Cho in fact has never missed any opportunity to extend such invitations to RK ever since his first political intervention in 1996.

52. *PS Study 2002* was conducted in Andipatti assembly constituency in two rounds. The first round was done prior to the campaign by Jayalalithaa and Karunanidhi. Data collection throughout the constituency with a sample of 1208 persons was completed on 12 February 2002, and the report was released to the press on 15 February 2002. The second round was carried out immediately after the campaign by Jayalalithaa and Karunanidhi. This round of study included a sample of 1105 persons, and the data collection was completed on 18 February 2002. The report was released to the press the next day. A comparative look into the findings of both the rounds indicates: (*a*) the campaign of the star leaders Jayalalithaa and Karunanidhi has had a visible impact on the voters, with Jayalalithaa's relatively greater than Karunanidhi's; and (*b*) Jayalalithaa's lead over her rival has become

252 ■ POPULAR CINEMA AND POLITICS IN SOUTH INDIA

irreversible and was ever on the increase even after Karunanidhi's campaign. The actual polling was on 21 February 2002, and the results were only a logical extension of the trend forecast: Jayalalithaa (ADMK) — 58.22 per cent, and Vaigai Sekar (DMK) — 27.64 per cent.

53. Since the whole question of 'RK versus Jayalalithaa' in the electoral battlefield was only hypothetically posed, one cannot say that things might not have changed in RK's favour, had he also gone for direct campaign. However, we can reasonably surmise based on the data that RK's popularity cannot be overstretched to the extent of making candidates he supports win. This is what has happened to Vijayakanth also: when he fielded candidates in 2006 solely relying on him, none could win except him.

54. See *Thina Thanthi* (2002). A fortnight later, RK's spiritual guru settled in the US Swami Satchidananda, said in an interview RK was sure to come to politics. See *Thina Thanthi*, 13 August 2002. RK himself announced, when the film's going was very demoralising, that he would quit cinema for good if *Baba* was made a success. See *Thina Thanthi*, 4 September 2002.

55. RK resorted to several tactics to promote the film. One such thing was to publish as ads and news stories the testimonials from celebrities, politicians and common people as well (imagine the 'super star' being in need of endorsement!), painting RK with a political colour and to give the impression that the film was already a hit. For example, a 'news story' said that in Chennai screens, *Baba*'s collection for the first 18 days exceeded *Padaiyappa*'s collection for the first 50 days; as could be expected, the story did not talk about how much the theatre owners had paid (*Thina Thanthi*, 4 September 2002). As a prelude to the release in Karnataka RK employed another tactic of trying to 'please' the people by criticising the 'sandalwood' Veerappan as 'rakshasha' (demon) for kidnapping the thespian Kannada actor Rajkumar two years before! (Veerappan kept Rajkumar under his custody in the forest from 30 July to 15 November 2000, demanding ransom. See *Thina Thanthi*, 11 August 2002). Unfortunately, the issue boomeranged in Thamizh Nadu, several politicians including Thirumavalavan accused RK of double standards in Veerappan case (*Thina Thanthi*, 14 August 2002). It may not be out of place here to mention that this has been the publicity style of RK, saying something apparently to please the people which in turn boomerangs by raking up a controversy. For example, in 2010 in the context of screening *Enthiran* in Mumbai, RK met Bal Thackerey and said he was 'like god' to him, a statement which many did not relish; earlier in 2008 in the context of release of *Kuselan* in Bangalore, he gave a televised interview apologising for hurting the sentiments of the Kannadigas, which became an issue in Thamizh Nadu. (In fact, the Kannadigas were offended in the first place because of a statement he had made to please the Thamizhs in Cauvery waters issue.)

POLITICS BEYOND POLITICS ■ 253

56. RK held a press meet on 11 April 2004 in his Raghavendra Kalyana Mandapam, in which he read out a two-part statement, the first part being emotional, and the second, rational. The statement was apparently written in a hurry, with plenty of mistakes, in a style mixed with spoken Thamizh; it neither had any headline nor any date. It ended with the slogan, 'Let rivers (be) interlink(ed)! Let India shine! Jai Hind', and carried no signature. Recalling the incident years later (in his birthday function on 13 December 2012), RK said he had opposed the PMK to prove that he was not a 'coward'. He justified his action saying that though what they had demanded was right, the way they said it was not acceptable.

57. The *PS Study 2004*, planned and executed by me in the context of elections to the parliament, was done in three phases: the *pre-alliance* phase conducted well before the formation of alliances (data collection: 17–30 December 2003, sample size: 4500, report released to the media on 9 January 2004), the *mid-campaign* phase (data collection: 13–23 April 2004, sample size: 5408, report released to the media on 25 April 2004), and the *post-election* phase (data collection: June-July 2004, sample size: 6546, report released to the media on 21 July 2004). The samples were collected from all the 39 parliamentary constituencies of Thamizh Nadu, and the lone Pondicherry constituency.

58. The maturity of the Thamizh Nadu voters could be seen in the way they have responded to the PMK's cultural policing, as revealed by the *PS Study 2004* (post-election phase): around three-fourths of voters (74.7 per cent) did not approve of the PMK's intolerance shown to the criticisms of actors RK and Vijayakanth. To another question regarding disruption of screening films by actors critical of politicians, the majority opinion (58.7 per cent) was not to link politics and cinema. A significant one-fifth (21.7 per cent) felt it was okay to block films promoting a decadent culture, and a little above one-tenth (12.4 per cent) thought the actors did not have the credibility to criticise politicians.

59. Two clarifications are in order here: (*a*) The 6.7 per cent vote share of the PMK at the State level in 2004 parliamentary elections could be misleading because it does not really reflect the strength of the party at the State level — the PMK after all contested only in five constituencies in Thamizh Nadu and all of them situated in the northern part of Thamizh Nadu where the *Vanniars* are thickly populated. The PMK is yet to become a State party in the true sense of the term. (*b*) The PMK has not been the most favoured party among the *Vanniars*. The maximum support the party could muster in the so-called '*Vanniar* belt' was witnessed in Pennagaram by-election (2010) in which the PMK went on its own and emerged as the runner-up with nearly one-fourth vote share, relegating the ADMK to the third position (DMK — 45.48 per cent, PMK — 24.17 per cent,

ADMK — 15.68 per cent, DMDK — 6.67 per cent). The *PS Study 2010* conducted in Pennagaram constituency (data collection: 29–31 January and 19–21 March; sample size: 1725) the findings of which were released to the media on 24 March registered a slightly higher support among *Vanniar* voters who constituted 71 per cent of the sample: DMK — 44.5 per cent, PMK — 27.6 per cent, ADMK — 15.7 per cent, DMDK — 2.3 per cent. Thus, Pennagaram serves as the benchmark for the *maximum* support the PMK could ever get among *Vanniars*, if concentrated and concerted efforts are made. It may be worthwhile to remember that the PMK was routed in the very *Vanniar* belt in the 2011 assembly elections that followed, and earlier in 2006 a strong candidate of the stature of Vijayakanth could win in Viruthachalam, a constituency believed to be RD's fort.

60. There have been exceptions, however. For example, the MGR government in 1980 was arbitrarily dismissed as soon as the Congress won the general elections but, as we know, MGR bounced back to power in the following assembly elections.

61. It is worth remembering in this context that RK and his fans could achieve nothing much even when the party they supported came to power in 1996. Had the DMK wanted, it could indeed have done a lot of favours to them in reciprocation, since the State was under its absolute control.

62. Incidentally, in an interview to NDTV on 30 June 2007 on the occasion of the release of his film *Sivaji*, to a question comparing him and Amitabh, RK said: 'In the cinema world, Rajinikanth is only a king — probably a king — but Amitabh Bachchan is an emperor'. It is only natural that his fans expect what he is in the 'cinema world' to be translated into the political world as well. It may be reiterated that for RK's fans *he* is the emperor, and nobody else.

63. According to the *PS Study 2004* (pre-alliance phase), Sonia Gandhi was in fact lagging behind Vajpayee by 23 points (Sonia — 60.5, Vajpayee — 83.2). This reflected the then prevailing mood of the voters across the nation, which was rightly gauged by many pollsters, and RK as well. But the 'India Shining' campaign wrecked the prospects of the BJP, which RK and other pollsters failed (or avoided) to observe (or acknowledge).

64. The 'India Shining' campaign after an initial kick-start turned out to be a national fiasco, because, but for a miniscule minority, India was not that shining after all. L K Advani, considered the master brain behind the campaign, later confessed that it was his 'mistake' and regretted that he should have called the campaign 'India Rising', not 'India Shining'. See *News Track India,* 2011, 'India Shining Campaign a Mistake: Advani', 3 December, http://www.newstrackindia.com/newsdetails/253122 (accessed 10 August 2014).

POLITICS BEYOND POLITICS ▪ 255

65. Precisely this is what RK also did in 1996 and reaped a harvest richer than what he deserved. Though elections were held in 1996 for both parliament and assembly, RK focused *only* on Thamizh Nadu and attacked *only* Jayalalithaa, without any reference to PM candidates or national politics. The perfect cinelation of hero versus villain apparently appealed to the voters. It may be mentioned that the Thamizh Nadu voters see RK primarily as a state, and not a national-level player. For the same reason, the voter response probably would not have been so adverse to RK in 2004, if only had he directed a part of his scathing attacks on RD towards Jayalalithaa, a villain on par with RK. However, the Thamizh Nadu voters have been very consistent in putting on top the national interests as perceived by them when it comes to parliamentary elections and have made the best possible choice from the available options: in 1996 they did not have any worthwhile reason to re-elect the INC (which was a 'silent' spectator to the demolition of Babri Masjid, and an active player in horse-trading the MPs) and so they voted it out, and voted in the Thamizh Nadu context for the best available alliance (DMK–TMC combine), which eventually played a pivotal role in the formation of the government at the Centre. Similarly, in 2004, people had no convincing reason to re-elect the BJP; conversely, there was no reason to rule out a chance for the INC. Also, people made use of this occasion to warn the ADMK government to mend ways, otherwise face a similar fate in the soon-to-come assembly election. The same pattern of voter behaviour is detectable also in 2009 and 2011 elections, as would be explained later.

66. However, a sizable number (17 per cent) attributed the success of the DMK merely to the kind of alliance it had forged, viz., to the arithmetic game of vote shares of constituent parties.

67. According to the *PS Study 2004* (mid-campaign phase), the viewership shares of various channels were: Sun TV — 71.5 per cent, Jaya TV — 7.6 per cent, Doordarshan — 6.8 per cent, Vijay TV — 4.1 per cent, K-TV — 2.0 per cent, Raj TV — 1.5 per cent, and Sun News — 1.1 per cent. Thanks to the mushrooming of channels which have eaten into the viewership of Sun TV, its share over the years has drastically come down to around 40 per cent, but it remains unsurpassed to date. Interestingly, while different channels vie for the second place at different times, the share for the second place has remained more or less constant at 6–7 per cent.

68. In terms of political allegiance, Sun TV has been the 'unsaid official' channel of the DMK party, till the feud between 'MK families' and 'Maran families' acquired irreconcilable public dimensions, giving rise to several political and business realignments, including the floating of Kalaignar TV in September 2007 as a rival to Sun TV. But the DMK continues to

256　■　POPULAR CINEMA AND POLITICS IN SOUTH INDIA

depend on Sun TV because of its sheer reach several times larger than Kalaignar TV, and Sun TV in turn plays its cards safely and strategically: it supports the DMK during the election times, and at other times, particularly when the DMK is not in power, it attempts to project itself as a 'neutral' channel by being politically correct in its news coverage and design (for example, the news about the chief minister Jayalalithaa comes first and Karunanidhi, only next).

69. Other political parties also resort to the technique of *re-presenting*. For example, the ADMK's Jaya TV and PMK's Makkal TV have employed this technique. But when the incumbent re-presences what had happened in the previous regime (when the present opposition had been in power), such a campaign only augments the arguments of the opposition because the tendency is to read everything of the past, irrespective of the fact whether it happened in the present regime or the previous regime, against the background of the 'present' which can refer only to the sitting government. Theoretically, evoking the 'just-yesterday' feel through re-presencing technique works better if it concerns anti-incumbency. This remains as yet another area to be further studied.

70. RK's strategy in 2004 was ill-conceived because, as explained earlier, the motive attributed to his intervention was too narrow and self-centred. There was more anger and reaction against the PMK than any serious, proactive thinking and planning for the State. Comparatively, there was at least a semblance of altruism in his intervention in 1996 (though it apparently started as a personal enmity which later took on political contours; the contents of the interview was a personal attack on Jayalalithaa) he spoke of 'saving Thamizh Nadu'.

71. In my opinion, the most opportune moment for RK to enter politics was the occasion of elections in 1996. The second best was Andipatti by-election in 2002 when he had the opportunity to take Jayalalithaa head-on. Assembly elections in 2001 and 2006 would have been better than the parliamentary elections in 1998, 1999 or 2004. In 2006, however, Vijayakanth would have been a serious contender to RK.

72. When actors get involved in election campaigns in support of a party, very often they are rewarded if the party they support wins. But when it loses, depending upon the status of the actor, s/he has to face a lot of difficulties, including not booking them for any film. It is also not rare that the contracts already made are also cancelled. Curiously, such steps are more often than not taken by the filmmakers as a pre-emptive measure lest they earn the wrath of the new party that has come to power. The recent classic example is the popular comedian Vadivel, who was so suddenly and abruptly blacked out of the silver screen immediately following the

POLITICS BEYOND POLITICS ◂ **257**

very announcement of the results of 2011 elections. Vadivel, it may be recalled, campaigned aggressively against the DMDK chief Vijayakanth.

73. When the same question was repeated in 2005 after the release of *Chandramukhi*, a blockbuster after *Baba* fiasco, only 12.1 per cent answered in the affirmative, 22.7 per cent said that even if he came, people's support would not be there; but the largest response (62.2 per cent) was he would not come. The *PS Study 2005* was a state-wide, 'state-of-the-State' study done between 27 April 2005 and 10 May 2005 with a sample size of 3167.

74. At the same time, thanks to the success of *Chandramukhi*, according to the *PS Study 2005*, majority (59.5 per cent) thought that he would continue to act (but in November 2004, it was only 17.6 per cent).

75. It has become fashionable in Thamizh Nadu political circles to deride the 'Dravidian' parties and talk about an 'alternative' to them. Political leaders like RD go a step further to suggest to the DMK that the word 'Dravida' in the name 'Dravida Munnetra Kazhagam' be changed to 'Thamizhaga' (see *Thamizhoasai*, 18 March 2012). Vijayakanth on his part has been talking about being an 'alternative' to DMK and ADMK but not necessarily with an ideology alternative to the 'Dravidian' one. First of all, his party itself has the word 'Dravida' in its name. Second, being a Telugu, Vijayakanth would need this 'Dravidian' cover to hide his non-Thamizh origins. However, Vijayakanth has been acting in films championing the cause of the Thamizhs — even though ironically he cannot pronounce the *zha* sound in the word '*Tha-mi-zh*' properly — and for the people of Thamizh Nadu he has come across as a Thamizh only. According to the *PS Study 2006* (pre-alliance phase), majority of the people (71.2 per cent) opine that his Telugu origin will not be a hindrance to his political activities. Interestingly, the language policy of the DMDK (as stated in the manifesto issued in 'the first state-level political meeting' in Madurai) gives a pan-Indian outlook to language in contrast to the DK/DMK/ADMK: 'protect mother language; learn all languages' (*annai mozhi kaappoam, anaiththu mozhiyum karpoam*). Third, Vijayakanth is fond of using the title *karuppu* MGR — MGR who was a 'Dravidian' of Malayalee origin! — which means he desires to be another MGR or emulate MGR. But the critical question here is to what extent he can achieve this. MGR was able to be successful because he emerged from within the DMK and cleverly projected an alternative leadership to Karunanidhi for 'Anna's party' (and not as an alternative party); in other words, he only wanted to liberate 'Anna's party' from the clutches of Karunanidhi, and as a DMK official he had the moral authority to do so. Moreover, in MGR's time, an alternative to the DMK was possible because, by the time MGR started his party, the INC was so weakened by intraparty squabbles (such as Kamaraj leaving the party) that the competition was effectively narrowed to DMK and

258 ■ POPULAR CINEMA AND POLITICS IN SOUTH INDIA

ADMK. As an interesting paradox the INC tacitly supported the formation of the ADMK, wishing that it would weaken the DMK so that it could have a comeback in the state. Unfortunately for Vijayakanth now there are too many — at least two (ADMK and DMK) — strong contenders to be faced. In my opinion, the only attempt that could have had the potential to have evolved into a real alternative in the recent decades was the TMC which we have already referred to.

76. The formation of the pre-poll alliance of the ADMK and the DMDK was the need of the hour even to equal, if not outweigh, the DMK–INC alliance. It was an unwilling partnership between two strong egos, and the alliance broke off at the earliest excuse. The ego clash between Jayalalithaa and Vijayakanth was publicly displayed in a mud-slinging assembly session on 1 February 2012 and Vijayakanth's press-meet in his party office the next day. Both the leaders indulged in a verbal duel and said they were ashamed of having entered into this alliance. Though personally they did not want this alliance, they revealed, it was done because their party cadres wanted it. This indeed is an amazing revelation because it shows that the ordinary party cadres could dare to think differently and prevail upon the charismatic and strong, if not autocratic, leadership to take crucial decisions against his/her own personal agendas.

77. The one thing that is inextricably linked up with the Indian/Thamizh Nadu politics for sure is caste, and no charisma however great can afford to ignore it. Even MGR, as noted earlier, did not exclusively depend on his charisma. Moreover, the fact that MGR was an outsider and he did not fit in the caste system of Thamizh Nadu worked in his favour because no one could blame him of caste favouritism. RK also has the same advantages like MGR in this regard. In contrast, Vijayakanth is identified with the powerful Telugu-speaking caste group in Thamizh Nadu (Naidu and Reddy), and some embittered DMDK party-men have already started accusing him of favouring his caste-men in assigning party posts.

78. There is a strong link between politics and education in Thamizh Nadu. Many of the deemed universities and professional colleges here are run by the families of present or former politicians such as Viswanathan, Jeppiar, Jagathratchagan, A. C. Shanmugam, Ponmudi, RD, and the list indeed is endless! Education is a safe business easily defensible as a 'noble service' and so no wonder the politicians turn to it to invest and multiply their money allegedly not always earned through legal means. The so-called educationists turn to politics allegedly to safeguard their wealth amassed through collecting enormous capitation fees for admissions rather than to do any committed social service. As of now, education is, probably after politics, an effective shortcut to earning quick money.

79. *Parkavakulam* is an umbrella term like *Mukkulam* and includes castes such as Udayar, Moopanar and Nathaman. Pachamuthu started also a weekly

POLITICS BEYOND POLITICS 259

magazine and a 24-hour TV news channel both named *Puthiya Thalaimurai* (New Generation), and a general entertainment channel *Puthu Yugam*. Recently he has floated *Vaenthan Movies* (styled after Sun Movies), and *Vaenthar TV*, another full-fledged entertainment channel.

80. A very sensitive issue that might have been legally resolved but remained emotionally unresolvable concerns the traumatic dismissal and reinstatement of the government employees. The wound was so deep that even after many reconciliatory moves by the government they were in no mood to forgive Jayalalithaa and in the elections in fact they not only voted against her but also, as booth officials, worked against her.

81. While it is true that the arrest of Kanchi Sankaracharya was offensive to the caste elite, majority of the general public, according to the *PS Study 2004 November*, expressed their appreciation for the Thamizh Nadu government for treating everyone equally (57.7 per cent); another significant size cautioned that since this arrest was a political action, it should not be blown up as a religious issue (16.1 per cent). The voice condemning the arrest was rather feeble (5.2 per cent), while another small section stated that even if it was necessary to arrest the Sankaracharya, the way he was treated was not proper (10.7 per cent). Incidents such as this arrest, and the alleged encounter-killing of 'sandalwood' Veerappan boosted the image of Jayalalithaa as a 'bold' leader. Compared to Karunanidhi, people in general perceive Jayalalithaa as a bolder person.

82. There is reason to believe that these measures had considerable impact on the people. The *PS Study 2004* (November) observed that the people had started looking at the ADMK government more and more kindly, with as many as 42.2 per cent expressing satisfaction with its functioning.

83. The 2006 election manifesto of the DMK was considered the 'hero' of the 2006 election by many including P. Chidambaram the then finance minister at the Centre. (See http://www.rediff.com [accessed 11 March 2006]). While releasing the 2011 manifesto, Karunanidhi said that the 2006 manifesto was the 'hero' while the 2011, the 'heroine.' (See http://www.ndtv.com [accessed 20 March 2011]).

84. According to the *PS Study 2009 April*, as many as 47.5 per cent expressed satisfaction with the state government, while 44.6 per cent felt unhappy with it; 7.9 per cent did not find the incumbent any different from its predecessor. A similar response pattern was seen with regard to the government at the centre as well.

85. According to the *PS Study 2009 April*, as many as 47.5 per cent expressed satisfaction with the state government, while 44.6 per cent felt unhappy with it; 7.9 per cent did not find the incumbent any different from its predecessor. A similar response pattern was seen with regard to the government at the Centre as well.

260 ■ POPULAR CINEMA AND POLITICS IN SOUTH INDIA

86. Muthukumar, a 26-year-old journalist, self-immolated in support of the cause of the Sri Lankan Thamizhs on 29 January 2009 in Chennai in front of Shastri Bhavan, a complex that houses central government departments. Before killing himself, he distributed a 4-page document in Thamizh stating his fourteen demands. (For an English translation of the full text, visit: http://www.tamilnet.com/art.html?catid=79&artid=28208 [accessed 9 September 2014]). The news of his death spread like wild fire across the State, particularly among the college students, reminiscent of the bygone anti-Hindi agitations. But the DMK government swiftly came down on the agitating student organisations, closed down all the colleges indefinitely and ordered all the students to vacate the hostels immediately. Thus the DMK managed to diffuse the situation and was able to avoid earning the displeasure of the INC leadership.

87. According to the *PS Study 2009 January*, as high as 85 per cent said they felt angry when they heard the news about the happenings in Sri Lanka: angry with our central and state governments (44.5 per cent), with Rajapaksa government (22.5 per cent), with the international community (12 per cent)), and with the LTTE (3 per cent).

88. Ironically this included also the INC which was accused of supporting the war. Some even alleged that the war was fought by India for Sri Lanka! The INC however wanted to play it safe till the elections were over. On the one hand, the INC-led government of India had never confirmed or denied in unambiguous terms its involvement in the war; on the other hand, the INC defended itself in its election campaign by describing the war as 'the war against the terrorist movement LTTE' which had murdered Rajiv Gandhi a former Indian prime minister, and further accused the LTTE of causing the death of civilians by using them as cover. It also had a tacit understanding with Sri Lanka to slow down or at least to give the impression that the civilians were not affected till the general elections here were over so that its alliance partners were able to save their face in front of the public. The gory, sadistic face of the Indian involvement became evident in the manner in which the electoral victory of the Sonia-led INC and the war victory of the Rajapaksa-led Sinhalese military were announced. This is the chronology of events: declaration of the election results favouring the INC (16 May), the butchering of thousands of Thamizhs (17 May), the news of the death of the LTTE chief Prabhakaran (18 May), and the death anniversary of Rajiv Gandhi (21 May). If this sequence was just a coincidence, it was a dreadful coincidence indeed. It looked that the whole war was masterminded and led by the Indian government controlled by Sonia Gandhi and family to avenge her husband's death by eliminating Prabhakaran before the death anniversary of her husband. But for most of the Thamizhs, avenging Rajiv's death could never justify the most brutal genocide massacring over 50,000 (many put

POLITICS BEYOND POLITICS **261**

it at 150,000) innocent civilians in a single night at Mullivaikkaal, which, according to some, even outwitted Hitler's ethnic cleansing at Auschwitz. This has made the people of Thamizh Nadu harden their position towards the Nehru–Gandhi family (to whom they had been favourably disposed for years). The stand of Thamizh Nadu voters has been vindicated by the 'Report of the Secretary-General's Internal Review Panel on United Nations Action in Sri Lanka' released on 14 November 2012; earlier, on 22 March 2012 the UN Human Rights Council had adopted a resolution urging Sri Lanka 'to investigate alleged abuses during the final phase of war' with the LTTE.

89. The fast which lasted only for a few hours — starting after breakfast and ending before lunch-time — was declared a 'success' because, Karunanidhi claimed, the Indian government prevailed upon Rajapaksa who consented to stop employing heavy artillery against the civilians. It turned out to be a cruel joke because the Sri Lankan government only intensified the war to the finish not bothering about the civilian casualties with the support of the Indian government! But, of course, Rajapaksa saw to it that no media dared to report this.

90. When asked if the Sri Lankan Thamizh issue would play a major role in the elections, there was no consensus among the voters, according to the *PS Study 2009 January*. Only 30 per cent thought it would be an important election issue in Thamizh Nadu, and another 30 per cent thought it might be an election issue but local/internal issues such as price rise and lack of basic needs and infrastructures would dominate the election campaign. Other responses include: since elections were fought based on factors like money, caste and alliance, this issue might not have a say in the election (18 per cent); since every party showed interest in this issue, this might not emerge as an election issue (5 per cent); its importance would depend on the situation that would prevail at the time of polling (12 per cent).

91. The 'Alagiri Formula' or the 'Thirumangalam Formula' derives its name from the way Karunanidhi's son Alagiri, in-charge of the affairs of the DMK in the southern region of Thamizh Nadu, spearheaded the electioneering during the by-election to Thirumangalam assembly constituency. He allegedly paid huge sums — as much as ₹5000 per vote — and devised innovative methods to hoodwink the EC (Ref.: the India Cables from the Wikileaks published in *The Hindu*, 16 March 2011). It may be reiterated that many things attributed to Alagiri — including distributing cash for votes — are routinely practiced by many, if not all, of the contestents in *all* the parties. When it comes to by-election, the entire state machinery together with the battalion of 'honourable' ministers is geared to electioneering as if making the ruling party candidate win is their official mandate; and usually the ruling party candidate only wins.

262 ■ POPULAR CINEMA AND POLITICS IN SOUTH INDIA

The *PS Study 2009 January* noted that the voters were expecting a good amount per vote modelled on Thirumangalam. Giving/getting money for voting in fact has become an integral part of the election culture. For example, when asked how many have received money at least once in the recent elections, according to the *PS Study 2011 March*, as many as 47.9 per cent answered in the affirmative, though ironically 80.5 per cent have stated it is unethical to vote for cash.

92. In the context of the 2009 general elections, one of the two critical factors identified in the *PS Study 2009 April* as exerting crucial impact on the exercise of voting concerned the efforts of parties at the constituency level to lure voters. The parties were so desperate to woo the voters that they resorted to all sorts of tactics — legal, metalegal, paralegal or illegal — transforming as a result the election season into an extended and extensive gala festival. The second critical factor impinging on voting was the direction and the momentum the Sri Lankan Thamizh issue was going to assume as the campaign progressed. But how a conflagration of contra and multi-directional signals from parties effectively neutralised the voters' position has already been discussed.

93. The stand of the other national party BJP on the Sri Lankan Thamizh issue was very much similar to the INC's: against the separate Thamizh Eezham and the LTTE; even in the final war against the Thamizhs the BJP was very much with the INC.

94. The Thamizh voters were clearly in a dilemma as to whom to vote in this election. While they were somewhat ready to condone the DMK for its strategic blunders because the ADMK's championing of the Thamizh's cause was such a surprise that it remained unconvincing, they showed their displeasure and anger towards the INC by defeating a few of their prominent candidates starting with the TNCC president K. V. Thangabalu to the outspoken and controversial EVKS Elangovan, Mani Shankar Aiyar, a friend of Rajapaksa, and R. Prabhu, one-time Central minister. In the case of P. Chidambaram, the initial result reported on TV was that he lost; but it was immediately withdrawn and a while later it was 'officially' announced — after a 'recount' it was said — that he won the seat with a slim margin of 3354 votes, which is the thinnest of all the margins of victory in this election. The runner-up filed a case challenging the victory of Chidambaram and the high court in its ruling on 04.08.11 rejected Chidambaram's plea to dismiss the case against him and cleared the way for the hearing to go on.

95. The top-most reason for the humiliating rout of the INC according to the *PS Study 2011 June* was its double standards in the Sri Lankan Thamizh issue (61.5 per cent). Other reasons include: inner-party rivalries (20.3 per cent), and alliance with the DMK (11.7 per cent). That most, if not all, the

POLITICS BEYOND POLITICS ■ **263**

people of TN *continue to feel* hurt and humiliated by the Sonia-led UPA government which goes out of its way to please Rajapaksa in the name of 'foreign policy' was obvious by the spontaneous agitations against inviting Rajapaksa as chief guest to Sanchi to lay the foundation stone for a Buddhist university (21 September 2012). A sad twist to this issue is that the Madhya Pradesh BJP government ignored the protests by the Thamizhs — Vaiko led a group of protesters to Madhya Pradesh itself — stating it was a cultural event organised by the state. In an attempt to express his anguish over this issue, 28-year-old Vijayaraj from Salem self-immolated and died on 18 September 2012. See *The Hindu*, 19 September 2012. When Channel 4 News came up with a second expose on 19 February 2013 shocking the world with gory visuals especially of the child Balachandran, son of Prabhakaran, being shot dead point-blank, the Indian government closed its eyes, while hundreds of agitated students were fasting unto death across the state. Again, in the context of Commonwealth Summit in Colombo (November 2013), the people of TN demonstrated their anguish through widespread agitations and the TN assembly passed a unanimous resolution on 24 October 2013 demanding the Indian government to boycott the Summit; The Channel 4 News 'another chilling expose' that the LTTE journalist Isaipriya was not killed 'in a combat'as stated by Colombo but caught alive, gang-raped and murdered by the Sinhala military (see http://www.youtube.com/watch?v=nwrj7_OdOio, published on 31 October 2013 [accessed 10 August 2014]) added to the frustration and anger of the people. The centre's response was only partial — the PM did not go, but India was represented in the Summit — satisfying none, including the UPA partner DMK.

96. Besides, the Election Commission was very strict in implementing the code of conduct. So much so, many parties, particularly the ruling DMK, accused the EC of high-handedness and targeting only the DMK candidates, with a special eye on Alagiri the election strategist par excellence. During the field work for the *PS Study 2011 March*, the research team noted that the festive mood common during any election season was totally absent now; it looked as if the whole state was under siege, and an undeclared emergency was in force.

97. According to the *PS Study 2011 June*, the two top-most reasons for the defeat of the DMK alliance are: the family rule of the DMK leadership (49.7 per cent), and the corruption and bribery in government departments (42.9 per cent); the much-publicised 2G-spectrum scam takes the third place (31.5 per cent), followed by current cut (27.8 per cent), and price rise (20.7 per cent).

98. Prior to the 2006 assembly elections, while speaking in the *Chandramukhi* audio release function, RK compared himself to a horse, and said, 'I am

264 ■ POPULAR CINEMA AND POLITICS IN SOUTH INDIA

a horse, not an elephant; when I fall, just like that I get up and run'. He reiterated the same point in the function to mark the completion of 200 days of running of the same film.

99. Also, probably RK wanted to wait and see how Vijayakanth, a person considered in the initial years as worth enough only to be his dupe in films, was going to perform in politics. But already by 2006 Vijayakanth had firmly established himself as a better CM-stuff than RK. The *PS Studies* done during this time clearly map the steady ascendancy of Vijayakanth in the popularity scale, effectively replacing RK whose decline has been irreversible. In terms of competence to be the CM and in terms of chances of becoming the CM, according to the *PS Study 2001* (pre-alliance phase), RK figured in the third place (but there is a chasm of difference in scores between the third rank and the first two ranks occupied by Karunanidhi and Jayalalithaa), whereas Vijayakanth was in the 9th place in competence and 7th in chance. According to the *PS Study 2004 (November)*— study done after the parliamentary elections — Vijayakanth retained his 9th place, whereas RK slid to 10th place. Vijayakanth's popularity went up when he was seen as a potential party leader, as demonstrated in the *PS Study 2005 April–May* (sample size: 3167), according to which Vijayakanth shot up to the 4th place just a few points lower than Stalin, the Deputy CM, while RK was in the 7th place. As the election fever set in, and with Vijayakanth as an actual party leader, according to the *PS Study 2006* (pre-alliance phase), Vijayakanth jumped to the third place, relegating Stalin to the 4th and humbling RK with the 10th.

100. See http://www.youtube.com/watch?v=WTwl8e1dEuI, titled, 'Superstar Rajinikanth's Request/Apology in Kannada to Kannadigas' (accessed 10 August 2014). It is a pity that in spite of all such efforts the film was an utter flop at the box-office causing heavy losses particularly to the exhibitors who had over-valued the film because of the excessive hype. According to some, *Kuselan* was almost a kind of repeat of *Baba*.

101. My translation of RK's press statement in Thamizh. For a reporting of his statement, see http://www.thehindu.com/todays-paper/no-one-can-compel-me-to-enter-politics/article1356414.ece (accessed 11 September 2014). RK's reaction to his fans was understandable, because he was upset with the disappointing reception to *Kuselan*, and the subsequent demand from some exhibitors to compensate for the losses. Even in the case of his previous mega-budget *Sivaji*, the actual financial returns did not correspond to the high hopes created by the extravagant publicity given to it. RK obviously was under duress to make his next film a box-office hit.

102. *The Hindu*, epaper dated 7 February 2010.

POLITICS BEYOND POLITICS ■ **265**

103. See http://www.nakkheeran.in/Users/frmNews.aspx?PVN=51807 (accessed 10 August 2014).

104. See *Junior Vikatan*, 26 October 2011.

105. It may be reiterated that particularly after the humiliating political debacle in 2004 it is others who have evinced greater interest in RK entering politics, invariably on apolitical occasions. For example, the Telugu Desam Party supremo Chandrababu Naidu welcomed RK to join the Third Front during a preview of *Sivaji* in Hyderabad in June 2007. See *The Hindu*, online edition, epaper dated 15 June 2007. As another example, Cho Ramaswamy repeated the invitation to RK in the context of the release of a populist biography of RK in March 2008, saying, 'If Rajini enters politics, Thamizh Nadu will go one step ahead of everybody'. See http://sudhishkamath.com/2008/03/13/the-name-is-rajinikanth-making-of-the-superstar (accessed 10 August 2014). Actor Karunas prophecied during RK's birthday celebrations on 13 December 2012 that the five-lettered Shivaji Rao (RK) should be next in the line of Thamizh Nadu CMs whose names are five-lettered (in Thamizh).

106. The public manifestation of RK as a potential political threat to Jayalalithaa, the then CM happened in 1995 in a function presided over by Jayalalithaa the CM (to facilitate actor Sivaji), and soon he shot to prominence through his statement, 'if this lady (*intha ammaa*) comes to power again, even god cannot save Thamizh Nadu'. In an ironic twist the denouement for his politiking came in 2012 in a similar function (to commemorate the 14th anniversary of Jaya TV) presided over by Jayalalithaa the CM, where an aged, drained out RK addressed her as 'Puratchi Thalaivi' and wished that 'the Chief Minister should become famous not only at India level but also at international level'. See *Dr. Namathu MGR*, 31 August 2012.

107. In spite of the appalling reception to *Koachadaiyaan,* because the shrewd RK offset the damage by quickly announcing his next film *Lingaa*; also, the fact that a prime ministerial candidate, now the Prime Minister, went to his residence to meet him has contributed to keep his 'super star' image intact.

108. As described by the anchor in the intro to RK's interview on the eve of the release of *Sivaji* telecast on NDTV 24×7 on 30 June 2007. RK's interview to media was telecast on other channels as well.

109. RK said this in a televised interview on 17 January 2008 on the occasion of the 'NDTV Indian of the Year Awards' function, in which he accepted the 'Entertainer of the Year' award. He further added, 'If he (god) gives me a politician's role, definitely I will do it'. See http://www.rediff. com/movies/2008/jan/18rajni.htm (accessed 10 August 2014). Somewhat similar was his response when Balachandar interviewed him

266 ■ POPULAR CINEMA AND POLITICS IN SOUTH INDIA

at *D40* referred to earlier. To the question, 'Will you come to politics or not?' RK responded, 'That is in the hands of God'. See http://tamil.oneindia.in/movies/specials/ 2010/10/24-kb-interviews-rajinikanth.html (accessed 10 August 2014). It may not be too much to say that it has become a worn out cliché that in every public function involving RK one staple, ritual component is the question, 'When will you come to politics?' and RK parroting as answer, 'It's in the hands of god'. Sometimes this cliché would almost border on ridiculing RK!

110. Stated by RK in a function to felicitate director S. P. Muthuraman on 29 October 2011. See http://www.nakkheeran.in/users/frmNews.aspx?PVN=64180 (accessed 9 September 2014).

111. That the people also have come to perceive him as more fit to be an actor rather than a political leader or a social worker is evident from the *PS Studies*. According to the *PS Study 2007* (done in November–December, after the successful reception to *Sivaji*, involving 3,281 samples), when asked which would be the most appropriate field for RK to pursue in the future, full-time acting in cinema tops the list with 45.2 per cent, followed by full-time spirituality (23.8 per cent), full-time social service (14.2 per cent), with direct politics taking the last place with 11.3 per cent. When the question was repeated in the *PS Study 2008 September* to a sample of 2,709 persons (done after the release of *Kuselan*), again full-time acting tops with 45.8 per cent. However, the people's disappointment with *Kuselan* is reflected in the response — a significant one-third (32.5 per cent) have said it would be better for him to retire. Other options include: full-time spirituality (10.7 per cent), full-time social service (5.2 per cent), with direct politics taking the last place with a negligible 4.3 per cent.

112. The Speaker of the House reprimanded Vijayakanth for his behaviour violating the decorum of the House and suspended him for 10 days from the assembly. Vijayakanth reacted to this by announcing, like his predecessors Jayalalithaa and Karunanidhi (as opposition leaders) that he would henceforth boycott all the assembly sessions throughout this regime and go directly to the people. True to his resolve, he did in fact go to the people, visiting the constituencies of his MLAs. Interestingly, even this action was promptly criticised by the ADMK in the next session of the House. See *Thina Thanthi*, 9 September 2012.

113. The DMDK came fourth after the ADMK, the DMK and the MDMK at Shankarankoil, and forfeited its deposit. At Pudukottai, the situation was different: the CPI whose constituency it was, did not contest, and the major opposition party, the DMK, boycotted the election. So it was a straight contest between the ADMK the ruling party and the DMDK

POLITICS BEYOND POLITICS ◀ **267**

the opposition party. But the DMDK was able to muster only 21.3 per cent as against the ADMK's 71 per cent, though to the annoyance of the ADMK supremo Jayalalithaa it retained its deposit. The DMDK did not contest in Yercaud by-election held on 4 December 2013; but in a queer move it contested at the same time in 11 seats for the Delhi assembly (mustering 2285 votes in all).

114. Even to continue as the 'captain' of his own party, he has to learn a lot, particularly in the context of increasing discontentment with the leadership. Between October 2012 and June 2013, for example, seven MLAs have 'met' the CM openly defying his authority. The climax came when the Chairperson of the party Presidium Panrutti Ramachandran resigned on 10 December 2013, and the emergency meeting of the party's executive committee on 12 December 2013 decided to abolish the post of Chairpersonship from the party structure itself. While this being the case with Vijayakanth, it seems RK is being conscripted into politics again, this time by an aggressive BJP determined to make Thamizh Nadu its bastion; and leaders like Pon. Radhakrishnan already talk about capturing power in the forthcoming 2016 assembly elections. Visit http://www.youtube.com/watch?v=xftEiqK7taE (video uploaded on 20 July 2014 on *Dinamalar* website; accessed 11 September 2014). Now that the special court's verdict on 27 September 2014 has unceremoniously unseated Jayalalithaa from chief ministership and barred her from contesting in elections in for next 10 years, the BJP is set to push its agenda hard. The media on their part are ripe with rumours that RK would be the BJP's cheif ministerial candidate (see for example, *Nakkeeran*, 27(39), 30 August–2 September 2014). If that happens, then the 'super star' of cinema has to forego that title in politics, because the real 'super star' in politics is Narendra Modi in the BJP. If RK floats his own party, again, he could be another Vijaykanth, may be with a slight edge over him. (Recall also the discussion regarding a similar hypotheical situation in the context of the 1996 elections.) It may be noted here that the recent verdict against Jayalalithaa may not in any significant way alter the political course of Thamizh Nadu, because whether she is in office or not, it will be her government ('governing those who govern the government') and she will remain the supreme power centre of the party in power. Apparently, the quantum of the punishment has only helped create an immediate mass sympathy for her. Finally, for the sake of argument, if RK were to win the contest against Jayalalithaa and Vijaykanth, would it not vitiate and counter the very myth that the voters are carried away by cine stars?

MGR's Filmography

AananthaJoathi / 1963 / V. N. Reddy and A. S. A. Samy
AasaiMugam / 1965 / P. Pullaiah
Aayiraththil Oruvan / 1965 / P. R. Pantulu
Abhimanyu / 1948 / M. Somasundaram and A. Kasilingam
AdimaiPenn / 1969 / K. Shankar
Alibaabaavum Naarpathu Thirudarkalum / 1956 / T. R. Ramanna
Anbae Vaa / 1966 / A. C. Thirulogachandar
Annamitta Kai / 1972 / M. Krishnan
Anthamaan Kaithi / 1952 / V. Krishnan
Arasakattalai / 1967 / M. G. Chakrapani
Arasilamkumari / 1961 / A. S. A. Samy
Ashok Kumar / 1941 / Raja Chandrasekar
Bhagdad Thirudan / 1960 / T. P. Sundaram
Chakaravarththi Thirumagal / 1957 / P. Neelakandan
Chandroadayam / 1966 / K. Sankar
Dakshayagnam / 1938 / Raja Chandrasekar
En Annan / 1970 / P. Neelakantan
En Kadamai / 1964 / M. Natesan
En Thangai / 1952 / C. H. Narayanamoorthi and M. K. R. Nambiar
Enga Veetu Pillai / 1965 / Chanakya
EngalThangam / 1970 / Krishnan–Panju
GuleBakaavali / 1955 / T. R. Ramanna
Harichandra / 1943 / Nagabushnam
Indru Poal Endrum Vaazhha / 1977 / K. Sankar
Iru Sagoatharargal / 1936 / Ellis R. Duncan
Ithaya Kani / 1975 / A. Jaganathan
IthayaVeenai / 1972 / Krishnan–Panju
Jenoavaa / 1953 / F. Nagoor
Kaanji Thalaivan / 1963 / A. Sivalingam

FILMOGRAPHY ◄ 269

Kaathal Vaakanam / 1968 / M. A. Thirumugam
Kaavalkaaran / 1967 / P. Neelakantan
Kalai Arasi / 1963 / A. Kasilingam
Kalankarai Vilakkam / 1965 / K. Sankar
Kanavan / 1968 / P. Neelakandan
Kannan En Kaathalan / 1968 / P. Neelakantan
Kanni Thaai / 1965 / M. A. Thirumugam
Koduththu Vaiththaval / 1963 / P. Neelakantan
Koondukkili / 1954 / T. R. Ramanna
Kudiyiruntha Koayil / 1968 / K. Shankar
Kudumpa Thalaivan / 1962 / M. A. Thirumugam
Kumaari / 1952 / R. Padmanabhan
Kumari Koattam / 1971 / P. Neelakantan
Maadappuraa / 1962 / S. A. Subburaman
Maattukkaara Vaelan / 1970 / P. Neelakantan
Mahaadaevi / 1957 / Sunderrao Nadkarni
MalaiKallan / 1954 / Sriramulu Naidu
Mannaathi Mannan / 1960 / Natesan
Manthiri Kumaari / 1950 / T. R. Sundaram and Ellis R. Duncan
MarmaYoagi / 1951 / K. Ramnath
Maruthanaattu Ilavarasi / 1950 / A. Kasilingam
MathuraiV eeran / 1956 / T. R. Ramanna
Mathuraiyai Meetta Sunthara Paandiyan / 1978 / M. G. Ramachandran
Maya Machindraa / 1939 / Raja Chandrasekar
Meenava Nanpan / 1977 / Sridar
Meeraa / 1945 / Ellis R. Duncan
Moahini / 1948 / Lanka Sathyan
Mugaraasi / 1966 / M. A. Thirumugam
Naadoadi / 1966 / B. R. Pantulu
Naadoadi Mannan / 1958 / M. G. Ramachandran
Naalai Namathae / 1975 / K. S. Sethumadhavan
Naam / 1953 / A. Kasilingam
Naan Aanaiyittaal / 1966 / Chanakya
Naan Yaen Piranthaen / 1972 / M. Krishnan
Naetru Indru Naalai / 1974 / P. Neelakantan
Nalla Naeram / 1972 / M. A. Thirumugam
Nallavan Vaazhvan / 1961 / P. Neelakandan

270 ■ POPULAR CINEMA AND POLITICS IN SOUTH INDIA

Namnaadu / 1969 / Jambu
Navaraththinam / 1977 / A. P. Nagarajan
Neerum Neruppum / 1971 / P. Neelakantan
Neethikku Thalaivanangu / 1976 / P. Neelakantan
Neethikkuppin Paasam / 1963 / M. A. Thirumugam
Ninaiththathai Mudippavan / 1975 / P. Neelakantan
Oli Vilakku / 1968 / Chanakya
Oorukku Uzhaippavan / 1976 / M. Krishnan
Oru Thaai Makkal / 1971 / P. Neelakantan
Paasam / 1962 / T. R. Ramannna
Padakoatti / 1964 / P. Prakash Rao
Paiththiyakkaaran / 1947 / Krishnan–Panju
Pallaandu Vaazhha / 1975 / K. Sankar
Panakkaara Kudumpam / 1964 / T. R. Ramanna
Panakkaari / 1953 / Ramanathan
Panam Padaiththavan / 1965 / T. R. Ramanna
Panaththoattam / 1963 / K. Sankar
Parakkum Paavai / 1966 / T. R. Ramanna
Parisu / 1963 / Yoganand
Pattikkaattu Ponnaiyaa / 1973 / P. S. Ranga
Periyaldaththu Penn / 1963 / T. R. Ramanna
Petraalthaan Pillaiyaa / 1966 / Krishnan–Panju
Prahalaathaa / 1939 / P. N. Rao
Pudumaippiththan / 1957 / T. R. Ramanna
Puthiya Poomi / 1968 / Chanakya
Raajaa Daesingu / 1960 / T. R. Raghunath
Raajakumaari / 1947 / A. S. A. Samy
RaajaMukthi / 1948 / Raja Chandrasekhar
Raajaraajan / 1957 / T. V. Sundaram
Raaman Thaedia Seethai / 1972 / P. Neelakantan
Raani Samyuktha / 1962 / Yoganand
Rahasiya Police115 / 1968 / B. R. Pantulu
Rathnakumar / 1949 / Krishnan–Panju
Rikshawkaaran / 1971 / M. Krishnan
Sabaash Maappillai / 1961 / S. Raghavan
Salivaahanam / 1945 / P. N. Rao

Sangae Muzhangu / 1972 / P. Neelakantan
Sarvaathikaari / 1951 / T. R. Sundaram
Sathi Leelaavathi / 1936 / Ellis R. Duncan
Siriththu Vaazha Vaendum / 1974 / S. S. Balan
Sri Murugan / 1946 / A. S. A. Samy
Thaazhampoo / 1965 / M. S. Ramadoss
Thamizhariyum Perumaal / 1942 / Ramanathan
Thaai Magalukku Kattiya Thaali / 1959 / R. R. Chandran
Thaai Sollai Thattaathae / 1961 / M. A. Thirumugam
Thaaikkuppin Tharam / 1956 / M. A. Thirumugam
Thaaiku Thalaimakan / 1967 / M. A. Thirumugam
Thaali Paakkiyam / 1966 / K. P. Nagabushnam
Thaasippenn or Joathi Malar / 1942 / T. R. Raghunath
Thaayai Kaaththa Thanayan / 1962 / M. A. Thirumugam
Thaayin Madiyil / 1964 / A. Subba Rao
Thaedi Vantha Maappillai / 1970 / B. R. Pantulu
Thaer Thiruvizhaa / 1968 / M. A. Thirumugam
Thalaivan / 1970 / P. A. Thomas
Thani Piravi / 1966 / M. A. Thirumugam
Tharmam Thalai Kaakkum / 1963 / M. A. Thirumugam
Theiva Thaai / 1964 / P. Madavan
Thiudaathae / 1961 / P. Neelakantan
Thozhilaali / 1964 / M. A. Thirumugam
Ulagam Sutrum Vaalipan / 1973 / M. G. Ramachandran
Urimai Kural / 1974 / Sridhar
Uzhaikkum Karangal / 1976 / K. Sankar
Vaedavathi or Seethaajananam / 1941 / T. R. Raghunath
Vaettaikkaaran / 1964 / M. A. Thirumugam
Veera Jagathis / 1938 / T. P. Kailasam and R. Prakash
Vikramaathiththan / 1962 / T. R. Raghunath and M. S. Ramadass
Vivasaayee / 1967 / M. A. Thirumugam

In Other Languages

Ektha Raja (Hindi) / 1951 / K. Ramnath
Jenova (Malayalam) / 1953 / F. Nagoor
Sarvathikari (Telugu) / 1951 / T. R. Sundaram

272 ◼ POPULAR CINEMA AND POLITICS IN SOUTH INDIA

RAJINIKANTH'S FILMOGRAPHY

(Only Thamizh Films)

Aadu Puli Aattam / 1977 / S. P. Muthuraman
Aarilirunthu Arupathuvarai / 1979 / S. P. Muthuraman
Aaru Pushpangal / 1977 / K. M. Balakrishnan
Aayiram Jenmangal / 1978 / Durai
Aduththa Vaarisu / 1983 / S. P. Muthuraman
Agni Saatchi / 1982
Alaavudeenum Arputhavilakkum / 1979 / I. V. Sasi
Annaamalai / 1992 / Suresh Krishna
Annai Oar Aalayam / 1979 / R. Thiyagarajan
Anpukku Naan Adimai / 1980 / R. Thiyagarajan
Anpulla Rajinikanth / 1984 / K. Nataraj
Apoorva Raagangal / 1975 / K. Balachandar
Arunaachalam / 1997 / Sundar C.
Athisaya Piravi / 1990 / S. P. Muthuraman
Aval Appadiththaan / 1978 / S. Rudraiya
Avargal / 1977 / K. Balachandar
Baatshaa / 1995 / Suresh Krishna
Baba / 2002 / Suresh Krishna
Billaa / 1980 / R. Krishnamoorthi
Chandramukhi / 2005 / P. Vasu
Chiththiramae Chiththiramae / 1985
Ejamaan / 1993 / R. V. Uthaya Kumar
Ellaam Un Kairaasi / 1980 / M. A. Thirumugam
En Kaelvikku Enna Pathil / 1978 / P. Madhavan
Engaeyoa Kaetta Kural / 1982 / S. P. Muthuraman
Enthiran / 2010 / S. Shankar
Guest Appearances (Thamizh only)
Guru Sishyan / 1988 / S. P. Muthuraman
Ilamai Oonchalaadukirathu / 1978 / Sridhar
Iraivan Koduththa Varam / 1978 / A. Bhimsingh
Jaani / 1980 / Mahendran
Justice Gopinaath / 1978 / Yogananth

FILMOGRAPHY ◼ **273**

Kaali / 1980 / I. V. Sasi
Kaayathri / 1977 / R. Pattapiraman
Kai Kodukkum Kai / 1984 / Mahendran
Karjanai / 1981 / S. V. Rajendran
Kavikkuyil / 1977 / Devaraj
Kazhuku / 1981 / S. P. Muthuraman
Koachadaiyaan / 2014 / Soundarya Rajinikanth Ashwin
Koadai Mazhai / 1986
Kodi Parakkuthu / 1988 / Bharathi Raja
Kuppaththu Raajaa / 1979 / Ramana
Kuselan / 2008
Maangudi Mainar / 1978 / V. C. Kuganathan
Maappillai / 1989 / Rajasekhar
Maaveeran / 1986 / Rajasekhar
Manathil Uruthi Vaendum / 1987
Manithan / 1987 / S. P. Muthuraman
Mannan / 1992 / P. Vasu
Mister Bhaarath / 1986 / S. P. Muthuraman
Moondru Mudichchu / 1976 / K. Balachandar
Moondru Mugam / 1982 / A. Jaganathan
Mullum Malarum / 1978 / Mahendran
Murattukkaalai / 1980 / S. P. Muthuraman
Muththu / 1995 / K. S. Ravi Kumar
Naan AdimaiIllai / 1986 / Thuvarakesh
Naan Mahaan Alla / 1984 / S. P. Muthuraman
Naan Poatta Savaal / 1980 / Purachithasan
Naan Sikappu Manithan / 1985 / S. A. Chandrasekar
Naan Vaazha Vaippaen / 1979 / T. Yogananth
Naattukku Oru Nallavan / 1991 / V. Ravichandran
Nallavanukku Nallavan / 1984 / S. P. Muthuraman
Nandri Meendum Varuha / 1982
Natchaththiram / 1980
Netrikkann / 1981 / S. P. Muthuraman
Ninaniththaalae Inikkum / 1979 / K. Balachandar
Oor Kaavalan / 1987 / Mano Bala
Paandiyan / 1992 / S. P. Muthuraman
Paavaththin Sampalam / 1978
Paayum Puli / 1983 / S. P. Muthuraman

274 █ POPULAR CINEMA AND POLITICS IN SOUTH INDIA

Padaiyappaa / 1999 / K. S. Ravi Kumar
Padikkaathavan / 1985 / Rajasekhar
Pairavi / 1978 / M. Baskar
Panakkaaran / 1990 / P. Vasu
Pathinaaru Vayathinilae / 1977 / Bharathiraja
Periya Idaththu Pillai / 1990
Poakkiri Raajaa / 1982 / S. P. Muthuraman
Pollaathavan / 1980 / V. Srinivasan
Priyaa / 1978 / S. P. Muthuraman
Puthukkavithai / 1982 / S. P. Muthuraman
Puvanaa Oru Kaelvikkuri / 1977 / S. P. Muthuraman
Raajaa Chinna Roajaa / 1989 / S. P. Muthuraman
Raajaathi Raajaa / 1989 / R. Sundararajan
Raanuva Veeran / 1981 / S. P. Muthuraman
Ragupathi Raagavan Raajaaraam / 1977 / Durai
Ranghaa / 1982 / R. Thiyagarajan
Sankar Salim Simon / 1978 / P. Mathavan
Sashti Viratham / 1983
Sathurangam / 1978 / Durai
Sivaa / 1989 / Ameer John
Sivaji / 2007 / S. Shankar
Sivappu Sooriyan / 1983 / V. Srinivasan
Sri Raagavaenthirar / 1985 / S. P. Muthuraman
Thaai Veedu / 1983 / P. Thiyagarajan
Thaaimeethu Saththiyam / 1978 / R. Thiyagarajan
Thaayillaamal Naanillai / 1979
Thalapathi / 1991 / Mani Rathinam
Thampikku Entha Ooru / 1984 / Rajasekar
Thanga Makan / 1983 / A. Jeyganathan
Thanikkaattu Raajaa / V. C. Loganathan
Thappu Thaalangal / 1978 / K. Balachandar
Tharma Thurai / 1991 / Rajasekhar
Tharma Yuththam / 1979 / R. C. Sakthi
Tharmaththin Thalaivan / 1988 / S. P. Muthuraman
Thee / 1981 / R. Krishnamoorthi
Thillu Mullu / 1981 / K. Balachandar
Thudikkum Karangal / 1983 / Sridhar

FILMOGRAPHY ◼ 275

Un Kannil Neer Vadinthaal / 1985 / Balu Mahendra
Uruvangal Maaralaam / 1983
Uzhaippaali / 1993 / P. Vasu
Vaelaikkaaran / 1987 / S. P. Muthuraman
Valli / 1993
Vanakathirkuriya Kaathaliyae / 1978 / Thirulokachandran
Veeraa / 1994 / Suresh Krishna
Viduthalai / 1986 / K. Vijayan
Yaar / 1985

OTHERS' FILMOGRAPHY

(Only Films Referred to in the Study)

Ajith (acting)

Mangaaththaa / 2011 / A. Venkat Prabhu

Anna (screenplay)

Nalla Thampi / 1949 / Krishnan-Panju
Sorka Vaasal / 1954 / A. Kasilingam
Vaelaikkaari / 1949 / A. S. A. Sami

Dhanush (acting)

Yaaradi Nee Moahini / 2008 / Mithran Jawahar

Kamal Haasan (acting)

Anbae Sivam / 2003 / Sundar C.
Avvai Shanmugi / 1996 / K. S. Ravikumar
Dasavathaaram / 2008 / K. S. Ravikumar
Guna / 1991 / Santhana Bharathi
Hei! Ram / 2000 / Kamal Haasan

Sathi Leelavathi / 1995 / Balu Mahendra
Thaevar Magan / 1992 / Bharathan
Unnaipoal Oruvan / 2009 / Chakri Toleti
Vasool Raja MBBS / 2004 / Saran
Vishwaroopam / 2013 / Kamal Haasan

Kannadasan (screenplay)

Illara Jothi / 1954 / G. R. Rao

M. Karunanidhi (screenplay)

Manohara / 1954 / L. V. Prasad
Paraasakthi / 1952 / R. Krishnan
Raajaa Raani / 1956 / A. Bhimsingh
Pillaiyoa Pillai / 1972 / Krishnan-Panju

Mani Ratnam (direction)

Iruvar / 1997

N. S. Krishnan (direction)

Manamagal / 1951
Panam / 1952

Murasoli Maran (screenplay)

Annayin Aanai / 1958 / Ch. Narayana Murthy

Sathyaraj (acting)

Englishkaaran / 2005 / Shakthi Chidambaram

Shah Rukh Khan (acting)

Ra. One / 2011 / Anubhav Sinha
Chennai Express / 2013 / Rohit Shetty

S. Shankar (direction)

Anniyan / 2005
Jeans / 1998
Mudhalvan / 1999

Sivaji Ganesan (acting)

En Thamizh En Makkal / 1988 / Santhana Bharathi
Paalum Pazhamum / 1961 / A. Bhimsingh
Paasamalar / 1961 / A. Bhimsingh
Paava Mannippu / 1961 / A. Bhimsingh
Veerapaandiya Kattabomman / 1959 / B. R. Panthulu

Vijayakanth

Captain Prabhakaran / 1991 / R. K. Selvamai

Others

Soothu Kavvum / 2013 / Nalan Kumarasamy
Thamizhpadam / 2010 / C. S. Amudhan

SELECT BIBLIOGRAPHY

Akbar, M. J. 1997. 'From Awara to Yes Boss: A History of India', *Asian Age*, 3 August.

Anand, Mulk Raj. 1957. *The Hindu View of Art*. Bombay: Asia Publishing House.

Armes, Roy. 1987. *Third World Filmmaking and the West*. Los Angeles: University of California Press.

Armour, Robert A. 1980. *Film: A Reference Guide*. Connecticut: Greenwood Press.

Austin, Bruce A. 1989. *Immediate Seating: A Look at Movie Audiences*. Belmont: Wadsworth.

Azhagesan, R. K. 1999. *Thamizh Cinemaavum Thamizhar Vaazhkaiyum*. Chennai: Manivasagar Pathippagam.

Bakhtin, M. M. 1981. *The Dialogic Imagination*. Austin: University of Texas Press.

Balasubramanian, P. C. and Raja Krishnamoorthy. 2010. *Rajiniyin Punch Tantram*. Chennai: Kizhakku Pathippagam.

Barnett, Marguaraite Ross. 1976. *The Politics of Cultural Nationalism in South India*. Princeton: Princeton University Press.

Barnouw, Erik and S. Krishnaswamy. 1963. *Indian Film*. New Delhi: Orient Longman.

Barry, Peter. 1999. *Beginning Theory: An Introduction to Literary and Cultural Theory* (Indian reprint). Manchester: Manchester University Press.

Barthes, Roland. 1972 [1957]. *Mythologies*. New York: Hill & Wang.

————. 1981. *Camera Lucida*. New York: Hill & Wang.

Baskaran, S. Theodore. 1981. *The Message Bearers: The Nationalist Politics and the Entertainment Media in South India, 1880–1945*. Madras: Cre-A.

————. 1996. *The Eye of the Serpent: An Introduction to Tamil Cinema*. Madras: East West Books.

Bate, Bernard. 2009. *Tamil Oratory and the Dravidian Aesthetic: Democratic Practice in South India*. New Delhi: Oxford University Press.

Baudrillard, Jean. 1983. *Simulations*. New York: Semiotext(e).

————. 1988. *The Ecstasy of Communication*. New York: Semiotext(e).

Bazin, Andre. 1967. *What is Cinema*. California: University of California Press.
Beck, Brenda E. F. 1972. *Peasant Society in Konku: A Study of Right and Left Subcastes in South India*. Vancouver: University of British Columbia Press.
Berger, John. 1972. *Ways of Seeing*. London: Penguin.
Bignell, Jonathan. 1997. *Media Semiotics: An Introduction*. Manchester: Manchester University Press.
Bose, Devlin, Partap Sharma and C. K. Razdan et al. (eds). 1976. *Film Miscellany*. Pune: Film and Television Institute of India.
Brosius, Christiane and Melissa Butcher (eds). 1999. *Image Journeys: Audio-Visual Media and Cultural Change in India*. New Delhi: Sage Publications.
Burra, Rani (ed.) 1981. *Film India: Looking Back, 1896–1960*. New Delhi: The Directorate of Film Festivals.
Chakravarty, Sumita S. 1996. *National Identity in Indian Popular Cinema — 1947–1987*. Delhi: Oxford University Press.
Collins, J. 1989. *Uncommon Cultures: Popular Culture and Postmodernism*. New York: Routledge.
Comstock, George, Steven Chaffee, Natan Katzman, Maxwell McCombs, and Donald Roberts. 1978. *Television and Human Behaviour*. New York: Columbia University Press.
Daniel, E. Valentine et al. 1987. *Fluid Signs: Being a Person in the Tamil Way*. Berkeley: University of California Press.
Das Gupta, Chidananda. 1981. *Talking About Films*. New Delhi: Orient Longman.
———. 1991. *The Painted Face: Studies in India's Popular Cinema*. New Delhi: Roli Books.
David, C. R. W. 1983. *Cinema as Medium of Communication in Tamil Nadu*. Madras: Christian Literature Society.
Dehejia, Vidya (ed.). 1999. *Representing the Body: Gender Issues in Indian Art* (2nd impression). New Delhi: Kali for Women.
DeNitto, Dennis. 1985. *Film: Form and Feeling*. New York: Harper and Row.
Dentith, Simon. 1995. *Bakhtinian Thought*. London: Routledge.
Denzin, Norman K. 1991. *Images of Postmodern: Social Theory and Contemporary Cinema*. London: Sage Publications.
———. 1995. *The Cinematic Society: The Voyeur's Gaze*. London: Sage Publications.
Derrida, Jacques. 1976. *Of Grammatology*. Baltimore: Johns Hopkins.
———. 1978. *Writing and Difference*. Chicago: University of Chicago Press.
———. 1993. *Memoirs of the Blind: The Self-Portrait and Other Ruins*, trans. by Pascale-Anne Brault and Michael Naas. Chicago: University of Chicago Press.
Dickey, Sara. 1993a. 'The Politics of Adulation: Cinema and the Production of Politicians in South India', *The Journal of Asian Studies*, 52(2).

280 ■ POPULAR CINEMA AND POLITICS IN SOUTH INDIA

Dickey, Sara. 1993b. *Cinema and the Urban Poor in South India*. New Delhi: Foundation Books.

———. 2008. 'The Nurturing Hero: Changing Images of MGR', in Selvaraj Velayutham (ed.), *Tamil Cinema: The Cultural Politics of India's Other Film Industry*. London: Routledge.

Doane, Mary Anne. 1991. *Femme Fatales: Feminism, Film Theory, Psychoanalysis*. New York: Routledge.

Drew, Donald J. 1974. *Images of Man: A Critique of the Contemporary Cinema*. Illinois: Inter Varsity Press.

Dwyer, Rachel and Divia Patel. 2002. *Cinema India: The Visual Culture of Hindi Film*. London: Reaktion Books.

Easthope, A. (ed.) 1993. *Contemporary Film Theory*. Harlow: Longman.

Eco, U. 1977. *A Theory of Semiotics*. London: Macmillan.

Editorial Board of Manimekalai Pirasuram. 1987. *Iyakkunar Sikaram K Balachandar*. Chennai: Manimekalai.

———. 1990. *History of A.I.A.D.M.K. Party/A.Thi.Mu.Ka.vin Thoatramum Valarchchiyum* (in Thamizh, 2nd edition). Chennai: Manimekalai.

———. 1991. *Purachi Selvi Jayalalitha* (2nd edition). Chennai: Manimekalai.

———. 1994. *Puratchi Nadikar MGR* (2nd edition). Chennai: Manimekalai.

———. 1995. *Nadikar Thilakam Sivaji Ganesan*. Chennai: Manimekalai.

Edgar, Andrew and Peter Sedgwick. 1999. *Key Concepts in Cultural Theory*. London: Routledge.

Erens, Patricia (ed.) 1990. *Issues in Feminist Film Criticism*. Bloomington: Indiana University Press.

Featherstone, Mike. 1990. *Consumer Culture and Postmodernism*. London: Sage Publications.

———. 1997. *Global Culture: Nationalism, Globalization and Modernity* (Reprint). London: Sage Publications.

Featherstone, Mike and Scott Lash (eds) 1999. *Spaces of Culture: City — Nation — World*. London: Sage Publications.

Fidler, Roger. 1997. *Mediamorphosis: Understanding New Media*. Thousand Oaks, California: Pine Forge Press.

Field, Syd. 2005. *Screenplay: The Foundations of Screenwriting*. New York: Bantam Dell.

Fiske, J. 1989. *Understanding Popular Culture*. Boston: Unwin Hyman.

Foucault, Michel. 1970. *The Order of Things*. New York: Vintage.

———. 1975. *The Birth of the Clinic*. New York: Vintage.

———. 1977. *Discipline and Punishment*. New York: Pantheon.

———. 1980. *Power/Knowledge*. New York: Pantheon.

Frankel, Francine R. and M. S. A. Rao (eds). 1989. *Dominance and State Power in Modern India,* vol. 1. Delhi: Oxford University Press.

SELECT BIBLIOGRAPHY 281

Friedman, Lester D. (ed.) 1991. *Unspeakable Images: Ethnicity and the American Cinema*. Illinois: University of Illinois Press.

Gabbard, Krin and Glen O. Gabbard. 1987. *Psychiatry and the Cinema*. Chicago: University of Chicago Press.

Gamman, Lorraine and M. Marshment (eds). 1989. *The Female Gaze: Women as Viewers of Popular Culture*. London: The Women's Press.

Garga, B. D. 1996. *So Many Cinemas*. Mumbai: Eminence Designs.

Gaul, Madan. 1973. *Other Side of the Coin: An Intimate Study of Indian Film Industry*. Bombay: Trimurti Prakashan.

Gledhill, Christine. 1987. *Home is Where the Heart Is: Studies in Melodrama and the Women's Film*. London: BFI Publishing.

Gokulsing, Moti and Wimal Dissanayake. 1998. *Indian Popular Cinema — A Narrative of Cultural Change*. New Delhi: Orient Longman.

Gopanna, A. 1999. *Kamaraj Era/Kamaraj Aatchi* (in Thamizh). Chennai: Surya Publications.

Gough, Kathleen. 1981. *Rural Society in Southeast India*. Cambridge: Cambridge University Press.

Government of India. 1969. *Report of the Enquiry Committee on Film Censorship*. New Delhi: Ministry of Information and Broadcasting.

———. 1979. *Symposium on Cinema in Developing Countries*. New Delhi: Publications Division, Ministry of Information and Broadcasting.

———. 1980. *Report of the Working Group on National Film Policy*. New Delhi: Ministry of Information and Broadcasting.

Grossberg, Lawrence. 1992. *We Gotta Get Out of This Place: Popular Conservatism and Postmodern Culture*. London: Routledge.

Guerin, Wilfred L., Earle Labor, Lee Morgan, Jeanne C Reesman, and John R. Willingham. 1992. *A Handbook of Critical Approaches to Literature*. Oxford: Oxford University Press.

Gupta, V. S. and Rajeshwar Dyal. 1996. *National Media Policy*. New Delhi: Concept Publishing Company.

Guy, Randor. 1990. 'MG Ramachandran: The Man of the Masses', in *Impact: MGR and Films* (bilingual). Madras: Movie Appreciation Society.

———. 1991. *History of Tamil Cinema*. Directorate of Information and Public Relations, Government of Tamil Nadu, Chennai.

Habermas, Jurgen. 1992. *The Structural Transformation of the Public Sphere: An Inquiry into a Category of Bourgeois Society*. Cambridge: MIT Press.

Hardgrave Jr., Robert L. 1965. *The Dravidian Movement*. Bombay: Popular Prakashan.

———. 1975. *When Stars Displace the Gods: The Folk Culture of Cinema in Tamil Nadu*. Occasional Paper Series, No. 3, Centre for Asian Studies, The University of Texas, Arlington.

282 ◾ POPULAR CINEMA AND POLITICS IN SOUTH INDIA

Hardgrave Jr., Robert L. and Anthony C. Neidhart. 1975. 'Film and Political Consciousness in Tamil Nadu', *Economic and Political Weekly*, 11(1).

Harriss, Barbara. 1984. *Meals and Noon Meals in South India: Food and Nutrition Policy in the Rural Food Economy of Tamil Nadu State*, Occasional Paper 31, School of Development Studies, East Anglia.

Hatmann, Paul, B. R. Patil and Anita Dighe. 1989. *The Mass Media and Village Life: An Indian Study*. New Delhi: Sage Publications.

Hunter, Allan. 1996. *The Wordsworth Book of Movie Classics*. Wordsworth Editions Ltd, Hertfordshire.

Ilamathi, Sivalai. 1997. *Sariththira Naayakar Em. Gi. Aarin Saathanaikal* (2nd edition). Chennai: Manimekalai.

———. 1998a. *Kalaignar Mu.Karunanidhi* (2nd edition). Chennai: Manimekalai.

———. 1998b. *Thi.Mu.Ka.vin Thoatramum Valarchchiyum* (3rd edition). Chennai: Manimekalai.

Irschick, Eugene. 1969. *Politics and Social Conflict in South India: The Non-Brahmin Movement and Tamil Separatism, 1916–1929*. Berkeley: University of California Press.

———. 1986. *Tamil Revivalism in the 1930s*. Madras: Cre-A.

Jameson, Fredric. 1991. *Postmodernism or The Cultural Logic of Late Capitalism*. Durham: Duke University Press.

———. 1992. *The Geopolitical Aesthetic: Cinema and Space in the World System*. Indiana: Indiana University Press.

Jarvie, I. C. 1959. *Towards a Sociology of Cinema*. New York: Routledge & Kegan Paul.

Jayakanthan. 1980. *Oru Ilakkiyavaathiyin Kalaiyulaga Anubavangal*. Madras: Thean Mozhi Pathipagam.

Jeyababu, S. V. 2000. *Punnakai Vallal MGR Ninaivukal 2000*. Chennai: Jeyababu.

Josephine, J. 1991. *Importance of Film Medium in Social Change: A Study of Women's Films made in India During the International Women's Decade, 1976–1985*, unpublished PhD thesis. Madras: University of Madras.

Kakar, Sudhir. 1989. *Intimate Relations: Exploring Indian Sexuality*. New Delhi: Viking.

Kaur, Ramindar and Ajay Sinha (eds). 2005. *Bollyworld: Popular Indian Cinema through a Transnational Lens*. New Delhi: Sage Publications.

Kazmi, Fareed. 1999. *The Politics of India's Conventional Cinema: Imaging a Universe, Subverting a Multiverse*. New Delhi: Sage Publications.

Kesavalu, V. 1990. *Impact: MGR and Films/Thamizhar Vaazhvil MGR* (bilingual). Chennai: Movie Appreciation Society.

Khedekar, R. G. 1986. 'A Financial Analysis of the Film Industry', *Screen*, Bombay, 7 March.

SELECT BIBLIOGRAPHY ■ 283

Kishen, P. (ed.) 1981. 'Indian Popular Cinema — Myth, Meaning and Metaphor', *India International Centre Quarterly*, Special Issue, 8(1).

Lewis, Lisa A. (ed.) 1992. *Adoring Audience: Fan Culture and Popular Media*. London: Routledge.

Lyotard, Jean-Francois. 1984. *The Postmodern Condition: A Report on Knowledge*. Minneapolis: University of Minnesota Press.

Macdonald, M. 1995. *Representing Women: Myths of Femininity in the Popular Media*. London: Edward Arnold.

Madsen, Roy Paul. 1973. *The Impact of Film: How Ideas are Communicated Through Cinema and Television*. New York: Macmillan.

Mahar, J. M. (ed.) 1972. *The Untouchables in Contemporary India*. Tucson: University of Arizona Press.

Mahmood, Hameeduddin. 1974. *The Kaleidoscope of Indian Cinema*. New Delhi: Affiliated East West Press.

Mast, Gerald and Marshall Cohen (eds). 1985. *Film Theory and Criticism: Introductory Readings*. New York: Oxford University Press.

Masud, Iqbal. 1987. 'Genesis of Popular Cinema', *Cinema in India*, 1(1).

Mathrubootheswaran, S. S. 1999. *Thannampikkai Tharugirathu Rajinikanth Vaazhkkai Varalaaru*. Chennai: Narmadha Pathippagam.

Mayne, Judith. 1990. *The Women at the Keyhole: Feminism and Women's Cinema*. Bloomington: Indiana University Press.

Metz, Christian. 1974. *A Semiotics of the Cinema: Film Language*. New York: Oxford University Press.

———. 1982. *The Imaginary Signifier: Psychoanalysis and the Cinema*. Bloomington: Indiana University Press.

Meyyappan, A. V. 1986. *Enathu Vazhkai Anupavangal*. Chennai: AVM Trust.

Mishra, Vijay. 2002. *Bollywood Cinema: Temples of Desire*. London: Routledge.

Mitra, Ananda. 1999. *India Trough the Western Lens: Creating National Images in Film*. New Delhi: Sage Publications.

Mittal, Ashok. 1995. *Cinema Industry in India: Pricing and Taxation*. New Delhi: Indus Publishing Company.

Mohandas, K. 1992. *MGR: The Man and the Myth*. Bangalore: Panther Publishers.

Monaco, James. 1981. *How to Read a Film*. New York: Oxford University Press.

Movie Appreciation Society. 1990. *Impact: MGR and Films* (bilingual). Madras.

Mulvey, Laura. 1989. *Visual and Other Pleasures*. Bloomington: Indiana University Press.

Naidu, M. D. Narayana. 1995. *N.T.R. — The Man of the Masses*. Tirupathi: Shobha Lata Publications.

Nandy, Ashis (ed.). 1998. *The Secret Politics of Our Desires: Innocence, Culpability and Indian Popular Cinema*. Delhi: Oxford University Press.

284 ■ POPULAR CINEMA AND POLITICS IN SOUTH INDIA

Narayanan, Aranthai. 1981. *Thamizh Cinemaavin Kathai*. Madras: NCBH.
———. 1994. *Thiravidam Paadiya Thiraippadangal*. Chennai: NCBH.
———. 1996. *Suthanthirappoaril Thamizh Thiraippadam* (2nd impression). Chennai: NCBH.
———. 1998. *Pattukottai Kalyanasundaram*. New Delhi: Sahitya Akademi.
Naveena Netrikkan, 2001, 'Something has happened to Rajini' (*Rajinikkuennamoa aayiduchchu*), 7–31, 26 October, pp. 4–7.
Neale, Steve and Frank Krutnik. 1990. *Popular Film and Television Comedy*. New York: Routledge.
Nichols, Bill (ed.). 1993. *Movies and Methods* (in 2 vols). Calcutta: Seagull Books.
Niranjana, Tejaswini. 1994. 'Roja Revisited', *Economic and Political Weekly*, 21 May.
Pandian, M. S. S. 1989. 'Culture and Subaltern Consciousness: An Aspect of MGR Phenomenon', *Economic and Political Weekly*, 24(30), 29 July.
———. 1992. *The Image Trap: MG Ramachandran in Film and Politics*. New Delhi: Sage Publications.
Pandian, M. S. S. and Geetha V. 1989. 'Jayalalitha: "Sworn Heir"', *Economic and Political Weekly*, 24(11), 18 March.
Pendakur, Manjunath. 2003. *Indian Popular Cinema: Industry, Ideology and Consciousness*. New Jersey: Hampton Press.
Penley, Constance (ed.) 1988. *Feminism and Film Theory*. New York: Routledge.
———. 1989. *The Future of Illusion: Film, Feminism and Psychoanalysis*. Minneapolis: University of Minnesota Press.
Pfleiderer, Beatrix and Lothar Lutze (eds). 1985. *The Hindi Film: Agent and Re-agent of Cultural Change*. New Delhi: Manohar Publications.
Polti, Georges. 2010. *The Thirty-Six Dramatic Situations* (Classic Reprint Series), Forgotten Books.
Postman, Neil. 1985. *Amusing Ourselves to Death: Public Discourse in the Age of Show Business*. New York: Viking Penguin.
Prasad, Madhava. 1998. *Ideology of the Hindi Film: A Historical Construction*. Delhi: Oxford University Press.
Pribram, Deidre E. (ed.). 1988. *Female Spectators: Looking at Film and Television*. London: Verso.
Prince, A. (ed.). 2008. *Anna Oru Samuthaya Sirpi*. Chennai: Kaavya.
Propp, Vladimir. 2010. *Morphology of the Folktale* (2nd edition). University of Texas Press.
Radway, Janice A. 1984. *Reading the Romance: Women, Patriarchy, and Popular Literature*. Chapel Hill: The University of North Carolina Press.
Rajadhyaksha, Ashish. 2003. 'The "Bollywoodization"of the Indian Cinema: Cultural Nationalism in a Global Arena', *Inter-Asia Cultural Studies*, 4(1): 25–39.

SELECT BIBLIOGRAPHY ▪ 285

Rajadhyaksha, Ashish and Paul Willeman. 1994. *Encyclopaedia of Indian Cinema*. London: British Film Institute.

Rajadurai, S. V. and V. Geetha. 2000. 'DMK Hegemony: The Cultural Limits to Political Consensus', in T. V. Sathyamurthy (ed.), *Region, Religion, Caste, Gender and Culture in Contemporary India*. New Delhi: Oxford University Press.

Rajanayagam, S. 1994.'Psychoanalytical Study of MGR Phenomenon', *Silampam*, no. 11.

―――. 1995. 'Social-Psychological Dynamics of Learning Sex and Violence through Media Porno', *Silampam*, no. 23.

―――. 1997a. 'Anthropological Inquiry into Cine-viewing Context', *Wavelength*, 7(2).

―――. 1997b. 'Portrayal of Women in Media', *Annai Velanganni*, 14(1).

―――. 1998a. 'Andro-media and Gyno-criticism', *The Rally*, 75(7).

―――. 1998b. *Kaalamatra Kaalam*. Chennai: Tharasu Veliyeedu.

―――. 1999. *Sila Mudivukalum Sila Thodakkangalum*. Bangalore: Kaavya.

―――. 2000a. 'Cine Politics of Pirated VCDs', *Vannak Kathir*, 12 March.

―――. 2000b. 'A Semiotic Analysis of *Hei! Ram*', *Sembaruti*, May.

―――. 2000c. *Samikkannu Ena Sila Manitharin Kathaigal*. Trichi: Ilayananthan Pathippagam.

―――. 2000d. *Thamizh Iraiyiyal Kalangal*. Dindigul: Vaigarai.

―――. 2002. *Kudumpa Uravil Kanavuth Thirai*. Chennai: Illidam.

―――. 2003. 'Drama, Dreama, Trauma: Media from a Psycho-Techno Perspective', *The Rally*, 79(8).

―――. 2004a. *Thamizh Iraiyiyal Thadangal*. Dindigul: Vaigarai.

―――. 2004b. 'Female Body @ Box Office Hits', *Mediagraph*, 1(1).

―――. 2004c. 'Kids Wanna Grow up Fast: A Few "Bits"of "Byted" Images', *Mediagraph*, 1(2).

―――. 2004d. 'Foto-Graffiti: An Unfinished Short Story', *Mediagraph*, 1(3&4).

―――. 2004e. 'Cine Song Massage', *Mediagraph*, 1(5&6).

―――. 2006a. 'Carnival Dreama', *Culture & Communications*, 4(15).

―――. 2006b. '*Devas* vs. *Asuras*: An Inquiry into the Villain', *Culture & Communications*, 5(16).

―――. 2006c. 'Through Violence... Some Questions, Some Answers, Some Questions', *Silampam*, 40.

―――. 2006d. 'Media Consumption of the Youth: A Political-Psychological Perspective', *Silampam*, 41.

―――. 2008.'The Depiction of Social Conflicts in C N Annadurai's Screenplays', in *Anna Oru Samuthaya Sirpi*.

―――. 2013. *Neeroattam: Arasiyal Panpaadum Panpaattu Arasiyalum*. Chennai: People Studies, Loyola College.

Rajanayagam, S. et al. (eds). 2000. *Rajini: Sila Mukangal*. Chennai: Silampam Veliyeedu.

Ramachandran, T. M. and S. Rukmini (eds). 1985. *70 Years of Indian Cinema [1913–1983]*. Bombay: CINEMA India-International.

Rangoonwalla, Firoz. 1970. *Indian Filmography: 1897–1969*. Bombay: J Udeshi.

———. 1983. *Indian Cinema: Past and Present*. New Delhi: Clarion.

Ray, Satyajit. 1976. *Our Films, Their Films*. New Delhi: Longman.

Rittaud-Hutinet, Jacques (ed.). 1995. *Letters: Auguste and Louis Lumiere*, trans. by Pierre Hodgson. London: Faber and Faber.

Ross, Andrew. 1989. *No Respect: Intellectuals and Popular Culture*. New York: Routledge.

Samuel, Stephen. 1983. *Film and Politics in Tamil Nadu: 1947–1980*, unpublished PhD thesis. Madras: University of Madras.

Santhanam, S.M. (ed.). 1998. *Makkal Virumpi Paarththa Marakkamudiyaatha Thiraippadangal*, vol. 1. Chennai: Manimekalai.

———. 1999. *Makkal Virumpi Paarththa Marakkamudiyaatha Thiraippadangal*, vol. 2. Chennai: Manimekalai.

Sarkar, Kobita. 1975. *Indian Cinema Today: An Analysis*. New Delhi: Sterling Publishers.

Sarojini. 1989. *Ilakkiyaththil Penn Neethi*. Dindigul: Arasi Pathippagam.

Sathyamurthy, T. V. (ed.). 2000. *Region, Religion, Caste, Gender and Culture in Contemporary India*, vol. 3. New Delhi: Oxford University Press.

Silverman, Kaja. 1988. *The Acoustic Mirror: The Female Voice in Psychoanalysis and Cinema*. Bloomington: Indiana University Press.

———. 1992. *Male Subjectivity at the Margins*. New York: Routledge.

Sivaji, Ganesan. 2006[2002]. *Enathu Suyasarithai* (My Autobiography), compiled and edited by T. S. Narayana Swamy. Chennai: Sivaji Prabhu Charities Trust.

Sivathamby, Karthigesu. 1981. *The Tamil Film as a Medium of Political Communication*. Madras: NCBH.

Somasundaram Pillai, J. M. 1959. *Two Thousand Years of Tamil Literature*. Madras: The South India Saiva Siddhanta Works Publishing Society (Tinnevely) Ltd.

Sreekanth, Gayathri. 2008. *The Name is Rajinikanth*. New Delhi: Om Books International.

Sreenivasan, Mukhtha V. 1993. *Thamizh Thiraippada Varalaaru*. Chennai: Gangai Puththaka Nilayam.

Srinivas, S.V. 2000. 'Devotion and Defiance in Fan Activity', in Ravi Vasudevan (ed.), *Making Meaning in Indian Cinema*, New Delhi: Oxford University Press.

Srinivasa Aiyangar, M. 1982. *Tamil Studies — Essays on the History of the Tamil People, Language, Religion and Literature*. New Delhi: Asian Educational Services.

SELECT BIBLIOGRAPHY ◀ 287

Stacey, Jackie. 1994. *Star Gazing: Hollywood Cinema and Female Spectatorship*. New York: Routledge.

Stam, Robert. 1989. *Subversive Pleasures: Bakhtin, Cultural Criticism and Film*. Baltimore: Johns Hopkins University Press.

Stam, Robert, Robert Burgoyne and Sandy Flitterman-Lewis. 1992. *New Vocabularies in Film Semiotics: Structuralism, Post-Structuralism and Beyond*. London: Routledge.

Telotte, J. P. (ed.) 1991. *The Cult Film Experience: Beyond All Reason*. Austin: University of Texas Press.

Thandavan, R. 1987. *All-India Anna Dravida Munnetra Kazhagam*. Madras: Tamil Nadu Academy of Political Science.

Thirunavukkarasu, K. 1990. *Dravidar Iyakkamum Thiraipada Ulagamum*. Madras: Manivasagar Pathipagam.

Thoraval, Yves. 2000. *The Cinemas of India*. New Delhi: Macmillan India Ltd.

Vachani, Lalit. 1999. 'Bachchan-alias: The Many Faces of a Film Icon', in Christiane Brosius and Melissa Butcher (eds), *Image Journeys: Audio-Visual Media and Cultural Change in India*, New Delhi: Sage Publications.

Vaidyanathan, T. G. 1996. *Hours in the Dark: Essays on Cinema*. Delhi: Oxford University Press.

Vasudev, Aruna. 1986. *The New Indian Cinema*. Delhi: Macmillan India Ltd.

———. (ed.). 1995. *Frames of Mind: Reflections on Indian Cinema*. New Delhi: UBS Publishers' Distributors.

Vasudevan, S. Ravi (ed.). 2000. *Making Meaning in Indian Cinema*. New Delhi: Oxford University Press.

Velayutham, Selvaraj (ed.). 2008. *Tamil Cinema: The Cultural Politics of India's Other Film Industry*. London: Routledge.

Vermorel, Fred and Judy. 1985. *Starlust: The Secret Fantasies of Fans*. London: W. H. Allen.

Vijayan, S. 1997. *Saathanai Naayakan M.G.R.* Chennai: Arulmozhi Pathippagam.

Virdi, J. 2003. *The Cinematic Imagination: Indian Popular Films as Social History*. Delhi: Permanent Black.

Wadley, Susan S. (ed.). 1980. *The Powers of Tamil Women*. Syracuse: Maxwell School of Citizenship and Public Affairs, Syracuse University.

Wayne, Mike. 2001. *Political Film: The Dialectics of Third Cinema*. London: Pluto Press.

Weimann, Gabriel. 2000. *Communicating Unreality: Modern Media and the Reconstruction of Reality*. London: Sage Publications.

Williams, Christopher. 1980. *Realism and the Cinema: A Reader*. London: Routledge and Kegan Paul.

Woods, Tim. 1999. *Beginning Postmodernism*. Manchester: Manchester University Press.

Zvelebil, Kamil. 1973. *The Smile of Murugan: On Tamil Literature of South India*. Leiden: Brill.

Newspapers and Magazines

Cinema Express (Thamizh), 2001
India Today (Thamizh), 1998–2014
Ithaya Kani, 2001
Junior Vikatan, 2001–14
Kumudham, 1970–2014
Murasoli, 1970–2014
Nakkeeran, 2001–14
Naveena Netrikkann, 2001
New Indian Express, 2001–14
Outlook, 2001–14
Thamizhoasai, 2011–12
The Hindu, 1991–2014
Thina Malar, 2001–11
Thina Mani, 2001–14
Thina Thanthi, 1970–2014
Thinakaran, 2001–14
Times of India, 2006–14

ABOUT THE AUTHOR

S. Rajanayagam is a field-based researcher, a well-known psephologist, and a teacher of media studies, committed to ongoing studies in political culture and cultural politics in the context of Tamil Nadu. He has authored over a dozen books practically in all literary genres — poems on feminist themes, short stories particularly revolving around children, postmodern and Dalit novels, stage plays, essays in media studies and theology — besides many video documentaries and short films, and lyrics for several audio albums. He is the Founder–Director of People Studies, and a pioneer in designing Visual Communication and Media Arts degree programmes in the state.

INDEX

Aayiraththil Oruvan 76, 136, 147, 152, 157
Abdul Latheef, M. 222
acterance 118, 120–21, 143–44
acting xvi, 9, 15, 23, 34, 147, 155–56, 192, 233–34
action hero image 25, 55, 126, 200
actors xx, xxii, xxiv, xxvii, 28, 100, 147, 191–92, 195–97, 233–34, 242
Adimai Penn 50n5, 70, 75, 78, 152, 159
ADMK (JL) 217
ADMK (JR) 191, 217
ADMK–BJP bandwagon 232
ADMK–INC alliance 194, 215, 217–18
adulations 35–36, 91, 135, 148, 175
Advani, L. K. 250n43
'aezhai pangaalan' 162
'Aezhaiyin sirippil Iraivan' 137
'affable darling' xxv, 55, 60n4, 129
aham 55–56
Ajith 182n19, 195, 241
Akila Indhiya Samathuva Makkal Katchi 236
All India Anna Dravida Munnetra Kazhakam (AIADMK/ADMK) xxvii, 116, 152–53, 163–66, 169–70, 172, 188–89, 191–92, 208–15, 217–27, 235–40; government by 203, 218, 225

alliances 205–06, 215, 217, 221, 225, 229, 231–32, 236, 239
Ananthan, Kumari 222
Anbae Sivam 9
Andipatti 173, 226, 233, 256n71
Anna. *See* Annadurai, C. N.
Annaamalai 18, 23, 37, 39, 67, 73, 79, 96, 100, 147, 170
Annadurai, C. N. xxi, xxvi, 5, 24–26, 128–29, 149, 154, 156–63, 165–66, 185, 203–07, 244n7; ascendancy in politics 244n7; DMK Phase 163–67; memory as political motif 159; *padi arisi* scheme 167n10; party 165
Annai Oar Aalayam 60n1
Anna-ism xxi
Anna–MGR–Karunanidhi triangular relationship 161
Annamitta Kai 67–68
Annayin Aanai 25
Anniyan and Hazare-style 180n10
Anpulla Rajinikaanth 147
anti-Brahmin 24
anti-hero image xxii, 9, 54, 126, 138, 169, 189, 194
anti-Hindi agitations 116, 165, 210
anti-Jayalalithaa wave 172, 218–19
anti-North 24–25, 204
anti-Thamizh riot xvi
anti-women behaviour 44
Apoorva Raagangal 168

INDEX 291

Arasa Kattalai 158
archetypes 144, 187
Arunaachalam 23, 27, 73–74, 100, 128, 131, 172–73
assemblage structure 150n2
assembly elections xxii, xxvii, 166, 191, 197, 212, 214–17, 222, 224–25, 233–38, 240–41
Athisaya Piravi 74, 170
audiences in Thamizh Nadu xxvii–xxviiin2
Avvai Shanmugi 9
Azhagiri, M. K. xxii; Formula of 261n91, 238–39

Baatshaa 23, 27–28, 36, 67, 71, 77, 100, 168, 171
Baba 26, 100, 138, 168, 173, 195, 226–29, 234; collection for 252n55; fiasco over 228–29; target of male politicians 229
Babbar, Raj xvii
Bachchan, Amitabh xvi–xvii, xix, 194, 242; election of xxx19
Bachchan, Jaya xvii
'Bad Habits' 83–84, 87, 90, 93
Bali, Vyjayanthimala xvii
barren 51–52, 54–55
'Bhagwan Rajini' 173
Bharathi, Alandur 218
Bharathiraja 227
Bharati 25
Bhava 10n2
Billaa 16, 36, 92
BJP alliance 225, 230, 239
BJP xvii, 178, 186, 219, 221–22, 224–25, 227–31, 236–37, 239–40, 242
body xxv, 33–35, 37–39, 46–49, 51, 64, 84, 131, 158, 161, 242; presentation of 33; of sister 48
Bollywood xxixn15

Bollywoodisation xviii, xxix–xxx n16
bribe 94, 160
by-elections 164, 211–13, 226, 243

Cable TV 248n31
campaign 24–25, 155, 191, 197, 202, 214–15, 217–18, 223, 239–40
Carnival 105–06, 108–10, 203
caste 39, 72n1–2, 99, 107, 109, 122n6, 125, 133–34, 166, 195–96
caste-based parties 249–50n41
castration anxiety xxv, 54, 56
Central Board of Film Certification (CBFC) xxviiin 6
centripetal triangle 138–39
Chandra Babu 18
Chandramukhi 168, 174, 234, 240
Chandran, S. S. 197
Chandrasekhar, Maragatham 213
channels 232, 238; film-based 121n1; film-based comedy 121n1; film-based music 121n1
characters 4, 6–7, 9, 15, 27, 34, 36, 48, 107, 118, 147–48
charismatic artistes 10
Chennai 93, 204, 217, 227
Chidambaram, P. 218–19, 222
Chiranjeevi xvi, xxixn11
cigarette 84, 87
cine songs 18–20, 22
cinelation, models of xxvi, 187–93, 220, 224; MGR's way of 188; Models of 187; Sivaji model of 189
cinelitic 21, 161, 169, 173, 184–89, 191, 193–95, 229
cinema theatres xx
cinematic 19–20, 68, 105, 116, 170–71, 187–89, 193–95, 229
cinemenon 108–10, 113

292 ■ POPULAR CINEMA AND POLITICS IN SOUTH INDIA

climax 6, 27, 45, 179, 218
Clothing 34
clubs xxiii, 109, 113, 147
coalition government 212–13, 221, 223, 230
comedians 17–18
comedy xxv, 12, 16–18, 41, 113, 118, 150; of heroism 28n1 29n7; and Inversion 16–18
commercial films 3, 5
concubines 48, 51–52, 125
conflicts 6, 45, 47–48, 62, 73, 97, 153, 230
confrontational scenes 24
Congress 153, 155–57, 188, 190–91, 201–02, 205–08, 210–14
Congress Jananayaka Peravai 222, 250–51n46
conscience 16, 71, 82, 88–89, 96–97, 175
corruption 161–62, 165, 171, 210, 213, 223; MGR's crusade against 210
CPI 206, 210–12, 221–22, 224, 235
culture xvii, 4–5, 44, 68, 84, 87, 93; sources of 5
custodians xxv, 80–81, 84, 87, 89
cycle 110, 113–15

Daesiya Murpoakku Dravida Kazhakam (DMDK) xvi, 235–36, 239–40, 243
darshan 123n12
'delay-expectation-arrival' technique 27
Desai, Morarji 213
Dharmendra xvii
DMK–INC combine 237
DMK–TMC alliance 194, 219
documentary footage 25
do-gooder action hero 14, 77, 117, 128, 152, 209

dominant class 64, 70–72
'don't cheat; don't get deceived' 159
donor xxvi, 135–37
double acting 16, 68, 70
Double Climax 5–7
double voyeuring 107
double-bodied migrantcy 62, 64, 80, 99, 203
'double-roles', or 'double-acts' xxv, 12, 15–17, 40, 92, 154, 164, 178
dramatic Entry 26–27
Dravida Kazhakam (DK) xxi, 115–16, 157, 202
Dravida Munnetta Kazhakam (DMK) xxi–xxii, xxvi–xxvii, 115–16, 153–60, 162–65, 185–86, 188–95, 200–15, 217–26, 231–32, 235–39; alliances with 172, 197, 221, 224–25, 231–32, 238; films by 154–55; ideology of 153, 185–86; as 'Karunanidhi katchi' 163
Dravidian Nation 203
Dravidian parties 205, 235
dreama/dreamatic 109, 112, 126, 143
drinking 44, 83–84, 87, 161, 227
duality 37, 155
Dutt, Sunil xvii

eating *mannsoaru* 181n12
education 70–71, 157, 175
'eeramulla irumpu nenjam' 132
Eezham Thamizhs Rights Protection Conclave 204
Ejamaan 54, 135
electioneering 188, 238
elections xvi, xxii–xxiii, 132, 162, 168, 193, 195–96, 201, 205–09, 211–26, 228–40; campaigns 157–58, 196, 216, 239
Emgeeyar Pictures 153, 155

INDEX 293

'en raththaththin raththamaana' 127
En Thamizh En Makkal 190
End-Clips 27–28
enfant terrible xxv, 54, 58–59, 60n4, 129
Enga Veettu Pillai (EP) xxv, 3–4, 9, 18, 39–40, 55, 65, 68, 70, 77, 81, 147, 152, 156–58, 160–61, 185, 228–29
Engal Thaesa Katchi 190
ennai vaazhavaikkum theivangalaakiya Thamizhaha makkal 131
Enthiran, 34, 168, 177–78, 181n15, 181–82n16–18, 20, 241–42
eunuch 53–54
eve-teasing 5, 59, 89, 118
exercise of power 97–100
exhibitionism 120
exposure anxiety xxv, 54, 57–58

fan clubs xvi, xxiv, 108–10, 112, 138, 147, 184, 187, 207, 209
fan-bond xxvi, 138
fan-following and box-office returns xxviiin5
fans, foreign 177
fantasy–politics interface xxvi, 125
fanzines 109, 139
fear 46, 51, 55, 94, 96, 120, 153, 162, 203, 233–34
feature Films, annual output of xviii; of MGR and RK 7, 14, 16, 35–36, 46–48, 54, 65, 73, 77, 97, 132
film viewing 105
first-past-the-post xxvi, , 249n39
Flynn, Errol 40
folk heroes 4, 115
folktales 5

Gandhi 25, 89, 160

Gandhi, Indira xvii, 116, 191, 205–06, 210, 213–15
Gandhi, Rajiv xvi, xix, 190, 192–93, 213, 215, 217, 225
Gandhi, Sonia 225, 231, 238
Ganesan, Sivaji. *See* Sivaji Ganesan
Gemini 208
gender politiking 201, 216–21
god xxvi, 137–38
good-evil interface 14–15
guilt 89, 96, 120
Gule Bakaavali 25
Gupta, Das xix; on films by MGR xxxn22
Guru Sishyan 89, 168–69

Haasan, Kamal xxii, xxiv, 4, 9–10, 15, 40–41, 169–70, 193–94; experimentation and innovation of 9
Haroon, J.M. 222
Hasya 29n7
Hei! Ram 9
henchmen 13, 92, 96
Hero versus Villain 75–77
Hero vis-à-vis Aide 79
Hero vis-à-vis Heroine 77–79
Hero-centricity 7–8
heroes 4, 14, 33, 49, 71, 75, 80–84, 97, 114–15, 117, 143; semi-mythological folk 4
heroine 4, 7, 15, 18, 27, 35–38, 45, 47–48, 56, 75, 77–79; worshipping 123n11
heroism 71–72
hero–villain continuum 14–15, 98, 187, 189
hero-worship xxii–xxiii, xxvi, 112–13, 115–16
Hindi films xvii–xviii
hostile lovers 57–59

294 ■ POPULAR CINEMA AND POLITICS IN SOUTH INDIA

Identi-fi ction vis-à-vis Identif-action
117–21
Illara Jothi 25
image discriminative xxvi, 200
image politics xxi–xxiii, xxvi, 12,
125, 129, 135, 143, 147
Inbak Kanavu 156
INC–DMK alliance 191, 213
Indhiya Jananayaga Katchi 237
'India Shining' Campaign
254–5n63–4
Indian National Congress (INC)
xvi–xvii, xix, xxi, 190–93, 201,
205–07, 211–15, 217–19, 221–
22, 224–25, 235–39
Indian National League 222
Indian Union Muslim League 222
Indian Uzhavar Uzhaippalar Katchi
222
Inheritance versus Earning 74
'inside-insider' phase 171–74
'inside-outsider' phase 174–79
Iruvar 244n11
isomorphism 188–89
Ithaya Kani 18, 25–26, 78, 130–31,
136, 154, 164, 185

Janaki xxvi–xxvii, 169, 191–92,
200, 217
Janata Party 186, 190–91, 212–13
Janata–ADMK combine 213
Jayalalithaa xxvi–xxvii, 116, 169–72,
189, 192–95, 216–19, 223–34,
226–27, 232–33, 237–39, 242–
43; attacks on 245–46n23, 100;
'price-less rice' (*vilai-illaa arisi*)
167n10; Puratchi Thalaivi as
prefix toxxxin26; Rajini's warning to 170
Jeans 15
Jekyll-and-Hide 16

justice xxv, 5, 80–81, 91, 94–95,
97, 99, 160

kaavadi 181n12
Kaavalkaaran 74, 136, 167n9
kaavya 4–5
Kalaivaanar 18, 208
kalavu 55
Kamaraj, K. 5, 167n3, 192, 202,
206–07, 210–12
Kambar's Ramayanam 39, 55
Kanchi Sankaracharya, arrest of 237,
259n81
Kannadasan 25, 153
Kanni Thaai 38, 84, 136
karpu 55, 130, 154, 156
Karthick 236
Karunanidhi, M. (MK) xxi–xxii,
24–25, 127–28, 130, 159–64,
185, 188–89, 193–95, 209–13,
223–25, 242; arrests of 122–
23n8; scripted *Raajaa Raani*10n9,
see also Pillaiyo Pillai
Karuppiah Moopanar, G. 190,
192–93, 213, 219, 223
Khanna, Vinod xvii
kinthanaar kathaakaalakshepam 25
'kitsch' xxvii– xxviiin2
knowledge revolution 155, 157
Koachadaiyaan xxiii, 183n22, 242
kolhai paadalkal 22
Kondrai Vaenthan 46
Kongunadu Makkal Katchi 222
kooththaadikal 5, 170
*Koaththu*3–5, 10n3, 109; meaning
of 4
Krishnan, N. S. (Kalaivaanar) (NSK)
18, 25, 29n7, 208
Krishnaswamy, K. A. xxxin26
KTV 121n1
Kudumpa Thalaivan 36

kulak kalvi 155, 157, 202
kulakkalvi-fame Rajaji 205
Kumar, Sarath xxvii, 188, 195, 197, 236
Kumari Koattam 26, 45, 47, 68, 70, 77, 79, 84, 136
Kuselan 175–77, 195, 241

'law for' vis-à-vis 'law as' 93–97
'liminal spurts' xxv, 64, 66
'looks' and 'style' 40–41

maanam 73–75, 91, 115–16, 130, 153, 156; *versus* wealth 73–74
Maappillai 58, 87, 172
Maattukkaara Vaelan 40, 67, 70, 74, 77, 132, 152
Mahaadaevi 34
main villain 13
Makkal Thamizh Desam Katchi 222, 224
Malai Kallan, 77, 136, 152; smoking 'traditional pipe' in 101
male body 34, 36–40, 43, 62; exhibition 33–36; gaze at 36–39
Malini, Hema xvii
mandrams xxvi, 112, 163, 189–90, 192–93, 207, 209
Mangaaththaa 182n19
Manithan 89, 144
Manithaneya Makkal Katchi 236
Mannan 15, 18, 23, 26, 38, 45–46, 49n1, 67, 79, 136, 152–57, 166–67
Manohara 25
Manorama 197
Manthiri Kumaari 25
Maran, Murasoli 25, 231
Marathi films xxixn15
marketing cinema 179
Marma Yoagi 23, 25, 152
*Masala*xxv, xxvii– xxviiin 2, 7, 174

Mathurai Veeran 5, 25, 152
Mathuraiyai Meetta Sunthara Paandiyan 26, 34, 152, 166
MDMK 221–22, 224–25, 235, 237, 239–40
Meenava Nanpan 26, 35, 66–67, 99, 152, 166
meta-culture xvii, 244–45n15
meta-texting 149
MGR Kazhagam 219, 222
MGR mandrams 163, 207, 209, 218
MGR Munnani 218
MGR (M. G. Ramachandran):arrest of 244n5; as custodian 87–89; death of 168–69, 190, 192, 217; delay his arrival to meetings 244n11; and DMK ideology xix, 153; DMK phase of 153–56; as do-gooder 14, 153; as Dravidian' of Malayalee origin 257n75; films titles of 140–41n7; legacy of 192; as *Makkal Thilakam*10n9; marital life of 60–61n5; as Mr Perfect' xxii; phenomenon of xvi; political charisma 245n21; politiking formula 125–26; as Puratchi Nadikar xx,xxxin26 as Puratchi Thalaivar xx; wives of 141n14
MGR-ADMK 221–22, 224, 249n36
mini-narrative xxv, 12, 24–26, 160
minor offences 83, 87–90, 89, 93
minor parties 221–34
Mister Bhaarath 28, 96
Modi 239–40; Rajinikanth wishing 242; Vijay visit to 240; visit to Rajinikanth 240
Mohideen, Khader 222
Moonru Mugam 87, 89, 94
moral economy 80, 96–97, 134
moral-legal system 95–96, 117

mother xxv, 36–37, 46, 51–52, 54, 56–60, 87–88, 91–94, 118, 125–26, 137–38, 166

motifs xxvi, 5, 125, 138, 144

Mudhalvan 174

Mullum Malarum 71, 79, 89, 135

mupperum vizhaa 204

Murattukkaalai 70, 75

'Muththamizh Selvan Mu Ka Muthu Rasigar Mandrams' 163

Muththu 23, 35, 73–74, 131, 148, 168, 171–72

Muthu, Mu. Ka. 162–63, 188, 209

Muthukumar 237

Naadaazhum Makkal Katchi 236

Naadoadi Mannan (NM) 15, 18, 23, 26, 67, 136, 152–57, 166, 185

Naam Thamizhar Katchi 239

Naan Aanaiyittaal 84, 157

Naan Adimai Illai 74, 87, 131

Nadukal Politics 115–16

nadukal worship xxvi, 115–16

Naetru Indru Naalai 164

Nalan 182n19

Nalla Thampi 18, 25

Nallavan Vaazhvaan 34

Nallavanukku Nallavan 28, 35, 48, 100, 131, 144, 169

Nam Naadu 26, 160–62

Nambiar 188

Napoleon 188, 195, 197

narcissism 120

Nargis xvii

narrative: autonomy 17; mini-narratives 24–26; superfluity 16

nava rasas xxiv, 3

Nazir, Prem xvi

Nedunchezhiyan 192

Neethikku Thalai Vanangu 25, 56, 68, 90, 135–36, 165

Nehru 25, 202, 215

Netrikkann 16, 35

new wave xv, 4

Nutritious Noon Meal Scheme 215

octa-motifs xxvi, 125, 138, 152, 159, 161, 169

oedipal attachment 56, 59

Oli Vilakku 26, 49, 55, 77, 84, 134, 150, 152, 158

Onrae Kulam — Oruvanae Thaevan 137

orphan/orphan-hood xxvi, 37, 69, 74, 92, 94, 125, 132–35, 138, 174

our household darling 157

'outside-insider' phase 169–71

'outside-outsider' phase 168–69

Paalum Pazhamum 60n1

Paandiyan 36–37, 74, 94, 96

Paasamalar 60n1

Paattaali Makkal Katchi (PMK) 168, 186, 221–25, 227–30, 235, 237–38, 240

Paava Mannippu 60n1

Paayum Puli 144

Pachamuthu 237

Padaiyappaa 18, 23, 26, 34–35, 38, 43, 77, 87, 100, 172–73, 229; targetted Jayalalithaa 229

Padaiyappaa Rajini Rasikar Mandram 147

Padikkaathavan 71

Padmini 208

Panakkaara Kudumpam 70, 84

Panakkaaran 65, 71, 73–74, 131

Panam Padaiththavan 55, 78, 84, 99

Pappaiya, Solomon 181n11

Paraasakthi 24, 40, 165

parliamentary elections xxii, xxvii, 166, 168, 190–91, 212, 214–15, 217–19, 221, 235–36, 239–41

INDEX ◼ 297

party politiking 185, 194
Patnaik, Biju 186
Pazha Nedumaran 231
People Studies xxiv, xxxin28
People's Alliance 224
'Pepsi' Uma, temple built for 123n11
Periya Idaththu Penn 26, 70, 99
Periyar, E. V. R. 227
Pillaiyoa Pillai 162
Poakkiri Raajaa 89, 144
politician-cum-actor model xxvi, 187
politiking formula xxvi, 125, 138
ponmana chemmal 144
Ponnar Sankar 242
poor: hero 75–77, 79; heroine 78–79
Praja Rajyam Party xvi, xxixn11
'precipitation' technique xxv
private realm 144
'pro-ammaa' wave 239
prohibition of liquor 210
propaganda films 190, 193
prostitutes 48, 51–52, 54, 59, 125
public appearances 123–24n13
public realms 55–56, 144, 163
punch dialogues 23–24
'Punyam' versus wealth74–75
puram 55–56
Puthiya Needhi Katchi 222

Raaja Kumaari 25
Raajaa Chinna Roajaa 33, 87, 170
Raajaa Daesingu 16
Raajaathi Raajaa 36
*Raaman Thaediya Seethai*18, 39, 49–50n3, 74, 78, 99, 147
Radha, M R 130, 197, 198n4
Radhakrishnan,Pon. 267n114
Radhika 197
radicalism-turned-rhetoric 201–08
Raghavendra Kalyana Mandapam 253n56

Raguvaran 193
Raja Rani 25
Rajaji 167n3
Rajendar, T. xxvii, 188, 195–96, 236
Rajendran, S. S. 208
Rajinikanth (Super Star/Shivaji Rao) xvi, xxi, 35, 41, 144, 146–47, 169–70, 173–77, 196, 232, 250n42; bizarre reaction at Amman festival 178; foreign fans to 177; as go-getter angry hero 117; on Hogenekkal drinking water project 241; image 14, 129, 194, 224, 228; Japanese fans 177; versus Jayalalithaa 220, 252n53; as 'management guru' 29n9; members deserting party for 247–48n29; on *Outlook* cover as 'Global hero Rajnikanth' xxxin27; political interventions of 132, 168, 173, 184, 187, 220, 224, 233; popularity 226
'Rajinikanth rasigar narpani mandram' 112
Rajkumar xvi
Rama Rao, N.T. (NTR) 235
Ramachandran,M. G.*See* MGR (M.G. Ramachandran)
Ramachandran, P. 212
Ramachandran, Panrutti 267n114
Ramadoss, Anbumani 228
Ramadoss, S. 227–30, 240; and *Vanniar Sangam* 249n34
Ramaiyadoss, Thanjai 25
Ramamurthy, Vazhappadi 221, 249n35
Ramarajan 188, 195
Ramasamy Naickar, E. V. (Periyar) xxi, 202
Rao, Gundu 190
Ra-One, of Shah Rukh Khan 242

Ravi, Radha 193, 195, 197
real politiking xix, 136, 161, 173, 184, 186–90, 200
renunciation xxvi, 133–35, 137–38, 157
're-presencing' 232
rich: hero 75–78; heroine 77–78;villain 75–77
Rikshaakaaran 25, 67, 70, 89, 152
'rite of passage' 112
Robin Hood-ist activities 77, 83, 118, 136
romancing 38, 70, 118

Samajwadi Party xvii
Sampath, E.V.K. 206, 210
Sangae Muzhangu 70, 74, 94, 130
Sangam/literature 5, 36, 39, 55, 135, 222
satellite twin centres xxvi, 186–87
Sathi Leelavathi 9
Sathyanarayana 246n25
screen image xxiii, 110, 126, 134, 200, 219, 221
screen realms xxvi, 136, 144, 147
screenings 106, 109, 112, 164, 228
Seemaan 239
Sekar, Vaigai 226
self-immolation 116, 122–23n8
self-reflexivity 144
Senthil 18
sentimental transtexting 150
serious crimes 84, 90–93
Seshan, T. N. 218
Shankar 174, 177, 240, 242; and AVM 180n9
shyness 55, 120
Silambam 41n6
Singh, Charan 213
Singh, Manmohan 228
Sinha, Shatrughan xvii

Siriththu Vaazha Vaendum 16, 27, 39, 73, 84, 93, 136, 164
sister 37–38, 47–49, 71, 90, 94–95, 125, 132, 135
Sivaji 23, 240, 242
Sivaji as precursor to Hazare 180n10
Sivaji Ganesan (*Nadikar Thilakam*) xvi,xxii, xxiv, xxvii, 4, 9–10, 10n9, 15, 40, 169–70, 188–93, 208–09, 217
Sivaji *mandram* 190
smoking 44, 83–84, 87
Snowball Dynamics 8–10
social body xxv, 62
Social positioning 10n8
Song Massage 18–23
Soothu Kavvum 182n19
Sorka Vaasal 25
Soundarya 182n21
Sri Lankan *Thamizh* extremists 217
Sri Ragavendra 138
Sri Ragavendra Trust 137
Srikanth 208
star-Chief Ministers xix
star-images xv
star-intervening-politics model xxvi, 188, 193
stealing 46, 87–89, 93, 134, 136
stunt sequences xxv, 3–4, 35–36, 113, 118, 150, 156; and villainy 12–15
style 10, 23, 34–36, 40–41, 59, 72, 87, 117–18, 121, 164, 204
subaltern identity xxvi, 20, 66–71, 80–81, 83–84, 93, 96, 128–29, 138, 148, 154
Sun Network 121n1, 172, 219, 232
subtexting 150n1
Sundarrajan, Major 208
supra-legal 91, 96, 168, 171, 194, 230
Swami, Subramanian 218, 221, 224
Swaminathan, R. V. 190

INDEX 299

Swamy, A.S.A. 25
Swatantra Party 205
'synonymisation' xvi, 147, 151n4, 161

tactexting xxvi, 23, 143–44, 149, 152, 171, 184, 188, 200, 229
tactical texting xxvi, 143
Tamil Nadu Theatre Owners' Association 182n19
Tamilaga Rajiv Congress (TRC) 221,249n35
taming of the shrew 77,
tea-stall politiking 19, 21–22
Telugu Desam Party (TDP) xvi
Telugu-speaking politicians 244n6
terrain switching 99
Thaai Kulam 125–26
Thaai Magalukku Kattiya Thaali 156
Thaai Meethu Saththiyam 60n1
Thaai Sollai Thattaathae 60n1
thaaikulam xxvi, 37, 125, 128, 138, 217
Thaalamuththu 165
Thaayai Kaaththa Thanayan 60n1
Thaayin Madiyil 60n1, 74, 99
Thaevar Magan 9
Thaikkuppin Thaaram 18
Thalapathy 54, 77, 92, 100
Thambikku Entha Ooru 68
Thamizh culture 39–40, 44, 51, 55–56, 68, 74, 130, 132, 135, 153, 156
Thamizh Eezham Supporters Organisation (TESO) 204
Thamizh films xxiii, 17, 130; archetypal characters in 5
Thamizh Maanila Congress (TMC) 219, 221–23, 225, 246n24
Thamizh Nadu Congress Committee (TNCC) 190, 192

Thamizh Nadu Mutharaiyar Sangam 222
Thamizh Thaesa Katchi 190
Thamizhaga Makkal Katchi 222
Thamizhaga Muslim Iykkya Jamaat 222
Thamizhaka Munnaetra Munnani (TMM) 190–91
Thamizhar Bhoomi 222
Thamizharasu Kazhakam 205
Thamizhness xxvi, 129–30, 132
Thamizhpadam 28n1
Thampikku Entha Ooru 38, 77, 131
Thani Piravi 27, 36, 70, 88
Tharma Thurai 71
Tharma Yuththam 77
theatre system 107
Thee 71
thennakam 129
thiraavidam 129–31
Thiru Vi Ka 25
Thirudaathae 25–26, 79, 87, 89, 99, 136, 152
Thirumangalam Formula 238, 261n91
Thirumavalavan 238
Thirunavukkarasar, S. 249n36
thiruvizhaa 107–10, *see also* carnival
Thondar Congress 222
Thozhilaali 36
Thuglak Cho Ramaswamy 251n51, 265n105
ticket 109, 112
trans-image voting behaviour xxvi
TV watching 121–22n2–4
'twin centre' politiking xxvi, 184, 186
twin-leaves, AIADMK's symbol of 25, 242

udanpirappu ('co-born') motif 126–28, 140n3, 158

Ulagam Sutrum Vaalipan 25, 34, 38, 40, 78, 130, 136, 164, 174, 209
union of lovers 27, 38
Unique Selling Proposition (USP) 23–24, 172
Unnaipoal Oruvan 9
Urimai Kural 18, 34, 67, 128, 186
Uthaya Sooriyan 148

vaaththiyaar 18, 144, 146–47, 160
Vaelaikkaari 24
Vaiko (Vai Gopalasamy) xxii, 231, 240
Vajpayee 224–25, 228, 231
valour 34–35, 39–40, 55, 153
vanthaaraivaazhavaikkum Thamizhaham 131
Vasool Raja MBBS 9
Veeraa 74
veeram 116, 130, 153, 156
Veerappan, R. M. 198n8, 218–19, 222, 246n26
Venkataraman, R. 190
Vetri Thirumagan by 198n8
vetri vizhaas 154, 220, 229
Vettavalam' Manikandan 222
Viduthalai Chiruthaikal Katchi (VCK) 222, 235, 237–38
viewing ambience 105
Vijay, 'Ilayathalapathi' 4, 90, 195, 240

Vijayakanth, Captain/'*Puratchi Kalaignar*'/*Karuppu* MGR xvi, xxvii, xxxin 26, 4, 151n4, 189, 195, 200, 235–36, 239–40, 242–43, 264n99; House suspension of 266n112
Vijayan 218
Vijayaraj, self-immolation 262–63n95
villain 6–7, 12–16, 48–49, 56, 64, 75–77, 79–82, 84, 94–99, 187–89, 193–95; elimination of 94
'villainesque' 178, 182n18
virgin 51, 53–54
Vishal, 'Puratchi Thalapathi' xxxin26, 4
Vishwaroopam 9
voyeurism 120

wealth xxv, 39, 69, 73–77, 79, 82, 97, 134, 137, 165, 210; as burden 73;*versus* peace 73
websites 109, 113
women/female body xxv, 27, 36–40, 43–47, 50–51, 54–56, 59–60, 62, 71, 87, 93, 126; as beauty 55; as daughter 48; as fiancée 46–47; as haughty 43–44, 79, 194; ideal 18, 78–79; as mother 46; as prostitute 48–49; as seducer 47; as sister 48; as terrifying 51–52; as widow 49, 51–52, 54–55, 125; as wife 38, 47–49, 51–55, 74, 94, 225